MW00619366

Diagonal Advance

The Veritas Series

VERITAS

Diagonal Advance

Perfection in Christian Theology

Anthony D. Baker

J.J.—
I'm so glad to meet you,
and look forward to being
colleagues in theological education
—Tony

CASCADE *Books* · Eugene, Oregon

DIAGONAL ADVANCE
Perfection in Christian Theology

Veritas

Copyright © 2011 Anthony D. Baker. All rights reserved. Except for brief
quotations in critical publications or reviews, no part of this book may be
reproduced in any manner without prior written permission from the publisher.
Write: Permissions, Wipf and Stock Publishers, 199 W. 8th Ave., Suite 3, Eugene,
OR 97401.

First published in Great Britain in the Veritas series, by SCM Press, 13–17 Long
Lane, London EC1A 9PN, England.

First U.S. edition published by Cascade Books under license from SCM Press.

Cascade Books
An Imprint of Wipf and Stock Publishers
199 W. 8th Ave., Suite 3
Eugene, OR 97401
www.wipfandstock.com

ISBN 13: 978-1-61097-815-6

Cataloging-in-Publication data:

Baker, Anthony D.

    Diagonal advance : perfection in Christian theology / Anthony D. Baker.

    xvi + 332 p. ; 23cm. —Includes index.

    Veritas
    ISBN 13: 978-1-61097-815-6

    1. Perfection—History of doctrines. 2. Deification (Christianity). I. Title.
II. Series.

BT766 .B29 2011

Manufactured in the U.S.A.

VERITAS

Diagonal Advance

Perfection in Christian Theology

Anthony D. Baker

J.J.—
I'm so glad to meet you,
and look forward to being
colleagues in theological education
—Tony

CASCADE *Books* · Eugene, Oregon

DIAGONAL ADVANCE
Perfection in Christian Theology

Veritas

Copyright © 2011 Anthony D. Baker. All rights reserved. Except for brief quotations in critical publications or reviews, no part of this book may be reproduced in any manner without prior written permission from the publisher. Write: Permissions, Wipf and Stock Publishers, 199 W. 8th Ave., Suite 3, Eugene, OR 97401.

First published in Great Britain in the Veritas series, by SCM Press, 13–17 Long Lane, London EC1A 9PN, England.

First U.S. edition published by Cascade Books under license from SCM Press.

Cascade Books
An Imprint of Wipf and Stock Publishers
199 W. 8th Ave., Suite 3
Eugene, OR 97401
www.wipfandstock.com

ISBN 13: 978-1-61097-815-6

Cataloging-in-Publication data:

Baker, Anthony D.

    Diagonal advance : perfection in Christian theology / Anthony D. Baker.

    xvi + 332 p. ; 23cm. —Includes index.

    Veritas
    ISBN 13: 978-1-61097-815-6

    1. Perfection—History of doctrines. 2. Deification (Christianity). I. Title. II. Series.

BT766 .B29 2011

Manufactured in the U.S.A.

For Allison, Lev and Anya

God approached and revealed Himself to men in Christ in such a manner that it became possible to set as one's way, limit, and goal the supreme commandment: 'Be ye . . . perfect, even as your Father which is in heaven is perfect.' . . . [Thus] the necessary diagonal of the earthly and the heavenly, of the temporal and the eternal, is known by every man only in his own creative activity.

Sergei Bulgakov, *The Lamb of God*

Contents

Contents

Centre of Theology and Philosophy

www.theologyphilosophycentre.co.uk

Every doctrine which does not reach the one thing necessary, every separated philosophy, will remain deceived by false appearances. It will be a doctrine, it will not be Philosophy. Maurice Blondel, 1861–1949

This book series is the product of the work carried out at the Centre of Theology and Philosophy at the University of Nottingham.

The COTP is a research-led institution organized at the interstices of theology and philosophy. It is founded on the conviction that these two disciplines cannot be adequately understood or further developed, save with reference to each other. This is true in historical terms, since we cannot comprehend our Western cultural legacy unless we acknowledge the interaction of the Hebraic and Hellenic traditions. It is also true conceptually, since reasoning is not fully separable from faith and hope, or conceptual reflection from revelatory disclosure. The reverse also holds, in either case.

The Centre is concerned with:

- The historical interaction between theology and philosophy.
- The current relation between the two disciplines.
- Attempts to overcome the analytic/Continental divide in philosophy.
- The question of the status of 'metaphysics'. Is the term used equivocally? Is it now at an end? Or have twentieth-century attempts to have a post-metaphysical philosophy themselves come to an end?
- The construction of a rich Catholic humanism.

I am very glad to be associated with the endeavours of this extremely important Centre that helps to further work of enormous importance. Among its concerns is the question whether modernity is more an interim than a completion – an interim between a pre-modernity in which the porosity between theology and philosophy was granted, perhaps taken for granted, and a postmodernity where their porosity must be unclogged and enacted anew. Through the work of leading theologians of international stature and philosophers whose writings bear on this porosity, the Centre offers an exciting forum to advance in diverse ways this challenging and entirely needful, and cutting-edge work. Professor William Desmond (Leuven)

VERITAS

Series Introduction

'. . . the truth will set you free.' (John 8.32)

Pontius Pilate said to Christ, 'What is truth?' And He remained silent.

In much contemporary discourse, Pilate's question has been taken to mark the absolute boundary of human thought. Beyond this boundary, it is often suggested, is an intellectual hinterland into which we must not venture. This terrain is an agnosticism of thought: because truth cannot be possessed, it must not be spoken. Thus, it is argued that the defenders of 'truth' in our day are often traffickers in ideology, merchants of counterfeits, or anti-liberal. They are, because it is somewhat taken for granted that Nietzsche's word is final: truth is the domain of tyranny.

Is this indeed the case, or might another vision of truth offer itself? The ancient Greeks named the love of wisdom as *philia*, or friendship. The one who would become wise, they argued, would be a 'friend of truth'. For both philosophy and theology might be conceived as schools in the friendship of truth, as a kind of relation. For like friendship, truth is as much discovered as it is made. If truth is then so elusive, if its domain is *terra incognita*, perhaps this is because it arrives to us – unannounced – as gift, as a person, and not some thing.

The aim of the Veritas book series is to publish incisive and original current scholarly work that inhabits 'the between' and 'the beyond' of theology and philosophy. These volumes will all share a common aspiration to transcend the institutional divorce in which these two disciplines often find themselves, and to engage questions of pressing concern to both philosophers and theologians in such a way as to reinvigorate both disciplines with a kind of interdisciplinary desire, often so absent in contemporary academe. In a word, these volumes represent collective efforts in the befriending of truth, doing so beyond the simulacra of pretend tolerance, the violent, yet insipid reasoning of liberalism that asks with Pilate, What is truth? – expecting a consensus of non-commitment; one that encourages the commodification of the mind, now sedated by the civil service of career, ministered by the frightened patrons of position.

Diagonal Advance

The series will therefore consist of two 'wings': 1, original monographs; and 2, essay collections on a range of topics in theology and philosophy. The latter will principally be the products of the annual conferences of the Centre of Theology and Philosophy (www.theologyphilosophycentre. co.uk).

Conor Cunningham
Peter Candler
Series editors

Acknowledgements

My debts to three people in particular in the following pages are extensive. In fact, if I felt as confined intellectually by twenty-first century consumerist culture as I generally do economically, I should be tempted to file bankruptcy and avoid my creditors altogether. However, here at least, I choose to receive their aid as gift and to return it in a small way simply by thanking them publicly. John Milbank has read and commented tirelessly on versions of these ideas since long before they were recognizable as chapters, and knew just when a word of critique needed to be replaced by a word of encouragement. It was he who first suggested the title 'Diagonal Advance'. Alan Gregory has lent me so many ideas and alerted me to so many texts as to nearly deserve a special index all his own. The material on English holiness literature especially shows his influence, although also the line in the Thomas section about trees clapping their hands, which I consider to be the best sentence in the whole book, is nearly a direct quote from one of our Latin Lunches at the Red River Café. And Tarah Van De Wiele: when I observed her penchant for theology and her skills as a reader of texts, I quickly approached her about working as my research assistant. I had not expected to get a writing coach, muse and (rather heavy-handed) editor in the process, but this book may not have emerged from the dark and cavernous virtual into the light of actuality, had it not been for that fortunate excess.

In addition to these three, many others have made contributions, great and small, to these pages. Scott Bader-Saye gave a generous amount of hours to reading and critiquing the first chapters. Ashley Brandon, Erin Warde and Teri Daily served as research assistants, reading, critiquing and tracking down sources. It is due to Ashley's efforts that, just to take one example, this book on perfection can include in its footnotes the writings of a man named Goodenough. Joe Behen read and commented on an early version of the Hellenism chapter. Alison Milbank once reminded me what I was writing about just when I was all but lost in the forest. Brian Sholl and I had a long discussion about *theosis* one afternoon and actually did wind up lost in a forest. Carey Newman at Baylor Press spent time discussing the layout of my book with me at a crucial time in its nascency, even though it was already contracted elsewhere. The library staff at Seminary of the Southwest spent unconscionable portions of their weeks making sure I got the strange and disparate texts I needed. Students in various classes at the seminar, and at churches around Austin, have been patient and gracious as I tried out these ideas on them. The administration and faculty of the seminary has been extremely supportive of my research. Nita and Ken Shaver opened the doors of Casa de la Playa for me to come and write in the serenest of settings. And then there have been countless conversations with friends and colleagues: Angel Mendez, Catherine Pickstock, Conor Cunningham, Craig Keen, Creston Davis, David Burrell, Dr Ross Miller, the Revd Edward Hopkins, Father Al Ajamie, Father David Barr, Gene Rogers, Jay Carter, Michael Hanby, Nathan Jennings, Pete Candler, Phil Turner, Rich Potts, Rocky Gangle and Willis Jenkins. Doug Harrison's influence shows up in various ways through these pages, as well as in my life more generally. Natalie Watson at SCM Press has been gracious and patient as she guided this project in for a landing. Thanks go to Lawrence Osborn, Valerie Bingham and Rebecca Goldsmith for their work on text. My parents have been conversation partners for this material over the years, as has my Uncle Ronnie. And finally, Lev, Anya and Allison, to whom this book is dedicated, have patiently endured a home invaded by stacks of Malory and Philo, meanwhile waiting for me to get on with fixing that broken light, building a doll's house, and relearning backup guitar chords. I'm all yours now.

Several chapters or sections of chapters below began life in another form. Some were papers for various occasions, and the feedback from those settings has been invaluable to me in developing them into their final state. Olivier Boulnois read, heard and critiqued material from the Third Movement below, as did his students Yann Schmitt and Chirine Raveton, along with the rest of his seminar at the Sorbonne in the Spring of 2008. I delivered a later version of that same material at the Grandeur of Reason conference in Rome that year, and comments from the attendees, Steve Long in particular, were of great assistance to me. Also that spring, the Department of Religion and Theology at Nottingham invited me to present a version of my Grail chapter, and the discussion that followed, ranging from Deleuze to Philippians to Dickens to Phoebe Palmer, was both dizzying and inspiring. The faculty of Seminary of the Southwest listened to and discussed a later portion of this same chapter. Some of the material on Thomas Aquinas below appeared in my article in *Political Theology* 10.1.

This project started years ago as a dissertation at the University of Virginia, and I remain appreciative to the Center for Religion and Democracy there, who gave me a generous grant for that work. Very little of the original project survived the revision, though I have carried over some of the material on Lossky in the Exposition below, and Neoplatonism in the First Movement.

With all that support and dialogue, it only remains to deliver the standard caveat, which is nonetheless especially true in this case: any shortcomings of the following text are only evidence of my own shortcomings and have nothing to do with any of those who have assisted me along this journey.

Prelude

Being human, as Aristotle says, takes practice (*Nichomachean Ethics* 2.4)[1]
but what is the performance for which we are warming up? It would be
a useful thing to spend a season rehearsing Mussorgsky's *Boris Godunov*,
unless of course we discover as we enter the pit on opening night that we
are actually billed to play Ellington's *Black, Brown and Beige*. Without
some sense of the whole, the *telos*, there is no way of knowing when we
are improving at being human. When does our practice make perfect, and
when is it just a series of disconnected instrumental exercises?

We are no longer able, for reasons this book will suggest, to think
through this question of a human *telos* very coherently. We have largely
forgotten what tune it is that we are playing. In fact, we have in modern
times come upon the sheet music to a very different orchestration and have
convinced ourselves that this is how to play the human song. From this
new discovery, two basic strategic options follow:

1 Play the arrangement before us according to the clearly defined no-
   tation and without improvisation, all the while ignoring a creeping
   sense that this music we play is not, in fact, very good. If the audience
   abandons us after intermission, or if those who do return give confused and hesitant applause at the end of each movement, this ought
   not distract us from the central goal: play what is on the stand in
   front of you. In the end, we may play a poor symphony; still, we will
   have succeeded in playing *this* symphony. There is a goal in this strategy, though it is entirely neutral in its relation to 'the good'. Thus,
   we may identify this mode of human practice as one of *teleological
   imperfection*. It achieves its *telos* precisely in its willing acceptance of
   mediocrity.

2 Play music of our own invention, rejecting the stale arrangement on
   the stand before us. Even more: the piece we play must not only refuse
   to align with the aim of the composer, but of the conductor, the audience and our fellow players in the pit. We might even come to expect
   that our own conception of the music's end owes too much to the
   bad music we have been asked to play. Even if we gather a chamber
   set from among the musicians around us to follow our lead, the point

---

1 See Terry Eagleton, 2003, *After Theory*, London: Penguin Books, pp. 6, 78.

remains that no end can be allowed to determine the direction of our play. Only music free of external parameters is good; the less it is governed by a predetermined end, the better. Thus, according to this strategy, the human music is an *ateleological perfection*. It achieves perfection precisely to the point that it rejects all *teloi*.

If we go on practising being human according to these new strategies, it cannot be long, regardless of which strategy we choose, before we forget the older music.

This is not to suggest that there is a pre-modern practice of being human that could come back to us now as a single sheet of music or a unified symphony. On the contrary, the 'older music' was an evolving style of being human that emerged along with the beginnings of philosophical and theological enquiry. This style of play entailed a named end, a *telos*, and also, eventually, as the style developed, a mode of engagement that allowed the players to experience their own music as good. As experience always involves a degree of improvisation, this style took a degree of skill, instrumentalists who knew their scales and riffs, but could also cue one another to take the lead with a look and a nod, and change rhythms seamlessly and in tandem with one another. There was an end in sight, but the end took shape in the course of the playing itself. The stakes of the performance, then, in this older style, were somewhat higher than in the newly determined strategies: classically, one played the human music in quest of a *teleological perfection*. This book tells the story, in four movements, of this perfection's emergence, and also of its distortion, culminating in the newly bifurcated strategies.

Before beginning, a note on my reading of texts. C. S. Lewis wrote that the task of the literary historian is to open a classical text without prejudicing the enquiry with that text's later intellectual heritage: to 'see the egg as if he did not know it was going to become a bird'.[2] If this is true, the task of the theologian who turns to historical documents is rather different. Here one must focus on the developed idea itself and then discern its scope and possibilities by combing through its ancestry. The theologian, that is, must rather see the bird, and then attempt to piece together the fragments of a shell that once formed the egg. When I read the classical texts below, I read with the assumption that a bird has hatched, and I investigate the shell fragments for evidence of when and how this hatching occurred.

In the following investigation, then, I proceed with the notion that there are, in fact, to return from ornithology to musicology, two symphonies: the one that emerges in the ancient world, coming to full expression in Maximus and Thomas, and the second, which comes to replace it in the late medieval and modern world. This notion prejudices my reading of Plato, Aristotle and the priests of Israel, as it does of Duns Scotus and John

---

2 C. S. Lewis, 1954, *English Literature in the Sixteenth Century Excluding Drama*, Oxford: Clarendon Press, p. 5.

Milton. I am not attempting to explain the full intellectual systems of any one of them, but am rather concerned only with the role they play in the ancestry of a single question: what is the end of the human being?

The Exposition, below, outlines the contemporary situation of perfection, prior to tracing either emergence or distortion: it illuminates the new sheet music. This new conceptualization structures the human practice in a way that makes it almost entirely different from the creature that the ancients wrote of. If Aeschylus, Aristotle, Augustine and Aquinas were to stumble upon a group of us now, practising at being human, would they recognize the melody? Or would they shrug their shoulders in common bewilderment and, despite their differences, go off to the other side of the pit and begin sharing and rehearsing the melodies that once flowed from their own pens, mouths and lives?

Exposition

He but requites me for his own misdeed
Kindness to such is keen reproach, which breaks
With bitter stings the light sleep of Revenge.
Submission, thou dost know I cannot try:
For what submission but that fatal word,
The death-seal of mankind's captivity,
Like the Sicilian's hair-suspended sword,
Which trembles o'er his crown, would he accept,
Or could I yield? Which yet I will not yield.

-Percy Shelley, 'Prometheus Unbound'

Somniloquent Cursings

When, in the early nineteenth century, the poet Percy Shelley retold the
ancient story of the war between Prometheus, the Titanic benefactor of
humans and Jupiter, his Olympian captor, he did so with a characteristic perversity that altered the tale entirely. His interest in 'completing'
the Prometheus cycle, as he said, was not simply to bring closure to a
long lost body of literature, but in fact to imagine a conclusion that the
tragedians never could have produced. Because his lyrical drama was to
be a *figura* of the moderns' great victory over against their intellectual
predecessors, a new ending was necessary. The ancient world could only
imagine the great prehistorical conflict between the Titan and Olympian to be resolved by the latter's mercy and the former's submission;
Shelley held that 'the moral interest of the fable . . . would be annihilated
if we could conceive of [Prometheus] as unsaying his high language and
quailing before his successful and perfidious adversary.'[1] Prometheus, for
Shelley, needs to win.

Shelley's Titan sees all too clearly that his stolen fire is the gift that has
become the innermost essence of his fashioned humans. Any compromise
that involves the return of fire, which stands for reason, the arts and even

---

1 Shelley's own 'Preface' to his 'Lyrical Drama in Four Acts', in George Edward
Woodberry (ed.), 1901, *The Complete Poetical Works of Shelley*, Boston: Houghton
Mifflin Company, p. 163.

the entire array of imaginative human culture,[2] would mean a destruction of the forms for which he has surrendered his own eternal freedom. So when Mercury pleads with him to submit to Jupiter's will, Prometheus points out that it is beyond his power to do so: he cannot agree to the destruction of the human race, and Jupiter will settle for nothing less.

> Submission, thou dost know I cannot try
> For what submission but that fatal word
> The death-seal of mankind's captivity,
> Like the Sicilian's hair-suspended sword,
> Which trembles o'er his crown, would he accept,
> Or could I yield? Which yet I will not yield. (*Prometheus Unbound*,
> 1.395–400)[3]

The gods are locked in a battle to the death: either Jupiter, the personification of transcendent and sublime oppression, must fall, or Prometheus, which is to say humanity as such, must submit.[4] Prometheus's curse of Jupiter, uttered in a rage of delirium and rehearsed for him by Mother Earth, awakens the Demagorgon, who then arrives in the heavens to depose Jupiter just as the latter is asserting his near-perfect omnipotence. 'Alone the soul of man, like unextinguished fire, burns toward heaven' he laments, 'hurling up insurrection, which might make our ancient empire insecure' (*Prom. Unb.* 3.1–49). And from the soul of humanity's benefactor comes just such an insurrection. Jupiter flees from the demon of the shadows, Prometheus is unbound, and along with him, all human powers and possibilities.

Shelley's Prometheus is an icon of human perfection. He is 'the type of the highest perfection of moral and intellectual nature impelled by the purest and the truest motives to the best and noblest ends'.[5] These 'best and noblest ends' require revolt, Prometheus's journey is an insurrective perfection. Only by emptying the human sphere of any sovereign governance will the human powers achieve their fullest. The brilliance of the young poet is that he appears to understand the implications of the appeal to archetypal insurrection better than many atheists and revolutionaries who come after him. It is not simply religious or monarchial authority that must be cast down if the human spirit is to be freed to achieve its highest possible good, but the very authority of language itself. Words, ideas, even logical notions, as he notes in an essay written as he was composing his great lyrical drama, can become a 'painted curtain' that eclipses the real dramatic activity of free human thought and imagination (see Shelley's *On*

---

2 Joseph C. McLelland, 1988, *Prometheus Rebound: The Irony of Atheism*, Waterloo, Ontario: Wilfred Laurier University Press, pp. 16, 20, 23.

3 Shelley, *Complete Poetical Works*, p. 171.

4 McLelland, *Rebound*, pp. 114–15.

5 Shelley, *Complete Poetical Works*, p. 163.

Life).[6] His Prometheus does not ride up to Olympus to depose Jupiter, since that would itself be a submission of a certain kind, a confrontation with the sovereign that would take the form, initially, of an acknowledgement that Jupiter is, in fact, the one to be deposed. In this sense, Shelley is already bending Hegel in a Deleuzian direction: true freedom is found beyond the master–slave dialectic, in the refusal of the master altogether. We encounter freedom in the affirmation of a human form that is neither positively or negatively under God (political sovereignty, logical or linguistic control), but instead recognizes beforehand the illegitimacy of any transcendent governor. Jupiter is as good as overthrown when Prometheus refuses to submit, since for Shelley the refusal of a heavenly encounter is itself the insurrection.

How, though, can this benign insurrection count as a perfection of the human form? Once he is unbound, could Prometheus not stride off on a path of world- and self-destruction as easily as toward its 'best and noblest ends'? We find a clue in the plot-twisting curse that he utters in his delirious state. For Shelley, if the human form is entirely unbound by God, Queen and all the formalities of human language, the motives that will rise to the surface of our nature will always be the praiseworthy sort. Prometheus must rebel, but his rebellion will not be a blinding hatred of Jupiter so much as collateral damage brought on by his maddening love for human beings. His only conscious cry is for 'truth, liberty, and love', virtues that will free themselves from tyrants who rush in and sow 'strife, deceit, and fear'. (*Prom. Unb.* 1.651–3). Prometheus himself is a perfection of love, and so only his love, not hate, can overthrow the heavens. So it is that his curse of Jupiter, which awakens the spirit that rides to Olympus to finish the coup, comes from his lips unconsciously, while he is talking in his sleep. Awake, he has no memory of the hateful words. Shelley's widow captures the centrality of his optimism when she writes that he 'believed that mankind had only to will that there should be no evil, and there would be none . . . That man could be so perfectionized as to be able to expel evil from his own nature, and from the greater part of the creation, was the cardinal point of this system.'[7] Her own 'modern Prometheus' shows an awareness of the darker potencies that lie within the wilful human spirit.[8]

---

6 Shelley, 1965 [1815], *On Life*, in *The Complete Works of Shelley*, vol. 6: *Prose*, New York: Gordian Press, p. 194. See Jerrold E. Hogle, 2006, 'Language and Form', in Timothy Morton (ed.), *The Cambridge Companion to Shelley*, Cambridge, UK and New York: Cambridge University Press, pp. 146–7.

7 Mary Wollstonecraft Shelley, in her notes on *Prometheus Unbound*, quoted in McLelland, *Rebound*, p. 116.

8 Still, though, the text of *Frankenstein* oozes with confidence in the powers of unbridled science and human creativity to produce pure goodness. McLelland thinks Mary Shelley's book is an argument for the rebinding of Prometheus (p. 115). But this judgement ignores those passages that present the 'monster' as a pure infantile form, growing in love for humans and the natural world. Doctor Frankenstein's failure is not in his 'Promethean' urge to create life, but in rejecting the life that he created, a move that makes the novel into an intentional reversal of Milton, where

Percy Shelley's poem is thus situated on the rise between modern and postmodern narratives of the human form, or, to be more precise, between the nineteenth century's Romanticism and the twentieth century's linguistic turn. His optimism about humankind's ability to achieve intellectual and moral perfection, once transcendence is subtracted, sounds to our ears like naïve Arcadianism; alternatively, his poetic crafting of a revolt that evades conscious utterance already recognizes the impossibility of the perfection that Prometheus performs, and leaves us in the space of a Wittgensteinian unspeakable or a Derridian messianic Logos. Shelley thus assists us in seeing that the accounts of the human journey from both centuries are varieties of Prometheanism, since the postmodern awareness of the textuality of the real is still the Romantic insistence on unbound freedom, even if the former attempts to school the latter in the multitude of invisible chains that still hold it fast.

A bit more recently, Michel Houellebecq, in his novel *Les particules élémentaires*, tells the story of humanity's end, in both the teleological and cessational senses of the word. *Soixante-huit* was, the author says, the inevitable next step in a long history of social erosion and relational fragmentation, such that the children born to that generation come of age as an almost literal manifestation of Deleuzian singularities. If in one sense the novel is thoroughly Shelleyan, following characters who seem to know and agree intuitively that the perfection of humanity is love, it is also pessimistic precisely where Shelley is optimistic. The formation of a sexual partnership, a family bond, a loyal city or a universal society around the virtue of love is precisely what modern humans are utterly incapable of doing. Thus the perfection of humanity is nothing less than the annihilation of humanity: in order to be the loving beings they desire to be, humanity must give way to a new species. So the novel concludes with the creation of a posthuman form, children of a 'perpetual afternoon' who refer to themselves, 'with a certain humour, by the name' their ancestors 'so long dreamed: gods'.[9]

---

it is the created life that rejects its creator. A better Frankenstein, a more perfect Prometheus, would have been less bound by the unscientific criteria of human loveliness, and would have embraced the creature that his elixir had awoken. Thus Mary is, like Percy, quite hopeful that the unbinding *can* perfect, even if she is not so confident as her husband that it *will* perfect. See Michael J. Hyde, 2010, *Perfection: Coming to Terms with Being Human*, Waco: Baylor University Press, pp. 98–106 and Marilyn Butler, 2003, 'Frankenstein and Radical Science', in Judith Wilt (ed.) *Making Humans*, Boston and New York: Houghton Mifflin Company, pp. 307–19. I am indebted to Alan Gregory for many conversations on the works of both Shelleys and especially for the idea that the tragic outcome of *Frankenstein* hinges entirely and simply on the monster's ugliness.

9 Michel Houellebecq, 2000, *The Elementary Particles*, trans. Frank Wynne, New York: Alfred A. Knopf, pp. 6, 263. Many thanks to my friend Brian Sholl for making me aware of this remarkable book.

If the 'end' of humanity is no longer a human, is that end really a perfection? This hesitation brings us to the very centre of the philosophical question of perfection. The Latin *perfectus*, from *facere*, is to be 'thoroughly made', as in the French phrase 'tout à fait'. Victorian English also retains a sense of human-making as a reaching of potential, even if our less than adequate attempts to name and construct that end mean that 'a made man' is a phrase that one utters only with a degree of irony. The ever-insightful Dickens, for instance, can give us this encounter:

> 'If at that time you could have helped us, Mr. George, it would have been the making of you.'
> 'I was willing enough to be "made," as you call it,' says Mr. George . . . 'but on the whole, I am glad I wasn't now.'[10]

Mr George's potential benefactor wants to bring him to *perfectus* through a series of shady financial dealings; if this is human perfection, Mr George wants none of it.

'Make', in its turn, bears an old English echo of 'match', such that a thing is only 'made' when it is 'matched', or well-coordinated for its particular purpose and peculiar environment. To be *perfectus*, then, has to do in part with how we are suited to the world around us. This is a flavouring still retained, and with no less irony, in the Elizabethan era. So Lady Macbeth admonishes her husband that his courage to be a man 'and so much more the man' before time and place availed the opportunity was laudable; now, when time and place are at last matched to his aspirations, with the sleeping Duncan before him as a made-to-order regicide and power-grab, his courage fails. Thus time and place 'have made themselves, and that their fitness now/ Does unmake you' (*Macbeth*, 1.7.52–3).[11] Macbeth's perfection is only ethereal, she says, until the fitting opportunity comes to 'make him' in the flesh. If he refuses now, he will be unmade, imperfect, because his dream to be 'more than man' will miss the single intersection of history with which it is matched.

But surely the difficulty, leading to ironic formulations, is in the idea of perfection itself.[12] Making a thing, seeing it fully made, is perhaps a simple enough thing when it is a matter of flowerpots and wave transmitters, but we hesitate when it comes to the purpose of a human, to finding 'make and match' by which we might inspect one another or ourselves and determine whether we meet all regulations. We hesitate to declare a human made because humans tend to experience themselves as unmatchable. The

---

10 Charles Dickens, 1964 [1853], *Bleak House*, New York: Signet Classics, p. 311.

11 W. G. Clark and W. Aldis Wright (eds), 1979, *The Complete Works of William Shakespeare*, vol. 2, Garden City and New York: Nelson Doubleday, Inc., p. 797.

12 See Newton Flew, 1934, *The Idea of Perfection in Christian Theology*, Oxford: Oxford University Press, especially pp. 52ff, where he considers the problem of 'the ideal' in Saint Paul.

human soul, Aristotle says, is 'in a manner all things' (*De Anima* 430a 14).[13] How then can it ever match this end? 'We are human', as a recent study on bioethics puts it, 'but can imagine gods'.[14] So are we fully made, perfected, when we achieve what we imagine, when we become all things, when we become gods? But if so, then we seem to have lost the very thing that once desired its own perfection: as in Houellebecq, the incomplete and desiring human has vanished. Are we then perfected only when we reject this imagined end (as the bioethics study in fact concludes is our ethical obligation)?[15] But a rejected end is a resignation to brokenness, no different than if acorns refused to become oak trees, or swallows refused to welcome in the summer.

Shelley rejects any resignation of this sort. His Titan achieves perfection to the extent that he rebels against all forms of sovereign control; he does not so much steal fire from the gods as steal the fire that constitutes divinity. Thus, modernity's ideal of perfection splits on an ethical wedge: should Prometheus steal the fire and become the god he imagines, in spite of the fact that he is (in Shelley at least) a creature of earth, or should he go on being human and bid farewell to the dream of deification? This is the question of perfection, as modern thought poses it. If in this Exposition we explore both strategies for determining the human vocation, it is only in service of suggesting, throughout the rest of this book, that the modern Promethean question is not in fact the question at all, but represents an imposition of a foreign *mythopoesis* on an older narrative of human ends.

Post-Enlightenment[16] thought is heavy with impulsive raids on the divine hearth. The 'Promethean complex' has settled deeply within the modern and postmodern psyche, so much so that he has become for us the 'figure of future human potential projected to the utmost degree of idealization'.[17] Said otherwise: the classical philosophical and theological discourse on human perfection, which sets out the possibilities for individual and communal achievement of the highest good, is in our age almost entirely colonized by the figure of Prometheus.

For instance, Freud is still a Romantic Promethean, as his account of dream interpretation shows. The stolen fire in this case takes the shape of an unbarricaded self-knowledge for his analysands. The subject who brings

---

13 R. D. Hicks (trans.), 1907, *Aristotle: De Anima*, Cambridge: Cambridge University Press.

14 *Being Human: Readings from the President's Council on Bioethics*, Chapter 1: 'The Search for Perfection', http://bioethics.georgetown.edu/pcbe/bookshelf/index.html (accessed 3 August 2010). See Hyde's thorough discussion of the report in Perfection, pp. 211–42.

15 See below.

16 Taking the Enlightenment as an era that was already waning at the end of the eighteenth century. See John R. Betz, 2009, *After Enlightenment: Hamann as Post-Secular Visionary*, Oxford: Wiley-Blackwell.

17 William Keach, 2006, 'The Political Poet', in Timothy Morton (ed.), *The Cambridge Companion to Shelley*, Cambridge, UK and New York: Cambridge University Press, p. 127.

to the session narrative material produced in self-conscious contemplation is, he insists, quite hopeless. To approach self-observation with 'tense attitude' and 'wrinkled brow', is to unwittingly suppress what she considers undesirable raw material, and thus she unavoidably exercises an extrinsic control over the interpretive process.[18] The subject, conversely, who simply observes her own psychic processes with a certain detachment, allows even the undesirable to come to the surface. An unlimited number of ideas now rise to the surface, and they become grist for the analytic mill, as all that is now suppressed is censorship itself. Dream interpretation can now proceed, beginning with the undesirable ideas that are of course, for the analyst, most desirable.[19]

The subject, for Freud, serves as its own Jupiter, policing the subconscious with the authoritarianism that disallows any real human flourishing. His solution, though, repeats the Shelleyan optimism, since his prescribed method of freeing the psyche through therapy only replaces the newly discovered intrinsic tyrant with another external tyrant, namely, the analyst himself.[20] The therapist can offer the new positivism of a doctrine that will unveil the true self. This has been demonstrated by a variety of critical texts on Freud, and perhaps nowhere as fully as in Deleuze and Guattari's *Anti-Oedipus*. 'What a mistake,' they write, 'to have ever said *the* id'.[21] The unbinding of Prometheus must entail, for them, an act of psycho-ontological unbinding, since the human type itself is only held together by its act of submission to authority. Once all the chains are truly off, we find the subject to be a limitless series of productions, a cacophony created by the whirlings and clankings of 'desiring machines'.[22] A finger that desires a stimulating surface to touch, a toe that desires warmth, a throat that desires water, a mouth that desires something to chew or suck. But many steps are required to say *I* want to hold your hand or put on a sock, or *I* want a drink or a piece of gum. It is not, most basically, the objects of my desires that I lack, but the objectivity of myself, 'the objectivity of man'.[23] This objectivity must be produced if it is to exist, and this fact reveals for them the bill of goods that is Freudian analysis. The discovery of the Oedipus complex was in fact the discovery of the external mechanism by which

---

18 Sigmund Freud, 1913, *The Interpretation of Dreams*, trans. A. A. Brill, New York: The Macmillan Company, p. 84.

19 See Fish's account of the coercive character of Freud's 'persuasive technologies'. Stanley Fish, 1989, *Doing What Comes Naturally: Change, Rhetoric, and the Practice of Theory in Literary and Legal Studies*, Durham, NC and London: Duke University Press, pp. 525–93. Thanks to Scott Bader-Saye for bringing this text to my attention.

20 Richard Webster, 1996, *Why Freud Was Wrong: Sin, Science, and Psychoanalysis*, New York: Basic Books, pp. 311–17.

21 Gilles Deleuze and Felix Guattari, 1985, *Anti-Oedipus: Capitalism and Schizophrenia*, trans. Robert Hurley et al., Minneapolis: University of Minnesota Press, p. 1.

22 Deleuze and Guattari, *Anti-Oedipus*, p. 9.

23 Deleuze and Guattari, *Anti-Oedipus*, p. 27.

the analyst can unite the many conflicting and co-terminal desires of the patient and give to her a self that she can confront. 'Say that it's Oedipus, or you'll get a slap in the face. The psychoanalyst no longer says to the patient: "Tell me a little bit about your desiring machines, won't you?" Instead he screams, "Answer daddy-and-mommy when I speak to you!"'[24] I manifest as a unity, and thus as 'perfectible' along a traceable trajectory, only when I emerge over against the other two sovereign members of the divine family, mommy–daddy–me.[25]

Freud, in short, 'doesn't like schizophrenics'.[26] But Prometheus unbound is in fact schizophrenic, and to ignore this situation is to bind him, tacitly and ideologically, once again. In this way, the postmodern philosopher exposes the hidden undoing of Romantic perfection: like the cat in the folk song, the deposed sovereign simply comes back through some unforeseen opening. Jupiter returns disguised as a sublime virtue or a rigidly analytic ideology and so gives the lie to Prometheus's insurrection. How then does postmodern psychoanalysis deal with the sovereign's return?

Deleuze and Guattari can, in fact, be brought up on their own charges without too much difficulty, revealing them to be 'Postmodern Prometheans', not all that far removed from the Romantic. For in the summoning of an image of foundational schizophrenia, they appeal tacitly to a transcendent order of things in general and of the human thing in particular. Being itself, they say, is schizoid, and any move toward functional unities on the part of those agencies that emerge within it will always be secondary. I, and we, exist in a realm of actuality that can freeze within the endless chaos of virtual, but will be always be 'untrue' to the formless being that issues it.[27] Why and how is this simply the case? It could only be because virtuality itself, the depths of ontological schizophrenia, stands sovereign over us in the way that God and the Id once did.[28] The unmanaged array of desiring machines is a new ontological positivism, and insurrection against this order of things is futile. Just as Mercury tries to convince the chained Titan, the only possible existence under the aegis of this unassailable God comes through submission.

The trouble with the Promethean complex is that any attempt to name an ideal towards which Prometheus may stride, or even to name the ontological arena in which he does stride, will always cycle back into a naming of transcendence. Shelley himself seems only to have been half-aware

---

24 Deleuze and Guattari, *Anti-Oedipus*, p. 45. See also Webster, *Why Freud*, pp. 278–95.

25 See especially *Anti-Oedipus*'s second chapter, 'Psychoanalysis and Familialism', pp. 51–138.

26 Deleuze and Guattari, *Anti-Oedipus*, p. 23.

27 See Deleuze, 1994, *Difference and Repetition*, trans. Paul Patton, New York: Columbia University Press, pp. 197–221.

28 See Alain Badiou, 1999, *Deleuze: The Clamour of Being*, trans. Louise Burchill, Minneapolis: University of Minnesota Press. Badiou attempts to solve the problem of the givenness of the ontological situation, but can do so only by confining the universal to a certain kind of particularity. I shall have more to say about this in the Fourth Movement, below.

of this difficulty, since he celebrates a human nature that is now free to become 'its own divine control' (*Prom. Unb.* 4.401), without recognizing that human nature now becomes, indeed, its own divine control. A humanity that frees itself through titanic rebellion will always wind up chained to a rock in the Caucasus again. This will be our fate, regardless of whether we map the journey romantically or postmodernly. To the extent that we chart the human form as in the least bit active, engaging the world in such a way as to register achievement, to that same extent we rely upon a goal that exceeds the form and lies extrinsic to it. This is one of the difficulties raised in Iris Murdoch's *The Time of the Angels*, which could be read as a novel situated under the sign of the Titanic unbinding. Here humans left with an empty heaven attempt to find a new trajectory toward the good in the midst of a relentless terrestrial fog, which gives the unsettling impression that 'life has no outside'.[29] One aspiring academic in the novel captures the difficulty precisely, in a manuscript to which he has given the working title, *Morality in a World without God*:

> I come now to a more serious and thought-provoking objection. If the idea of Good is separated from the idea of perfection it is emasculated and any theory which tolerates this severance, however high-minded it professes itself to be, is in the end a vulgar relativism. If the idea of Good is not severed from the idea of perfection it is impossible to avoid the problem of 'the transcendent.' Thus the 'authority' of goodness returns, and must return, to the picture in an even more puzzling form.[30]

The only alternative the author can see that refuses a transcendent perfection is vulgar, because it would consist in an attempt to escape from any shared grammar of critical thought, and thus an attempt to hide from the implications of our named desires in a non-existent private language. This though is simply a newly fashioned neurotic self-binding. Wishing to avoid such vulgarism, what option do we have besides understanding our shared sense of goodness as a donation from a universal and transcending 'perfect'? Prometheus unbound is either an isolated figure on a white plain, or a player in a symphony he did not invent. Either way, Prometheus freed is Prometheus bound.

Resisting the Flames

Could it be that the entire strategy of freeing ourselves from extrinsic determination is wrong-headed? Perhaps humans ought to give up the tyranny of auto-poetic perfection, and play the music we inherit. Perhaps Prometheus is better off bound.

---

29 Iris Murdoch, 1966, *The Time of the Angels*, New York: Viking Press, p. 30.
30 Murdoch, *Time*, pp. 123–4.

Therapeutic imperfection

This point is made rather convincingly by Bruno Bettelheim, a Freudian who catches the admiration of Deleuze and Guattari, even if he 'has a noticeable bias in favor of Oedipal or pre-oedipal causality'.[31] His study of child rearing, *A Good Enough Parent*, attempts to free contemporary childcare givers from the very notion of perfection. The psyche, in Freudian and post-Freudian doctrine, is not a blank slate, but rather an inheritor of a host of complex identifiers: ontogeny recapitulates phylogeny, in the still mythological teaching of early psychoanalysis; or, to say the same thing in the post-Mendelian paradigm, individuals inherit genetic information.[32] Bettelheim uses psychoanalysis against that brand of rigorous behaviourism that suggests that children are formed entirely by the actions and reactions of their caregivers in earliest years, the notion that human children are 'Skinnerian pigeons'.[33] This school of thought, which he suggests is still prevalent in performance-driven North Atlantic society (at least), drives an anxiety about finding the perfect blueprint that will produce the perfect child, and thus make the caregivers into the perfect parents. The mechanistic image, he suggests, is part of the problem. We think of parenting as we think of designing the perfect machine: with enough tinkering, we will get the outcome we desire.[34] Perfect parenting is the doomed project of crafting our children *ex nihilo*. The good enough parent, then, will reject the search for a blueprint, and will instead create an environment in which the distinct potencies of identity that are already the child's can develop and be expressed in non-anxious, self- and other-respecting modes.[35]

Following Bettelheim, then, a new option emerges: rather than the Romantic-cum-postmodern quest for a perfection that erases all objectifiable parameters as tyrannical, should we not opt for the more common-sensical plan of discarding perfection itself as a kind of tyranny? Human beings are bound by layers of inheritance and even by seemingly random personalities. Certainly as a therapeutic measure for those searching frenetically for a ruse against these limits (and which of us, parents or not, are immune to this *frenetique*?), the honest and painful acknowledgement of the boundedness of life in time and space, and of the inconstancies of human desires, is central to any possible happiness.

But when Bettelheim asks us to acknowledge that good enough is better than perfect, he is in fact asking us to accept a new and only tacitly articulated *telos*. Having rejected perfection as pathology, 'good enough'

---

31 Deleuze and Guattari, *Anti-Oedipus*, p. 37.

32 Bruno Bettelheim, 1987, *A Good Enough Parent: A Book on Child-Rearing*, New York: Random House, pp. 9–10. Thanks to Dr Ross Miller for first bringing this book to my attention.

33 Bettelheim, *Good Enough*, p. 9.

34 Bettelheim, *Good Enough*, pp. 15–18.

35 Bettelheim, *Good Enough*, pp. 10, 149–65.

can become the new perfection. If it is to serve, we must learn to 'listen' to the genetic inheritances that are the nebulous identities of our children and then surround them with those patterns of behaviour that therapy determines will aid human flourishing.[36] However, this means that we still situate ourselves in relation to a goal of ideal parenting, and it is still limited by our ability to imagine an ideal of human flourishing. Has the therapist fully contemplated our economic, political and intellectual situation, including metaphysics and theology, so that she is equipped now to offer us a reliable new perfection of the good enough? And has she considered whether her identified goal of the good enough is, from a broader philosophical perspective, good enough? Even in the least ideological environment, the new end will most likely be constructed accidentally and on the fly, by a particular culture, social group or therapeutic community, even if its meta-role of 'endness', or perfection, is explicitly rejected. For instance, what keeps Bettelheim's 'most desirable result of psychoanalytic education', namely, 'to love well and to work well',[37] from translating into practice as the goal of experiencing enough easing of relational anxiety that one can continue to be a productive member of a capitalist economy. Is this 'good enough'? If not, then in spite of an initial rejection of perfection as pathological, it is not clear that Bettelheim (or we) can settle for less.

It would seem this is the *mise en scène* for the introduction of a theology of perfection, which could mitigate our dilemma by challenging the limitations of the Promethean-Jupiter dialectic with a counter-narrative, construing a human end which is a gift and so not the sort of thing we can either steal or refuse to steal. The trouble, though, is that the theological seems to have missed its cue. In a variety of traditions, Orthodox, Catholic and Protestant, and a variety of constructions, the human end envisioned within modern and contemporary theology is still implicitly or explicitly a riff on the Promethean *mythos*.

Perhaps this is to be expected. Like any complex that holds power in any age, we can either exemplify it or reject it; either way, our past narratives and future possibilities will be scripted by it. To live in mortal fear of the Oedipus archetype is the surest guarantee that I will fall in patricidal love with my mother; in fact, this is the inescapable point of the oracle's diagnosis in the Sophoclean sequence, since Oedipus himself is the original refuser of the Oedipal.

A reactionary anti-Prometheanism is apparent, first of all, in less explicitly theological contexts such as in the United States' President's Council on Bioethics, mentioned above, which was commissioned to lead a large-scale evaluation of the ramifications of the posthuman question for contemporary legal and moral imperatives. The authors of this report are understandably critical of engineered attempts to abolish human vulnerability and finitude. In their final report, they acknowledge that these efforts have a basis in an anthropological quandary: 'We are human, but can imagine

---

36 Bettelheim, *Good Enough*, pp. 332–44.
37 Bettelheim, quoting Freud affirmatively, *Good Enough*, p. 12.

gods.' When they formulate from this the key ethical question, however, they opt for a particular vocabulary: 'Should we try to mould the imperfections we have been (given?)' through genetic modification, embryonic stem cell research, etc., 'into something closer to our ideal?'[38] Finitude and vulnerability here are not seen as goods that allow human communication and culture, but rather as 'imperfections', and the report's conclusion argues that we should satisfy ourselves with our own distance from the perfection we imagine: 'An appreciation of the giftedness of life would constrain the Promethean project and conduce to a much-needed humility.'[39]

The contrast of 'the Promethean project' with the virtue of humility reveals the extent to which the authors' vision of a human good is limited by this complex. Of course humility in itself is a laudable trait, especially in light of the body-transforming perfectionism of posthuman genetics; but to counsel resigned humility over against the project of unlimited groping of human minds and fingers is to accept fully the disjunction of Olympianism versus Titanism as set forth in Shelley's poem, and simply to vote against his outcome. For Shelley, to be human is to strive for perfection, freed from extrinsic governance; for the Council, to be human is to be imperfect, and to strive for perfection is to violate the right order of things. In this way a contemporary allergy to perfection stems from an acceptance of this very disjunction.

As a further example: theologically tinted therapeutic literature often opts against the recovery of perfection, and takes the Bettelheimian path wherein perfectionism is a pathology, counselling instead a spirituality that is 'more a journey toward humility than a struggle for perfection'.[40] Texts on addiction from the Alcoholics Anonymous school suggest that 'trying to be perfect is the most tragic human mistake'. Instead of striving to be Godlike, the way to freedom and flourishing is through an embracing of human imperfection.

In direct contradiction of the serpent's promise in Eden's garden, the book Alcoholics Anonymous suggests, 'First of all, we had to quit playing God.' According to the way of life that flows from this insight, it is only by ceasing to play God, by coming to terms with errors and shortcomings, and by accepting the inability to control every aspect of their lives that alcoholics (or any human beings) can find the peace and serenity that alcohol (or other drugs, or sex, money, material possessions, power, or privilege) promise but never deliver.[41]

---

38 *Being Human,* Chapter I, Introduction.

39 *Beyond Therapy: Biotechnology and the Pursuit of Happiness,* from the same commission. http://bioethics.georgetown.edu/pcbe/reports/beyondtherapy/chapter6.html (accessed 3 August 2010). Again, see Hyde, *Perfection,* pp. 211–42.

40 Ernest Kurtz and Katherine Ketcham, 1992, *The Spirituality of Imperfection: Storytelling and the Search for Meaning,* New York: Bantam Books, p. 5.

41 Kurtz and Ketcham, *Spirituality,* p. 5.

In spite of the undeniable wisdom in this advice, the formulation begs an important question. The above excerpt assumes quite boldly that the quest for perfection is synonymous with a desire to play God. The pitting of a benevolent embracing of limitation over against the serpent's promise from Genesis is one that is typical of modern Christian language, though not of the Church Fathers. In the older tradition, the serpent's promise was deceptive precisely because the Godlikeness that he offered was the gift that God had always intended to give. By stealing it, the Eden dwellers ruined the gift of deification and were cursed with the limiting names that they had, by their theft, already given themselves. Thus the idea that humans sin by desiring too much is in fact a complete reversal of the older understanding, where the primordial sin was an attempt to be human through a resignation to any end other than the gift of Godlikeness. In fact, according to Scholastic angelology, even Lucifer's fall was not a matter of an overactive Promethean complex, but rather a pathetic desire to settle for less than was his share. By attempting to reify himself as a stabilized angelic form on the divine throne, rather than continuing in the endlessly deifying progression of sharing in the divine nature and rule, Lucifer becomes Satanic.[42] We can only finally accept the wisdom of a 'spirituality of imperfection' if we reject this deeply rooted Christian notion that perfection is the journey towards Godlikeness.

Popular theologies like these assume a certain image of perfection in order to reject it. Perfection, for them, is an unbridled pursuit of autonomy, self-creation and the rejection of any *telos* beyond the subjective will. Rightly recognizing the conflict between this sort of perfectionism and Christian morality, they reject the idea of perfection as such, assuming that this goal will always take the form of an unwarranted theft of the Olympian fire. Instead, we should embrace our earthly imperfection. What these authors are unable to see is that in this very rejection they fully accept the modernists' account of perfection. Perfection is always titanic, and they choose the side of Jupiter.

But we are getting ahead of ourselves, already tracing out the perfectionism that the modern Promethean *mythos* eclipses. Here it is only my aim to show that the seemingly prudent teaching 'that trying to be perfect is the most tragic human mistake' is philosophically incoherent at best, ethically reproachable at worst.

Philosophically incoherent simply because it begins by begging the question, *what is perfection?* Human perfection, for Aristotle, is simply that end toward which humans, as distinct from acorns and horses as well as from soldiers and doctors, strive. It is formally identical with the object of our striving, since the goal of a doctor is to accomplish perfectly the tasks of the medical practice and the goal of a human is to accomplish perfectly the tasks of the human practice (*Nichomachean Ethics*,

---

42 See Henri de Lubac, 1998, *The Mystery of the Supernatural*, trans. Geoffrey Chapman, New York: Crossroads Publishing Company, pp. 29–32.

1094a–1109b).[43] The strangeness of the notion of an ultimate end within the endless continuity of temporal life is not lost on Aristotle, and so he invents the radical notion that *eudaimonia*, the infusion of divine happiness within a human life, is a kind of narrative arc that structures an entire life, not simply the epilogical reflection at the end.[44] The whole, with its contingencies and surprises, is the internal structure of the end. This radical notion that achieving an end has to do first of all with the manner in which one approaches it along the way becomes so intrinsic to the idea of perfection that the great Aristotelian Thomas Aquinas could suggest that God is not quite perfect. Only those who can become more fully actualized through (*per*) a process of making (*fectus*) can be perfect in the proper sense of the term. God is *actus purus*, and thus only retains a perfection of a rather ironic sort: perfect, though not 'by way of perfection' (*per modum perfectionis – ST* 1.4.1, *ad* 2).[45] In this light, the denial of perfection is coterminous with the rejection of any sort of responsiveness to a call to strive for an end.

Of course, the AA community, the therapist who suggests that we aim for 'good enough', or the singer who advises us to 'Ring the bells that still can ring/ Forget your perfect offering/ There is a crack, a crack in everything/ That's how the light gets in',[46] are not attempting to reject human agency and development. Rather, they are rejecting a pathological compulsion for a super-temporary level of performance, which ultimately compromises one's ability to pursue the good life. Yet in the older philosophical language, this is not perfection, but perfection's negation: perfectionism as a contemporary pathological phenomenon is anti-perfectionism in the classical vocabulary. In place of the classical motif of a life shaped by the pursuit of a commonly discerned human good, the 'addict of perfection' substitutes an obsession with a self-named *summum bonum*, an object seen, incoherently, as the great end which will raise her beyond all the partialities and losses of temporal life. But is the proper response to this pathology a new modern anti-perfectionism, which has not only the limitation of philosophical incoherence, but also of moral risk? Might we not rather attempt to sketch a new account of perfection that captures the participatory striving identified within the classical doctrine?

43 H. Rackham (ed. and trans.), 1956, *Aristotle* Vol. XIX, Loeb Classical Library no. 73, London and Cambridge, MA: William Heinemann Ltd and Harvard University Press.

44 See Robert Heinaman, 1993, 'Rationality, Eudaimonia, and Kakodaimonia in Aristotle', *Phronesis*, vol. 38, pp. 31–56. Also Robert Spaemann, 2005, *Happiness and Benevolence*, trans. Jeremiah Alberg, SJ, Edinburgh: T&T Clark, especially Part 1.

45 Fathers of the English Dominican Province (ed. and trans.), 1947, *Summa Theologiae*, New York: Benzinger Bros.

46 Leonard Cohen, 'Anthem', http://www.mp3lyrics.org/l/leonard-cohen/anthem (accessed 3 August 2010). Thanks to my friend and musical sage Bob Kinney for this lyric.

Pietistic imperfection

In order to demonstrate the moral risks in the loss of perfection, I turn to more explicitly theological texts. Adolph von Harnack's immensely influential studies on the development of Christianity make a related point to both the bioethics report and the text on addiction, a century prior. Using the proper name for Godlike perfection associated with the Greek Fathers, von Harnack writes: 'the notion of redemption as deification of mortal nature is subchristian.' 'The whole doctrine is inadmissible', he says, 'because it has scarcely any connexion with the Jesus Christ of the Gospel, and its formulas do not fit him; it is, therefore, not founded in truth,' but instead on an 'egoistic desire for immortal existence'.[47] Deification, the idea that created things have their proper goal in becoming gods, is for Harnack simply one of many false imports into Christianity, perverting the 'higher righteousness' of Semitic messianism with the insatiable appetite of Hellenistic philosophy. This higher righteousness was founded for him above all on the 'all important point' that ensured the integrity of Christian teaching: humility,[48] understood by Harnack as nothing less than the restraint from claiming deification as a human goal. The following chapters of this book will contest this judgement on nearly every point.

Contemporary theologian Reinhold Hütter follows the Harnackian way of thinking at least in this respect, rejecting what he takes to be a 'disastrous and deeply pretentious' exchange of attributes 'between God and humanity' in favour of a separation of the powers of sovereignty from the powers of created being. Recognizing the importance of the question of human ends for the identification of created humanity as such, he asks, 'What constitutes the human as human? What makes us who we essentially are?' For him, the Christian answer to this question is a freedom bound by divine charity, a freedom in which God remains sovereign, and humans are the contingent beings who refuse to attempt any violation of God's sovereignty. By contrast,

The epoch of modernity defined itself by rejecting Christianity's answer to the question, What is so great about freedom? Goethe's famous poem 'Prometheus' captures best the modern answer to this question: moral sovereignty and self-sufficiency. By heroically defying the gods, Prometheus claims freedom for himself and the whole human race. Moreover, he shows that freedom makes him Prometheus in the first place . . . I call this perspective, in which the Promethean 'I' imagines itself as sovereign, the *modern daydream*.[49]

47 Adolf von Harnack, 1901, *What is Christianity?: Sixteen lectures delivered in the University of Berlin during the winter-term 1899–1900*, trans. Thomas Bailey Saunders, London: Williams and Norgate, p. 235.

48 Harnack, *What is Christianity*, p. 73.

49 Reinhold Hütter, 2004, *Bound to Be Free: Evangelical Catholic Engagements in Ecclesiology, Ethics, and Ecumenism*, Grand Rapids, MI: Eerdmans, p. 7.

Though Hütter sketches in plain terms the moral and theological limitations of this 'Promethean "I"', he does not yet see the ways in which he remains caught within his very rejection of it. By accepting the contrast of Christian virtue with deification, which was understood by theologians like Augustine and Maximus the Confessor precisely as an exchange of attributes between God and creatures, he is accepting the terms as defined by the modern Prometheus and simply choosing to stay bound in the Caucasus rather than to storm the heavens. The human is constituted, for Hütter, in a refusal of the insurrective attempt to become Godlike, coming to terms instead with the chains that are more fitted to his nature.

The danger inherent here is that by refusing humankind one perfection, this theology inevitably substitutes another, lesser end. If human attributes are unexchangeable with divine, then they really belong to humans, and human perfection is achieved immanently, by developing those attributes to their fullest embodiment. By refusing to allow Prometheus to mount up to the heavens, to be deified, Hütter ensures that he will, in fact, have an earthly perfection. Moreover, the relation of this human perfection to the divine attributes will always be rather vague, as shown by the numerous attempts in the seventeenth and eighteenth centuries to divide God's attributes into lists of communicable and incommunicable. Even if we insist that divine grace is necessary to achieve this earthly end, we nonetheless construct it as a perfection belonging to humans and thus essentially bifurcate human perfection and the character of God. Human perfection will thus become a sort of vacuum in which anything but the holiness of God can form.

This is a point grasped by the twentieth century's premier Protestant theologian in regards to the tradition of Christian mysticism. Although deeply sceptical of the erotic God-talk of the mystics, Karl Barth notes that if it is entirely suppressed, 'we do not guard against the paganism of religious sentimentalism and religious *eros*. On the contrary, we open up the way for it. For this paganism finds its excuse in the vacuum created by such evasion and suppression. It flourishes all the more vehemently in this vacuum.'[50] We will return below to Barth's significant, if ultimately limited, contribution to the theology of perfection. But here we find him noting an irony which is also a moral risk that the theological rejection of perfection encounters: an allergic reaction to the idea of perfect fulfilment of human desire will give way to a host of unscripted, untraceable, imperfect desires that clamour for fulfilment.

Thus, though we now have a domesticated Prometheus who willingly submits to authorities beyond his control, resigning himself to an imperfect life from within the limits of the human situation, we are surprised to find that this very resignation involves him in various non-deifying perfections which we have given him licence to name autonomously. We have in brief authorized him to pursue any perfection he likes, so long as he stays bound to earth, the very sort of binding that will, in fact, keep his

---

50 Karl Barth, 1958, *Church Dogmatics*, Vol. 4: *The Doctrine of Reconciliation*, Part 2, trans. G. W. Bromiley, Edinburgh: T&T Clark, p. 798.

own attributes from mirroring God's. Thus pietistic anti-perfection has forgotten the lesson of Lucifer's fall, namely, that the demonic is precisely the desire for anything less than deification. Even Shelley kept the Titan more restrained, ensuring that only love counted as a truly human end. A bound Prometheus can, logically, be anything but loving, since love is the proper name of God's essence. In this way, if chained too tightly, the Titan will inevitably be radically unchained, 'free' to stride forth toward just the sort of autonomous and god-defying perfection that theologians want to keep him from attempting. Prometheus bound is thus more Titanic than ever.

If, as the previous section demonstrated, we reject any manifestation of a sovereign perfection only to see it reassert itself against us, we now see that we can reject human deification only to find that this very rejection manufactures an undisclosed insurrection against our now welcomed chains, in both cases, the repressed perfection returns. A fear of the first type of rejection, I suspect, lies embedded in the fabric of this second. Theologians, musicians and therapists have bought the contrast of humble submission versus the striving for Godlikeness, and their vision of the human good suffers a philosophical and ethical incoherence as a result.

Imperfect theosis

The Christianity that rejects deification however, as John Passmore notes, is only a portion of the story, since many theologians recognize in this term the proper name of the Christian end.[51] Von Harnack has in recent years come under rather intense critique for his 'Hellenization thesis' in general and for his critique of deification in particular. Norman Russell's painstakingly thorough tome now makes it impossible to accept either that deification was entirely present in the pre-Christian Greeks or that it was entirely absent in the Old Testament (the point having already been made by writers like Wayne Meeks that, by the time the New Testament was being composed, there were no unhellenized Jews).[52] In fact, Russell makes a persuasive case that deification was not a popular term or concept among the pagan Greeks at all until after they had been influenced by the New Testament and Apostolic writings.[53]

---

51 John Passmore, 2000, *The Perfectibility of Man*, 3rd ed., Indianapolis, IN: Liberty Fund Inc, pp. 85–9.

52 Wayne Meeks, 1986, *The Moral World of the First Christians*, Philadelphia: Westminster Press; Norman Russell, 2004, *The Doctrine of Deification in the Greek Patristic Tradition*, Oxford and New York: Oxford University Press; Stephen Finlan and Vladimir Kharmlamov, 2006, 'Introduction', in Finlan and Kharmlamov (eds), *Theosis: Deification in Christian Theology*, Eugene, OR: Pickwick Publications, pp. 7–9. See also Jules Gross's important text as well: Gross, 2002 [1938], *The Divinization of the Christian according to the Greek Fathers*, Anaheim: A&C Press, pp. 264ff.

53 Russell, *Deification*, pp. 8, 121ff.

Still, we must be slow about championing deification or *theosis* as our way out of the binding/loosing conundrum. *Theosis* is, as Stephen Finlan and Vladimir Kharmlamov have noted, an idea deeply seated in the ancient tradition which nonetheless lacks any clear definition.[54] It is possible to conceive of deification in such a way as to retain the exclusionary relation of humility and perfection. A mystical Orthodox theologian like Vladimir Lossky certainly stands 'at the opposite pole' from 'the line of Harnack's thinking',[55] since Lossky insists that deification is at the most basic layer of Christian teaching; but (and Finlan and Kharmlamov do not see this point) his account of deification is no closer to a theology of human perfection than is Harnack's moral imperative of humility.

Lossky is essential to the contemporary ecumenical thinking on deification since his texts, appearing in translation in the 1950s and 1960s, led the way in what has become a renaissance of eastern theology in the West. His account of deification begins in his understanding of the knowledge humans can have of God. Chief among his sources here is Gregory Palamas, whose own point of departure, according to Lossky, is 'the antinomy concerning the knowable and the unknowable in God',[56] seen in his signature distinction between divine *energia* and *ousia*. This antimony, says Lossky, has 'a real foundation in God', since via the energies God reveals himself in natural processions which are, strangely, neither exterior nor essential to God. The division is rather *within* God, between proper divinity and that which 'overflows'. Thus Lossky denies what a Catholic of the same era calls 'entitative participation',[57] while affirming what we might call *emanative* participation.[58]

Though Lossky refers to this terminological division as a 'real distinction', it actually has more the character, as we shall see below, of the Scotist 'formal distinction', as it serves to separate the territory in God in which we share from that which is forever closed off to us.[59] So the object of mystical experience is never

God in His essence, incommunicable and unknowable by definition; for if we could at a given moment participate to some degree in the essence,

---

54 Finlan and Kharmlamov, *Theosis*, p. 4.

55 Finlan and Kharmlamov, *Theosis*, p. 9.

56 Vladimir Lossky, 1974, *In the Image and Likeness of God*, eds John H. Erickson and Thomas E. Bird, Crestwood, NY: St Vladimir's Seminary Press, p. 53.

57 The phrase is Maritain's, quoted in Jean Borella, 2002, *The Sense of the Supernatural*, trans. G. John Champoux, Edinburgh: T&T Clark, p. 127.

58 Lossky seems inconsistent regarding this intrinsic division: in *Mystical Theology*, he says that 'the energies signify an exterior manifestation of the Trinity which cannot be interiorized, introduced, as it were, within the divine being'. Vladimir Lossky, 1976, *The Mystical Theology of the Eastern Church*, trans. Fellowship of St Alban and St Sergius, Crestwood, NY: St Vladimir's Seminary Press, p. 80. This construction is more modalistic than the 'gnostic' internalized division in *Image and Likeness*.

59 Lossky, *Image and Likeness*, p. 56. See Third Movement, below.

we would not in that moment be what we are, but gods by nature; but we are created beings called to become by grace what God is by His nature. If St. Peter (II. Peter 1:4) calls us 'partakers of the divine nature' (*divinae consortes naturae*), it is to the degree that this nature becomes participable in the energies, but not in itself.[60]

All that can be kataphatically attributed to God is attributable to energy alone: wisdom, goodness, even simplicity.[61] In terms of essence, only apophatic theology serves, which for Lossky means the denial of any and all attributes.

It is interesting to note that Lossky's writings, so characterized by attention to union with God, consist mostly in qualifications of this union. We read what 'the union to which we are called' is not: hypostatic, substantial, a sharing in divine essence. Instead, we are united to God 'in his energies'.[62] Lossky's theology appears characterized by an anxiety that the human will demand too much, desire too much, and so come unbound from its proper limitations. In this case though, the 'Protestant' problem returns: an end that is anything but a sharing in the divine perfections will install within creatures their own perfection. For if the energetic activity of God comes separate from the essential being of God, how is the divinity which we know and in which we share, reliably Godlike? Deification in this case only ensures a human end that is remote by some ambiguous degree from the perfection for which human form was crafted. Even if it is characterized by obedience to God, or the reflection of God's acts in history, the erecting of an antimony between these discernible energies and the indiscernible essence amounts to an insistence that God's creatures are given an end, suited to their nature, which will always make the praise of the divine essence an unnatural and transgressive human activity. As we shall see below, this pietistic anxiety is entirely foreign to the Church Fathers, and so their articulation of *theosis* requires no essential qualification.

In critiquing Western theology's accounts of divine knowledge, Lossky echoes a Harnackian humility which serves to safeguard divine essence from creaturely intrusion. For Thomas, he says,

> the antinomy [of essence and energy] does not exist; the positive and negative ways can and ought to be harmonized or, rather, reduced to a single way, that of positive theology; the negative way then would be nothing more than a complement, a corrective to the positive way, which would simply indicate that all affirmations touching the nature of God ought to be understood in a more sublime sense.[63]

---

60 Lossky, *Image and Likeness*, p. 56.
61 Vladimir Lossky, 1995, 'The Procession of the Holy Spirit in Orthodox Trinitarian Theology', in Daniel B. Clendenin (ed.), *Eastern Orthodox Theology: A Contemporary Reader*, Grand Rapids: Baker Book House, p. 177.
62 Lossky, *Mystical Theology*, p. 87.
63 Lossky, *Image and Likeness*, p. 53. See Lossky, *Mystical Theology*, pp. 23–43.

Thomas claims to know too much, and only negates as a gloss on the affirmed. In other accounts of deification, Lossky sees a danger originate in epistemologically confounding the two planes of thought, which is to say, incorporating in the intra-Trinitarian relations what can only be attributed to the economy.[64] By contrast Palamas, according to Lossky, offers a theology that is grounded in apophasis: in what we do not know, and cannot become.[65]

To what extent is this account of deification faithful to Palamas? Though this is a rather complex question, passages from Gregory's writings at least give us reason to hesitate in taking Lossky's reading to be the obvious one. Palamas is certainly critical of the Messalian doctrine that perfection amounts to passing 'as far as one wills unto the ineffable mysteries of God'.[66] But this is not to say that the positive naming of God takes place in a different order from the negative. Rather the divine names themselves withdraw from their naming, such that God's essence is excessive of the energies within which it is revealed. Theology is negative from start to finish not because God is most basically negative (beyond, without or otherwise than being), but because God is excessive being. Thus that which is unseeable is 'the fullness of this divine beauty' unseeable even if one should stare at it forever.[67] The essential divine 'darkness' is not that of a God beyond God, but a 'dazzling darkness' that is the overwhelming radiation of pure light.[68] Divine *energia* is much more the brilliance of divine essence than its antinomy, and participation in the divine energy is simply a way of

---

64 Vladimir Lossky, 2001, *Spor o sofiologii v russkom zarubezh'e 1920–1930 godov*, ed. N. T. Eneeva, Moscow: Institut vseobshchei istorii, pp. 12–22. See Rowan Williams, 1975, 'The Theology of Vladimir Nikolaievich Lossky: An Exposition and Critique', Ph.D. diss., Oxford University, pp. 48–56. Lossky comes closest here to Modalism, as Bulgakov implies, in offering a protection of the Father's transcendence that makes the Son and Spirit *effects*, participants in the Father/essence, and only nominally consubstantial. Sergius Bulgakov, 2001, *Bride of the Lamb*, trans. Boris Jakim, Grand Rapids, MI: Eerdmans, pp. 18–19. The doctrine of the monarchy of the Father is buttressed for Lossky by the antinomy, as the energies are synonymous with the processions of Son and Spirit, and the Father, who does not proceed, is the essence of the Godhead (although the Son and Spirit share mysteriously in this essence). On this, see Lossky, *Mystical Theology*, pp. 82–6. God's essence, the Father, is utter darkness; his energies, all divinity that is not the Father, are alone given for our participation. See also the Losskian Leonid Ouspensky, 1992, *Theology of the Icon*, vol. 2, trans. Anthony Gythiel, Crestwood, New York: Saint Vladimir's Seminary Press, pp. 371–409.

65 See Vladimir Lossky, 1978, *The Vision of God*, trans. Asheleigh Moorhouse, London and Clayton, WI: The Faith Press and American Orthodox Press, pp. 124–37.

66 John Meyendorff (ed.), 1982, *Palamas: The Triads*, trans. Nicholas Gendle, New York: Paulist Press, p. 34.

67 Palamas, *Triads*, p. 31. See Rowan Williams, 2002, 'Deflections of Desire', in Oliver Davies and Denys Turner (eds), *Silence and the Word: Negative Theology and Incarnation*, Cambridge and New York: Cambridge University Press, pp. 130–5.

68 Palamas, *Triads*, p. 36.

safeguarding the infinite surplus of the divine essence. *Apophasis* cannot be a rule allowing the mystic admittance to some divine passages and not others, since God's being is infinitely simple. While Palamas's doctrine of God is complex enough to deserve a study of its own, we can at the very least say that there are no locked doors in the divine being for Palamas: just an infinite number of rooms, accessible via *askesis*, whose far wall is ever just out of our range of vision.[69]

Here Lossky seems to be less attuned to the subtleties of the Palamite distinction than to the Kantian subjection of ontology to epistemology: what can be is limited by what can be known. For the older tradition, and here again we are getting ahead of ourselves – God's being exceeds the limitations of our *modus cognoscendi*, just as our knowing is destined to be transformed by what we are called to become. 'Then I will know fully, even as I have been fully known' (1 Cor. 13.12).

The ancient idea of *theosis* as a union with God can be turned against an account of human perfection just as easily as the Protestant theology which is generally considered to offer an opposite account of human ends. When this happens, as in Lossky, the underlying assumption is that the best end for humans is a limitation of our desire for divine things and a satisfaction with the imperfection of those finite graces that are intended for us.

The grace of *theosis* is limited in a similar way in the work of Roman Catholic theologian Jean Borella. Borella sees quite clearly the irony of a humility that refuses union with God:

> To imagine that the creature remains irremediably enclosed in its own finiteness is, in a certain manner, to consign it to hell. But is not this just what we are exposed to if we are allowed to think that the creature should in some way 'keep its distance' vis-à-vis God, as if this entitative contact were somehow possible after all, but something to which we had no right?[70]

Borella here outlines a counter-*mythopoesis*, a narrative of human perfection located somewhere besides the dyadic script of Prometheus Bound/Unbound. Self-regulated to a distance from God, we are no nearer our intended purpose than if we set off barnstorming heaven and usurping the throne. The Blessed Virgin is Borella's counter-Promethean iconography, as 'the purest creature because she is most purely a creature, which is defined as having a given being and therefore a received being'.[71] Her *fiat* is the origin and type for our *fiat voluntas tua*, which is the utterance in which our natures find its supernatural end.

---

69 For a gesture to some of the complexity, see the final note in 'God's Lost Acreage', below.

70 Borella, *Sense*, p. 136.

71 Borella, *Sense*, p. 134.

A careful reader of de Lubac, Borella recognizes the centrality of the Thomistic thesis: grace perfects nature, it does not destroy it (*gratia perficit naturam non tollit: ST* I.1.8, ad 2). If the reception of grace signifies that we become something besides the knowing and desiring beings that we naturally are, then grace is our destruction. A rigorous doctrine of Christian perfection will entail a supernatural grace that allows us to be more fully who we are. The prayer for God's will and kingdom therefore cannot be a revocation of our nature; neither though is our natural desire capable of willing what it, paradoxically, wants. 'Now what does this being want if not itself? It wants itself, if it is not itself; and what it wants is its own reality, its own ontological affirmation. Such is the reason why the will wills. To want itself is to desire self-possession, to be for itself its own cause, its own origin.'[72] In this, Borella sees through the weaknesses of other accounts of perfection which allow nature its own pre-revelatory perfection. Dietrich von Hildebrand, to choose one influential example, argues that the 'natural' human 'merely wants to perfect himself within the framework of his natural dispositions', according to an '*exclusively* human' scope.[73] If this were the case, then the supernatural grace he encounters in Christ would begin by putting an end to natural desire and insert a new desire for the supernatural, elicited first within human nature through the extrinsic contact of revelation. We might and even ought to read the life of virtues that Hildebrand envisions as a recipe for saintliness, or even a sharing in divine holiness; we misread, though, if we take the virtues to be perfecting.[74] Purely elicited desire will never be perfecting, since grace of this sort encounters a nature that never 'lacked' it, since it never desired it, and indeed never needed it. On the contrary, the natural human thus was complete in its own sphere prior to divine revelation.[75]

Borella, following de Lubac, construes the relation of nature and supernature with a subtle difference from this: rather than suggesting that the will naturally desires an immanent end, he supposes that it desires perfection, though it supposes, wrongly, that this perfection will be 'exclusively human'. Union with God, says Borella, is the completion of the desire 'inscribed in the very substance of our being', since this perfection is always 'consummated by grace', there simply is no natural perfection.[76] The creature desires the self-possession that it can never have, because to

---

72 Borella, *Sense*, p. 138.

73 Dietrich von Hildebrand, 1990, *Transformation in Christ: On the Christian Attitude of Mind*, San Francisco: Ignatius Press, p. 3. I owe my awareness of this dense and rich text to Conor Cunningham.

74 In spite of his own claims to render transformation and perfection as theological synonyms (see *Transformation*, pp. 188–96), the point here is that for Hildebrand, in fact, they are not.

75 See John Milbank, 2005, *The Suspended Middle: Henri de Lubac and the Debate Concerning the Supernatural*, Grand Rapids, MI: Eerdmans Publishing, pp. 48ff.

76 Borella, *Sense*, p. 127.

be a creature is to depend upon other creatures, upon spatial and temporal location, ultimately on God. Only then, in the *Pater Noster*'s repetition of Mary's fiat, can we find our most basic natural desire perfected, and perfected through a plea for a supernatural gift: 'thy will be done'.

As we take a step forward towards a theology of perfection, however, a new difficulty arises, contained more or less awkwardly in the question of human experience. How does the existing Christian encounter this perfecting grace, without either domesticating it to the level of her own existence, or reverting to a pure self-humiliation in favour of the will to which she submits? If the supernatural gift which we cannot name on our own crosses out the natural desire for self-possession which we only ever experience as a confining hell, how is the very plea *fiat voluntas tua* not a destruction of our nature? If Mary is the icon of a metaphysically coherent perfection, does she fail to be also the icon of an existentially paradigmatic perfection?

Borella himself, having seen the problem of both a denial of natural desire and of supernatural union, is unable to construct a sufficient answer. For him, Mary's *fiat* is a pure renunciation that she cannot, in fact, encounter existentially as perfection. She is perfect only *sub specie aeternitatis*. Does deification, he asks, involve 'entitative contact' between humans and God?

> Surely not, for properly speaking such a 'contact' is quite simply impossible. Every contact presupposes limits across which different realities can touch one another, while the divine Substance is limitless . . . But by virtue of its limitlessness, divine Infinity includes all of the finite within itself. Only from the point of view of finite being is the Infinite outside.[77]

The denial of contact between the being of God and humans is an appropriate way, he says, to 'safeguard transcendence'.[78] It does not risk actually frustrating the union implied by deification, since the finite is always touching the infinite in view of the metaphysical inclusion of all things within God's infinity. Thus for God, the union will in fact take place; finite creatures, though, will only experience this union as a lack. And this must be the case, since any experience of union with God will, he believes, annihilate the creature as creature.[79] Therefore the prayer for God's will and kingdom will always take the form of a sublime request, *thy kingdom come, though I can never know it to have come*, since to ask otherwise would be to place ourselves illicitly in the heavens. Thus, to desire deification is to desire our perfection; but to desire to experience deification is to overstep the boundaries of our finitude. For Borella, human perfection is

---

77 Borella, *Sense*, p. 136.
78 Borella, *Sense*, p. 136.
79 Borella, *Sense*, pp. 135–40.

possible, but only God can experience it: something like a crown prince who stands to inherit the kingdom, but for the fact that everyone knows his mother will outlive him by at least half a lifespan.

Ironically, in this imperative of Catholic renunciation, we find Prometheus in his most aggressively Romantic posture: humans who are shut off from heaven nevertheless take it upon themselves to say what can only be spoken truly by the infinite God. For in Borella's construal, the very phrase 'union with God' would intrude upon our speech as another form of positivism, open to all the aporias of posited, inexperienced transcendence. Perfecting union would always be a lie when affirmed by finite creatures. This would be the case even if it were affirmed only as an eschatological hope, since the eschatological consummation, as Borella rightly insists,[80] does not dissolve the finite creature into the infinite God. But does this force upon us the conclusion that a natural desire for the supernatural is an ontological imperfection? Even as a mark of hope, in that case, the creature could never take its proper end to be union with God.

Our quest for a counter-Promethean perfection (as opposed to an anti-Promethean resignation) thus resolves into a problem of the mediation of divinity to humanity, of the encounter with the infinite perfections of God in the midst of our human finitude. As we turn to the Church Fathers in the pages below, we will see how they develop a distinction of Creator from creature that undercuts the modern problem of finite contact with the infinite, and thus allows for a real mediation of perfecting ends to the finite creature.

Unshared perfection

One final modern theological account of the Christian *telos* announces this problem and gestures towards its resolution, albeit somewhat unintentionally.

Karl Barth's account of sanctification, taking up some 350 pages of his *Doctrine of Reconciliation*, is certainly one of the most significant attempts of the last 100 years to sort through the question of the end that Christianity constructs for human beings. His initial warrant for the project is the need to take the entire question of the human reception and embodiment of divine holiness beyond a certain spiritual pathology, in which sanctification stands for one stage of the *ordo salutis* which the Christian is asked to perform, claims to have performed or frets over not having performed.[81] As such, Barth attempts to describe Christian holiness as something given to and for human beings, not stolen from heaven as a characteristic that belongs properly only to God. Determining how well his account accomplishes this will require us to linger briefly over his text.

---

80 Borella, *Sense*, pp. 127, 139–40.

81 Barth, *CD* IV.2, pp. 501–3. My reading of Barth has been most influenced by two of my teachers, Craig Keen and Gene Rogers.

In John Passmore's reading, the early Barth is a representative of Protestantism's rejection of humanity's perfectibility, while the later Barth softens, and begins to entertain the notion that humans are not entirely 'helpless, without God's grace, to take even the first step towards perfection'.[82] Passmore's account makes of Pelagianism a pivot of perfection, in much the same way that the texts treated in this chapter have used Prometheanism: if a certain author suggests that humans name and accomplish their own perfecting, then Passmore calls the author perfectionist or Pelagian. Authors who reject the human labour of self-perfecting are anti-perfectionist or anti-Pelagian. For him, Barth is initially a member of the latter camp, an uncompromising anti-Pelagian. He then makes some hesitating though significant strides toward a higher anthropology, making him in his later phase a kind of scared Pelagian.[83]

That this reading fails to do justice to the central project that Barth undertakes throughout his work is, in fact, illustrative of the central argument of this initial chapter. Barth clearly attempts to move beyond the impasse of a Promethean or Pelagian unbound perfectionism versus an anti-Promethean or anti-Pelagian denial of human perfection altogether. If an author as perceptive as Passmore, whose research has taken him into the depths of the philosophical and theological question, can ultimately provide no more complex assessment than a two-dimensional spectrum on which one is either Pelagian, anti-Pelagian or an unstable mixture of the two, then perhaps our ability to consider the entire question of the human *telos* has indeed been colonized by a modernized titanic mythology.

As a historical observation, it is true enough to note that there is a shift in Barth's work from an anthropology that sketches human nature and its purpose more or less entirely in the negative, to one that begins to give more attention to the goodness of human culture and expression, even in a pagan or pre-revelatory mode of existence.[84] Yet many things do not change, and included among them is his position on deification. If the *Römerbrief* of 1922 rejects any notion of the exaltation of humans into kinship with God,[85] this language is only intensified in the *Doctrine of Reconciliation* over 30 years later. Though he himself was celebrated for rehabilitating a high Christology, in this late volume he laments some of its unforeseen and problematic consequences. An Alexandrian doctrine can, like a Trojan horse, invite an invasion, in that it can lead to a '"high-pitched" anthropology; to the doctrine of a humanity which is not only capable of deification, but already deified, or at any rate on the point of

---

82 Passmore, *Perfectibility*, p. 114.

83 Passmore, *Perfectibility*, pp. 130ff.

84 Hans Urs von Balthasar, 1992, *The Theology of Karl Barth*, trans. Edward T. Oakes, San Francisco: Ignatius Press, pp. 44ff. A related shift, it should be said, was obvious to Barth as well. See Karl Barth, 1960, *Humanity of God*, Richmond: John Knox Press, pp. 37–8.

85 Karl Barth, 1933, *Epistle to the Romans*, trans. Edwyn C. Hoskyns, London: Oxford University Press, p. 30.

apotheosis or deification'.[86] This is still essentially Harnack's Hellenization thesis, since Barth takes deification here to be a false import to the gospel from paganism, though his espousal of Nicene Christianity does not leave open to him Harnack's option for a liberalization of theology out of this Hellenistic dress.

At the same time, it is in his Christology, and in particular in founding a doctrine of sanctification on a Christocentricity, that Barth does go beyond Harnack. 'We have merely taken seriously what Calvin called the *participatio Christi*, making it the ultimate foundation of his whole doctrine of sanctification.'[87] Jesus Christ is, as he states in the earlier volume on creation, the 'real man', while

> Christians, then, are the men to whom Jesus Christ, and in Him their own completed sanctification, is revealed and present as this new, true man, and who know that they are co-ordinated with Him as their first-born Brother and subordinated to Him as their King instituted from all eternity.[88]

Christ is the perfect expression of human nature; he loves perfectly, which means in unrestrained self-giving,[89] and as such he is, and Barth does not hesitate here to use the Hellenistic vocabulary, if somewhat ironically, 'a happy man, a man who is to be counted blessed'.[90]

The difficulty comes, as Barth is well aware, in translating the perfection of Christ into some vision of a general human end, in other words, in reading Calvin's *participatio Christi* as an actual participation and not simply a nominalism based on Christ's perfection.'The break made by God in Jesus must become history,'[91] and the saints, gathered first of all as *ecclesia*, manifest this becoming-history of God's revelation in Christ. As he attempts to speak to this becoming, however, his images and metaphors are less participatory, and he begins to conjure certain images familiar to his readers from the pages of the *Römerbrief*: the holy life is 'a birth from above' whose occurrence is its own possibility, lacking any *dunasthai* in human nature;[92] it is 'unlike any direction which one man may give to others', and 'falls vertically, as it were, into the lives of those to whom it is given'.[93] Any residue of an Aristotelian cosmic *telos* is rejected, since this would imply for him that the natural energies of the created order have their own

---

86 Barth, *CD* IV.2, p. 82.
87 Barth, *CD* IV.2, p. 581.
88 Karl Barth, 1960, *Church Dogmatics*, Vol. III *The Doctrine of Creation*, Part 2, trans. and ed. G. W. Bromiley and T. F. Torrance, Edinburgh: T&T Clark, p. 729.
89 Barth, *CD* IV.2, p. 823.
90 Barth, *CD* IV.2, p. 788.
91 Barth, *CD* IV.2, p. 544.
92 Barth, *CD* IV.2, p. 563.
93 Barth, *CD* IV.2, p. 523.

Godward directionality. In this way, though, his concern to emphasize the uniqueness of God's gift gives him cause to develop an account of grace that threatens to undermine his reflection on the saints. Only a shared sense of discerning God's will, drawn analogically from encounters and experiences through which the community has passed together and separately, allows God's people to share in the 'becoming history' that is God's revelation in Christ. How does Barth allow for the 'horizontal' development of 'true humans', if holiness is a vertical drop?

In spite of Barth's awareness that human nature cannot be abolished by the act of God, he never manages to account for the central dynamic of perfecting grace in his own thinking. An 'obediential perfection',[94] a *telos* based entirely in simple obedience to a self-eliciting call, is no perfection at all, since it cannot recover the nature as the *dunamis* completed through divine grace.

This impasse is clearest in Barth's account of the 'problem of Christian love'. For him there could never be a natural desire for the supernatural, since desire itself is 'the direct opposite of Christian love – the love which seeks and attains its end as the self-giving of the one who loves to the object of his love'.[95] If Christian *agape* is this paradigm of self-giving, *eros* is that 'other kind of love' which 'does not have its origin in self-denial, but in a distinctively uncritical intensification and strengthening of natural self-assertion'.[96] To desire at all is to strain for self-completion, for a 'union with the beloved' that at base wants to consume the beloved, 'like the wolf when it has devoured, as it hopes, both Red Riding Hood and her grandmother'.[97]

When Barth returns, in good Barthian fashion, to nuance his perhaps overstated dichotomy of *agape* and *eros*, his means of doing so makes this point with even greater clarity. The Christian 'loves with erotic as well as Christian love',[98] but this is not because something of her natural desire is completed or even transformed in the dynamic of *agape*. Rather, the presence of the two kinds of love in her are evidence that she is *simul justus et peccator*. *Eros* plays the role of the Pauline 'old man' who must be put to

---

94 This is Passmore's phrase. Here Barth may rely too much on Bonhoeffer, who tends to describe discipleship as an immediate responsiveness that undercuts any temporal mediation, a 'simple obedience to the will of God as it has been revealed'. Dietrich Bonhoeffer, 1995 [1937], *The Cost of Discipleship*, trans. Fuller and Booth, New York: Simon and Schuster, pp. 72ff. Barth admits to being 'tempted simply to reproduce . . . in an extended quotation' the chapter on 'Simple Obedience' from Bonhoeffer's *Nachfolge*', CD IV.2, p. 533.

95 Barth, CD IV.2, p. 735. Cf. Maximus the Confessor's 'Centuries on Charity' 1.9–10, in which *eros* is the name given to an *agape* that is reaching toward God. Berthold (trans and notes), 1995, *Maximus: Selected Writings*, Mahwah, NJ: Paulist Press, p. 36.

96 Barth, CD IV.2, p. 734.

97 Barth, CD IV.2, p. 734.

98 Barth, CD IV.2, p. 751.

death so that the new man can live the Christoform life.[99] *Eros* is present only as that lingering influence of the 'sloth and misery'[100] that shapes human life outside of Christ. Desire has no place in our perfection.

This leads to one of the most revealing passages in all of Barth's writings, a portion of which I quoted above in response to the post-Enlightenment idea that all pagan desire must be eradicated with Christianity. Here he acknowledges the very impasse that I am attempting to sketch. Mystical prayer for union with God, he says, often 'smacks of religious eroticism . . . But how arid would be our hymn books if we were to purge out all elements of this kind!'[101] Realizing that the hard contrast he has established between *eros* and *agape* will lead to just such a posture, he warns of its danger with a bit of self-effacing criticism.

> If a choice has to be made, is it not better to say a little too much and occasionally to slip up with Nicolai and even with Zinzendorf and Novalis than to be rigidly correct with Kant and Ritschl and my 1921 *Römerbrief* and Bultmann, but in so doing to create a zone of silence in relation to the central matter of which the former rightly or wrongly tried to speak . . . ?[102]

What I am suggesting here is that we take Barth at his word. He sees the centrality of *eros*, of natural human desire, for liturgical and vocational sanctification, but he can find no other way to preserve it than by calling it a 'slip up' that is preferable to the 'rigidly correct' alternative. He simply lacks the language that would allow him to wander down the theological pathways that he correctly perceives to be the necessary ones.

This shortcoming is indicative of the limits of a Barthian Christocentricity. When he erects a strict barricade between the perfection of Christ and the human participation in that perfection, he is turning, as he seems to be at least partially aware, from Alexandria's Christology as well as its anthropology. By suggesting that theology mistakenly overlooks 'the irreversibility of the relationship between God and man',[103] he is arguing against the Patristic language that linked deification with the incarnation: 'God became human so that humans might become gods.' To rely on this formula amounts to a 'heaven-storming doctrine of the humanity of the Mediator', which opens the door for the illicit deification of humans.[104] He prefers instead the relation of covenant, a term which allows him to keep imperfect humanity at a distance from the perfect God. In other words, sharing in divine holiness is ultimately a Promethean goal, and must be rejected in favour of Christian humility. But then Barth fails to answer his

---

99 Barth, *CD* IV.2, p. 736.
100 Barth, *CD* IV.2, pp. 378ff.
101 Barth, *CD* IV.2, p. 798.
102 Barth, *CD* IV.2, p. 798.
103 Barth, *CD* IV.2, p. 83.
104 Barth, *CD* IV.2, pp. 82–3.

own insightful critique: how can he avoid opening a vacuum in which paganism and wolfish consumption flourish 'all the more vehemently'?[105]

To be sure, Barth's theology is less a systematic theology or what the scholastics called a *summa theologiae*, than an extended treatise on Christian faith and formation. As such, his account of sanctification is a work of rhetoric, intended to encounter his audience in a way that will unveil aspects of the gospel that have become shrouded. If post-Reformation conversations on holiness are dominated by questions of degrees of sinlessness and the possibility or impossibility of self-conscious perfection on earth, Barth's reliance upon humility, calling the saint a 'disturbed sinner' whose past may still intrude upon his present,[106] goes some distance in allowing a true reception of *participatio Christi* as a gracious gift. At the same time though, this anti-perfectional humility, manifesting itself in 'simple obedience' to a revelatory positivism, turns out to be not only theologically and philosophically suspect, but makes for poor Christian formation as well. Simple obedience is always a complex endeavour, and ignoring this will inevitably lead to abstraction from existentially located beings, just as Mary's pure renunciation, in Borella's account, constructs an ideal of human offering that dislocates the human from the context in which any such offering could be made. Surely *participatio Christi* involves acts of construction, of discernment, analogy, conjecture, even trial and error: human activities, even as they are perfected by divine action. The call to holiness is always in some sense part of the craft of creatures, since any call that encounters our ears and imaginations will involve the host of powers that comprise human understanding. Obedience to God's will likewise must necessarily include some strong element of what one might call 'guessing at God'. Ignoring this factor will, to return an earlier argument, inevitably involve a pathological return of the repressed.

Theoria amid the Wreckage

The Romantic and postmodern mythos offers as human *telos* the breaking of all visible and invisible chains that bind the human archetype; the theological response, even where it avows perfectionist language most avidly, attempts to keep Prometheus enchained by his nature and let what perfection may come arrive supernaturally, as an inexperienceable gift from Jupiter. Nevertheless, both cycle back on one another, evidencing their symbiotic relationship: Prometheanism relies upon a tacitly posited sovereign, sooner or later, while humble anti-Prometheanism cannot help but fill in the vacuum with an undisclosed immanent *telos*.

The following chapters will suggest that classical Christianity, harvesting the religious and philosophical bounty of Greece and Israel, introduces a perfection for humanity that is neither Promethean nor anti-Promethean,

---

105 Barth, *CD* IV.2, p. 798.
106 Barth, *CD* IV.2, pp. 524ff.

but of a different order of mythopoesis altogether. In a sense, though, Shelley has already begun pointing us in this direction. As we saw above, his Prometheus cannot ride up to heaven and dispose of Jupiter, not only because his motivation for insurrection must be love, but also because, as Shelley says elsewhere, 'nothing exists but as it is perceived'.[107] The Jupiter who appears to the prisoner is but a spectral figure, who comes in answer to Prometheus's own beckoning. The 'actual Jupiter' cannot be perceived, because the entire point, for Shelley, is that this sort of posited transcendence simply does not exist: there is no actual Jupiter. But this means that there ought to be no 'new Jupiter' either, like Shelley's own 'love', which intrudes upon the lyrical drama as a positivistic human ideal will, in turn, stand sovereign over humanity. If Shelley is blind to the limits of his own insurrective impulses, there remains another element at work in his poem that begins to indicate a way beyond the fatalistic return of the Promethean complex.

In the poem's final stanza, the Demagorgon offers a litany of blessings to the gathered spirits and elements, a calling for each to carry on in such a way that love might fold 'over the world its healing wings' (4.561). Among the spells that will 'reassume an empire o'er the disentangled gloom' is the particular vocation given to humanity:

> To suffer woes which Hope thinks infinite;
> To forgive wrongs darker than death or night;
> To defy power, which seems omnipotent;
> To love, and bear; to hope till Hope creates
> From its own wreck the thing it contemplates . . . (4.569–74)

What might it mean for hope, which the first line of the excerpt tells us is unable to see an end to human suffering, to then contemplate this unseeable object, and then even to create it from its own wreckage? Any object of hope that is first passively received before subsequently becoming the blueprint for humanity's self-fashioning would fail, precisely by being a new Olympian transcendent, nonhuman in its very arrival. Is it possible, though, that there could arrive within human existence a contemplatable perfection, at one and the same time fashioned by human hope, and given from beyond hope's creative reaches? Could Prometheus advance towards this *telos* neither vertically nor horizontally but on a diagonal? Shelley seems to be grasping for a sort of conjectural *telos* that does not reduce to Murdoch's fictional vulgarism. But even as he grasps thus, his Pyrrhonic rejection of traditioned patterns of thought and imagination place this contemplative *telos* just beyond his fingertips.

These final remarks may be taken as signposts for the following journey. Conjecture, a non-positivistic transcendence, a rhetorically constructed object of worship, a perfection made theurgically from the wreckage

---

107 Shelley, *On Life*, p. 194.

of human cultural impulses, a diagonal advance: these are images that we will revisit in the chapters below. Before returning to Shelley's half-completed project, though, we must retrace the path that perfection itself took through the human imagination. A religious and philosophical image of perfection as a particular sort of boundedness emerges among the ancient Greeks; a rather different sort of binding comes to us from ancient Israel. How were these images transformed by the Fathers of the Church into a uniquely Christian perfection, and transformed again by later generations of theologians in such a way that would allow the Prometheus myth to compromise the earlier Christian vision?

Inceptions

I

Divine Suspension: Perfection in Athens

Philosophy begins in the Platonic love for the divine measure.

Eric Voegelin

Bonds of Kinship

If Shelley's Prometheus is iconic of the modern and postmodern wreckage of perfection language only through an intentional perversion of the classical myth, the ancient myth itself is an obvious place to begin looking for the older form. What was perfection in the lyrical and philosophical tradition that issued from the first Prometheus cycles?

The tragedies of Aeschylus mark the headwaters of philosophical enquiry into human perfection. What are humans for? How do kings and cities decide for particular human ends without ignoring a general and universal end of human beings as such? By the era of the Athenian Academy these questions will occupy such a central place that they seem to us now to be consistent with the birth of philosophy itself. From Plato, through the writings of the New Testament, to the Cappadocians, Augustine, and Medieval and Renaissance Christianity, the answers also will move in a recognizable direction. Somehow, humans are for the gods and the gods are for us, and our perfection is a matter of rightly discerning theirs. This is the pre-classical insight that gives birth to philosophy and through it shapes the Christian account of humanity's end.

In Aeschylus's *Prometheus Bound*, among the earliest extant dramas in Western literature, Hephaestus chastises the Titan for the sin of over-gifting, as he regretfully chains him to the rock on Zeus's orders: 'Thou, a god not fearing the wrath of gods, hast given to mortal men honors beyond their due' (*Prometheus Bound*, 29–30).[1] The stolen Olympian fire is in this sense both superhuman and the core of the new human essence, since when brought down to earth, it initiates all that is distinctive to the

---

1 Aeschylus, *Prometheus Bound*, in Whitney J. Oates and Eugene O'Neill, Jr (eds), 1938, *The Complete Greek Drama*, Vol. I, trans. Paul Elmer More, New York: Random House.

human creature: science, numbers, letters, history, astrology and 'all human arts are from Prometheus' (*Prom. Bd.* 505). Hephaestus's evaluation of the sentencing is shared by his brothers Oceanus and Hermes, if with an added pinch of spite: humans have their place in the order of things, and the Promethean burglary has given them the means to transgress these limits (*Prom. Bd.* 283–399, 944–1078b).

Is there not something remarkably unjust in this evaluation, though? After all, Prometheus the Titan is older than Zeus the Olympian, and the former's endowment of humans with heavenly fire has a good claim for being the original 'naturing' of humans. Has Prometheus really given humans what is beyond their due, or has Zeus rather substracted from us the end that is our original inheritance? In Sappho's version, in fact, the human is Prometheus's own creation, not Zeus's, and thus given a nature that precedes the Olympian coup in the order of being, even if not in the order of temporal events.[2] Any naming of human perfection according to Zeus's law will only be after the fact, an imposition of a nature on a thing that contains a trace of the preternatural.[3] Even in Aeschylus, Prometheus has a good argument for grandfathering his creatures into the Olympian-ruled world under an older Titanic code.

What is Aeschylus's tragedy saying about justice and human *telos*? Are the other Olympians right, and is Prometheus something of a late adolescent among Titans who needs to follow the ancient wisdom of the Delphic oracle and know himself, his place and the place of his craftsmanship better? Or are we to recognize the appeal of his claim to a supernature in humanity, which would then endow humankind with a spirit of rebellion at the core of its essence? The ambiguity is heightened for post-classical readers, since *Prometheus Bound* is only the first instalment of a dramatic trilogy whose sequels, *Prometheus Unbound* and *Prometheus the Fire-Bringer*, are lost from the literary annals. The text does, however, offer us a few clues that point towards a 'moral' quite different than the one Shelley reacts so strongly against.

One clue comes in the character of Io, who is in effect, like Heraclitus and Hermes, another study of Zeus from afar. Her encounter with the king of Olympus has left her mad and deformed, roaming the world in search of her ever-elusive place. Most immediately, the cause of her tormented state is the jealousy of Hera; the chorus of Oceanus's daughters, however, is not fooled. They know her demise was prescribed the moment Zeus's eye caught hers, which is why they sing, 'Never may one of the gods/ Descend from the skies for my love' (*Prom. Bd.* 898–9). Wealthy noblemen should not marry the daughters of craftsmen; neither should a god grow amorous for a human. How then is Zeus not guilty of bestowing upon 'mortal men

---

2 Sappho, *Fragment 207*, in David A. Campbell (ed. and trans.), 1982, *Greek Lyric*, Vol. I, Loeb Classical Library no. 142, Cambridge, MA: Harvard University Press.

3 Eric Voegelin, 1957, *Order and History*, Vol II: *The World of the Polis*, Baton Rouge: Louisiana State University Press, pp. 255–6.

honours beyond their due', the very sin for which he has condemned Prometheus? In this light, Aeschylus seems to be siding with Prometheus, since it is not the Titanic supernatural, but the Olympian 'natural' that represents the real transgression.

Yet again, though, there is a subtlety to the argument that, though perhaps made explicit in the later dramas, remains subterranean here. Prometheus appeals to Themis, his mother, for judicial oversight in his affair: 'O holy mother mine, O thou firmament that dost resolve the common light of all, thou seest the wrongs I suffer' (*Prom. Bd.* 1091–3).[4] Themis is divine justice, or eternal righteousness, or Gaia, 'one form she hath but many names' (*Prom. Bd.* 212). Besides Prometheus, she is also the mother of Dike, human justice, whom Hesiod before Aeschylus sketches as one promoted to Zeus's side to be his everlasting companion.[5] This sister becomes the ordained *nomos* of human affairs: a daughter of divine justice, given charge over the affairs of earth. However, Prometheus makes no appeal to his sister, but only their mother. In one sense this is not surprising, given that only Themis's rule would do for a Titan. Yet it is surprising since the subject of the conflict is that of human justice, of precisely what is due to human beings.[6] Dike's brother goes over her head. In doing so, does he behave rightly, or does this appeal betray a stubborn insistence upon the very transgression that got him chained to the Caucasus in the first place? Is Prometheus being Promethean once again?

We might frame the key question in this way: Is the human *telos* divine participation, in this case a sharing in the order of the pre-Olympian Saturnine cosmos? Or in making this appeal to Themis by ignoring the ordained human *nomos* of Dike, does Prometheus desire something greater than human perfection for his beloved humans?

Though we cannot remain with the Promethean cycle to find a resolution to this question, another of Aeschylus's works provides some illumination. In *The Suppliants*, Io and Zeus are pitted against one another again, now through a geopolitical renarration of the ancient rape. The drama opens as Danaus is fleeing with his 50 daughters from his brother Aegyptus, who has commanded his 50 sons to force their cousins into a union *en masse*. The daughters return to the ancient homeland of Io, now Argos, and appeal for aid to its ruler, King Argos. They begin their supplication with prayers to the Olympians, being sure to remind the gods of their own specific kinships and similarities with themselves. So the chorus of daughters sings to 'bright Apollo, exiled once from heaven' (*Suppliants*, 214),[7] and Danaus their father assures them, 'The exiled god

---

4 Aeschylus, *Prometheus Bound*, in Herbert Weir Smyth (ed. and trans.), 1956, *Aeschylus*, Vol. I, Loeb Classical Library no 145, Cambridge, MA: Harvard University Press. Unless otherwise noted, translations are from the LCL version.

5 Voegelin, *Order and History* II, pp. 139–40.

6 Voegelin, *Order and History* II, pp. 255–6.

7 Aeschylus, *The Suppliants*, in Whitney J. Oates and Eugene O'Neill, Jr (eds),

will pity our exile' (*Suppl.* 215). The daughters then recount the narrative of Io, identifying themselves with the maiden in flight: 'like her I wail and wail in soft Ionian tones' (*Suppl.* 68). When they lay their suppliant wands at the feet of the Argonian festal gods in the sacred grove, their appeal is complete: though we are foreigners to your land, they are saying, your gods know our gods, and they remember our ancestors. In light of the kinship of Argonian and Aegyptian gods, the king must give the daughters sanctuary.

The king, however, finds the situation much more difficult to discern, and at several levels. In terms of typology, it matters a great deal which Io they are, so to speak. If they are, as they claim, Io in flight from Hera, upon whom Zeus bestowed his grace, then the people of Argos who honour Zeus ought also to act gracefully toward the daughters. On the other hand, they might be Io the unperturbed maiden by the river, suddenly spotted and pursued by Zeus (*Suppl.* 291–302). If the latter is the case, why should the Argonians not simply wink away the imminent rape with a knowing wag of the head towards Zeus and a 'boys will be boys'? Legally, perhaps the sons have a right to this wedding, and perhaps their female cousins are improperly influenced by the excesses of the Amazon tribe (*Suppl.* 287). To make matters more complicated, Argos knows that if the island offers the maidens protection, the ship which brings the sons of Aegyptus to his shores will also bring his land's destruction: 'If ill fate chance, my people then may say – *In aid of strangers thou the State hast slain*' (*Suppl.* 400–1).

When the maidens appeal to Dike, proconsul to Zeus and font of human justice, King Argos responds that it is unclear just whose side she is on.

Chorus: Dike protects her champions.
King: True, if she had a part therein from the first. (*Suppl.* 343–44)[8]

In response, the daughters change their prayer: 'Yea, indeed, may Themis, daughter of God the Apportioner, Themis who protecteth the suppliant, look upon our flight that it bring no mischief in its train' (*Suppl.* 359–61).[9]

Argos reflects, 'A deep, a saving counsel here there needs – an eye that like a diver to the depth of dark perplexity can pass and see, undizzied, unconfused' (*Suppl.* 407–10). Although he sees the need for such a discernment if both city and suppliant maidens are to be saved from a band of marauders, still he quickly back tracks and makes a decision: Argos

---

1938, *The Complete Greek Drama*, Vol. I, trans. Paul Elmer More, New York: Random House. Unless otherwise noted, all translations come from this volume.

8 Aeschylus, *The Suppliant Maidens*, in Herbert Weir Smyth (ed. and trans.), 1956, *Aeschylus*, Vol. I, Loeb Classical Library no. 145, Cambridge, MA: Harvard University Press.

9 I have modified the translation only to emphasize the goddess to whom they appeal. See Voegelin, *Order and History* II, pp. 247–53.

would never recover from such a war, and his duty lies in the protection of the people of his realm (*Suppl.* 437–54). This announcement sets the stage for what is surely one of the most dramatic passages in the tragedians, a desperate appeal by the maidens that gives Argos reason to reconsider:

> Chorus: Hear now the end of my manifold appeals for compassion.
> King: I hear; say on. It shall not escape me.
> Chorus: I have breast-bands and girdles wherewith to gather up my robes.
> King: Such things are proper, no doubt, to womenfolk.
> Chorus: In these then, be sure, I have a rare contrivance –
> King: Tell me what speech thou hast in mind to utter.
> Chorus: If thou wilt not engage thyself to give some pledge unto our company –
> King: What is the contrivance of the sashes to effect for thee?
> Chorus: To adorn these images with tablets of strange sort.
> King: Thy words are riddling; come, explain in simple speech.
> Chorus: To hang ourselves forthwith from the statues of yon gods. (*Suppl.* 455–65)

The threat of the daughters of Danaus to hang themselves by their own girdles from the festal gods in the grove motivates King Argos to take the deep council he has already said is needed. He takes the matter to his people, the *demos*. The people of the realm ultimately decide for the maidens, despite the probability that it will almost certainly (and in the end does, apparently, though here again we have only one part of a three-part drama) bring all the devastation of an unwinnable war on their land. When the invasion finally occurs, the atheism of the sons of Aegyptus vindicates the king in his decision. They sweep into the sacred grove and shout mockingly that their ship is the only shrine they hold sacred. 'I am host to no sacrilegious hands' (*Suppl.* 927) says the king, now realizing that the men who have no kinship with his gods have no kinship claims upon him (*Suppl.* 919–25).

Importantly though, it is neither the sacrilege of the sons nor the threat of the daughters that decides the case. The former affirms the decision, the latter initiates it. But the 'deep saving counsel' in between is where king and *demos* take the side of the daughters.[10] What do these depths reveal, this unconfused secret only discernible to an eye 'like a diver'?

As the image suggests, the righteousness of the gods lies 'above', like the sky is above the inhabited land, or the water's surface above the infinite teeming of the sea. The daughters have asked the king to sort out the aspects of kinship, legality and obligation in their case, and this calls for a passage from the divine surface through the human depths. They have appealed dramatically to the festal gods; the king and the *demos* must determine the precise shape of the human justice which suspends from such

---

10 Voegelin, *Order and History* II, pp. 249–50.

an appeal. This is why their appeal to Themis becomes, strangely, an appeal to the king to take Dike 'to thy side' (*Suppl.* 395). Dike is not other than Themis, but is 'deeper' in the fabric of human existence. She is an incarnation, suspended from the neck of her transcendent mother, born to meet the variant needs of the human order. In some ways she is less stable, since the depths that she governs are murkier, and she must be subject to revisions and amendations. Dike is nonetheless reliable, since she is, in effect, the human face of her divine mother, and will show this face to the one who plumbs the depths.[11]

Though the drama does not follow the king into his convocation with the people, the king reports afterwards that 'with one assent the Argives spake their will', naming Zeus, and therefore themselves, as the suppliants' guard (*Suppl.* 605-24). The strophe that concludes the thanksgiving of the maidens notes this entanglement of praise of the gods and right discernment of the ways of humans: 'And to the Argive powers divine/ The sacrifice of laurelled kin/ By rite ancestral, pay' (*Suppl.* 704-5b). The king and his people will continue to discern the order of human justice as long as they continue to honour the gods, since there is no law of Dike that is not also a window onto the world of Themis. The liturgies of Argos determine the morality of Argos, and the one law of Dike that founds and judges all others is 'the mighty law: Your gods, your fathers deified, ye shall adore' (*Suppl.* 708-9a). Beyond this law there is no justice, because human life itself is not established on the stable turf of an uncomplicated *nomos*, but is suspended precariously from the divine righteousness. We hang by our own belts, Aeschylus says, from the necks of the gods we name.

What then of the fire-thief? Is Prometheus prepared to make such a dive? Does he understand this divine suspension? Though he is right to appeal the human case to a super-Olympian court, perhaps he still lacks an important insight into the *telos* of his progeny. The just ways of humans are not the ways of the Titanic gods *or* the Olympian tyrant. They are not simply 'natural' creatures given *eidos* and *ethos* under the new cosmic order, nor are they supernatural creations whose ways are identical to those of the Titan Themis, as Prometheus himself seems to hope. They are a depth creation, whose ends must be discerned from within the midst of history by these beings themselves, but only as they call upon the gods. Humans are bound upon the earth, but this very binding is also a suspending, so that Dike and Themis, human good and divine perfection, must be traced together, their throats joined by the ends of a single leather strap.

The Holy Fool and the Water Clock

Plato gives voice to the insight in his explanation of the origin of the dialectic itself, the tool with which humans can discern truth in the world. So

---

11 Voegelin, *Order and History* II, pp. 139-40, 255-7.

Divine Suspension: Perfection in Athens

Socrates says in the *Philebus*,

> A gift of gods to men [θεωνμενε ανρωπουζ δοσιζ], as I believe, was tossed down from some divine source through the agency of a Prometheus together with a gleaming fire; and the ancients, who were better than we and lived nearer the gods, handed down the tradition that all the things which are ever said to exist spring from one and many and have inherent in them the finite and the infinite. (*Philebus*, 16c)[12]

The evolution of Prometheus here is significant. The stolen fire is still the spark of human understanding, but the theft itself has begun to fade into the mythological background. The human fire is now a *dosis theon*, a gift of the gods. Which? Does Zeus himself wish to share his Olympian embers? Are all the gods in on the gift? Plato wrestles with this question, as I will demonstrate, throughout the dialogues, and can only begin to sketch its answer. But the answer is crucial, since, by his own admission, the dialectical – that is, philosophical – knowledge that perfects humans in wisdom begins and ends in the discernment of this gift.

How divine does Plato take human perfection to be? In *Theaetetus*, in the midst of a conversation on what it means to judge some people as wiser or more excellent than others, Socrates leads his fellow dialecticians on a digression about the vocation of the philosopher. The philosopher interests himself in a certain kind of perfection, but this veers rather drastically from the sort of perfection pursued so doggedly by the other visible characters in the city. The latter engage in their work at a pace that gives them no leisure – leisure, for instance, to stand around the marketplace and discuss wisdom and excellence and then to digress from that discussion to enquire about the relative excellencies of various *teloi*. Lawyers and other public figures could never pause to reflect on the shape of the good that their lives map out, since they 'are always in a hurry – for the water flowing through the water clock urges them on' (*Theaetetus*, 172e).[13] Though ostensibly free, this sort of man 'does not know how to wear his cloak as a freeman should, properly draped, still less to acquire the true harmony of speech and hymn aright the praises of the true life of gods and blessed men [ἀνδρῶν εὐδαιμόνων]' (*Theaet.* 175e-6a). The truly free citizen will not be a slave to the water clock, but will engage in leisurely pursuits, not because there is nothing important to do, but because hurrying to accomplish the tasks of the day will be meaningless, unless he can make room to

---

12 Plato, *Philebus*, in Harold N. Fowler and W. R. M. Lamb (ed. and trans.), 1925, *Plato*, Vol. III, Loeb Classical Library no. 164, London and New York: William Heinemann Ltd. and G. P. Putnam's Sons. Concerning *Meno*, see also Catherine Pickstock, 2004, 'Eros and Emergence', *Telos* 127, pp. 97–118.

13 Plato, *Theaetetus*, in Harold N. Fowler (ed. and trans.), 1921, *Plato*, Vol. VII, Loeb Classical Library no. 123, London and New York: William Heinemann Ltd. and G. P. Putnam's Sons.

articulate the way in which the tasks themselves harmonize with the life of the gods and the blessed.

It is this harmony that the philosopher pursues, even though he will most often fail to embody it with any recognizable finality:

> Why, take the case of Thales, Theodorus. While he was studying the stars and looking upwards, he fell into a pit, and a neat, witty Thracian servant girl jeered at him, they say, because he was so eager to know the things in the sky that he could not see what was there before him at his very feet. (*Theaet.* 174a)

If even servants understand the world better than Thales, those who mind the water clock will give him up for a lost cause. From time to time he may draw another person up into a view of the city 'from above', where this disciple can ask about the meaning of wealth and work as such and what it might mean to call a human being happy. When that happens, though, this disciple is likely to turn fool himself: 'he stammers and becomes ridiculous', entirely unable to articulate what he discovers in the language of the masses (*Theaet.* 176d). The world 'there before him at his very feet' becomes utterly strange, and even its language fails him. Granted a vision of higher things, he becomes a kind of holy fool, unable any longer to navigate the rhythms below.

Readings of the dialogues often miss the degree to which acosmism is a tragic necessity.[14] Fleeing the body is not an imperative condemning embodiment itself, since the writing consistently, in both subject matter and attention to details of their settings,[15] commends a life that dwells within the material – for Plato, the habits and patterns of life in and around Athens. The things to flee, rather, are the embodied rhythms of mundane *teloi*, the primary obsessions of lawyers and politicians. A body itself is not

---

14 As Gross does, in *The Divinization of the Christian according to the Greek Fathers*, Anaheim: A&C Press, 2003, pp. 39ff. For the critique, see Hans-Georg Gadamer, 1986, *The Idea of the Good in Platonic-Aristotelian Philosophy*, New Haven and London: Yale University Press, pp. 63ff. Also see Adrian Pabst, *Metaphysics: The Creation of Hierarchy* (forthcoming from Eerdmans), Chapter 1. My reading of Plato on this issue has been greatly influenced by a series of lectures by Catherine Pickstock at the University of Virginia in 1999.

15 Catherine Pickstock, 1998, *After Writing: On the Liturgical Consummation of Philosophy*, Oxford: Blackwell, Chapter 1. This is one of the key aspects of Plato that Cicero picks up on in *De Finibus*. He even mimics the style in the fifth dialogue, when he and several friends go for a walk through the gardens of the Academy, and suddenly, 'the remembrance of Plato comes into my mind, whom we understand to have been the first person who was accustomed to dispute in this place; and whose neighbouring gardens not only recall him vividly to my recollection, but seem even to place the man himself before my eyes'. Cicero, *De Finibus (On Ends)*, in H. Rackham (ed. and trans.), 1914, *Cicero* Vol. XVII, Loeb Classical Library no. 40, London and New York: William Heinemann Ltd. and G. P. Putnam's Sons.

metaphysically enslaving to the soul, but bodies controlled by the dripping of the water clock are. So, in the *Theaetetus* digression, the summary of the contrast of the stammering philosopher and the slavish lawyer comes as a sort of resigned moral injunction:

> Theodorus: If Socrates, you could persuade all men of the truth of what you say as you do me, there would be peace and fewer evils among mankind.
>
> Socrates: But it is impossible that evils should be done away with, Theodorus, for there must always be something opposed to the good; and they cannot have their place among the gods, but must inevitably hover about the moral nature and this earth. Therefore we ought to try to escape from earth to the dwelling of the gods as quickly as possible; and to become like God so far as this is possible [φυγή δέ ὁμοίωσις θεῷ κατά τό δυνατόν], and to become like God is to become righteous and holy and wise . . . There is nothing so like him as that one of us who in turn becomes most nearly perfect in righteousness. (*Theaet.* 176b–c)

What are we to make of the note of pessimism that initiates Socrates' suggestion here that the best end is a kind of *homoi-theosis*? If this note holds consistently throughout the dialogues, then we shall be forced to say that Godlikeness is a kind of anti-perfection in Plato, since he makes it the last resort of an imperfectible *polis*. As it happens, he does not consistently hold to this escapism, and so we cannot rest with any easy proto-gnostic reading of Platonic *theosis*.[16]

The *Republic*, written prior to *Theaetetus*,[17] is a good example of this contrast, since it supplies some of the images that the later dialogue will take up and revise. Here we again meet the philosopher in the role of the enlightened one rather out of step with *hoi polloi*. Having escaped the cave of shadows and looked into the rays of the sun, he returns to the cave in order to draw out his fellow men (*Republic*, 516e).[18] While he receives no great welcome either, and indeed this time the laughter of the slaves is followed by the threat of execution (*Rep.* 517a), a certain confidence in the persuasiveness of the form of the good prevails over the entire dialogue.

So, like Thales, the lawgiver of the *Republic* fixes his gaze vertically rather than horizontally, and 'will endeavour to imitate' the eternal order and its celestial inhabitants 'as far as may be, to fashion himself in their likeness

---

16 As, for instance, Gross's reading. See the original: Jules Gross, 1938, *La divinisation du chretien d'apres les Peres Grecs: Contribution historique a la doctrine de la grace*, Paris: J. Gabalda, pp. 43ff.

17 I follow the chronology mapped out in Voegelin, 1956, *Order and History*, Vol. III: *Plato and Aristotle*, Baton Rouge: Louisiana State University Press, Part One. See also Gadamer, *Idea*, pp. 22–32.

18 Plato, *Republic*, in Paul Shorey (ed. and trans.), 1956, *Plato*, Vol. VI: *Republic*, Vol. II, Loeb Classical Library no. 276, London: William Heinemann Ltd and Cambridge, MA:.Harvard University Press.

and assimilate himself to them' (*Rep.* 500c). Unlike Thales, however, the philosopher now turns this work of assimilation not just on himself, or even on a fellow disciple, but upon the entire city, offering public and private patterns of Godlikeness to all citizens (*Rep.* 500d). His 'Phoenecian tale' of the origins of different classes within the city in common clay and precious metals is designed to allow the various orders in the city to see one another as 'akin' [ὁμοίους] (*Rep.* 415a)[19] and so able to observe a common good of the whole in spite of their sub-political differences.[20]

When Socrates bans the poets and sophists from the city, this seems at first glance to be a supremely 'Olympian' move: he asserts the 'new legal' for his city by excluding the primordial and preternatural. But this exclusion is only a half-measure, necessary because the poets are corrupting the youth of the city by teaching them to speak impiously of the Gods (382ff). In effect they are setting a false *telos* before the youth (the gods deceive, ergo deceit is divine, ergo . . .). Ultimately, though, Socrates readmits the poets, since no *polis* can be a peaceful, eudaimonic city (*Rep.* 420b), without 'hymns to gods and the praises of good men' (*Rep.* 607a). With such tools, the citizens can build a city that will perfect their souls, even as their soul-building perfects the city.[21] Thus true poetry does not battle against true philosophy, since the lover of wisdom loves also the beauty of *poesis*.[22] The city itself becomes this hymn to the gods, and therefore the making of the city is the *poesis* of a poem.

This optimism returns later in the *Laws*. There, as in the *Republic*, divine participation does not require an escape from the social and political entanglements that make up the life of embodied humans. The worship of divinities is essential to the happy life [εὐδαίμονα βίον] (*Laws,* 716d),[23] not just for the good public order it brings to the *polis*, but also and primarily because liturgy makes us temperate and just with a share in the temperance and justice of God. Such a one is therefore dear to God, since he is like him ['ὅμοιος γάρ] (*Laws,* 716d–17b). *Eudaimonia* is, as its etymology suggests,[24] a participation in the heavenly orders of being; and this is ultimately as good for the city as it is for the saint.

19 Plato, *Republic*, in Paul Shorey (ed. and trans.), 1946, *Plato*, Vol. V: *Republic*, Vol. I, Loeb Classical Library no. 276, London and Cambridge: William Heinemann Ltd. and Harvard University Press.

20 Voegelin, *Order and History* III, pp. 104–8.

21 See Voegelin, *Order and History* III, pp. 93–4; Pabst, *Metaphysics*, Chapter 1; and Hans-Georg Gadamer, 1980, *Dialogue and Dialectic: Eight Hermeneutical Studies on Plato*, trans. P. Christopher Smith, New Haven and London: Yale University Press, pp. 39–72.

22 See Raymond Barfield, 2011, *The Ancient Quarrel between Poetry and Philosophy*, Cambridge and New York: Cambridge University Press, pp. 13–18. Many thanks to Scott Bader-Saye for bringing this book to my attention.

23 Plato, *Laws*, in R. G. Bury (ed. and trans.), 1926, *Plato*, Vol. X: *Laws*, Vol. I, Loeb Classical Library no. 187, London and New York: William Heinemann Ltd. and G. P. Putnam's Sons.

24 Robert Spaemann, 2005, *Happiness and Benevolence*, London: T&T Clark, p. 8.

How then do we read the 'fleeing' motif of the later text? The difference in the *Theaetetus* is simply that there Socrates is less confident in the philosopher's ability to persuade the citizens that divine participation is their proper end.[25] From the *Republic* to the *Theaetetus*, the Godlike philosopher changes from prophet-king into holy fool, from celebrated lawgiver to Thales in the pit. This pessimism develops, in fact, throughout the dialogues. So in the early *Apology*, the Academy is established as a kind of true *polis* within the degraded *polis* of Athens; the *Republic* and Middle Dialogues bear a strong measure of hope in the ability of this other city to emanate divine wisdom to the masses; in the later work, Plato seems more certain that the Athenians will always condemn the divine Socrates to death, and follow the drippings of their all-too-human water clock to their own deaths. Even the *Laws*, the last dialogue, establishes the city ordered in liturgy and festival not as a deified city, where gods and sons of gods might dwell, but as the next best thing: 'It will be clear to him who reasons it out and uses experience that a State will probably have a constitution no higher than second in point of excellence' (*Laws*, 739a).[26]

There is, then, no nascent Gnosticism in Plato, even where he is most emphatic about escaping from the body. To use an analogy from Hebrew Scriptures: Plato's disgust with embodied life in Athens is no more a sign of a metaphysical disdain for bodies and cities than are Yahweh's announcements that he will destroy Israel and Judah a sign of metaphysical disdain for his elected nation, just the opposite, in fact. Just as Yahweh binds himself to the Israel he curses, Plato and Socrates bind themselves to the embodied life of the city that seems to revel in its imperfection. Platonic perfection is not about fleeing *polis* and *soma*, but rather the assimilation of the community of temporal beings, as far as possible, to the eternal Good that transcends them. If the city refuses to become like the gods, then the Philosopher must turn from it towards the heavens; this, though, will be a rather imperfect perfection.

Two questions stand as yet unresolved in this formulation. First, the question of perfection's philosophical coherence, posed in the Exposition above. How can we become like the gods and still be human? An apple does not become perfect when it is most like a peach, even if a gardener considers the latter to be the more excellent fruit. The perfect apple perfects the form of the apple itself, and to be human is to have a human perfection. How does *theo-mimesis* avoid destroying the integrity of the human form? This is still an Aeschylian question, since it folds within it the claim of the Daughters of Danaus that humans are accountable to divine measures of

---

25 Voegelin, *Order and History* III, pp. 143–9.

26 For the importance of the chronology of the *Dialogues* and its implications on the question of embodiment, see Voegelin, *Order and History* III, pp. 92, 218–22. One could argue, alternatively, that the difference is not attributable to any supposed change in Plato's view through time but subject matter. The *Republic* makes a political fiction of the soul in order to show the hierarchical mechanisms which can save it; the digression in *Theaetetus* is more straightforward and simply speaks of the difficulty of saving souls.

justice, as well as the claim of Prometheus that earthbound creatures can be recipients of divine fire.

The second question is not simply 'how can mimesis be a perfection,' but, assuming that there is some measure of legitimacy to Prometheus's appeal to Themis, an answer to the first question, that is, which affirms its possibility, we must ask about degree. How much mimesis is entailed by perfection? How like the gods are humans to become, how assimilated ought we expect them to be? This will take us beyond the question of the integrity of various forms and into the realm of cosmic forces that war against the perfection, not just of humans, but of all informed beings: the *Theaetetus*' 'evils which inevitably hover above the moral nature and this earth' (176a). This is also still a Promethean question (though Prometheus now of the ancient tragedies, not of the Romantic poems), and below its surface we can hear echoing the ancient agonistics of preternatural Titanism and world-historical Olympianism. Plato's treatment of this material, however, demonstrates a development of Aeschylus's Prometheus that slightly alters the sense of the older drama. Said otherwise: Plato's response to the second question undermines his response to the first. I will treat these two questions in order.

Alchemania

All good things have their source in the good; the attentive dialectician knows that no limited end can be cut off entirely from the vision of the *idea tou agathou*. Admittedly, as Socrates suggests in the *Republic*, the good is 'hardly seen' (*Rep.* 516b) and can be discerned for the most part only in its effects. The good harvest, good speech and good citizens all share in a way of being that is mediated through each but circumscribed by none (*Rep.* 516b–c). Still, though, the idea of the good can be the object of contemplation for the philosopher, since these very mediations suggest the shape of their transcendent source. So the philosopher imitates the good so far as he is able and also offers the *polis* a constitution made in its image. For the good *polis*, just like the good person, derives its true character (*eidos*)[27] from being informed by this transcendent goodness.

Is this account of participation entirely coherent, though? Particular goods are called 'good' not because they manifest all possible goodness, but because they show a fittingness to the circumstances surrounding them. The best speech does not smell like the best rose or look like the best dance

---

27 Warrant for this use of *eidos* can be found in several places; see Voegelin, *Order and History* III, p. 94, for instance: 'Plato's use of the terms *eidos, idea,* and *physis* suggests an empirical search for characteristics, which derive their quality of essentials from the constancy of their occurrence in things of a common sense class under observation.' See also Pabst, *Metaphysics*, chapter 1, Gadamer, *Idea*, pp. 63–125, and Gail Fine, 1988, 'The Object of Thought Argument: Forms and Thoughts', *Apeiron* 21, pp. 105–45.

or even sound like any other good speech. It is good because it manifests a rhetorical excellence that corresponds precisely with the occasion, the place and the audience. How does Plato's account of participation in the transcendent good attend to the particular harmonies of any measurable good? What does it look like, in Socrates' city, for located and embodied citizens to hang suspended from the necks of gods, who themselves hang suspended from the neck of the universal Good? Plato's most developed answer comes in the *Philebus*, where he casts Socrates in the humorous role of the Timean demiurge and charges him with the creation of a philosophical mixture that will make up the most perfectly divine human (*Phil.* 59d–e).

This dialogue opens rather strangely for a Platonic discourse: Socrates actually states what he thinks. The characters agree at the outset to engage in a dialectical pursuit of the greatest human good, and Philebus insists that perfection lies in the life of pleasure. His side in the argument will take the form of an appeal to the goddess Hedone, though Philebus wrongly identifies her as Aphrodite (*Phil.* 12b). Socrates himself says perfection lies in the purview of Athena: in *nous* rather than *soma*, and so in the life of wisdom [φρόνησις]. In the end, surprisingly, neither is entirely correct: 'In this argument, then, both mind and pleasure were set aside; neither of them is the absolute good, since they are devoid of self-sufficiency, adequacy, and perfection [τελέου]' (*Phil.* 67A).[28] Instead, the proper *telos* is some sort of mixture of the two, and so they must all say a prayer to Dionysius or Hephaestus, or whoever turns out to be the god of mixtures (*Phil.* 61b–c).

Perfection is a kind of mixture, not because it lies halfway in between Hedone and Athena, but because the virtues championed by both are lacking a common element. What is missing from both pleasure and wisdom is limit. The universe is, in fact, defined and maintained by the gift of limit. An unnamed goddess, Socrates says, took pity on the formlessness of a world in which there was no measure, and established the limitation of law and order. 'You say she did harm; I say, on the contrary, she brought salvation.' (*Phil.* 26b–c). The best life is not the one that shares directly in the idea of good via infinity, even the infinity of the virtues, but rather through 'all the things which belong to the infinite, bound by the finite' (*Phil.* 27d). So the *bios miktos*, a mixture not of wisdom and pleasure but of infinity and finitude, is the best.[29]

This is not to say that infinity in itself is an imperfection, but only that it is a cosmic imperfection. It is true, of course, that human wisdom cannot 'contain the good' (*Phil.* 22c) any more than human pleasure, even if it has a greater share in the good. But when Philebus rightly points out that Socrates' Athena has not won out any more than his own goddess (whom he apparently has now accepted is not Aphrodite), the response is playfully subversive:

---

28 Of course, Socrates may not be surprised by his inaccuracy, since he begins to turn the conversation in this direction already near the beginning of the dialogue, at 22d.

29 Gadamer, *Idea*, pp. 111ff.

Philebus: Neither is your 'mind' the good, Socrates; it will be open to the same objections.

Socrates: My mind, perhaps, Philebus; but not so, I believe, the true mind, which is also divine. (*Phil.* 22c)

Mind and wisdom in themselves are synonymous with the good itself and so are as limitless as the *idea tou agathou*. But this identity occurs only in the divine, and the dialecticians have agreed to enquire into human perfection. Socrates is willing to admit, then, that his answer needs revision for human perfection, but not that infinite wisdom and the good itself are separable. Divine goodness is infinite wisdom; our participation in the good manifests itself in infinite virtues enjoyed in finite measure.

Once they have determined that the best life is the *bios miktos*, the philosophers agree to try their hand at discerning the human recipe. They first agree that the truest sorts of wisdom, for instance about the nature of justice in itself, belong in the best kind of life (*Phil.* 62a). But Socrates then asks whether that is enough, or whether this star-gazing Thales will still lack perfection:

Now will this man have sufficient knowledge, if he is master of the theory of the divine circle and sphere, but is ignorant of our human sphere and human circles, even when he uses these and other kinds of rules or patterns in building houses? (*Phil.* 62a–b)

It is now Protarchus who replies, since Philebus the hedonist has left the discussion (*Phil.* 12a–b; one wonders where he is off to). The one concerned only with divine things, Protarchus says, cuts a rather ridiculous figure. 'If any man is ever to find his own way home', then the human mixture must include impure knowledge as well as pure (*Phil.* 62b): divine and subdivine knowledge, pure pleasures as well as any lesser sorts which wisdom will allow. Socrates agrees, and at this point he and Protarchus turn into maniacal alchemists, throwing into the great human mixing pot everything that seems convenient to the form, until finally all the stops are pulled: 'I, then, like a doorkeeper who is pushed and hustled by the mob, give up, open the door, and let all the kinds of knowledge stream in, the impure mingling with the pure' (*Phil.* 62c). The metaphor has apparently got mixed here as well.

The key to the mixed life is not simply attunement to the highest good, but measure [μετριότης] and proportion [συμμετρία], since any compound that lacks these will be nothing but a jumble (*Phil.* 64d–e). Finitude is the arena of the measured, and perfection lies within it as the way of proportionately measured beauty. They cannot, in fact, 'catch the good with the aid of one idea' (*Phil.* 64e–5a) at all, since this would be a sort of knowledge proportionate only to the gods. What they can do, though, is 'run it down with three – beauty, proportion, and truth' (*Phil.* 65a), since the truth-seeking philosopher will be able to discover the symmetries that issue in the most perfect of human lives. Though the *idea tou agathou* continues to elude us, we can approach it through the well-measured mixture, since 'the power [δύναμις] of the good has taken refuge in the nature of the beautiful' (*Phil.* 64d).[30]

Thales in his pit is clearly not the icon of perfection in the *Philebus*. Is this then a self-critique of the more 'ethereal' dialogues? Is Plato distancing himself from an early notion that perfection is the *theoria* of divine forms? Gadamer reads the *Philebus* as marking that sort of evolution: 'What is viewed from the perspective of the *Republic* (or the *Symposium*) as the pure unmixed good or beautiful "beyond being" is here determined to be the structure of "the mixed itself"'.[31] For the good to take refuge in the beautiful, he claims, it must cease to be an idea in itself, becoming instead 'the being of the ideas generally', not mediated by them, but immediately identical to them.[32] Even more radically: 'The good is no longer the one',[33] since it is proportioned out into the beauty of non-mediating existence. In short, Plato is here 'turning from the realm of the ideal to what is best in reality'.[34]

Gadamer is here combating the debased modern reading of Platonism as acosmic transcendence, discussed above. He is thus correct to insist upon a concretizing Platonism in which bodies and cities are the irreducible sites for the manifesting of the good. However, he fails to take account of a religious gap that overlays the contemplation of perfection throughout the dialogues.[35] The Good is still the One, and remains the proper end of human contemplation throughout. 'Then, if we are not able to hunt the good with one idea only, with three we may catch our prey; . . . and these taken together (σὺν τρισὶ λαβόντες. . .οἷον ἕν] we may regard as the single cause of the mixture, and the mixture as being good by reason of the infusion of them' (*Phil.* 64e–5a).[36] The Jowett translations bring out a cycling back upwards that is less explicit in the Fowler, and missed by Gadamer: the three do not replace the one, but gesture back to it, triangulating its

---

30 For an account of the intermingling of the Good and Beautiful in Plato, see Jean-Louis Chrétien, 2004, *The Call and the Response*, trans. Anne A. Davenport, New York: Fordham University Press, pp. 6–12. The Fourth Movement, below, discusses this account in Chrétien.

31 Gadamer, *Idea*, p.115.

32 *Idea*, p.124.

33 *Idea*, p.115.

34 *Idea*, p. 30.

35 For the notion of a religious gap in Plato, see Voegelin, *Order and History* III, p. 255, and John Milbank, 2006, *Theology and Social Theory*, 2nd ed, Oxford and Cambridge, MA: Blackwell, p. 329. It could be argued that Gadamer's approach is still too Heideggerian: that is to say, that he is suspicious of transcendence, and so suspicious of a religious Plato, and tries to bring Plato closer to immanentized Aristotle.

36 Plato, *Philebus*, in B. Jowett (trans.), 1911, *The Dialogues of Plato*, Vol. III, New York: Charles Scribner's Sons.

otherwise invisible location. *Sun trisi, oion en*: with these three taken as one, we will find the good, and the ultimate origin and *telos* of our mixture. The One's elusiveness is not a sign that it has collided immediately with finitude, but rather that it stands beyond them, in just the way that it stands 'beyond being' in the Republic. The One/Good is not a world-negating unparticipated form, as Gadamer fears it may become, but neither is it multiplied out into 'the structure of the mixed'.[37] It is, rather, the donator of all beings, the source and cause of all beautiful measure, the invisible one that makes a *harmonia* of the many. The good takes refuge in the beautiful because all beautiful forms are a graceful refracting of their informing good.[38] 'A *dosis* of gods to men, as I believe, was tossed down from some divine source through the agency of a Prometheus together with a gleaming fire' (*Phil.* 16c).[39] This *dosis* is particularly fitting for human perfection, since we are made to face the good, and thus find our own unique mixtures as refractions of that transcendent idea. Only in the divine mind will we find infinite wisdom and an unmediated good. But this only means that finitude is not a true opposition to infinity, nor is the many in opposition to the one. Multiplied beauty is a refracting of the One/Good, as the finite is a 'movable image of the Eternity' (*Timaeus*, 37d).[40] The many forms of the *bios miktos* are icons (*Phil.* 59b) of the transcendent virtues, themselves refractions of the *idea tou agathou*.

There is then a 'secondness' to human perfection in the *Philebus*, just as there is in the *Laws*. Plato is not, however, suggesting that less than perfect is good enough, nor is he reducing the transcendent idea into more manageable parts. There is a key difference between a reductive second best and one that is second because it sees the perfect good from afar, and the *Philebus*, at least, unambiguously gestures toward the latter:

Socrates: We must, then, gain a clear conception of the good, or at least an outline of it, that we may, as we said, know to what the second place is to be assigned.
Protarchus: Quite right.
Socrates: And have we not found a road which leads to the good?
Protarchus: What road?
Socrates: If you were looking for a particular man and first found out correctly where he lived, you would have made great progress towards finding him whom you sought.
Protarchus: Yes, certainly.
Socrates: And just now we received an indication, as we did in the beginning,

37 Gadamer, *Idea*, p. 115.

38 See Pabst, *Metaphysics*, Chapter 1 and Spaemann, *Happiness*, p. 6.

39 Plato, *Philebus*, in Harold N. Fowler and W. R. M. Lamb (eds and trans.), 1925, *Plato*, Vol. III, Loeb Classical Library no. 164, London and New York: William Heinemann Ltd. and G. P. Putnam's Sons.

40 Plato, *Timaeus*, in R. G. Bury (ed. and trans.), 1999, *Plato*, Vol. IX, Loeb Classical Library no. 234, London and Cambridge, MA: Harvard University Press.

that we must seek the good, not in the unmixed, but in the mixed life. (*Phil.* 61a–b)

The mixed life is not good in and of itself, but rather good insofar as it leads to *ton agathon*, as a path leads to the home of a lost friend. Protarchus understands this clearly a few lines further, when, as I quoted above, he insists that the pseudo-circle and other forms of lesser wisdom be admitted to the mixture on the grounds that they are necessary 'if any man is ever to find his own way home' (*Phil.* 62b). He means Thales, first of all, who will perennially end up in the pit if he cannot remember the stone wall where he should turn left, and which gate to pass through into his own garden. But 'home' is also the transcendent and evasive idea, the dwelling place of the many gods and even of the transcendent divinity, the *idea ton agathon*. Thales is right to desire this more ultimate home, even if he forgets, in his contemplations, how to make his way there as an earthbound being. The gap that separates God from human life is the gap that separates the dialectical fire from the hand of God who gives it, and the multiplicity of discernible forms from the Good from which it derives. The finite mixtures of secondness, then, are the way home to the idea of the good because they are the only hope for creatures on earth who desire to dwell with the gods, 'to become like God so far as this is possible'.

Liturgical rebellion

We have, the reader will recall, a final question to ask of Plato. How 'second' is this secondness? How far is it possible to become like God within the limits of finitude? How perfect is Platonic perfection?

Consider again the passage from *Theaetetus* cited above:

> Theodorus: If Socrates, you could persuade all men of the truth of what you say as you do me, there would be peace and fewer evils among mankind.
> Socrates: But it is impossible that evils should be done away with, Theodurus, for there must always be something opposed to the good; and they cannot have their place among the gods, but must inevitably hover about the moral nature and this earth. Therefore we ought to try to escape from earth to the dwelling of the gods as quickly as possible . . . (*Theaet.* 176b–c)

Most Athenians are unpersuaded by Socrates' call to a philosophical life. They will, of course, ultimately condemn this self-proclaimed gadfly, and the charges will be, variously, teaching the youth to believe in no gods or teaching them to believe in extra-civic gods (*Apology*, 27d).[41] In

---

41 Plato, *Apology*, in Harold N. Fowler (ed. and trans.), 1977, *Plato*, Vol. I, Loeb Classical Library no. 36, London and Cambridge, MA: Harvard University Press.

Theaetetus, Socrates gives the reason for the general obstinacy of his fellow citizens: evil powers will always exist in opposition to the good. Since they have no share in the good, these powers must hover at a distance and collect around the earth, around servant girls, lawyers and other enslaved Athenians. A few lines later he expresses the matter succinctly before finally ending the digression: 'Two patterns (παραδειγμάτων), my friend, are set up in the world, the divine, which is most blessed (εύδαιμονεστάτου), and the godless, which is most wretched' (*Theaet.* 176e).

Is this reference to hovering and non-participating evils a literary device, a kind of allegorizing of Plato's impatience with his sluggish co-citizens, or is it a metaphysical doctrine? If the former, it may need no more consideration than a simple acknowledgement that 'the road home will be difficult'. If the latter, the mixed life of humans must also include, in the depths of their ontological make-up, a fundamental imperfection.

The *Timaeus's* demiurge provides a typology for the mixers of the *Philebus*, and this dialogue too suggests that the cosmic mixture includes a preternatural and metaphysical evil. In the *Philebus*, the alchemists craft a human nature that is suited for the mediation of the true, proportionate and beautiful, so that they can reject as evil all those pleasures of Hedone which have no share in the Good (*Phil.* 62e–3c). The divine demiurge of Timaeus's mythological poem also has to sort through chaotic and unparticipating motions in order to make a well-ordered world. However, since he is making the original cosmic mixture, he cannot simply sift out the chaos and allow the true ingredients in. The entire universe is unformed chaos, and his mixture makes proportion and harmony for the first time: 'he took over all that was visible, seeing that it was not in a state of rest but in a state of discordant and disorderly motion' (*Tim.* 30a). A kind of raw becoming, the cosmos awaits the hand of the creating God, which introduces *logos* to it (*Tim.* 30a–b). God patterns the new order on his own being, and so invites cosmic theosis: 'Being devoid of envy He desired that all should be, so far as possible, like unto himself' (*Tim.* 30a). Becoming is an icon of being, Timaeus says, since the original work of the divine craftsman took unbecoming chaos and directed it towards his own likeness.[42]

However, in one of the most significant and dramatic breaks in Plato's writing, the myth-maker of the *Timaeus* stops his account of cosmic origins after saying that becoming is an icon of being, and starts over.[43] The trouble is that he suddenly realizes that the chaos itself is a kind of pure and ateleological becoming that does not, in fact, imitate the goodness and beauty of true being (*Tim.* 48a–9b). His first telling had attended to the order of a logified cosmos, but not to the way in which God manages to turn the raw becoming into Godlike being. When he begins again, he claims that

---

42 See Gadamer, *Dialogue and Dialectic*, p. 163.

43 On the literary motivations and effects of the 'new beginning', see John Sallis, 1999, *Chorology: On Beginning in Plato's* Timaeus, Bloomington and Indianapolis: Indiana University Press, pp. 91–8. See also Gadamer, *Dialogue and Dialectic*, pp. 169ff.

the missing element is the most important in the entire myth. God orders the cosmos not by stamping himself upon its raw material, but by persuading (πειθειν, *Tim.* 48a) the chaotic movements toward himself. He fashions the whole within a kind of cosmic nursery (*Tim.* 49b) so that the *genesis* can also be a *telos*. Without the nursery, divine-likeness would only be a foreign end imposed upon the chaos. The chaotic becoming lacks an end, and lacks also the temporalizing and localizing structures that would allow the primordial dischordant becoming to become something. Thus the *khora* of the myth's new beginning allows Godlikeness to be also a perfection.

The ateleological, alogical *genesis*, the chaotic becoming that has no time or space, is the cave-dwellers of the *Republic* and the servant girl of *Theaetetus*, now transcribed as a primordial cosmology.[44] Like the literary break in the dialogue itself, the new *telos* of deification struggles against this chaos, since the *telos* governs an older, more elemental rebellion. *Telos* attempts to rule a world of becoming that it did not create, and the task of philosophy as a whole is to persuade the powers hovering around the earth to form themselves according to the likeness of the creating God.

In pressing this structure of metaphysical conflict, Plato makes use of the tragic mythology, though already in a slightly altered form.[45] Prior to the Olympian coup, in the age of Saturn, humans and animals lived together in *eudaimonia* (*Laws*, 713e). There were no states, no kings, only the God himself who shepherded the people and the many gods under him who governed various aspects of creaturely life (*Statesman*, 271e–2a).[46] But when that paradisal age came to its own fated completion, the gods withdrew, and the universe began spinning in reverse, a reversal which was always 'an inevitable part of the earth's motions' (*Stat.* 269d). It is at this point that Zeus looked upon the chaos that had descended upon the Saturnine Age and persuaded, as in the *Timaeus*, the spiralling cosmos to take on a new order.[47] This is the order of kings, cities, laws. Properly respected and followed, Olympian order will make humans like gods. It will, however, never annihilate the evils that hover, because 'unpersuaded necessity' remains, even as the new theotic order urges the cosmic agents in the other direction. So Zeus and his ilk are Thales and Socrates, fighting against the inevitable command of the 'late Saturnine' water clock.

Does Plato then side unequivocally with Zeus in the war against Prometheus? Was the Titan wrong to give us the divine fire that, even if ontologically deserved, still gave 'to mortals honours beyond their due'? Even here we must step carefully. Plato certainly rejects any notion of a return to a pure Saturnine age, and even refuses to say whether that first paradisal state was better than the Age of Zeus which followed the reordering of the

---

44 Voegelin, *Order and History* III, pp. 202.

45 Voegelin, *Order and History* III, pp. 151–69.

46 Plato, *Statesman*, in Harold N. Fowler and W. R. M. Lamb (eds and trans.), 1925, *Plato*, Vol. III, Loeb Classical Library no. 164, London and New York: William Heinemann Ltd. and G. P. Putnam's Sons.

47 Voegelin, *Order and History* III, pp. 204, 255.

world (*Stat.* 272 b–e). Yet the *Laws* sketches for us a more complex image. Here the Athenian stranger insists that we should in fact imitate the Saturnine Age: 'we ought by every means to imitate the life of the age of Cronus, as tradition paints it, and order both our homes and our States in obedience to the immortal element within us, giving to reason's ordering the name of "law" (*Laws*, 713e–14a). We should imitate the pre-Olympian, though not by lawlessness, but by a worship of prehistoric divinities which issues forth in a lawgiving of our own discernment. This is the mythopoetic register of the mixed life.

Plato gives an indication here of the depths into which King Argos must dive. In the *Suppliants*, the king had to discern which party in the dispute had the greater share in the local gods of the sacred grove. In the *Laws*, Plato puts his citizens in a city with no king, where the liturgical orders form the heart of citizenship. Zeus, the lawgiver of the Cretans, along with Apollo, lawgiver of the Lacedaemonians (*Laws*, 624a), are both eclipsed by an unnamed Athenian lawgiver. This divine benefactor seems, perversely, to be Dionysius, the God who is less interested in the order of the state than in the ecstatic and eudaimonic life.[48] Participation in God is in this case more a matter of liturgical play than of law-abiding seriousness. Those affected by the divine powers are suspended from the gods now not tragically, by their own belts, but comically, by a golden cord that is able to make them sing and dance like heaven's marionettes (*Laws*, 644d–5b, 803d–e).[49]

The citizens in search of this rapturous *eudaimonia* will still observe an order of justice and law, but they will do so not so much out of obeisance to the Olympian order as in an act of riotous harmonization with what is best, even the transcendent and pre-Olympian Good. Zeus will still act to persuade order out of chaos, but his acts will be mediated through a liturgical exchange that transcends his operations. The citizens will still 'cling to Dike' (*Laws*, 716a), his governor of human justice, but she will now act as a vicar of a higher order, and will mediate the prayers, songs and orgies of the citizens beyond the throne of Zeus, toward the supra-divine court of Themis and the other children of Saturn from which they originate.

We must add a final ingredient, then, to the kettle of the *bios miktos*: the Dionysian as a limiting structure upon a Zeus-governed Olympus.[50] But Dionysius limits in the way that liturgy limits human emotion, which is to say only by shaping it into an icon of the divine. Thus limitation is also a transgression. With the festival God as lawgiver, the human mixture follows

---

48 I am assuming here that the second book, beginning with an invocation of both Apollo and Dionysius, and ending with a brief discourse on music, dance and wine, is meant to imply the identity of the unnamed lawgivers. See Voegelin, *Order and History* III, p. 255.

49 See the punning of *paidia* (play) and *paideia* (education) in the *Laws*, noted in Voegelin, *Order and History* III, p. 232.

50 I am influenced here by the discussion of the Dionysian in Terry Eagleton, 2005, *Holy Terror*, Oxford: Oxford University Press, pp. 13–17.

the secondary order of law only by going beyond, celebrating the way in which it mediates the higher: Dike, as a manifestation of Themis. In this way, even as he insists that Zeus must win out over Prometheus, Plato subversively hints that Prometheus's submission may win him the fire after all, since the order of justice proper to humans is precisely the one that mediates divinity.

The perfect life in Plato is, in one sense, always imperfect, since the order of perfection will endlessly wage war against the primordial chaos that precedes it. With this we arrive at the limits of Platonic perfection and the source of the metaphysical problems with which the Fathers of the Church will wrestle. And yet the consistent liturgical language with which Plato addresses this gap between human chaotic protology and our well-ordered *telos* offers a hint of the path that the Church Fathers will take: this gap can be spanned, not by the rigour of dialectic alone, but primarily in civic festivals and invocations. Human perfection at its fullest makes us better than the limited civic gods, and suspends us by our necks, by means of the sashes of our ritualized language, from the *idea tou agathou* itself.

A More Proximate Perfection

'Philosophy begins in the Platonic love for the divine measure.' If we can point to an original Academic teaching on human perfection, it is the teaching of the divine measure itself: the human end is the life that hangs suspended, so far as possible, from the gods. Plato's perfectly mixed life is one that discerns the material while contemplating the divine.

What happens to this understanding of human ends in that other pillar of the Athenian Academy? Does Aristotle think, as he is often supposed to have thought, that in giving humans such a share in the transcendent Plato 'hast given to mortal men honors beyond their due?' If so, then our search for an alternative to modern perfection's bifurcation ends here, where the tragic ironies of the ancient Prometheus are recast as an unambiguous option for a humble immanence; Aristotle would, in short, be the bridge between Aeschylus and Shelley.

This is, in many ways, the prima facie reading of Plato's intellectual offspring. In the well-known beginning of the *Nicomachean Ethics* he charges his master with losing the temporal by over-attending to the eternal, of placing relative goods in a univocal fog of a 'common Idea' which is incapable of distinguishing 'the absolutely good and the relatively good' (*Nic. Ethics*, 1095a22–4).[51] Plato's idea of the good, we might say, recalling the critique of the Exposition above, is both logically and ethically flawed according to his student. Logically, since it hides an equivocation under a blanket of indemonstrable *methexis*: thus, a good god, a good idea and a good home for a duck make use of divergent senses of the word good,

---

51 Aristotle, *Nicomachean Ethics*, in H. Rackham (ed. and trans.), 1956, *Aristotle*, Vol. XIX, Loeb Classical Library no. 73, London: William Heinemann Ltd and Cambridge, MA: Harvard University Press.

each generating an evaluation that is limited to the definitive function of its ascriptive subject. To say that all share in the idea of the good, Aristotle says, is to misunderstand what we actually mean when we say these various things are good, which is simply that they fulfil a particular end which is included in their definitions. Obviously then, 'there cannot be a single and universal notion' (*Nic. Ethics*, 1095a26–9) that preserves the sense of the particular categorical predications.

Further, Platonic perfection is flawed ethically, since, 'even if the goodness predicated of various things in common really is a unity of something existing separately and absolute, it clearly will not be practiceable or attainable by man'. The transcendence of Plato's idea is just what makes it moot for a discourse on ethics, and this allows Aristotle to make his new beginning: 'the Good which we are now seeking is a good within human reach' (*Nic. Ethics*, 1096b30–5).

If the good is within human reach then there is no longer any need for an act of religio-political discernment, like Argos's dive into the depths between divine and human justice. Even where he concedes to Plato the deifying power of human happiness, Aristotle insists that the participation of the human in the divine is beside the point:

> Now if anything that men have is a gift of the gods, it is reasonable to suppose that happiness is divinely given – indeed of all man's possessions it is most likely to be so, inasmuch as it is the best of them all. This subject however may perhaps more properly belong to another branch of study. Still, even if happiness is not sent us from heaven, but is won by virtue and by some kind of study or practice, it seems to be one of the most divine things that exist. For the prize and end of goodness must clearly be supremely good – it must be something divine and blissful. (*Nic. Ethics*, 1099b11–18)

Gone here is the irony of the Platonic city, where humanity reaches its natural *telos* while forgetting itself in liturgical ecstasy. Aristotle can suppose that God gives *eudaimonia*, but still argue that its important feature for ethics is not the ecstasy of its discovery in liturgical rites, but a much cooler intellectual recognition. If we were to force the entire thought into a syllogism, it would read:

> The better something is, the more godlike;
> Perfection is the name for the best achievement of humankind;
> Perfection is the most godlike thing that humans can attain.

The human who has achieved a virtuous and happy end may not even realize that she is divinized via this proximity to God. Human beings, like the sciences they fashion, 'all aim at some good, and seek to make up their deficiencies, but they do not trouble about a knowledge of the Ideal Good' (*Nic. Ethics*, 1097a5–8). A certain theological vision of human perfection thus remains intact here, but religion no longer seems to operate in a way that informs this vision in any of its content.

The critique of Plato even reads in certain passages, in spite of the transcribed character of the text, like a philosophical farce, a send up in the spirit, if not the style, of Sophocles' *Clouds*. If Plato means the story of Thales and the Thracian girl to be a biting critique of the false wisdom of Athenians, Aristotle redresses it as an account of the useless wisdom of the stargazing philosopher. His own hesitation to critique Plato of the pit then becomes part of the act: 'Such enquiry goes against the grain because of our friendship for the authors of the Theory of Ideas.' But which shall we prefer? Loyalty to friends, or the love of truth (*Nic. Ethics*, 1096a13–15)? And the *nouveau* Academics, waiting for their cue, are quick to prod the reformer on to his ground-clearing dispute with his own master. In the end, even his concessions are backhanded: Let us grant to Plato that all goods are in some discernible way participants in the eternal idea, 'it is not easy to see how knowing that same Ideal will help a weaver or carpenter in the practice of his own craft', nor indeed to see how it will help humans achieve their peculiarly proportionate end of being good humans (*Nic. Ethics*, 1097a8–10).

In Aristotle then, we observe an unmistakable severing of the Danaan girdles. Humans have their own end, their own virtues, their own courts of appeal, none of which should be confused with the goods relative to gods, any more than the goods relative to a hammer or a mango. Perfection is simply the actualization of form; goodness is the relative name for the actualization of each substance or species. Divine perfection is the divine good, but not the good of a human, a serving spoon or a habitat for birds. The only sense in which all these goods allow participation in the divine is the hypothetical one: happiness is the respective best good for humans, and so 'if anything that men have is a gift of the gods, it is reasonable to suppose that happiness is divinely given' (*Nic. Ethics*, 1099b11–13).

We can trace the basic divergence between the student and the master on this grid. Plato seeks the idea of the good, and sometimes finds that it translates into a civic good, and other times throws his hands up in resignation and flees embodied society altogether. However, philosophy has since Aristotle sought out the space between the water-clock-watching lawyer and the stargazing Thales. Ethics, from this point forward, ceases to follow the path of divine wisdom [σοφία], and instead is marked by the pursuit of practical human wisdom [φρόνησις] (*Nic. Ethics*, 1140b31–1141a9). In plotting human perfection, then, Aristotle moves quickly past the notion of sharing in the divine idea of the good, and fastens on to a secondary perfection, a *deutera eudaimonia*. 'The life of moral virtue on the other hand is happy only in a secondary degree' (*Nic. Ethics*, 1178a9–10). This is the proportionate end toward which the human alone is ordered. Only the second sort of perfection is useful for tracking down experienceable happiness, so only the second sort comes to play in an account of ethics.

Aristotle's school of liturgy

It may be surprising, in light of this critique, to hear Aristotle say that *phronesis*, the practical wisdom of shipbuilders and omelette-makers, is not 'in authority over' *sophia* at all, any more than 'Political Science governs the gods' (*Nic. Ethics*, 1145a10–12). At the end of the day, it is the activity of contemplation of divine wisdom alone that 'will constitute perfect happiness' in human beings (*Nic. Ethics*, 1177a15–18). Does he then wind up, after a rather over-inflated critique of the master, back at Thales in the pit as the ideal human? If the proper work of perfection is the fulfilment of the human form and thus something attainable and distinctly human, why is the contemplation of *sophia* the path to consummate and perfect happiness?

In order to come to terms with this apparent incoherence, we return to the notion that perfection is an actualization of a particular potential. In *Metaphysics* XII, Aristotle develops his earlier[52] account with the new suggestion that 'Therefore there must be a principle of this kind whose essence is actuality' (ἡ οὐσία ἐνέργεια, *Met*. 1071b20–3).[53] Here the Timaean notion that time is a moving image of eternity is worked out in a metaphysics in the most proper sense of the term, the 'above motion' which generates motion itself (*Met*. 1072a19–1073a13). Prior to this, he imagined actuality only as the progression of a potency.[54] If there are, though, only substances that move from potential to actual, then we will never gain a satisfactory view of the field of *energia* as such. What causes the motion that precedes any given actualization? Horses are perfected as they move from potentially good at jumping and bearing riders to actually good, and their movement from *dunamis* to *energeia* is caused by good nutrition, good training and the model of other perfected horses. A human is potentially a being who can practise the virtues and contemplate the gods, but the actualization requires the already actualized presence of a well-ordered *polis*, complete with good parenting and proper education (*Nic. Ethics*. 1091b12–1095b13). If everything moves and nothing puts it in motion, then Zeno may be right after all, and movement itself may be a kind of stillness.

Stated otherwise, in the terms of Timaeus's poetic do-over: the very notion that a thing *becomes* requires the added notion that it becomes *something*. A horse does not just change, it becomes a better or worse horse; if not, then it simply fluctuates among various characteristics that will soon melt into indistinction. To call a thing a horse is already to imply its *telos*,

---

52 Following Voegelin's chronology again, *Order and History* III, pp. 271–84.

53 Aristotle, *Metaphysics*, in Hugh Tredennick (ed. and trans.), 1958, *Aristotle*, Vol. XVIII: *Metaphysics*, Vol. II, Loeb Classical Library no. 287, London and Cambridge, MA: William Heinemann Ltd. and Harvard University Press.

54 David Bradshaw, 2004, *Aristotle East and West: Metaphysics and the Division of Christendom*, Cambridge and New York: Cambridge University Press, pp. 1–23; Jonathan Lear, 1988, *Aristotle: The Desire to Understand*, Cambridge and New York: Cambridge University Press, pp. 15–26.

and thus to chart its becoming on a particular scale. And what is good for the horse is good for all the animals on the farm: all movement shares at least this much in common, that it is a becoming toward an end.

Further, the notion of teleological becoming itself would fall into logical equivocation unless the horse-becoming of a horse and the habitat-becoming of a duck's nest shared a more universal structural orientation. They become, and so they commonly aim at *telos*. The argument for an unmoved mover in Aristotle bypasses the fragmentary particularization of the Good in a multiplicity of goods.[55] It is true that carpenters and soldiers have their own respective *teloi*; however, stepping beyond their respective *techne*, the very fact of 'having a *telos*' places a more universal claim on them. They are exigencies of *dunamis* en route to *energiea*. All being aims at this universal common end, since just as a horse cannot become without becoming a horse, potential being cannot become without becoming actuality. That end in turn draws the becoming toward it, as the idea of horse draws the formation of a horse. Just as there is 'pure horse' in the relative *telos*, there is 'pure act' in the universal. We can thus revise the earlier syllogism:

The more virtuous a human becomes, the more actual she is;
God is pure act, while the virtuous human is en route from potency to act;
Therefore, the more virtue a human has, the more Godlike she becomes.

Aristotle thus brings into unity the two beginnings of Timaeus's poem: it now goes without saying that every genesis is granted a *telos*. We do not need the sharp divide in the middle, since there is no ateleological genesis at all. In at least this sense, he moves beyond the tragic remainder in Plato, implying in this structural argument for an unmoved mover that there is no primordial war between the Titans and Olympians, between lawless freedom and the late assertion of order. The pure act causes all movement, from the cosmic cycles of the heavens to the virtuous progress of humans (*Met.* 1072a26–1072b14).

How, though, does the unmoved mover cause this motion? It cannot be only as an efficient cause, like a whip to the backside of a horse, since the whip itself must carry out a movement from potency to act in order to bring about the same effect in the horse that feels or hears it snap. The meta-mover moves, rather, more like objects of desire and objects of thought move us to desire and to think. The beautiful work of art can set my desire in motion without any development from potency to act on the part of the work itself, as can the knowledge of the parts of an aircraft engine: we see the whole, and are 'moved' by a desire to understand how it works. In fact, the painting and the engine move us the same way, since 'the primary objects of desire and thought are the same' (*Met.* 1072a28). We love what we know and wish to know better, and also only know actively as an

---

55 Bradshaw, *Aristotle*, pp. 24–44.

expression of the desire to understand and remember.[56] The unmoved in this way moves us to contemplate, which is our highest good, by being in itself desirable and so quickening our potential for knowledge. It 'causes motion by being an object of love, where as all other things cause motion because they are themselves in motion' (*Met.* 1072b4–5).[57] The object of desire is the final cause, the *telos* of motion, since by being knowable as desirable, this object invites the desiring motion of all other beings. Since 'God is that actuality' (*Met.* 1072b25–9), which stands as final cause of all motion, we can say in a remote sense that all cosmic perfection of potency into act is desire for God; more proximately, that the divine act causes humans to actualize their knowledge and love of actuality, a knowing and loving that takes bodily form as human virtue.

Perfection, then, is always an imitation of divine good. God takes pleasure in being pure act, and we 'see' the pleasure of actuality in seeing God, and learn to take pleasure in 'waking, sensation, and thinking', that is, our own manifestations of actuality (*Met.* 1072b17–19). We do not, for Aristotle, begin to arrive at our own *telos* by contemplating our own secondary good *in potentia* and then setting it into motion. We achieve our own *teloi* by imitating the divine good, so far as this is possible for us.[58] This is the meaning of the Aristotelian doctrine that actuality precedes potentiality (*Met.* 1071b4–20). The 'seeds' of potency always come from a prior actuality, and ultimately this is the case not in fruit trees and baby raccoons, where Aristotle of course knows that his argument is circular, but in God, where pure actuality is the parent that implants the seeds in all substances (*Met.* 1072b31–1073a3). To the all-important question of which came first, the chicken or the egg, Aristotle answers clearly: God. We awake desiring actuality, even before we know what it is to be human potentially. It is only after the fact, metaphysically speaking, that we come to see the fittingness of this desire, since, as it happens, the desire which awakens in us as the love of God is also the motion which carries our humanity to its perfection. There is only *energeia* in the heavens and on earth because the divine good is *energeia*, and the celestial spheres, waves of the sea and human beings all long for it, and thus find their own good in desiring the perfection of God.

Returning to the *Ethics*, we can see now why contemplation of divine wisdom is the particular good of the human after all. 'It is not really the case that Prudence (φρονεσις) is in authority over Wisdom (σοφια), or over the higher part of the intellect' (*Nic. Ethics*, 1145a7–10). Happiness is not simply an achievement of nameable goals connected to material culture, but also the actualization of 'the higher part of the intellect', or 'the best part of us' (*Nic. Ethics*, 1177a12–15), which happens to be *nous*. *Nous* is the thin place where the human is most herself in distinction from the world, but also most identical to the world, since the act of understanding

---

56 Lear, *Aristotle*, pp. 116–34.
57 Bradshaw, *Aristotle*, pp. 29ff.
58 Spaemann, *Happiness*, p. 46; Voegelin, *Order and History* III, p. 306.

is a formation of 'all things' within the soul (*de Anima*). This, though, is the human *dunamis*, and so in the activity of *nous* wherein she is most actualized as a lover of wisdom, she is at the same time most mimetic of the *purus actus*. If Delphic self-knowledge is the path to human perfection, then the highest part of the human must know itself as well; but since it is akin to the divine, the *nous* knows itself only in knowing itself as divine-like, and humans, the embodiments of *nous*, must likewise have their perfection in the contemplation of God.[59] If, on the other hand, human *phronesis* were our ultimate end, the *sophianic* that resides in our make-up would be incomplete, and humans would fail at perfection due to a kind of metaphysical incoherence.[60]

Nous is then the hidden depth of the human, and its act of desiring God is the single truly human act. To trace perfection as a human pursuit of a human end 'would be a strange thing', since it would suggest that *nous*-bearing human 'should choose to live not his own life but the life of some other than himself' (*Nic. Ethics*, 1178a2–5).[61] A human who lacks the divinity of *nous* is no human at all, and so a purely human perfection is no perfection at all. Perfection is the actualization of the full human *dunamis*, and the knowledge of the divine is the highest *energiea* that the soul can achieve.

This brings us to an Aristotelian 'suspension' after all, a perfection nameable only as a sharing in the divine life. The *bios theoretikos*

> will be higher than the human level: not in virtue of his humanity will a man achieve it, but in virtue of something within that is divine . . . Nor ought we obey those who enjoin that a man should have man's thoughts and a mortal the thoughts of mortality, but we ought so far as possible to achieve immortality, and do all that man may to live in accordance with the highest thing in him; for though this be small in bulk, in power and value it far surpasses all the rest. (*Nic. Ethics*, 1177b27–1178a1)

Aristotle takes up the Theaetetian claim here that our proper end is to become as divine as possible. The single difference is that actuality itself is mimetic of God in Aristotle, whereas in Plato the possibility of nonteleological acts always lurk around the edges of ordered, teleolological being.[62] Aristotle's critique of Plato, and whether he is right or wrong is not my present concern, is in essence that he has given too much *phronesis* away to the water clock, and that he hopes to find a pathway into the sophianic good somewhere other than in the crafty wisdom of the citizenry. For Aristotle, we achieve immortality 'so far as possible' not by ceasing the pursuit

---

59 Lear, *Aristotle*, pp. 302-3.

60 Voegelin, *Order and History* III, pp. 364-6. But Voegelin maintains that Aristotle does not avoid incoherence on this point, while I am suggesting that he is coherent, in view of his metaphysic of mediation.

61 Which is, at it happens, exactly the point of the critique of mimetic poetry in the *Republic* (392c–394b).

62 See Voegelin, *Order and History* III, pp. 284ff.

of secondary *teloi* and placing ourselves in immediate relationship to the Good, but by passing through the mediations themselves. Thus he can turn his attention toward the more proximate perfection, even creating from *'telos'* the neologism *entelechos*,[63] without closing off access to the perfect itself. A substance can have its own relative and internalized end because the proximate always registers its desire for the pleasure of pure actuality that is God's. Perfection, Aristotle is at pains to tell us, will not enter human horizons anywhere but through human *energeia*; the perfection that does enter in this way, though, will deify.

The point about swallows and the summer (*Nic. Ethics*, 1098a17–20) after all is that perfection is not an immediacy, but a 'long revolution' whose 'end' always exceeds its own parameters. For all the swallows do not make it summer any more than one does, since once all the swallows have come, it is autumn. 'One fine day' will not make a person happy, but neither will all the days, since then the 'happy thing' will be dead. *Eudaimonia* names the arrival of divine actuality within the moment-by-moment ethos of a lived life; 'happiness' is simply what it means for humans to touch the Good by becoming human. Thus, in spite of his critique of the idea of the Good as basically useless, Aristotle arguably allows a fuller and less tragic participation in it than does Plato. Every movement from *dunamis* to *energeia* imitates, and through imitation shares in, supreme, super-genetic actuality.[64]

This is the point at which the religious gap appears in Aristotle's ethics, and this in two distinct ways, relative to the two happinesses. The first happiness of humans, the *bios theoretikos*, depends upon the reception of a gift that no human, even the philosopher, can achieve. If the *Ethics* states that *telos* is either from God or else so Godlike as to be 'like as' from God, the *Metaphysics* sees more clearly that God must be the cause of all *teloi*, since he is the teleological cause of all actuality. So our becoming is our 'wanting' to be actuality. The divine is always in a state of pleasurable activity, and this is its simplicity; we, however, are complex beings, and so cannot enjoy actuality constantly: 'Its life is like the best which we temporarily enjoy' (*Met.* 1072b14–16; see *Nic. Ethics*, 1154b21–31). Act for us is always mixed with potency, just as *nous* is mixed with body and appetite. Thales will not be able to stare all day at the stars, because he is both more and less than pure act: less because the potencies of embodied life are always secondary to actualities of any sort, and more because he is a compounded being, and cannot enjoy a simple perfecting state (*Nic. Ethics*, 1141b6). These interventions of actuality that he does enjoy, within the confines of embodied life, are a sign for the philosopher that happiness comes not simply from putting the human form into motion, but from following the *nous*

---

63 See Gerasimos Santas, 1989, 'Desire and Perfection in Aristotle's Theory of the Good', *Apeiron* 22(2), pp. 75–99.

64 Spaemann, *Happiness*, pp. 64–5. See also Robert Heinaman, 1993, 'Rationality, Eudaimonia, and Kakodaimonia in Aristotle', *Phronesis* 38(1), pp. 31–56.

in its desire for a higher kind of actuality. Our pleasure in *bios theoretikos* is inconsistent because we are human; that it comes at all must mean that our desire for it has been set in motion by something beyond our own nature. The first sign of the gap, then, is the excess of actuality over the potency through which we contact it.

Secondly, the religious gap appears in the *deutera eudaimonia*, and this in perhaps a less obvious fashion. The perfect life within human grasp is the life of habitualization of all the 'other' virtues that are inferior to the activity of nous (*Nic. Ethics*, 1177b27–1178a): courage, temperance, justice, *phronesis*, etc. These virtues are habits which shape us, and what belongs to a nature cannot be altered by habit. Thus the moral and intellectual virtues are not really ours by nature any more than the highest virtue of *theoria* is. On the other hand, they are not counter to our nature either, since we have a certain suitability for them. Rocks cannot be trained to climb stairs, since their nature is to fall to the earth. We can be trained to act virtuously, and so these traits are neither natural nor against our nature, but the received activity for which our natures are most fit. So our souls and bodies are 'perfected by habit' [τελειουμένοις δὲ διὰ τοῦ ἔθους] (*Nic. Ethics*, 1103a26);[65] we are not, at least in terms of our ontological make-up, *transformed* by habit. 'The best part of us' touches the divine; *nous* is not pure act, but it is how human mimesis shares in pure actuality. The virtuous habits allow the coming-to-be-godlike, which our souls and bodies began craving the moment they began to exist.

So the shoemaker achieves perfection by attaining the virtues especially relevant to her calling, and in doing so becomes a kind of embodied mapping of the highest, motionless actuality. The deutero-*eudaimonia* is a mediation of the proto-*eudaimonia*, and this mediation is so radical that any talk of the idea of the Good in itself, apart from the mediations, is out of bounds. There is no pure *telos* for the cobbler, the soldier, the lawyer or the philosopher: there are only the relative *teloi* in which, through the gift of their becoming, are the sites of the coming of *telos* itself into the world.

Suspended rhetoric

Is it not just here, though, that Aristotle allows that ancient whisper of the tragic back in to the construal of human perfection? We saw above that he roots out all metaphysical tragedy by collapsing the distance between 'becoming' and 'becoming something'. Still though, a certain vocational tragedy returns, and must return, given his structuring of teleological orientation as necessarily mimetic.

This is the case because the 'highest part' of the cobbler and the physician will, though ordered to the highest perfection, only attune itself

---

65 My translation.

to the second perfection relative to cobblers and physicians.[66] They will never know themselves as Godlike, even at their most perfect. The consequences of this ignorance are in fact worse than the old puzzle about Socrates and the satisfied sow, since it is questionable whether true happiness can be found in the mud at all. The one who perfects the *techne* of bread-making is becoming more like God; but if the non-contemplative bread-makers' guild goes on 'perfecting' their craft without actively maintaining this *mimesis* (and how can they, since it has nothing to do with the material or understood *telos* of their craft?), they may perfect it in a way that in fact rebels against the *actus purus*: making bread, say, that is thin and bleached to the point of insubstantiality and sealed in polka-dotted plastic. In other words, though metaphysically there is no room for a becoming that is free from its teleological cause, in practice there is, simply because the narrowed vision of practical ethics fosters a forgetting of the highest good.

Just as Plato's philosopher returns to the cave to inform the slaves of the sun's existence, so Aristotle's philosopher makes it his business to contemplate the highest happiness and to consider the gap between this and the relative ends of all other vocations. Ideally, the philosopher lives and thinks among those citizens who have been brought up and educated with an appreciation for what is better, so that his work will be that of a kind of shepherd of virtue. But the world is not ideal, Aristotle knows, and more often than not the question of 'best' is up in the air, 'something on which either people hold no opinion either way, or the masses hold a contrary opinion to the philosophers, or the philosophers to the masses, or each of them among themselves' (*Topics*, 104b3–6).[67] In these cases the philosopher must be more than a shepherd. He must also be a prophet; or, in Aristotle's term, a rhetorician.

Rhetoric is the science that aims to educate *hoi polloi* on the ethos of the good, and thus to urge cobblers and statesmen toward the liturgy of perfection, and away from the slavery of the water clock.[68] The purpose of a treatise outlining the method of proper public address is not, Aristotle says, simple persuasion, but rather the 'detection of the persuasive aspects of each matter' under discussion (*Rhetoric*, 1355b).[69] Persuasion alone is sophistry; the rhetorician is also always a philosopher, and so has glimpsed the truth in both its material and formal aspects. He may attempt to persuade the Athenians to fight a war, but he will do so only after contemplating the *telos* of Athens as such, along with the material capacities of the Athenian navy and infantry (*Rhet.* 1396a).

---

66 Spaemann, *Happiness*, pp. 59–60; Gadamer, *Idea*, p. 176.

67 Aristotle, *Topica*, in Richard McKeon (ed. and intro), 1941, *The Basic Works of Aristotle*, New York: Random House.

68 Voegelin, *Order and History* III, pp. 359–62.

69 Aristotle, *The Art of Rhetoric*, ed., trans. and intr. H. C. Lawson-Tancred, 2005, London: Penguin Books.

Before he can make his case, the rhetorician must engage in the more philosophically rigorous science of logic. He relies upon both analytic and material logic in order to identify and pursue the *telos* toward which he will urge his future audience. The syllogism must be flawless, and the knowledge of categories into which things and words fit must be as complete as possible. These sciences, though, serve the rhetoric, and not the other way around, as the *Topics* makes plain, and so the rhetorician requires, in addition to material knowledge and tight syllogisms, a special kind of logical tool.

Argument always arises in the need for like-mindedness at one level or another, when it is lacking. While on occasion the pressing problem that comes before the rhetorician may be the conflict between philosophers, in which case the full syllogism will be the tool of choice, more often it will be common citizens who are 'unable to take a general view of many stages, or to follow a lengthy chain of argument' (*Rhet.* 1357a1–12). In other words, when the bread-makers' guild has lost sight of the way its own becoming mirrors a universalizable good. The orator must in these cases adapt his reasoning to the ears and minds of his audience. For this reason, not the syllogism proper, but the 'enthymeme' will be the most useful and even most powerful logical tool of the philosopher (*Rhet.* 1355a). Enthymemes, syllogisms shortened and loosened so as to indicate a conclusion in a general way, are the rhetorician's deductive demonstrations. He can mould and revise them in order to fit the purposes of persuading a particular audience on a particular point. They are, in effect, the tools that will equip Plato's philosopher for his return trip into the cave, where he must attempt to persuade those who remain in chains that there is a world above, with a sun and sky.[70] The tight syllogism of the strict dialectic may not avail him, especially as the cave-dwellers have not been made aware of the many facets of the gift that 'some Prometheus' handed down to humans; the well-crafted enthymeme, however, may just do the trick. So rather than a major, minor and deducted conclusion, he shortens his delivery: The chains on your bodies also bind your souls, since they limit your will to the world you can see.

The rhetorician is King Argos, who has made the dive into the depths of humanity's share in the divine and must now speak to the gathered crowd who awaits the verdict. Do we hang from the gods? How can our activities and actualizations acknowledge this suspension? Are our lives a measure of the divine? The shoemakers and physicians who concern themselves with the relative goods of their trade will not have traversed these depths. They must be given material examples and partial syllogisms in order to be persuaded in matters of the common good. But how this good hangs suspended from God is something only the philosopher will see. So the philosopher must be a logician, he must be a political scientist, but if he is going to be of any use to the city, and not be either a Thales in a pit or Socrates in a prison cell, he must finally be a rhetorician.

---

70 Voegelin, *Order and History* III, p. 362.

Lost Belts

Aristotle thus uses the science of rhetoric as a way to overcome the despair of the later Plato, who turned his philosopher into a fool in order to maintain his lifelong insistence that the Promethean fire can arrive in human hands, human cities, and can materialize as a human *telos*. Three centuries later, Cicero will challenge the Athenian Academy on precisely these points and accuse the Stoics of forgetting the teachings of Plato and Aristotle on the good life. The Stoics abolish liturgy in the cities; by doing so, he insists, they lose the *Philebus*'s sense of the measured. They 'discard the body' (*De finibus*, 4.11.26) and attempt to participate in the divine with an immediacy that is entirely unsuited to material culture (*De fin.* 4.4.10). They prefer nothing over anything else, and so refuse to measure the relative pleasures that go into the mixing pot (*De fin.* 4.26.72–3). For them, to become divine is to become unhindered by the earthbound human nature (*De fin.* 4.15.41), which is why, in the end, Cato the suicide and Marcus the insatiable conqueror are equally true to the Stoic ethos.

Cicero's challenge to the Stoa is evidence for the judgement that, although 'philosophy begins in the Platonic love for the divine measure', yet 'the history of philosophy is the history of the derailment of Plato'.[71] Also though, it demonstrates the way in which the founders of philosophy were read during the long decline of the Athenian Academy. They were the ones who insisted that 'the Chief Good' is 'in the whole of man' rather than a part (*De fin.* 4.13.33); that bodies, friendships and cities are not outside the structuring *telos* of the divine nature simply in view of their tendency to misbehave (*De fin.* 4.25.68–71); that reaching a happy end ought to perfect our nature and all that our nature includes, not destroy it (*De fin.* 4.25.69). These elements contain, for us, a portion at least of the makings of a counter-narrative of perfection. Beginning in the tragedians, Greek philosophy narrates a *telos* for humanity in which the human becomes more divine precisely as she becomes more human. Even as she finds her journey haunted by metaphysical or practical ateleology, the wayfarer still manages to name her pathway as the *via perfectionis*; keeping to it, she escapes these spectres and shares in the life of God.

---

71 Voegelin, *Order and History* III, p. 277.

2

God's Long Journey:
Perfection in Jerusalem

> Memory is the sense of loss, and loss pulls us after it. God himself
> was pulled after us into the vortex we made when we fell,
> or so the story goes.
>
> Marilynne Robinson

Yahweh's Children

While Aeschylus was composing his tragedies in Greece, caravans of exiles were returning to the western edge of the Mediterranean from the lands of Babylon. In Jerusalem and the surrounding countryside, the reconfigured people of Israel began assembling old scrolls that told of Abraham, Moses and David into a new library that charted their journey through generations as the chosen people of the god Yahweh. In the hands of these compilers, the Hebrew Bible emerges as the narrative of a God who calls from mysterious darkness to summon the world toward its ultimate good, beyond any hovering evil.[1]

Their Scripture opens in a set of accounts that immediately raises the question of the divine–human boundary and its possible traversal. For instance:

> When people began to multiply on the face of the ground, and daughters were born to them, the sons of God saw that they were fair; and they took wives for themselves of all that they chose. Then the LORD said,

---

1 In the following chapter, I assume the validity of source criticism, but I read canonically, attempting to practise what Bakhtin calls 'novelistic consciousness'. Raymond Barfield, 2011, *The Ancient Quarrel between Philosophy and Poetry*, Cambridge: Cambridge University Press, p. 254, explains Bakhtin's hermeneutic as one in which 'voices remain themselves even in the cauldron, where they come up against other voices without being reduced or cancelled or synthesized or otherwise taken out'. See also Walter Reed, *Dialogues of the Word: The Bible as Literature According to Bakhtin*, Oxford: Oxford University Press, pp. 38–76. Thanks to Scott Bader-Saye and Alan Gregory for discussion of these texts, as well as of how to name my own hermeneutical process, above.

'My spirit shall not abide in mortals forever, for they are flesh; their days shall be one hundred twenty years.' The Nephilim were on the earth in those days – and also afterward – when the sons of God went in to the daughters of humans, who bore children to them. These were the heroes that were of old, warriors of renown. (Gen. 6.1–6)

How stable can the border between earth and heaven be, with the sons of God behaving this way? Under the pens of the post-exilic scribes, this fragment comes to serve as a prologue to the deluge cycle.[2] Noah is in fact introduced in the genealogy in the verses just prior to these (5.29–32), and the following verses take up his story proper, with God seeing the wickedness of his creatures and grieving at having fashioned them from dust at all (6.5–8). The pursuit of the daughters of humans by the sons of God is thus part of the warrant for the flood itself. The Nephilim are 'warriors of renown' (6.4), but in the Hebrew mythology this is not high praise, since 'making a name' is always an ambiguous activity. The builders of the tower attempt to do it in Genesis 11.4 with less than commendable results. Adam and Eve, likewise, are found guilty of something of this sort, since their proper name is 'image of God' (1.26–7), and on the advice of the serpent they take over their own destiny, naming themselves as autonomous eaters of fruit. To achieve renown for oneself is to take over the name-giving agency of God.[3]

Along with name-making, desire also operates in these texts as an element of a false blending of the heavenly and earthly. 'So when the woman saw that the tree was good for food, and that it was a delight to the eyes, and that the tree was to be desired to make one wise, she took of the fruit and ate' (Gen. 3.6). Like Eve with her apple, the Nephilic ancestors saw that the daughters of earth were fair. In both cases the language repeats the refrain of the first creation narrative: 'And God saw that it was good' (1.4, 10, 12, 18, 21, 25, 31). By 'seeing it was good', Eve, Adam and the Nephilim attempt to take on the role of God, thereby becoming the exiled and 'fallen ones'.[4] These three narratives, Eden, the sons of God and Babel, repeat a motif of boundary-crossing to which, in each case, God responds with decisive condemnations and re-bindings: the curses and geographic boundaries of Genesis 3, the flood and temporal boundary (120 years) of Genesis 6 and the scattering and linguistic boundaries of Genesis 11.[5]

---

2 E. A. Speiser, 1964, *Genesis*, in *The Anchor Bible*, New York: Doubleday, p. 46; Mark G. Brett, 2000, *Genesis: Procreation and the Politics of Identity*, London: Routledge, pp. 40–1. Noth suggests that it could even be a later edition to the completed Pentateuch. Martin Noth, 1981, *A History of Pentateuchal Traditions*, trans. Bernard Anderson, Chico, CA: Scholars Press, p. 28.

3 Brett, *Procreation*, p. 49.

4 David M. Carr, 1996, *Reading the Fractures of Genesis: Historical and Literary Approaches*, Louisville: Westminster John Knox, pp. 237–8. Alter states that 'fallen ones' is the most probable sense of the term Nephilim. Robert Alter, 1996, *Genesis*, New York: W. W. Norton, p. 27.

5 Alter, *Genesis*, pp. 26–7; Carr, *Fractures*, pp. 237–8.

It is already tempting to see in Israel's aboriginal mythology an anti-Prometheanism of the modern type. The creation of heaven and earth, on this reading, is the establishment of a hard and fast natural boundary; a 'law of territoriality' that puts into place a 'dichotomy between the divine and the human'.[6] The Edenic humans sin by violating this order in an attempt to climb to the heights of heaven, while the builders of the tower repeat this sin in a literal fashion.

At the same time, how can we avoid reading here a parallel to the Prometheanism of the ancient type? The rebellion of God's creation is not limited to the mundane, since these 'primeval titans' encourage the disorder by lusting after the women of earth.[7] The story almost demands the lament of Aeschylus's chorus, uttered in reply to Io's misfortune: 'Never may one of the gods/ Descend from the skies for my love' (*Prom. Bd.* 898–9).[8] Like Zeus, Prometheus falls in love, though with humanity as a whole rather than with a maiden by the water's edge, and in doing so he apparently gives 'to mortal men honors beyond their due' (*Prom. Bd.* 29–30). When gods descend from the heavens in pursuit of humans whom they find 'fair', humans will begin to think themselves capable of ascending to those same heavens and becoming gods. And this will only turn out badly, with humans morphing into spiders, falling to earth with melted wings or finding themselves exiled from paradise. If the modern *mythopoesis* condemns this ascent because it violates a stable order of being, the ancients, who had no notion of stable orders of being, simply indicate its fatedly tragic end: evils endlessly hover round our earthbound bodies, and the best that will come of this divine insemination is the madness of Io, the chimeric nomad.

Neither reading, however, is entirely warranted by the text. Israel's story is not Greece's tragic Prometheanism, for the simple initial reason that the descending gods are sons of the creating and ruling God, not his older brothers. Hellenism always includes a chaotic remainder, since Jupiter is himself a usurper of the Saturnine cosmos. Genesis is the story of children in rebellion, from God's angelic sons to the tricksters and deceivers in his earthly garden, to Adam and Eve's own son, and the children of Isaac, Jacob and Judah. There is no pre-creation narrative of the *agon* in heaven among those vying for sovereignty, only the God who creates a heaven and earth that he calls good. Chaotic powers of evil, springing from illicit acts

---

6 Susan Niditch, 1993, *Folklore and the Hebrew Bible*, Minneapolis: Fortress Press, p. 43.

7 See Speiser, *Genesis*, p. 46, whose connection of the sons in the Hebrew myth with the ancient divine ancestors of the Hellenic is not unique. See Alter, *Genesis*, p. 27, and Voegelin, 1956, *Order and History*, Vol. I: *Israel and Revalation*, New Orleans: Louisiana State University Press, pp. 20–1. Niditch, *Folklore*, p. 42, goes so far as to say that the God of Genesis is 'not unlike all the great heads of pantheons such as Odin or Zeus', since he 'can be tricked, becoming subject to the wiles of those whom he has created, such as Loki, Prometheus, the snake, Adam and Eve. He is, in short, a parent.'

8 Whitney Oates and Eugene O'Neill, Jr, 1938, *The Complete Greek Drama*, Vol. I, New York: Random House.

of his children, therefore have no legitimate place within this order.[9] There is no tragic remainder, and this permits a narrative of perfection that *in potentia* goes beyond the limits of Greek myth and philosophy.

Israel's story cannot be read straightforwardly as a condemnation of modern Prometheanism either. Though Genesis 1—11 seems to install a prohibition against godlikeness in creatures, certain elements of the Eden narrative point to a different interpretation. First of all, as I suggested in the Exposition, the role of the serpent here is like that of any worthwhile mythological trickster: he does not invite outright rebellion, but rather a subtle undermining of order.[10] 'You will not die' if you eat the fruit, he says, rather, 'you will become like God' (Gen. 3.4–5). As it happens, the first statement is true, since it is apparently the other tree in the garden's centre that wards off mortality (3.22). They will not die if they eat of the tree of knowledge, but only if they cease to eat from the tree of life. The second statement of the serpent is also true, as God's response to the transgression shows: 'See, the man has become like one of us' (3.22).

Not only is there an element of truth in the serpent's divination of the human future; his words also mark a certain fidelity to their past. 'You will be like God' refers back to the unique manner of the man and woman's creation, 'according to our likeness' (1.26). Becoming like God is what they are created for. So if God separates the light from the day in order to name the one 'day' and the other 'night' (Gen. 1.4–5), Adam separates the large four-legged grey beast from the large four-legged striped beast, and the grey one he calls 'donkey,' while the striped one he calls 'zebra' (2.19–20).[11] Like God, the man and woman will rule, and like God they will fill the earth with creatures (1.26–8). Imitation of God continues even outside of Eden, as the exiled ones are still fruitful and multiply, and generations continue to rule the earth, separate its territories and bestow names upon it. On both sides of the hedge we find accounts of boundary transgression marking the actions of both Yahweh and his creatures: God walks in the humans' garden (3.8); Enoch walks with God (5.22). Certainly the multiple rebellions of Genesis are perversions of order, but this order itself already includes a commerce between heaven and earth that is entirely foreign to the modern construct.

What, then, does this ancient text suggest about the end intended by Yahweh for his people, and, through them, for humankind as such? There is a vocation to Godlikeness alongside a prohibition; there are condemnable transgressions of cosmic orders of being, and also friendships and communications that cross these boundaries gracefully. What is the human *telos* in ancient Israel?

---

9 By the time of the rabbis, the opening of Genesis 6 was already taken as an account of the origin of evil. See Archie T. Wright, 2005, *The Origin of Evil Spirits: Genesis 6.1–4 in Early Jewish Thought*, Tübingen: Mohr Siebeck.

10 See Niditch, *Folklore*, p. 42.

11 See Brett, *Procreation*, p. 30.

An errant God

After losing control of his children in Genesis 1—11, Yahweh begins anew. His sons once descended to make a nation of name-making heroes; now he himself descends, adopts a new son out from the house of that man's natural father, and gives this adoptee a divinely crafted name:

> Now the LORD said to Abram, 'Go from your country and your kindred and your father's house to the land that I will show you. I will make of you a great nation, and I will bless you, and make your name great, so that you will be a blessing. I will bless those who bless you, and the one who curses you I will curse; and in you all the families of the earth shall be blessed.' (Gen. 12.1–3)

There is no heroic act or reference to riches that warrant the adoption of Abram, only an inscrutable election, echoing the preference for Abel's sacrifice.[12] Further, Abram does not need to make a name for himself, since God will give him his new name (17.5). In this way, Yahweh follows the path of the angels down to earth, not because he finds Abram to be fair, but rather to make him fair. This initiates a covenant upon which Yahweh will establish an anti-Nephilic order of perfection.

The narrative of the three visitors in Genesis 18—19 demonstrates the contrast between the old disruptive transgression and the new order of righteousness established within the divine descent. Three men appear to Abraham by the oaks of Mamre, and the text calls them 'Yahweh' (18.1). Abraham washes their feet and spreads a feast before them, and then hears them tell of the fate that awaits Sodom and Gomorrah. At this point the text apparently identifies only one of them as Yahweh, the one who stays to haggle over the fate of the cities (18.22), while the two who head there become first men, then angels (19.1). In Sodom, Lot repeats the hospitality of Abraham, while the men of the city respond to the presence of the visitors in a contrasting fashion: 'But before they lay down, the men of the city, the men of Sodom, both young and old, all the people to the last man, surrounded the house; and they called to Lot, "Where are the men who came to you tonight? Bring them out to us, so that we may know them"' (19.4–5). When Lot tries to protect his guests, even offering his own daughters to the mob, they turn on him: '"Stand back!" And they said, "This fellow came here as an alien, and he would play the judge! Now we will deal worse with you than with them." Then they pressed hard against the man Lot, and came near the door to break it down' (19.9). A Christian epistle later recognizes the parallel between Genesis 6 and 19 as a repetition of lust for 'strange flesh' (Jude 6–7, Authorized Version).[13] The angels of the

---

12 Brett, *Procreation*, p. 49.

13 See William Countryman, 2003, *Interpreting the Truth: Changing the Biblical Studies Paradigm*, Harrisburg, PA: Trinity International Press, pp. 47–8. See also 2 Peter, which I discuss in the Second Movement, below.

earlier story lust after the daughters of humans, while in the later it is the humans who lust for angels.

Perhaps more directly, though, Sodom is a repetition of Babel. If Eve and the sons of God perversely imitate God in seeing that earthly creation is good, the builders and the men of Sodom see that God, or the heavenly beings, are good.[14] The first type is a disordered desire for earth, the second a lust for the strange flesh of heaven.

What leads to the heavenly condemnation here? Is it the strangeness of the flesh, or the strangeness of the desire? Abraham and Lot, after all, 'desire' their unearthly visitors, though they express this longing with foot-washing and feasting rather than with attempted rape. If the desire of an earthly being for a heavenly being were simply illicit, then Abraham and Lot, as well as Noah and Enoch, would stand under this judgement, not to mention the composers of the Psalms and the Song of Songs. If the desire of a heavenly being for an earthly were unnatural, then God himself would be an outlaw alongside the Nephilim, simply for blessing the goodness of his own creation.

It is not the fact of desire, then, but rather the mode of desiring that lies at the root of the sin. Desire goes strange.[15] The contrast of Abraham and Lot with the men of Sodom underscores this point, as does that of Noah with the Nephilim before or the tower-builders after. Yahweh and his sons long for the company of the earthly beings; all too easily this desire turns to violent lust, and evening strolls through the garden turn to Sabine-like rape scenes. The creatures long for the presence of their creator, and this desire too takes on a monstrously lustful form. (Perhaps Babel as phallus is not simply a post-Freudian interpretation?) It is wrongly ordered desire that makes the flesh go strange.

In both the 'vertical' and 'horizontal' gazes, God's creatures tend, from Eve and the angels to the men of Babel and Sodom, to lose themselves in the desirable. Eve is not condemned for imitating the divine recognition of creation's goodness, but for recklessly consuming the good that she sees. By contrast, when God sees the goodness of the world he creates, he can rest and then enjoy the goodness of humans, trees, rivers and animals, by blessing them, taking walks with them and calling out to them. When Abraham desires the company of his visitors, he begs them to stay, and feeds them as God once fed the man and woman. Abraham does not rape or consume the good, but beckons it and coaxes it and serves it. He is, in this sense, a return to the Edenic likeness of God. Lot's hospitality repeats the Abrahamic posture, though by settling in a land of Nephilic desire (Gen. 13.12–13), he and his family are already stretched precariously in between the new adoption and the old inheritance.

Thus the world after Genesis 3 is a world exiled from its true home, and the adoption of Abraham works against this exile, re-establishing a divine

14 Carr, *Fractures*, pp. 190–1.

15 See Eugene F. Rogers, Jr., 1999, *Sexuality and the Christian Body: Their Way into the Triune God*, Oxford: Blackwell, pp. 256–60.

likeness on earth in the practices of righteousness, obedience and excessive hospitality. Just as in the earlier chapters, however, the heavenly God does not do violence to the earthly creatures by imposing his desires upon them. In the deluge cycle, Yahweh refuses to start over, to utterly destroy his creation, but instead will work through the fallen and exiled world itself in order to bring about its perfection. Adam and Eve are exiled, but still blessed; Cain is cursed, but protected; Noah plays the drunken fool, but is still God's friend; the builders are scattered, but scattered so that from this very diaspora a people can be chosen who will bring blessing to all (12.3).[16] Even Abraham's famous faith wavers as he awaits an heir (Gen. 16), and his earlier behaviour while passing through Egypt is at least questionable (12.10–20). Still, God has bound himself to this man and this people in such a way that imperfection is no barrier to perfection. Through the faith and failure of Abraham, all the nations will be blessed. God never destroys his offspring in the Hebrew narrative, but rather pursues them in order to bring them to perfection.

If Chapters 3 to 11 gesture towards this pursuit, after Abraham the trajectory only intensifies. Now that Yahweh has made a covenant with a family, he is bound to the name that these children create for him, and so their doubts and misdeeds implicate their adopted Father as well. Thus, we can say that Abraham's God deals with creation's disorderedness not only by working through, but identifying with the imperfections of Abraham's friends and family. This identification turns, at many points, to *mimesis*: so Lamech and Jacob bargain for daughters like God and Abraham once bargained for Sodom (Gen. 29.16–30); God can be coaxed into pacifity and mercy by good smells (6.21) as a man can be taken for a bowl of stew (25.29–34). The stories are filled with familial deceit: mothers betray their children (27.5–17), brothers turn against one another (37.18–28), and when a father-in-law betrays his son's wife, she responds with a deceit of her own (38.1–30). And all this trickery and betrayal no longer ends in divine judgement, since God seems more than ready to play the game on their terms.[17] God is the God of Jacob, who receives land and blessing dishonestly, not so much of Esau, who happens to come home hungry at the wrong time. 'Who was it then that hunted game and brought it to me, and I ate all before you came, and I have blessed him? – yes, and blessed he shall be!' (27.33). Is Isaac's blessing different than God's? Is God fooled by a hairy arm as well? The narrative gives us no cause to think otherwise. He has bound himself to a new family, and will follow them through all the drama of human existence in his attempt to find friends among his children.

The narratives of Genesis suggest that God responds to the boundary-crossing of the angels with a boundary-crossing of his own; that when Adam and Eve are sent into exile, their fertility and dominion can still be

---

16 See Hans Urs von Balthasar, 1991, *The Glory of the Lord: A Theological Aesthetics* Vol. VI: *Theology: The Old Covenant*, trans. Brian McNeil C.R.V. and Erasmo Leiva-Merikakis, San Francisco: Ignatius Press, pp. 178ff.

17 See Brett, *Procreation*, pp. 86–109.

an *imitatio dei*, because God has wandered out of the Garden after them. Yahweh has come unbound from the heavens, and enters the post-Edenic world in order to coax it out of its patricidal quagmire.

A retreating God

Those who first told tales of Yahweh–Elohim thus leave us with a God who follows Abraham's imperfect children in order to turn this family toward holiness. In the later narrations of the priestly redactors, though, this becomes only the initial stage of God's relation to this people. The descent of God culminates in a retreat of God back into the heavens, and their own appropriation of God's holiness must make some rather drastic adjustments. Though this retreat is foreshadowed in the separation motif of Genesis – God separates Abraham not just to fashion a new lineage, but ultimately because God himself is separate – it is not until we come to the Moses narratives that we discover the radicality of God's separation.

When the Israelites 'groaned under their slavery' in Egypt, and 'their cry for help rose up' to Elohim, 'God heard their groaning', and turned towards them. In this responsive turn, God does what he did among the Patriarchs, when he found himself appeased by burnt offerings, or answered to the summons of praying men and women, or painted a sign in the sky so that he would not forget a promise: 'and God remembered his covenant with Abraham, Isaac, and Jacob' (Exod. 2.23–4). When the new son/friend character of the Exodus is introduced into the story, however, the errant God of Genesis reveals a new dimension of his being. 'God said to Moses, "I AM WHO I AM."' He said further, 'Thus you shall say to the Israelites, "I AM has sent me to you"' (3.14). 'I appeared to Abraham, Isaac, and Jacob, but by my name "Yahweh" I did not make myself known' (6.3). Though the text gives God this name earlier, Exodus tells that the people themselves had no knowledge of it, knowing God only as the 'Elohim' of Abraham and his children.[18]

The new name ends all *mimesis*, both God's of his people and the people's of God. The priests allow the anthropomorphic language of the Genesis narrative to stand, even repeating it in the opening of Exodus (2.24–5), in order to emphasize the novelty of the Sinai revelation. At Sinai, God's true holiness is revealed as distant, nonhuman and removed from the intrigues and deceptions of the created image.[19] In Genesis, God sees, speaks, smells, appears, descends and remembers. In Exodus, God recedes into limited and ambiguous interactions with Moses alone, while the rest of Israel experience an impersonal cloud, a dangerous fire (13.21) or a deep rumbling thunder (19.16).

---

18 William H. C. Propp, 1999, *Exodus 1—18*, in *The Anchor Bible*, New York: Doubleday, p. 268.

19 Israel Knohl, 1995, *The Sanctuary of Silence: The Priestly Torah and the Holiness School*, Minneapolis: Fortress Press, pp. 124ff.

The second encounter between Yahweh and Moses on Sinai forms the 'Berith drama' at the heart of the priestly narrative.[20] Here especially secrecy and mystery shroud the new manifestation of God: 'Then the Lord said to Moses, "I am going to come to you in a dense cloud, in order that the people may hear when I speak with you and so trust you ever after"' (Exod. 19.8). On the morning of the third day, when Yahweh was to have shown himself to the assembly awaiting at the mountain's foot, there is only thunder and lightning and the warning 'not to break through to Yahweh to look' (19.21). 'Set limits around the mountain and keep it holy' (v. 23). Eventually it is Moses himself who comes down, and when he repeats Yahweh's words, first orally and then in writing on the stone tablets, the people take this to be God's self-revelation (24.3–4), as if they expected no more. The true Yahweh, the one whose name cannot be comprehended, descends from the heavens only in a cloud of darkness that hides his face even from the one anointed to enter his presence.[21]

The cult of atonement, revealed to Moses after Sinai in front of the tent of meeting (Lev. 1.1), brings Yahweh's withdrawal into liturgy. In Leviticus, while burnt offerings like Noah's remain, they are made at the entrance of the tent, and not taken into the inner sanctuary. The bulls are slaughtered and burnt in plain sight by the sons of Aaron, so that the people can see that God does not consume them (1.9).[22] The burnt offerings still give a 'pleasing odour to Yahweh', but a new distinction occurs between these, which function as a kind of constant offering up of the best crops and livestock, and purification and guilt offerings within the sanctuary, in which odour no longer plays a role. In this way, Leviticus announces the difference between Yahweh and any god whose blessing, like Isaac's, can be manipulated through pleasing smells. The way to this God's heart, one might say, is no longer through his stomach. The priests themselves eat the animals on the altar (7.5–10); similarly, they place bowls and vessels on the altar in the tent of meeting but leave them to stand empty, underscoring Yahweh's absence from the realm of sensuality and consumption. And when they bring the shewbread to the altar, they do not replace it several times a day as in the temple cults of the hungry Mesopotamian gods, but instead they leave it to stand for a week and then consume it entirely themselves, as if resigning themselves to God's absence (Exod. 25.29–30; Lev. 24.8–9).[23] The priestly cult of Israel is thus a liturgical narration of the superiority of a God for whom human bowls and loaves of bread are entirely useless.

In this way, a new sense of divine perfection enters our plot line. If the materiality of creation threatens to ruin the sanctity of the Greek gods, for Israel's cult God is beyond any such threat, even to the point of indifference.

---

20 Voegelin, *Order and History* I, pp. 415ff.

21 Knohl, *Sanctuary*, pp. 129–37.

22 Knohl, *Sanctuary*, p. 133.

23 Knohl, *Sanctuary*, pp. 132–7.

In addition to the removal of those rites that implicate God as an embodied recipient of atoning sacrifices, the Levitical instructions on atonement further distance God from the Temple cult by grammatical constructions that seem to make atonement a consequence of priestly performances rather than divine initiative.[24] So, for instance, in the expiation of the inadvertent sins of the whole assembly (Lev. 4), the anointed priest spreads the blood of a young bull on the veil and altar and, through this offering, the people are forgiven. It is not, however, a matter of Yahweh forgiving them, since this would involve him too intimately in the economy of persuasion through which Elohim met with the Patriarchs, and, furthermore, imply that their sins had somehow brought harm to God.[25] The priest himself makes atonement, and the people are forgiven (4.31): Yahweh remains on the exterior of the exchange. Thus a decisive element of God's separation from his creation is his absence from the economy of atonement.

Even if God is too holy to engage with them, can we not at least note that Israel becomes holy, thus sharing, even at a great remove, in Yahweh's holiness? In fact, no, due to the fact that the assembly of Israel is also, to a significant degree, absent from this economy. The more God withdraws from the scene, the less does the forgiveness appropriated by the people issue in any moral perfecting among them. Levitical atonement is not personalized in any real sense.[26] The priests do not place the blood of the offerings upon the sinner, but upon the holy place, as if the real emphasis of the rite is on the expiation of impurity from the sanctuary itself, rather than of sin from the sinner. Likewise, the scapegoat of Chapter 16 retains a sense of 'forgiveness' for the sinners only in a very general sense. The point is rather that through the act of expelling the goat, the sins of the people will not touch the consecrated objects at the centre of the assembly.[27] The altar is holy and the liturgical objects surrounding it are holy; the priests derive their holiness from these objects, rather than from an imitation of Abraham's character or his adoptive Father (Exod. 29.21, Lev. 6.27).[28]

Do the gathered people then become holy? Throughout the priestly writings, chiefly sections of Exodus and the first part of Leviticus, the divine name of Yahweh is taken to disallow imitation. 'Holy' takes on the explicit connotation of separate, and thus implies something close to a polarization of God's holiness and Israel's holiness.[29]

---

24 Knohl, *Sanctuary*, p. 135.

25 Knohl, *Sanctuary*, p. 135; Jacob Milgrom, 1991, *Leviticus 1–16*, in *The Anchor Bible* New York: Doubleday, pp. 45–7.

26 David P. Wright, 1999, 'Holiness in Leviticus and Beyond: Differing Perspectives', *Interpretation* 53, pp. 352–4.

27 Knohl, *Sanctuary*, p. 154.

28 Gary A. Anderson, 1992, 'Sacrifice and Sacrificial Offerings (OT)', in *The Anchor Bible Dictionary*, Vol. V, New York: Doubleday, p. 879.

29 See Walther Eichrodt, 1961, *Theology of the Old Testament*, Vol. I, trans. J. A. Baker, London: SCM Press, pp. 407–11.

Then Moses said to Aaron, 'This is what the LORD meant when he said,
"Through those who are near me
I will show myself holy,
and before all the people
I will be glorified."'
And Aaron was silent. (Lev. 10.3)

Israel does not become holy at all in the priestly writings, but her priests, holy places and ritual objects are made holy by new ritualized expressions of the old name-making power of God. Even the holiness of the priest lacks any ethical imperative, and is rather a matter of preparing them to perform the cult service without fear of reproof.[30] So, immediately following the sanctification of the priests, fire consumes the sons of Aaron; but not for social or personal defilement, rather for offering 'unholy fire before Yahweh, such as he had not commanded them' (10.1). In fact, all fire is unholy, just as the priests and all the people are unholy. The ritual obedience commanded by Yahweh from the cloud and the thunder is all that is holy in the world. The only sense, for the Priestly Torah, in which God remains a mimetic force at all is in the withdrawal of priests from the assembly,[31] which mirrors the divine withdrawal underway since the revelation of the new name to Moses at the bush.

Bilateral covenant language drops into the background in the priestly writings, and the unilateral language of *'edut*, testimony, comes to the fore.[32] Rather than a mutual bond issuing in mutual blessing, the withdrawing God offers a unilateral pact or testament, which instructs Israel in the often-obscure acts that will, in the darkness of the divine discernment, constitute her faithfulness. God, from the darkness inside the cloud, will ensure the terms of the covenant from both ends. It is this *'edut*, rather than a *berit*, that is inside the ark, so that the latter is not really an ark of the 'covenant' but rather, closer to the one-sided emphasis captured in the Authorized Version, an 'ark of the testimony': more literally, if less poetically, the priests carry on their heads an ark of the unilateral divine pact (Exod. 25.16–21).[33]

As distant from the covenantal faith of the Patriarchs, Yahweh is also beyond any need to reward Israel's goodness with blessing, in this sense perhaps even 'beyond good and evil'. Here earthly holiness is a purely passive reception of God's act of singling them out, which is thus meant to

---

30 Wright, 'Holiness', p. 354.

31 Knohl, *Sanctuary*, pp. 154–6.

32 Knohl, *Sanctuary*, p. 173.

33 The NRSV uses 'covenant' for both, thus skirting the key distinction. See Knohl, *Sanctuary*, p. 142; see also Baruch Schwartz, 'Israel's Holiness: The Torah Traditions', in Marcel J. H. M. Poorthuis and Joshua Schwartz (eds), 2000, *Purity and Holiness: The Heritage of Leviticus*, Leiden: Brill, pp. 47–59. Many thanks to Steve Bishop for helping me with the Hebrew here and for discussion of my research for this entire chapter.

challenge the pre-Sinaitic belief in a God who was imitable because not above tribal intrigue.[34] The God of the priests will not be imitated, conjured or associated in any way with the earthly agency of human beings. God has no ear for prayer and praise, so that even the sanctuary is silent.[35] For the priestly Torah, then, the consecrated Aaronites and objects, let alone the gathered assembly of Israel, cannot become the name they speak. The liturgical alphabet remains decidedly esoteric, and holiness remains the sole possession of God. Though this retreating God stands in contrast to the errant God of Genesis, the priestly redactors offer Exodus as an unfolding of the covenantal logic of the older texts. A God who is trustworthy as a partner in mutual exchange must be a God beyond the deceptive influences of that economy of exchange: a covenantal God must be always moving toward a self-redefining as a God beyond covenant.

For if Yahweh is not going to repeat the fall of the pre-Nephilic ancestors, he cannot, like them and like Eve, lose himself in pursuit of the good creation, nor indeed in pursuit of Israel. Even in Genesis, when God follows them out of the garden, thus surprising Eve with a child and inviting sacrificial prayers from her sons, he never intends to remain there as a nomad in self-exile. For the priests, neither the economy of sacrifice to appease divine anger, nor the persuasion or duping of Yahweh, are true images of Israel's God. He has followed them through his own pleasure out of Eden and continues to pursue them in a land overgrown with thorn and thistle, a land as unfit for him as it is for his people. Yahweh too must, in Genesis, labour in the land beyond the gates of the garden. Later, when the time comes to receive the revealed 'proper name' of Israel's God on the mountain, this pattern of divine involvement must come to an end. Through Abraham, and most spectacularly at Sinai, God begins to call the creatures out of Nod, of Sodom and of Egypt, back into the garden in which he first created them. In the meantime, however, even Israel must relate to God as a foreigner. Their entire alphabet of liturgical objects and significations presents a new language, one based not in worldly violence and chaos, but in divine order. The consecrated priest, consecrated altar and unholy people become part of Israel's secret and elusive vocabulary for speaking the secret and elusive name of God.[36]

Binding the Nephilim

The human potential to ascend to the heavens always intersects the divine potential to descend to earth. Let us pause briefly to underscore the novelty of the divine descent crafted within these texts, in relation to both the modern and antique Olympianism sketched previously.

Modern theism is prejudiced towards a God who is bound to the heavens in such a way that the intrigues of earthiness are beyond his character.

---

34 Schwartz, 'Traditions', p. 58.
35 Knohl, *Sanctuary*, p. 148.
36 Voegelin, *Order and History* I, pp. 134–5.

For this reason, Christian theists often make the incarnation into a transgression of divinity. Ancient Greek religion has no such prejudice: Homer envisions such an intersection between the heavens and earth that to imitate the gods might mean to become wise, and then again it might mean to commit adultery.[37] Even Plato, who envisions a much more rigorous theological education for Athens' poets and her youth, can only offer good gods who, like humans, find themselves limited by the evils that hover over a primordially chaotic cosmos.

The Hebrew Scriptures, by contrast, narrate a God who is neither bound to the heavens nor entangled with the stuff of earth, but rather relates to creatures in a dynamic motion of descent and withdrawal. Influenced by Harnack's contrast of Jerusalem and Athens, theologians continue to draw the line between the Hebrew and the Greek in terms of the immanent work of the Hebrew God in the world, and the transcendent otherness of the Athenian *agathon*.[38] Drawing exclusively on images of the Good in the *Republic*, Harnack and others fail to see how the Platonic and Aristotelian gods are radically present within the city, how all civic festivals and vocations are essentially divine repetitions among the city's heroes and governors and labourers. The Greek gods are immanent, we might say, in virtue of the incessant celebration of their transcendence. Likewise, pointing only toward passages like Abraham's bargaining success with Yahweh, theologians celebrate divine mutability within Israel's theology without attending to the way that the rest of the Torah takes up these texts.[39]

Though it would be no less anachronistic, it would in fact be more accurate to stand the Harnackian thesis on its head. The Hellenistic lack is not immanence, but the 'transcendence' necessary for the gods to claim final sovereignty of the cosmos. Likewise, if we measure the quantity of the Torah in which the priests insist upon the separation of Yahweh from the rest of creation – a separation referred to by shorthand with the phrase 'I am holy' – we could rather more accurately say that Yahweh is too transcendent, too perfect, to be present or immanent in the created order.

---

37 Ancient texts such as Heraclitus's *Homeric Problems* develop allegorical interpretation as a response to just this 'problem'.

38 Adolf von Harnack, 1904, *What is Christianity*, 3rd edn, trans. Thomas Bailey Saunders, New York: G. P. Putnam's Sons, pp. 193–230. See also Jenson, who, though less wooden in the distinction, still relies upon it in various contrasting pairs: act and being, economic and immanent, revelation and philosophy, pre- and post-Constantinian. See, for instance, Robert Jenson, 1988, *America's Theologian: A Recommendation of Jonathan Edwards*, Oxford: Oxford University Press, pp. 92–3; 1992, *Unbaptized God: The Basic Flaw in Ecumenical Theology*, Philadelphia: Fortress Press, pp. 132ff.; and 1997, *Systematic Theology*, Vol. I: *The Triune God*, Oxford: Oxford University Press, pp. 42–60, 75–81.

39 See Henry Jansen, 1995, *Relationality and the Concept of God*, Amsterdam: Rudopi Bv Editions, pp. 196 ff, for a treatment of this problem in Moltmann and Pannenberg. Colin Gunton as well flirts with an error of the sort in Colin Gunton, 2002, *Act and Being: Towards a Theology of the Divine Attributes*, Grand Rapids: Eerdmans, pp. 55ff.

But perhaps more accurately for Israel, considering that every indication of divine involvement is tied to the larger narrative of withdrawal and vice versa, we ought to say that the scribes and priests of Israel never envision a transcendence that fully occludes an immanence, any more than an immanence that denies a transcendence. Only the seventeenth-century humanist revisions of theology and metaphysics allow for such a distinction.[40]

The move toward divine separation relates to a cultic dynamic in Israel that theologians also tend to simplify. What does Yahweh's holiness mean for the gods of the nations? Like immanent/transcendent, the contrasting pair monotheism/polytheism is one that does not sit comfortably in Israel's Scriptures. The tribes are never simply monotheistic, if that term is meant to imply the belief that there is only one divine being in the heavens and on the earth. Prophets, seers and sorcerers exist outside of Israel, and thus apparently draw on powers besides Israel's God: Pharaoh's attendants mimic Moses' signs (Exod. 7.12), Saul contacts the deceased Samuel through a witch (1 Sam. 28). Even the language of the Decalogue leaves ambiguous the matter of heaven's population: 'You shall have no other gods before me' (Exod. 20.3; Deut. 5.7). While there is, as we shall see below, indication of the grounds for such a belief in the prophets, where for instance Yahweh's robes fill the heavens, the 'jealous anger' of Yahweh suggests that even here 'monotheism' is a polemical stance against rival cults, rather than a dogmatic rejection of rival powers.[41]

For although never simply monotheistic, Israel's Scriptures are, with unwavering consistency, monocultic. While there is never a single liturgical paradigm or even final agreement among the editors regarding the proper arena for the rites – Shiloh, Dan, Bethel, or only Jerusalem (Judg. 21, 1 Kings 12; 1 Sam. 1; Jer. 7)[42] – the texts are unified by the cultic veneration of a single God. Indeed, as the Jahwist/Elohist writings are expanded towards a broader notion of a more 'perfect' God, the Genesis narratives begin to bear interesting implications for the universality of their God's purchase on the world. When Adam and Eve leave Yahweh's garden, they find that there are other gods ruling and working in the land. The divine beings of Genesis 6, originally God's heavenly sons, have made their home in the world. They are Yahweh's kin, but have gone renegade, unleashing evils on the world by setting themselves up as 'other gods'. Since evil obviously survives the flood, the Nephilim do as well, reappearing in Canaan after the Exodus (Num. 13.33).[43] Something true and revelatory even lingers around the lesser gods of Canaan, since Yahweh–Elohim apes their patterns and behaviours in the stories of Noah, Abraham and Jacob. Even in their false name-making, the Nephilim, like Cain, bear the mark of their Father.

---

40 See Charles Taylor, 2007, *A Secular Age*, Cambridge, MA: Harvard University Press, pp. 221ff.

41 Thomas Römer, 2007, *The So-Called Deuteronomistic History: A Sociological, Historical, and Literary Introduction*, London: T&T Clark, pp. 172–5.

42 Römer, *So-Called*, p. 98.

43 Perhaps, as a student in one of my classes in Austin suggested, because they were so tall.

As Yahweh retreats, these other gods are seen for what they are: not rivals to his authority, but disordered trajectories of his own power. We can see this in the literary colonizations themselves. The deluge retells an ancient Mesopotamian story, but now it is the narrative of a god unlocalized in judgement, mercy and authority over creation. Isaiah's praises of Yahweh take up the Assyrian king's proclamation of his own eminence, but only in light of Assyria's fall, and their king's now all too obvious fallibility.[44] Abraham binds his son in the tradition of the Molech worshippers, but only as a prelude to an excessive generosity that outstrips the insatiable consumption of the Mesopotamian god: 'as it is said to this day, "On the mount of the Lord it shall be provided"' (Gen. 22.14). Molech himself must be recovered and even out-sacrificed, so that Yahweh might reveal his own unrivalled primacy.[45] The priests include this narrative not in order to show that Yahweh is appalled by human sacrifice: far from it, since this would encumber him with human passions. Rather, they simply want to demonstrate that even this radical gesture could not turn Yahweh's ear to Abraham. Abraham's God thus 'out-Molechs' Molech: where the Canaanite God hungers and consumes, Yahweh demands without need, and so can demand Isaac only to give him back, just as he can burn a bush without consuming it. Molech is no rival to this God, but a false image, a runaway child, whose theological self-image is in need of repair.[46]

As with Elijah and the prophets of Ba'al (1 Kings 18) or Josiah's discovery of the scroll and subsequent repentance for 'the sin of Jeroboam' (2 Kings 22–23), Yahweh's worshippers remain monocultic as an act of resistance against a cosmos filled with gods. Yahweh must critique and subdue and order these other gods, just as he critiques and orders and subdues those human beings in which evil has taken hold.[47]

Thus, according to Israel's hymnbook:

God has taken his place in the divine council;
    in the midst of the gods he holds judgment:
'How long will you judge unjustly
    and show partiality to the wicked? *Selah*

Give justice to the weak and the orphan;
    maintain the right of the lowly and the destitute.
Rescue the weak and the needy;
    deliver them from the hand of the wicked.'

They have neither knowledge nor understanding,

---

44 Römer, *So-Called*, pp. 67ff.

45 A theme important for Voegelin's thesis of the historical emergence of Israel and its religious claim. See *Order and History* I, pp. 111ff.

46 This paragraph benefited from a lively discussion with Professors Gregory and Bader-Saye.

47 Römer, *So-Called*, pp. 98, 172–5.

they walk around in darkness;
all the foundations of the earth are shaken.

I say, 'You are gods,
    children of the Most High, all of you;
nevertheless, you shall die like mortals,
    and fall like any prince.' (Ps. 82.1–7)

Yahweh's descent, says the Psalmist, culminates in this scene of ascending judgement, where he 'takes his place' and recovers the Nephilic disorder. The rival gods, whom we might have thought were the true princes of the nations, are unveiled as only the rebellious children of Yahweh. The chaotic injustice with which they fill the earth will not stand. They will die like mortals, and God will replace them with his adopted heir: 'I have set my king on Zion, my holy hill/ . . . 'You are my son/ today I have begotten you' (Ps. 2.6–7).

As Yahweh's chosen children, Israel will do what the rebellious children could not. She will bring praises to the one God who is over all. In this way, Israel develops a sort of divine *mimesis* of a certain kind after all. Her monocultism is a reflection of God's own project of theopolitical unification: As God stands in the divine council in order to rename creation as a unity under his rule, Israel takes her place among the council of nations, and names no other God before him. When the rival powers challenge Yahweh's authority, Israel's priest insist that this is but a call to rename him in liturgical craft, and thus also to help properly name the 'other gods' as the exiled heavenly beings that they are.

Parting the Cloud

Does this reclaiming, then, not already begin to suggest an internal critique of the priest's theology? The God beyond imitation has made his way into the Assembly: if Abraham's children allow themselves to be renamed by him, even in his wake, then their very names become Godlike, holy with the separate holiness of God. This is precisely the point made by yet another school of editors in Ancient Israel. Their 'Holiness Code' opens with words that could hardly stand in sharper contrast with the non-imitative disjunctives of Exodus and Leviticus 1 – 18: 'Yahweh spoke to Moses and said, Speak to all the community of the Israelites in these words: You shall be holy, because I, Yahweh your God, am holy' (Lev. 19.1–2). With these words, the darkness on Sinai lifts, and divine holiness is shared with the assembly below. This new language marks a final stage in the Torah's construction of Yahwistic dynamism.[48]

---

48 Knohl, *Sanctuary*, pp. 200–4. 'Holiness Code' is A. Klostermann's term. In what follows, I assume Knohl's ordering of the sources as JEDPH. At the same time, one must recognize the hint of self-fulfilling hypotheses in all source criticism.

Makers of a holy name

The Holiness Code assumes that by following the commandments, Israel will come to resemble God.[49] The authors thus overcome the priestly allergy to divine–human kinship, though not in such a way as to reimplicate Yahweh in the trickeries and negotiations of his children. The situation is now reversed, and Israel is implicated in the affairs of God. The older notion of a separating people under a separating God returns, as the new *mitvot* call the people to perform, in their economic and culinary practices, the same acts that Yahweh performs from on high. So, for example, as God has made a clear separation between Israel and the nations, Israel will make a clear separation between clean and unclean beasts (Lev. 27.11) as well as between various kinds of foods (Deut. 14.21) and the yarns they use for sewing cloth (Deut. 22.11). Their sexual ethic is mimetic as well: they will live in Yahweh's land as his sons and daughters, and their Father will not share them with other gods; neither then shall fathers within the tribes offer as prostitutes the daughters living in their houses (Lev. 19:29). The *mitvot* thus perform a rehearsal of all Yahweh's own actions toward Israel and, in doing so, develop a moral dimension missing from the earlier Levitical texts and Exodus tables. This new turn introduces one of the most obvious novelties of the Holiness Code, in the instruction that God's holiness be transmitted to the whole camp of Israel and not simply the consecrated objects.[50]

For the priestly redactors, again, Yahweh shares his holiness with liturgical objects and whatever or whoever touches them; for the Holiness School, Yahweh shares his holiness with the families and clans that make up the entire assembly. In marking this transition, the Holiness School underscores the excessive character of Israel's God. God consecrates priests not just to sanctify his own name, but in order to offer imitative holiness to all of Israel, just as God elects Abraham in order to bless the nations. For these authors, holiness as separation is always exceeded by holiness as an emanation beyond these divinely erected boundaries.[51]

In this case, for instance, if the Holiness School is the one who says 'be holy', then every instance of the text implying that Israel should be holy can be attributed to the Holiness School, even if it is otherwise out of place, for instance, Leviticus 11.44. All the same, the staying-power of the Wellhausen hypothesis in one form or another is surely significant. By adopting this particular ordering, I am interested only in the interchanges of the various theologies of holiness apparent within the Pentateuch, and it seems to me that a reordering of sources would only cause minor alterations in the reading I give here. Whether or not H is final is only a minor point: the major point is the new image of holiness that emerges in Leviticus 19, and that somehow manages to gloss other passages throughout the Law and Prophets as they now stand.

49 Knohl, *Sanctuary*, p. 173.

50 Jacob Milgrom, 2000, *Leviticus 17–22*, in *The Anchor Bible*, New York: Doubleday, pp. 1602–7; Knohl, *Sanctuary*, pp. 180–6.

51 This is the key point that Gammie misses in John Gammie, 1989, *Holiness in Israel*, Minneapolis: Fortress Press. I have benefited greatly from discussions of this text, as well as of the Holiness Code more generally, with Jeffrey Stackert.

This excess is most obvious in the symbol of boundedness par excellence in the Hebrew literature: the land. The space between the rivers is configured here as a geographic imitation of God, unique among all other tracts. 'When you reap the harvest of your land, you shall not reap to the very edges of your field, or gather the gleanings of your harvest; you shall leave them for the poor and for the alien: I am the LORD your God.' (Lev. 23.22) In this agricultural excess we find one of the most consistent images of the Hebrew Scriptures, in both the Law and the Prophets. The land itself flows with milk and honey (Exod. 3.8); rivers of wine run through the mountains, and the harvester and the sower race one another through the furrows of the field (Amos 9.13). The Holiness Code even suggests, surprisingly, that the mimetic vocation pre-dates God's calling to the children of Abraham: the land itself vomited out the Canaanites because they defiled its holiness, the same would happen to Israel, but for the new gift of laws which insist that people drive out the sinner from the land, before the land spews out the people (Lev. 20.22–22). Even beyond the Torah-practices of Israel, the inhabitants of the land between the rivers are sanctified for the imitation of divine excess.

How does the Holiness School maintain this new order of mimesis, without falling back on the old pre-priestly *mimesis* of Genesis? It does so, in part, with a creative use of the divine names. The priestly opening of Exodus invokes the name of Elohim in order to state a contrast between the old order and the new: 'I appeared to Abraham, Isaac, and Jacob as Elohim, but by my name Yahweh I did not make myself known to them' (Exod. 6.3). The priestly Torah henceforth drops Elohim entirely, thus marking the sharp distinction between the pre- and post-Sinaitic revelation.[52] The Holiness Code, however, takes up Elohim as an adjective used freely to modify the name Yahweh, or even as a name that can be used interchangeably: 'They shall be holy unto their Elohim, and not profane the name of their Elohim: for the offerings of Yahweh made by fire, and the bread of their Elohim, they do offer: therefore they shall be holy' (Lev. 21.6). The point here is not simply that Elohim is Yahweh somewhere in the mysterious depths of this unpronounceable name, but that Yahweh continues to be and act like Elohim: Israel's God is *yahweh-'elohaykem*.[53] The errant God who reaches into Israel through a self-degrading impropriety is still present, but now present as the unspeakable, 'perfect being' of Exodus 3. The enveloping dynamism of Israel's God thus does not end with withdrawn absence, but with the constant presence of this withdrawing, like letters from a friend abroad. Yahweh is with them as Elohim: the holy one as a pathway to their own holy end.

God is still wholly other, in the Holiness Code as in the priestly writings, so that his electing initiative cannot imply that he has found a potential co-worker among the people of earth. The constantly renewed choice for Israel, like the original adoption of Abraham, is always a unilateral gift to

---

52 Knohl, *Sanctuary*, pp. 124–5.

53 Milgrom, *Lev.* 17–22, pp. 1803–4; Knohl, *Sanctuary*, p. 173. Thanks again to Steve Bishop.

an entirely dependent assembly. However, in light of this gift, Yahweh has 'handed over his name'[54] more completely than even Genesis intimates. Thus when covenant returns in these texts, it brings new content. No longer suggesting a tribal God in need of assistance, persuasion or good smells, *berith* now implies the inexplicable act of the unnameable God. The covenant of holiness says that he binds his name so entirely to the name of Israel that they will not simply 'be his people and he their God', but they will do the name-making for him that he once did for Abraham. Thus yet another reversal: the liturgies of Israel 'make a name' for the one who alone gives names to human creatures. The order of imitation is at its highest point in Hebrew Scripture in this imperative.

The imperative is, at the same time, reason for a new concern about profaning God's name.[55] Yahweh's name is beyond human intrigue, and yet radically embodied in the assembly. And if there is a new layer of risk for the name of Yahweh, there is likewise a new layer of threat to the assembly to whom his name is bound. So, for instance, if someone gives a child to Molech (Lev. 20.2–5), this does not simply insert a wedge between him and the holiness of Yahweh; it actually makes the theologically disastrous claim that Yahweh, who has willingly given himself to be imaged by his people Israel, thereby offers his offspring to Molech. This man or woman must be cut off from the people, then, not simply to salvage the being of Israel, but now to rescue the divine being itself.

The account of the rebellion of Korah and his sons, non-priestly members of the tribe of Levi, is the clearest instance of this new binding of the name to the people.[56] The narrative is written in light of the new emphasis on the assembly's participation in Yahweh's holiness, as the rebels' protest makes plain: 'You have gone too far! All the congregation are holy, everyone of them, and Yahweh is among them. So why then do you exalt yourselves above the assembly of Yahweh?' (Num.16.3). Korah and his sons simply take the apparently logical step from a sanctified assembly to a desanctified priesthood, in effect challenging Moses to turn back to the Pre-Sinaitic order of revelation. Moses is clearly displeased, and so the text sets up a contest, foreshadowing the later showdown between Elijah and the prophets of Baal:

When Moses heard it, he fell on his face. Then he said to Korah and all his company, 'In the morning the LORD will make known who is his, and who is holy, and who will be allowed to approach him; the one whom he will choose he will allow to approach him.' (Num.16.4–5)

---

54 Von Balthasar, *Glory of the Lord* VI, p. 64.
55 Knohl, *Sanctuary*, pp. 124–5, 168–9.
56 For evidence that this is an H text, see Knohl, *Sanctuary*, pp. 73–87. The narrative, however, is enough on its own to prove the point, since it never would have occurred to the writers of Leviticus 1 – 18 to begin the showdown with the shared assumption that 'all the congregation are holy'.

Before any act can 'make known' the limits of holiness, however, Yahweh hesitates, in a way that combines the bargaining of Abraham in Genesis with the unapproachability of the God of Exodus:

> Then the LORD spoke to Moses and to Aaron, saying: Separate yourselves from this congregation, so that I may consume them in a moment. They fell on their faces, and said, 'O God, the God of the spirits of all flesh, shall one person sin and you become angry with the whole congregation?' And the LORD spoke to Moses, saying: Say to the congregation: Get away from the dwellings of Korah, Dathan, and Abiram. (Num. 16.20–24)

The entire congregation is now the 'ten righteous in Sodom', and Moses and Aaron successfully bargain them out of judgement. Korah's sin is in reducing the divine name to the name 'Israel' as if they were synonymous: in effect, he remembers the errancy of Genesis, but forgets the withdrawal of Exodus. It is still the retreating God who makes himself present in the congregation, and the priestly order remains in place, standing in Yahweh's wake and gesturing toward his back with their mysterious cultic alphabet.

Like the Korah narrative, the texts of the Holiness School challenge the priestly scribes by suggesting a different theological shift between the pre-Sinaiatic and the post-Sinaiatic. Whereas the early texts envision a God who imitates deceitful humans, the Holiness Code's reversal constructs Israel as imitators of and participants in the movements of God,[57] extending the act of holy-making out from the sanctuary to the entire assembly, as their proper vocation. Holiness is a matter of priest-craft, but also of agriculture, of cloth-making, of family structures and fidelities, and of festival. But binding herself to the things of earth, Israel can imitate the one who resides in the rarified air on the mountaintop.

Hearers of ten holy words

> Then Moses turned and went down from the mountain, carrying the two tablets of the covenant in his hands, tablets that were written on both sides, written on the front and on the back. The tablets were the work of God, and the writing was the writing of God, engraved upon the tablets. (Exod. 32.15–16)

---

57 Schwartz, 'Traditions', pp. 47–59, says that there is no real sense of *imitatio dei* in H. Milgrom, however, finds implicit evidence for a mimetic theology here, so long as 'one is careful not to take *imitatio dei* literally, but rather to follow the *text* of 19.2 literally, namely, strive for holiness ... and thereby approach God's holiness ...' With this qualification, 'the concept can be maintained: *imitatio dei* means live a godly life'. *Lev. 17–22*, p. 1605.

The tablets that Moses twice brings down from Sinai contain the central *mitvot* of the covenant. They are written by the hand of God, from within a darkness that looks like fire to the people at the mountain's base, and spoken to Moses in a divine voice that sounds like thunder. Are these Ten Words, then, a glimpse into the cloud on top of Sinai? Do they retain the priestly separation between Israel and her God, or do they follow the Holiness School in negotiating this distance through a mimetic structure? Is Yahweh their righteousness, or do the stone tablets provide them with a human ethic safely removed from the fire storms atop Sinai?

It has long been noted that the Decalogue does not entirely fit with the Priestly redaction, and recent scholarship suggests that it shows the hand of the Holiness School. Though cloud and thunder suggest divine withdrawal, the Words themselves are not meant only for Moses, or for Moses to pass along to Aaron and the Levites. They are meant for all: 'Yahweh said to Moses: Thus you shall say to the Israelites . . .' (Exod. 20.22). Every Israelite is now commanded to follow laws of godliness.[58]

Is this general order of godliness really 'godly', though? 'You shall not murder', 'you shall not steal', these are hardly unique prohibitions, and are perhaps more easily read as mores for communal order than as mimetic behaviours that will reveal the hidden nature of Yahweh. Does 'not stealing' even make sense as an attribute of God?[59]

The narrative location of the revelation of the two tablets provides a clue as to how to read them. The prohibitions against murder, adultery, theft, false witness and coveting all refer to acts done at one time or another by the Patriarchs and Matriarchs of Genesis. These deeds were more or less tolerated by God, since Yahweh was not yet adequately worshipped. On Sinai, however, the Temple and its orders are revealed, and so all bad mimesis is out: Cain, the Nephilim, the tower builders, Rebekah, Judah and Tamar, these are not their true mothers and fathers, and imitating them by murdering, deceiving and coveting will no longer do. The extra-liturgical prohibitions of the second tablet thus belong alongside the 'I am Yahweh your God' (Exod. 20.2) commands of the first. The one who withdraws on the mountaintop and in the tent of meeting is the one who adopted them, and so by separating themselves from the deeds of Abraham, Jacob and even Moses himself (Num. 20.12), they in fact honour their fathers and mothers in the Abrahamic lineage by bringing honour to their true Father.

The fourth commandment is the most explicitly mimetic. In the second version, from Deuteronomy, the day of rest is a performance of the Exodus, a day to 'Remember that you were a slave in the land of Egypt, and the LORD your God brought you out from there with a mighty hand and an outstretched arm' (Deut. 5.15). Rest is here a demonstration in protest of the false identity constructed for Israel by her enslavement in Egypt. Observation of the Sabbath is a way of remembering who they are not: slaves

---

58 William H.C. Propp, 2006, *Exodus 19–40*, in *The Anchor Bible*, New York: Doubleday, p. 167.

59 This is Schwarz's point, pp. 47–59, about *imitatio dei*. See note 57.

made to work without rest, a situation that led to their forgetting of God. In the earlier version, we find the ontology that lies behind this logic. The slaves must leave Egypt, because Israel is meant to imitate God who rested after his work:

> Remember the sabbath day, and keep it holy. Six days you shall labour and do all your work. But the seventh day is a sabbath to the LORD your God; you shall not do any work – you, your son or your daughter, your male or female slave, your livestock, or the alien resident in your towns. For in six days the LORD made heaven and earth, the sea, and all that is in them, but rested the seventh day; therefore the LORD blessed the sabbath day and consecrated it. (Exod. 20.8–11)

This is the sole instance in the Decalogue when a commandment is backed by the warrant that God is like the command itself. Israel's workless day will make her an image and likeness of the Creator. Here the congregation is allowed to peer into the cloud and see that what is holy for them is also holy for God; put more radically: as they work and rest, their very bodies become the holiness of God, thickening into fleshly form.

The Frozen Alphabet

Let us take stock of the many dynamics and reversals of our story thus far: Yahweh peoples the heavens and earth with children whose perfection is his own image and likeness; the children fall into errancy and exile; Yahweh follows them and adopts a new family, despite the rather Nephilic morality that they observe; Yahweh withdraws, announcing through moving pillars of cloud and fire that he will no longer follow his children, they will now follow him; Yahweh's shrouded presence settles on the mountain, and opens long enough to offer the mimetic ethic that will allow Israel to follow her God out of the land of Nod and into Canaan, a land so like the aboriginal world that its perfections begin to blend in the scribes' minds with the perfection of Adam and Eve's garden. Following Yahweh, Israel will leave the land of Sabbathless slavery and ungodly giants; she will 'go out in joy, and be led back in peace; the mountains and the hills' will 'burst into song, and all the trees of the field shall clap their hands' (Isa. 55.12). The cherubim with flaming swords will stand aside, reopening the path to the tree of life (Gen. 3.24). The evil gods will be bound within Yahweh's service once again, and no competitive *agon* will compromise the perfection of creation.

'By giving back the word to God in the unconditional act of praise, Israel is perfect, i.e. in the state in which God requires it to be in order to make out of the word of answer a word of God himself.'[60] This word, the fulfilment of the covenantal mutuality, allows God to be so unequivocally

---

60 Von Balthasar, *Glory of the Lord* VI, p. 207.

present in the praise of the people that their response is a spelling of his call, their voice a perfect imitation of his. And a perfect imitation of Yahweh is perfection itself, since here there is no celestial struggle from which Yahweh emerged as the vanquishing power. Yahweh 'is who is', and there is no prior order of being which can hover like a remainder over the summons to 'be holy as I am holy'.

Thus there is no 'Greek' problem here of a less than perfect God. And as the *telos* of a people will always be shaped by the perfection of their God, we can say that Israel's monocultism introduces a dazzlingly sublime perfection into human history.[61] They are the chosen people of the perfect God; the perfect God is their perfection.

With this sublimity, however, a new problem arises. How sustainable is the cultic performance of this perfection? Even without the experience of exile, when the word of praise lies dormant and the harps hang on trees (Ps. 137.2), the mimetic vocation survives always under the threat of its own dissolution. This is, after all, the God of the unpronounceable name, as Korah and his followers found out, even if 'Elohim of Abraham and Isaac and Jacob' will be his name for all generations. The Yahwistic remainder still threatens to take back the name that God has handed over, just as he does with Korah. How can the priests, let alone the sowers and weavers and merchants, perform in their lives and vocations an imitation not only God's electing presence, but also the constant threat of his withdrawal? The entire history of the covenant teeters on the edge of absurdity, like an alphabet that may comprise the basic elements of a meaningful language, and then again may simply be a string of sounds and symbols that is entirely useless for saying anything at all. Israel's liturgical-social-ethical-economic alphabet is both meaning-laden and beyond meaning at once, consistently and irreducibly; this is their predicament.[62]

For this reason, despite the complexity added by the Holiness Code and related texts, the post-exilic redactors return again and again to a more antiseptic vision of the Ten Words, as laws handed down from the far side of inconceivable gap, a gap that, precisely because it invites no contemplation, is the opposite of the religious gap of the Greeks. The Sinai code become a kind of *deutero-nomos*, but one no longer bearing the marks of the *proto-nomos*:

> Surely, this commandment that I am commanding you today is not too hard for you, nor is it too far away. It is not in heaven, that you should say, 'Who will go up to heaven for us, and get it for us so that we may hear it and observe it?' Neither is it beyond the sea, that you should say, 'Who will cross to the other side of the sea for us, and get it for us so that we may hear it and observe it?' No, the word is very near to you; it is in your mouth and in your heart for you to observe. (Deut. 30.11-14)

---

61 This is the principal point of Voegelin's reading in *Order and History* I.
62 See Voegelin, *Order and History* I, pp. 355ff.

The commandment is of the earth, and following it is a simple matter of obedience to a human path of righteousness. Their task is not the (ancient) Promethean ascent of Sinai into the presence, nor of an Argonian descent into the contemplative depths of human–divine participation: it is 'very near them'. When simple obedience of the temporal commandment replaces contemplation of its eternal and mimetic depths, the word spoken ceases to articulate divine holiness and thus ceases to retrace a human sharing in divine perfection.

The prophets of the exilic and post-exilic period recognize the unsustainability of divine *mimesis* most explicitly. They cast themselves often as new Moseses, re-encountering Yahweh in a new burning bush. They offer a new Law that addresses the unsettling and growing gap between the darkness on Sinai and the new calf-worshippers below. So, for instance, when Jeremiah stands outside the gate of the Temple making his proclamation to the passers-by on their way to worship, the prohibitions of the Decalogue form the basis for his condemnations: 'You steal, you murder, you commit adultery and perjury, you burn sacrifices to Baal, you run after other gods whom you have not known' (Jer. 7.9–10).[63] He then rehearses the Exodus account, with one significant alteration: Yahweh says, 'When I brought your forefathers out of Egypt, I gave them no commands about whole-offering and sacrifice; I said not a word about them. What I did command them was this: If you obey me, I will be your God and you shall be my people. You must conform to all my commands, if you would prosper' (7.22–3).

But of course Yahweh did say a word or two about offerings and sacrifices: namely, the entire book of Leviticus. In effect, Jeremiah draws a straight line from the Exodus to the Decalogue to the post-Babylonian period, bypassing the Temple cult entirely. Why does he do this?

There is an obvious 'editorial argument' at play here between the priests and the prophets.[64] Beyond this, though, we can trace deeper and more evasive theological issues in the fabric of the text. The prophets revise the Exodus not simply to usher in a new era of prophetic power, but because they perceive a broad-scale failure of the Aaronide alphabet to spell out the divine name. When yarn and agriculture and ephod have failed to pronounce Yahweh's name, the prophet short-circuits the Levitical scroll altogether, and with it the cultural mediation of divine perfection. Now his own words encounter the gathered assembly like new Tablets brought down from Sinai. He leads them back to the burning bush, which also takes on a radicalized manifestation: The first Moses saw the theophany on the mountain and stopped at a distance; now the fire is within God's very being and touches the lips of the prophets (Isa. 6). Ezekiel takes Yahweh's soothing promise to Moses, 'I will give you words to say', and advances upon them in a single giant step: 'He said to me, O mortal, eat what is offered to you; eat this scroll, and go, speak to the house of Israel. So I opened my mouth, and he gave me

63 Voegelin, *Order and History* I, pp. 431–2.

64 Jack Lundbloom, 1999, *Jeremiah 1–20*, in *The Anchor Bible*, New York: Doubleday, pp. 481–2.

the scroll to eat' (Ezek. 3.1–2). The consumed scroll now pronounces the holiness that the liturgies and replicative *mitvot* cannot.[65]

With these visions and symbolic acts, the prophets drive a wedge into the Deuteronomistic gap between the ethic of heaven and the ethic of earth. They order Israel to obey the commandments; but the experiences of exile and constant political threat have taught her that the name of Yahweh is capable of receding again, just as it did in Egypt and the wilderness. With this insight, they begin to consider, for the first time in Israel's intellectual history, the radical implications of worshipping a God who is uncontained by the land, by covenant and even by the particular election of their ancestor Abraham. The loss of the Temple does not eliminate the presence of Yahweh on earth, because Israel's God now exceeds both the space of Temple and the time of cult. Isaiah says this with a masterful touch with his pairing of the living God, whose train fills the Temple, with the dead king of Judah, whose train could not have filled more than a few yards of palatial staircase (Isa. 6.1).[66] His vision of cherubim and the smoke-filled temple intensifies many times over in the later apocalyptic visions of the prophets, in which living creatures, glowing amber, spinning wheels and flames, crystal domes, flashes of lightning and cracks of thunder, are all summed up in the deceptively pedestrian statement, 'This was the appearance of the likeness of the glory of the LORD' (Ezek. 1.28).[67]

A God so radically untranscribed will certainly stretch the old faith in the stability of land and throne. Deutero-Isaiah, continuing the new covenant motif,[68] goes so far as to condemn those who, like Lot's wife, look back on the 'former things' of pre-exilic Judah. The time has come for a new departure, a new Exodus:

> Thus says the LORD,
>> who makes a way in the sea,
>> a path in the mighty waters,
> who brings out chariot and horse,
>> army and warrior;
> they lie down, they cannot rise,
>> they are extinguished, quenched like a wick:
> Do not remember the former things,
>> or consider the things of old.
> I am about to do a new thing;
>> now it springs forth, do you not perceive it?
> I will make a way in the wilderness
>> and rivers in the desert. (Isa. 43.16–19)

---

65 See von Balthasar, *Glory of the Lord* VI, pp. 267–8.

66 Voegelin, *Order and History* I, p. 437.

67 Deceptive because its synthetic simplicity is loaded with increasingly intensifying prepositions, removing the appearance several steps from Yahweh himself. I owe this point to Alan Gregory.

68 Voegelin, *Order and History* I, pp. 468ff.

The previous incarnation of Israel is now 'Egypt', and the new Moses sings that its horse and rider have been drowned, just as the old Moses once sang of the old Egypt (Exod. 15).

In Amos, this vein of supersessionism only grows stronger, as the notion of a cosmic Yahweh begins to affect the narration of the election itself: 'Yahweh roars from Zion', and his word that comes to the shepherd of Tekoa places Israel and Judah in a long line of cities, kingdoms and people with whom God has apparently entered into a covenantal relation. They are all threatened and condemned alongside Israel, and so she is warned not to consider herself 'chosen' in a way that these others are not. The ninth chapter even insists that the Exodus is not a unique act of Yahweh toward Abraham's children:

Are you not like the Ethiopians to me,
    O people of Israel? says the LORD.
Did I not bring Israel up from the land of Egypt,
    and the Philistines from Caphtor and the Arameans from Kir?
    (Amos 9.7)

The prophets of Israel renarrate the election in order to indicate the tension between the universal glory of Yahweh and the particularity of the chosen tribes. 'It is too light a thing' (Isa. 49.6), they insist, to contain the glory within the tribes alone. God calls prophets 'over nations and over kingdoms, to pluck up and pull down, to destroy and to overthrow, to build and to plant' (Jer. 1.10). Israel and Judah, for better or for worse, find their place among these nations, as one of the many peoples 'planted', and now one of many ready for plucking.

How is a God who now dwells no longer on Sinai, but throughout the heavens and earth, to issue discernible commands for the perfecting of a people? The priests of the Holiness School envision a law issuing from a lifting cloud to a gathered nation below; the prophets see a law issuing from the fathomless heavens, to all nations and peoples. Could any language describe the divinity mediated by these commands? Or are all languages bound to fail, reverting into a social ethic void of any theological content?

None of this is to suggest that the Holiness revisions are completely missing in the prophetic literature.[69] The prophets themselves embody Yahweh's presence, somewhat like the Nazirites of the Torah: the whole assembly concentrated into a single character. The God of the prophets is certainly not above Genesis-like anthropomorphisms: Hosea 'is' God when he takes a prostitute home as his bride, and as he lies awake burning with jealousy

---

69 Knohl in fact, in *Sanctuary*, pp. 212ff, insists that they are so strongly present as to suggest a final revision of even the prophetic texts by HC. This, though, seems to ignore all the thematic differences highlighted by Voegelin, *Order and History* I, pp. 432ff.

when she absents herself from their covenantal bed night after night. The message that comes to Israel and the nations through the mouths of Jeremiah and Amos is of the Lord's anger over the sinfulness and injustices that he sees with his eyes and hears with his ears, rather like the Elohim of Genesis. And for all his anger, Yahweh might, as in the days of Noah and Abraham, bargain for the lives of the nations, and 'repent' of his ways, take back his curses, and spare the cities (Jonah).

And yet these incarnational narratives bear but little on the holiness prescribed for the people of earth. The shattered memories of Sinaitic and Davidic covenants figure only as the old paths of holiness, and the new will be an intensive obedience that only rehearses these memories in distant and abstract patterns. The less useful the kingship of David and the sacrifices of Aaron seem for constructing a language for post-exilic faith, the more inimitable the holiness of Yahweh becomes. In Isaiah's vision, the cherubim sing of Yahweh's holiness; the sharing of fire from an absent altar[70] is not construed as a sharing of holiness, but rather as a purgation, on the order of the indecipherable atonement in the first two-thirds of Leviticus. Isaiah is consecrated for mission like Aaron was consecrated for the cult, but he is not made holy. In Ezekiel's vision, in which 'the heavens were opened', revealing the dazzling vision of four-faced cherubim and spinning wheels, the fire is taken from 'in between the wheels' (10.2), with a 'liturgical solemnity'.[71] And yet this fire is specifically the fire of judgement on Jerusalem, which issues forth from a dense cloud that never opens in a way that might give the citizens a glimpse of their holy calling (10.3). Ezekiel's own call is likewise removed from the realm of holiness, since the heavens must close on the holiness of Yahweh before he can hear the voice of a man who summons him and helps him to his feet.[72]

What then is the perfection for the nations that gather in the train of the living and everlasting God? It certainly bears elements, as we have seen, of the old Decalogue, though without the imitative strictures. Now the law comes forth not even in a recognizable code, as this would fix the boundless Yahweh to a formula that would soon become 'too light a thing'. The 'new thing' is, in a word, obedience and is exemplified in the symbolic actions of the prophets as much as it is described in their diatribes. They are men called by a voice, often in spite of the unmanageability of the visions they perceive. They mark out the judgement of Yahweh with their bodies, when the language of sermon and liturgy has failed.

At that time the LORD had spoken to Isaiah son of Amoz, saying, 'Go, and loose the sackcloth from your loins and take your sandals off your feet,' and he had done so, walking naked and barefoot. (Isa. 20.2)

---

70 Von Balthasar, *Glory of the Lord* VI, p. 248.

71 Von Balthasar, *Glory of the Lord* VI, p. 274.

72 See the discussion of this character in Moshe Greenberg, 1983, *Ezekiel 1—20*, in *The Anchor Bible*, New York: Doubleday; also Von Balthasar, *Glory of the Lord* VI, pp. 267–8.

'Go, take for yourself a wife of whoredom and have children of whoredom, for the land commits great whoredom by forsaking the LORD.' (Hos. 1.2)

The spirit entered into me, and set me on my feet; and he spoke with me and said to me: Go, shut yourself inside your house. As for you, mortal, cords shall be placed on you, and you shall be bound with them, so that you cannot go out among the people; and I will make your tongue cling to the roof of your mouth, so that you shall be speechless and unable to reprove them; for they are a rebellious house. (Ezek. 2.4–6)

And you, O mortal, take a sharp sword; use it as a barber's razor and run it over your head and your beard; then take balances for weighing, and divide the hair. (Ezek. 5.1)

Von Balthasar summarizes this posture of the prophets, whose bodies stand in for the failed covenant language, as a 'stairway of obedience' that 'God wills to construct for himself in the men whom he has chosen'. Where human cultic language freezes in its ascent toward the heavens, and with it the human ability to respond to God as his covenanted partner, 'the history of the covenant of God becomes a history of God with himself',[73] performed in the scroll-eating and head-shaving acts of the prophets. Indeed, what other response is fitting for a God from whom human language, culture and political governance is increasingly alienated? If even the cultic naming of Yahweh by Israel is superseded, what way lies open to the reception of divine presence other than this radical obedience?

Rather than a participation in divine holiness, there is here a 'metastasis' that stalls the perfecting order of earth in reverence for the spinning wheels of divine glory.[74] Even the proximity of an 'earthly' morality begins to deconstruct itself, as the prophets realize the inadequacy of the Deuteronomistic solution to the gap between heaven and earth. Having seen the heavens opened by the river of Chebar, Ezekiel cannot be satisfied with the relative perfection of earth. The perfection of heaven, however, is too terrible even for his eyes. What can he do, then, but instrumentalize himself to the will of Yahweh, making of himself an intentionally 'uncurious vessel'[75] for divine agency?

---

73 Von Balthasar, *Glory of the Lord* VI, p. 223. I have benefited greatly from conversations with Ashley Brandon regarding the role of symbolic performance in the prophets.

74 Voegelin's term is meant to suggest that revelation came to be seen by the late prophets as an attempt 'to transform reality into something which by essence it is not'. *Order and History* I, pp. 453ff. See the discussion of this controversial term by Bernard Anderson and David Morse in William M. Thompson and David L. Morse (eds), 2000, *Israel and Revelation: An Interdisciplinary Debate and Anthology*, Milwaukee: Marquette Press, pp. 17–46, 164–90.

75 Von Balthasar, *Glory of the Lord* VI, p. 233.

What does this metastasis mean for human agency? If humble obedience is the last word of human action, so that God replaces Abraham as his own covenant partner, then creation is abolished by its own perfection. Ezekiel is the anti-Abraham, since he cannot engage in an economy of mutual blessing with God; but he is also the anti-Adam, since the Edenic human is created for the naming and stewarding of things and the prophetic human for the performance of acts that are resistance to human language and cultural activity.

Israel's narrative is, then, one of a return to the perfection of Eden, but in the end this return journey is shrouded in ambiguity. With each window onto the holiness of Yahweh, Israel sees something of her own holiness, since her holiness is one just as Yahweh is one. But with each shrouding of God's being and action in inexplicable mystery, the commandment given to them becomes something other than holiness, a 'way that is right' for them, perhaps, though not a passage into God's perfection that would constitute their own perfect end.

In this sense, the closing of heaven is always also the closing of earth. When the Sinai cloud descends over the divine presence, it descends over Eden as well, and the ineffability of Yahweh renders unpronounceable not only God's proper name, but Adam's too. The scribes and priests of Israel offer a vision of perfection that improves upon the perfection of Greece, where the gods themselves are an *agon* of metaphysical disharmony; but the price for uncompromising divine perfection is dear, as the worshippers of this God experience the failure of their liturgical symbols, their psalms and their social mores for sharing in this God's being. In Athens it is the hovering of a surd evil remainder which compromises human perfection; in Jerusalem, it is the hovering of the sublime and unrepeatable good.

Both the Hebrew and the Greek, though, we can at the very least say, offer a vastly richer vocabulary for the commerce between the human and the divine than the modern bifurcation can imagine. If they fall short of a fully coherent account of human perfection, this only suggests that our mapping of an alternative to the modern impasse cannot stop here, but must move on to that point in time when these texts are taken up by the tradition that issues from them.

3

First Interlude:
Yahwistic Deification in Philo
of Alexandria

The soul of man must quicken to creation.

T. S. Eliot

Mystical Kaleidoscope

Any simple attempt, of course, to compare the ancient Semitic and the Hellenic worlds will rely on the sort of generalizations and sleights of hand that doom analysis. In tracing the origin of a new path for the imagining of human perfection, the duality must, to some degree, remain unsynthesized and uncontrasted. Images may serve us better here than textual comparisons. On the one hand, the daughters suspended from the festal gods; on the other, the Law emerging from a dark cloud atop a mountain. The metaphysical imagining of perfection in the clearing of the Greek grove is a world apart from the revelation of the *derek* given from the fog on Sinai. Tertullian's rhetorical question still rules the discourse: in the end, 'what, indeed, has Athens to do with Jerusalem?' (*De Præscriptione Hæreticorum* 7).[1]

At the same time, comparisons are unavoidable, if only because these two horizons have in fact collided at various points – though not irreducibly – into a single 'language of biblical Hellenism'.[2] Since the first century after the birth of Christ, literary minds have negotiated and renegotiated the fused space created by this collision, and that has meant first of all asking what makes either one distinct. If we wish to contrast these horizons as a precursor to naming the result of the fusion, we might put it this way: Hellenism offers a participation in gods who are imperfectly divine; Israel

---

1 Though perhaps not quite the way he meant it, or the way it has been taken. The famous question from *De Præscriptione Hæreticorum* is collected in *Ante-Nicene Fathers*, Vol. 3, online at http://www.ccel.org/ccel/schaff/anf03.v.iii.vii.html (accessed 14 September 2010).

2 David T. Runia, 1993, *Philo in Early Christian Literature*, Assen; Van Gorcum and Minneapolis: Fortress, p. 154.

offers a God who is too perfect for our participation. In both, a vision of human perfection fails to emerge with any finality.

What happens, though, when the ancient world attempts to bring these two images together? The first significant attempt at a fusion came out of Alexandria midway through the first century of the Common Era, where the crossing of trade routes allowed for a 'kaleidoscope conversation' among various traditions and religious of the empire.[3] Human perfection is particularly important in the synthesizing project of Philo Judæus, since he recognizes that in the question of human ends lies perhaps the very basic tension between the traditions of Moses and of Socrates. The Torah prescribes the way of holiness for the people of the Torah, but does not suggest with any clarity what the way is for the nations, for the human. Something of the ecstasy of the festal rhythms is lacking, he perceives, in Judaism, where the prophet alone is initiated, and the city metastasizes in alienation from God's holiness. In this regard, Philo can recognize the great work of translating the Tanakh into Greek as the beginning of the universalization of the Sinaitic revelation. Through these translating efforts, God granted 'that the greater part, or even the whole, of the human race might be profited and led to a better life by continuing to observe such wise and truly admirable ordinances' (*De Vita Mosis*, 2.6.36).[4] Indeed, putting Moses into the Greek, the universal tongue, allowed for true fulfilment of the Mosaic Law, since the end of revelation had always, for Philo, exceeded the particularity of the Jews. Even on the mountain it was given for all, 'that he who would observe the laws will accept gladly the duty of following nature and live in accordance with the ordering of the universe' (*Vit. Mos.* 2.8.48).

Regardless of the perennial debate over whether Philo was more Jewish or more Greek, it is essential for our purposes to note that his intentional conjoining of traditions has the expressed aim of bringing the Hellenistic idea of a universal sharing in the being of the gods with the Jewish teaching of one true God. Philo is attempting to grant universal and mystical participation in the perfect God of Israel. As one scholar puts the matter, Philonic Judaism is not trying 'to find a Jewish Isis or Demeter, or a Jewish series of Amesha Spentas, it is trying to find within Judaism a symbolic basis by which it can express and achieve the Greek mystic goal'.[5]

---

3 E. R. Goodenough, 1963, *An Introduction to Philo Judaeus*, 2nd edn, New York: Barnes and Noble, p. 22.

4 Philo, *De Vita Mosis*, in F. H. Colson (ed. and trans.), 1950, *Philo*, Vol. VI, Loeb Classical Library no. 239, Cambridge, MA: Harvard University Press.

5 E. R. Goodenough, 1935, *By Light, Light: The Mystic Gospel of Hellenistic Judaism*, New Haven: Yale University Press, p. 20. Goodenough attempts to show the influence of the oracular and Hermetic traditions on Philo, a conclusion which he draws by insisting that religious rites and experience only become active in the Greek world centuries after Plato. Meeks agrees in principle, but argues that this could just as easily be counted as evidence, reciprocally, that Sinaitic theophanies were important for the birth of Hellenistic mysticism. Wayne Meeks, 1967, *The Prophet-King: Moses Traditions and the Johannine Christology*, Leiden: E. J. Brill, pp. 110ff.

Poetry in the Tabernacle

Moses is, for Philo, 'the greatest and most perfect of men' (*Vit. Mos.* 1.1.1). His greatness is not in the first place a measure of his heroic virtue, though, as we would expect to read in a Life of Hercules or Alexander; rather, Moses is great because of a great encounter. The ascent of Moses into the cloud on Sinai is always central to Philo's imagination,[6] and it is within this cloud, and on account of what he saw and what occurred to him there, that Moses achieved his laudable status.

[He] entered, we are told, into the darkness where God was, that is into the unseen, invisible, incorporeal and archetypal essence of existing things. Thus he beheld what is hidden from the sight of mortal nature, and, in himself and his life displayed for all to see, he has set before us, like some well-wrought picture, a piece of work beautiful and godlike, a model for those who are willing to copy it. (*Vit. Mos.* 1.28.158)

This Godlike work, the life of Moses itself, becomes in turn the measure of human perfection, our way of entry into the archetypal mysteries of the darkness:

Happy [εὐδαίμονες] are they who imprint, or strive to imprint, that image in their souls. For it were best that the mind should carry the form of virtue in perfection [εἶδος τέλειον ἀρετῆς], but, failing this, let it at least have the unflinching desire to possess that form. (*Vit. Mos.* 1.28.158–9)

The first thing we can observe from this passage is that Philo uses the traditional Greek ethical language to describe the event and implications of Sinai. Like the Philosopher of the *Republic* who rules the city in light of his contemplation of the form of the good, Moses is the lawgiver who is fit to rule in view of his initiation on the mountain. At the same time, Philo's text implies a more Aristotelian account of the good, since it is not ultimately the ineffable within the cloud that serves as a model for human virtue, but Moses himself. The lawgiver thus supplies us with an Aristotelian *deutero agathon*, accommodating the *idea ton agathon* into a visible object toward which we can strive.

While both lines of influence (oracular Hellenism to Judaism through Philo, Siniatic mysticism to Hellenic world through Philo) were most certainly active in the cross currents of the period, both Goodenough and Meeks overlook the mysticism, in the centrality of rites and divine participation, that was already active in Plato. To a significant degree, when Philo and the anonymous hermetic texts construct an account of humanity built upon sharing in God as the ultimate end, they are both being true to a basic Platonic imperative.

6 See Burton Mack, 1995, 'Moses on the Mountaintop', in John Peter Kenney (ed.), *The School of Moses: Studies in Philo and Hellenistic Religion*, Atlanta: Scholars Press, p. 18.

First Interlude: Yahwistic Deification in Philo of Alexandria

Just as for Aristotle, the secondary good is good insofar as it images the primary, and this leads Philo to an important revision of the received Sinaitic canon. The Moses who emerges from the cloud and among the people is discernibly Godlike, so much so that Philo calls him 'God and King [θεός καὶ βασιλεύς]' over the nation (*Vit. Mos.* 1.28.158). When Moses is atop the mountain, he is Godlike through his proximity to the ineffable; if he is Godlike also in his descent, then his human actions now carry the divine presence within them. Thus he does not simply receive divine revelation and speak and act in oracular obedience, but his words and actions now manifest the nature of Yahweh through the human form of the prophet.

This manifestation, for Philo, takes place most of all in the construction of the tabernacle. Exodus 25–30 records the instructions that Moses receives on the design of the sacred space, objects and vestments to be used in worship. In Philo's estimation, the long series of 'You shall make' commands are evidence that Yahweh is initiating Moses into the creative patterns of his own work. Creation itself is the paradigm of the tabernacle (*Vit. Mos.* 2.16.76), so that even the colours of cloth woven into the curtains are types of the four elements of creation identified by the *Timaeus* (53a). This correspondence is only fitting, if the worship space under construction is to name the maker of the universe. 'For it was necessary that in framing a temple of man's making, dedicated to the Father and Ruler of All, he should take substances like those with which that Ruler made them all [αἷς τὸ ὅλον ἐδημιούργει]' (*Vit. Mos.* 2.18.88).

The interior of the tabernacle becomes then an icon of the cosmos itself. The candles are 'the luminaries above', and their placement within the temple signals the path of the stars, sun and moon across the heavens. The twelve stones of the priest's ephod are the twelve patriarchs, but they are also the twelve signs of the zodiac, figuring the phases of 'colouring in the air and earth and water . . . and also in the different kinds of animals and plants' (*Vit. Mos.* 2.24.126). The entire cosmos, in this way, enters the Holy Place with the priest; he is the whole creation gone to worship. Even the Tetragrammaton, unspeakable except by purified tongues, can appear in the four incisions on Aaron's crown, and so point to the hidden geometric and musical harmonies of the spheres (*Vit. Mos.* 1.20.114–15).

The entire field of correspondences within and beyond the Temple cult demonstrates what is for Philo the key to the universalizing of Israel's cult for all humankind. God makes manifest his own creative activity in the 'You shall make' phrases addressed to Moses. Thus when Moses enters the cloud on Sinai, all is not dark. He can 'see' the ratios between the instructions given to him and the prototypical instructions given to the light, dark, earth, sky, waters and living things of the original six days. The making of the golden calf at the base of the mountain becomes the antitype to the making of the tabernacle: while Moses is in the divine presence learning the patters of true *poesis*, the people are collecting below, inventing a false *poesis* that does not share in the secret of the six days (*Vit.*

Mos. 2.32.167–8). The cloudless place at the foot of the mountain is now, ironically, the place of true darkness. Throughout Philo's entire allegorical project, extending through multiple treatises,[7] he attempts to illuminate the presence of the true demiurge, thereby bathing all shadowed lands in the new light of Sinai.

The creative work of Israel's God is so central to Philo's notion of the divine that he adapts the Aristotelian language of *energiea* to mean not simply actuality or actualized being, but also activity.[8] The resting of God on the seventh day is not inactivity, but a perfect *poesis*, since 'God never ceases making, but even as it is the property of fire to burn and of snow to chill, so it is the property of God to make [ποιεῖν]; in fact, more so by far, inasmuch as He is to all the source of action [ἀρχὴ τοῦ δρᾶν]' (*Legum Allegoriae*, 1.3.5–6).[9] The Sabbath becomes for Philo a divine festival, beyond the temporal contrast of work and activity, gift and reception, possession and expenditure:

> The principle is this. God alone in the true sense keeps festival. Joy and gladness and rejoicing are his alone; to Him alone it is given to enjoy the peace which has no element of war. He is without grief or fear or share of ill, without faint-heartedness or pain or weariness, but full of happiness unmixed. Or rather since His nature is most perfect, He is Himself the summit, end and limit of happiness. He partakes of nothing outside Himself to increase His excellence. Nay He Himself has imparted of His own to all particular beings from that fountain of beauty – Himself. For the good and beautiful things in the world could never have been what they are, save that they were made in the image of the archetype, who is truly good and beautiful, even the uncreated, the blessed, the imperishable. (*De cherubim*, 2.25.86)

The mixture of the Platonic with the Hebrew is here at its most refined. The God who is unlimited even by evils or the unformed elements is also the God who shares his being and his perfect festal happiness with his creation.

---

7 See Goodenough, *Philo*, pp. 47ff.

8 David Bradshaw, 2006, *Aristotle East and West: Metaphysics and the Division of Christendom*, Cambridge: Cambridge University Press, p. 62. But Bradshaw errs in looking to the active/passive distinction for the key to Philo's differentiation of Creator and creature. Citing the following passage from *De cherubim*, Bradshaw, p. 77, argues that Philo asserts, inexplicably, that creatures are not active makers: 'It belongs to God to act (ποειν), and this we may not ascribe to any created being. What belongs to the created is to suffer (πασχειν), and he who accepts this from the first, as a necessity inseparable from his lot, will bear with patience what befalls him, however grievous it may be' (p. 77). He neglects, however, to note that this comes in the context of commentary on Cain, who sins in attempting to possess all things at once, and thus to erase the receptivity of temporal life. Ontologically, for Philo, the creature is always a mixture of activity and passivity, as he states further down in *De cherubim*, 79.

9 Bradshaw, *Aristotle*, pp. 60–1.

If humans are suspended from the neck of this God, then our perfection is to share in the nature of the perfect itself.

The two tablets of the Decalogue stand as further evidence, beyond the tabernacle instructions, that Moses did in fact perceive divine perfection in the cloud. Though the first 'treats of . . . the monarchical principle by which the world is governed', and the second of human prohibitions for social order, the two together 'open out broad highroads leading at the end to a single goal' (*De Decalogo*, 12.50–1).[10] If the honouring of Yahweh in the first commandments were an injunction to be obeyed without any comprehension, the ends of the tablets would be two: revere God and live well together. In fact, the second tablet is more or less a commentary on the first, since refraining from murder and adultery and the like is simply the way of embodying the prohibition on taking other gods before Yahweh, or taking his name in vain. The fifth commandment, Philo insists, is the key to the linking of the tablets: if the first four tell us about the honour due to God the Father, the fifth tells us that an analogous honour is due to parents, 'who copy His nature by begetting particular persons' (*De Dec.* 12.51). The second tablet, then, is a human morality that opens in the space of the analogy of parenthood. If the perfect parent is pure creativity of gift-sharing, and all human beings are the issue of human parents, then all human activity is characterized at its most perfect as the giving and sharing of gifts.

Furthermore, the unity of the tablets supplies the reason that the ten words, the highest of all *mitvot* issuing from the gift-giving God, need not entail curses or punishments. Dike is 'sitting by' Yahweh, and in her, his own justice rules the earth (*De Dec.* 33.177).[11] The kings of earth, even the 'servants and lieutenants of God', must rely on threats and punishments in order to execute just measures on earth, since commands can issue from their lips only at a remove from the seat of universal good. When God makes a decree, however, no such threats are needed, since 'Thou shalt not' comes from the mouth of the one besides whom there are no others. Beyond the commandments, there is no higher good; these are not so much *deutero agathon* as humanly workable inroads to the idea of the good itself. Thus the kingly commander is also the 'guardian of peace' who will 'supply richly and abundantly the good things of peace' for the world that he governs (*De Dec.* 33.177–8).[12] His gifts can be trusted, and so, in their highest expression, they need no scaffolding of punishments on which to rely.

If from Aeschylus through Aristotle the problem of Dike and Themis persists, the problem, that is, of a court of divine justice whose relationship to the court of human justice is always in question, here the two become

---

10 Philo, *De Decalogo*, in F. H. Colson (ed. and trans.), 1950, *Philo*, Vol. VII, Loeb Classical Library no. 320, Cambridge, MA: Harvard University Press.

11 Philo, *De Decalogo*, in C. D. Yonge (trans.), 1993, *The Works of Philo*, Peabody: Houghton Mifflin, p. 533.

12 Colson (ed. and trans.), *Philo*, Vol. VII, p. 95.

one. The old Saturnine/Olympian chasm here collapses. Zeus, for the tragedians and philosophers, could only ever rule as a lieutenant, even when his coup was unquestionably a success. He still was ruling, through Dike, a natural sphere whose judicial order belonged to the transcendence of Themis her mother. In rolling Zeus into Saturn, Philo also rolls Dike into Themis, and the justice of the transcendent God is now the gracious decree of an order of justice that can rule the earth as well.[13] The girdles have here, for the first time in a Hellenistic text, been looped around the necks of the gods in the highest of heavenly groves.

As the creatures blessed to receive these good gifts, humans find in the mystery of the Sinai cloud not only a *Logos* that is the paradigm of their own being, but the feast-making that is the end of their own moral perfecting. The Sabbath commandment is a vocation. '"Always follow God," it says: "find in that single six-day period in which, all-sufficient for His purpose, He created the world, a pattern of the time set apart to thee for activity. Find, too, in the seventh day the pattern of the duty to study wisdom . . . and all that in thy own life makes for happiness [εὐδαιμονία]"' (*De Dec.* 20.100). Our summons to Godlikeness always implies the false possibility of a self-making that would refuse this vocation. The Nephilim of Genesis 6 are the souls who follow their passions toward a degenerate transformation, a sort of fall narrative underscoring the dangers of a *poesis* that divorces itself from the archetype. Nimrod the hunter is the figure of disordered deification, since his desertion of the better for the worse makes him into a giant, a sort of ironically monstrous likeness of the God of creation (*De gigantibus*, 12.55–6).[14] The giants are the unparented, those who make themselves on the false paradigm of murder, theft and covetousness, and thus become non-participating self-makers.

Attending to the calling to make ourselves and our world on the paradigm of divine craft, we become Godlike; failing to thus attend, we will continue the activity of making, but will make instead a garden of thorn and thistle inhabited by godless giants. Philo has provided here a significant signpost on the path toward an anti-Promethean perfection. Nimrod, like Cain, is indeed a Promethean figure of the classical type, who, 'fearing not Zeus, in self-will too much . . . honourest mortals' (*Prom. Bd.* 142–3).[15] But Cain is not Abel, and giants are only a perversion of the true alignment of desire for God with the reception of God's self-giving. To honour mortals too much is in fact to honour them too little, since by doing so we curse ourselves to become giants. The call to Yahweh's people is rather to become earthly repetitions of divine joy, sharers of the divine feast.

---

13 See also *De cherubim*, 37.123, where God's aseity implies his graciousness: 'But God is no salesman, hawking his goods in the market, but a free giver of all things, pouring forth eternal fountains of free bounties, and seeking no return. For He has no needs Himself and no created being is able to repay His gift.'

14 Yonge (trans.), *The Works*, p. 162.

15 Aeschylus, *Prometheus Bound*, in Paul Elmer More (ed. and trans.), 1899, *The Prometheus Bound of Aeschylus*, New York: Houghton Mifflin.

Sublime Sabbath

Having established that Philo of Alexandria articulates a new order of correspondence between human perfection and the divine, built on the analogical correspondence of human making to divine making, we must raise
a new question. Does this order of divine *poesis* take us fully into the order of divine perfection, or does the correspondence simply progress a few
steps deeper into the cloud, before ceasing at a new layer of metastasis? In
other words, can we call the divine creativity with which Moses' perfection
comes into alignment simply 'God', or is Yahweh still hidden, even as we
construct the tabernacle?

We have already noted the first bit of evidence that can guide us on
this question. In the instructions for Aaron's crown, Philo notes a layer of
symbolism gathered round the Tetragrammaton. Even if the name itself is
unspeakable except by the initiated, it still retains signifying force in the assembly. The four cuts in the crown are the four letters, which generate also
the cosmic fours of geometrical categories (point, line, plane and cube) and
the musical ratios of the octave (*Vit. Mos.* 2.23.115). The hidden name,
then, is not only sublime, since it generates a broader cosmic numerology.
Musical composition shares in the divine name, in virtue of its repetitions
and innovations on the musical scale. The architecture of the tabernacle,
which makes use of this geometry, thus becomes the materialization of the
unspeakable name.

On the other hand, however, the name itself remains unvocalizable, and
thus only the number of letters, and not the letters themselves, can generate
cosmic symbols (*Vit. Mos.* 2.23.115). Similarly, the name by which Yahweh
will be known, as he tells Moses, is 'the God of the three men whose
names express their virtue', that is, Abraham, who is the virtue of teaching,
Isaac, who is natural virtue, and Jacob, who is practical virtue (*Vit. Mos.*
1.14.75–6). These names are signs of the presented attributes of God, as are
the serpent, the leprous hand and the turning of water to blood (*Vit. Mos.*
1.14.77ff). God gives himself to be known by signs; but *ego eimi ho on* is
not so much a name as it is a vocal placeholder, signifying that 'no name
at all can properly be used of me' (*Vit. Mos.* 1.14.75–6). God allows his
name to be called, as one scholar puts it, but only by means of a 'deliberate
misuse of language'.[16]

Is this not fitting, though, as a theological marker of the limits of human
speech? Is it not imperative that Moses and the Israelites recognize the
transcendent gap between the Elohim of Abraham, Isaac and Jacob, the
God nameable by revelation, and Yahweh, the God whose name is ever
unpronounceable?

In fact, no. What is imperative for the theological integrity of Israel's
faith is the insistence that Yahweh and Elohim are simply one, and so the
God who is named through the virtues and accounts of the Patriarchs is just

---

16 David T. Runia, 1988, 'God and Man in Philo of Alexandria', *Journal of
Theological Studies* 39(1), p. 55.

as transcendent, even in those very virtues and accounts, as the 'new name' given to Moses. The separation of Elohim/Yahweh as revealed/unrevealed God, which is discernible after Philo in the early Rabbinic literature,[17] will always threaten to undermine Israel's monocultism. It will also threaten to undermine the theological integrity of human perfection, since the human can be perfected as human no further than the human can progress as a knowing, desiring creature. If it is not the 'perfect' God, but only the revealed God, who is manifest to humans, then humans will have a perfection that is quarantined from the being of God. Thus the Promethean problem of autonomy and extrinsic sovereignty returns.

What we find in Philo at this point is a translation of the Saturnine/Olympian division into a new, partially Aristotelian, partially Mosaic language of God's hidden essence and revealed attributes. So when Moses asks to see God's essence, Yahweh responds with a paternalistic and Delphic reprimand: 'Know thyself, then, and do not be led away by impulses and desires beyond thy capacity, nor let yearning for the unattainable uplift and carry thee off thy feet, for of the obtainable nothing shall be denied thee' (*De specialibus legibus*, 1.8.44).[18] When Moses asks a second time, his requests has altered: 'I beseech Thee that I may at least see the glory [δόξαν] that surrounds Thee, and by thy glory I understand the powers [δύναμις] that keep guard around Thee, of whom I would fain gain apprehension' (*De spec. leg.* 1.8.45). The response this time is a qualified no: 'While in their essence [κατὰ τὴν οὐσίαν] they are beyond your apprehension, they nevertheless present to your sight a sort of impress and copy of their activity [ἐνεργείας]' (*De spec. leg.* 1.8.47).[19] No one sees the essence of divine powers; but a copy of their activities will be discernible to Moses' eyes.

In the Septuagint's version of this narrative, it is the *doxsein* that are visible, while God's *prosopon* cannot be seen. But by introducing the *ousia–energeia* vocabulary, Philo creates a new order of distinction that alters the text significantly. In the actual Exodus narrative, not only is there no hint of the essence/energy terminology, but the entire exchange of requests and denials is also absent. Moses instead asks God to show him his ways and his presence, and God grants the request: 'I will do the very thing that you have asked' (Exod. 33.17). We should take the admonition 'you cannot see my face', then, neither as a limitation of Moses' potential divinization nor as a refusal of his desire for divine communion. The response is instead as much as to say, *you may see me in such a way as not to destroy yourself*: 'I will cover you with my hand until I have passed by' (Exod. 33.22). Indeed, when the encounter occurs the following morning, even this qualification seems to have evaporated: 'Yahweh descended in the cloud and stood with him there, and proclaimed the name, "Yahweh"' (Exod. 34.5).

---

17 See Runia, *Philo in Early Christian Literature*, pp. 12–16.

18 Philo, *De specialibus legibus*, Books I–III, in F. H. Colson (ed. and trans.), 1950, *Philo*, Vol. VII, Loeb Classical Library no. 320, Cambridge, MA: Harvard University Press.

19 Bradshaw, *Aristotle*, p. 63.

For Philo, by contrast, Moses asks to see what is not meant for his eyes, not once but twice. God must first lessen his desire, before granting him a blessing: 'Do not, then, hope to be ever able to apprehend Me or any of My powers in Our essence. But I readily and with right goodwill admit you to a share of what is attainable' (*De spec. leg.* 1.8.49).[20] The innovation modifies not only the Hebrew understanding of the knowledge of God, but the Greek as well, since for Plato and Aristotle, an essence is known by its *energiea*. Philo has in fact, via the now underscored Hebraic notion of the inscrutable name, used the fundamental principle of classical metaphysics to signify its own contrary: in the single case of God, the essence produces energies that render it unknowable.[21]

More promisingly, Philo implies in one place that the essence of creation itself is unknowable as well, which might lead us to conclude that human actualization retains an analogous purchase on divine actuality. The divine, as we saw above, has its essence in Sabbath rest, which is also perfect creative activity. The human, by contrast, must always labour in the time of the six days. But the seventh day is not only God's eternal and perfect dwelling, it is also the perfection of the world, since only on this day is creation complete. The manna in fact teaches Moses the Sabbath, since he sees enough of it fall on the sixth day to make gathering on the seventh superfluous. Reasoning analogously then from the creation of food in the desert to the creation of world out of nothingness, Moses comes to see that the Sabbath is a kind of transcendent space beyond creation itself: not really a day of creation, but the excess of the six days that comes both after and eternally before (*Vit. Mos.* 2.48.263–7). To the extent that Moses reads the divine signature in the manna, the difference between *ousia* and *energia* is less a prohibition than a separation-for-*theoria*. Like the religious gap in Plato, an excessive Sabbath marks the inability of human beings to accomplish their own perfecting. Moses discerns the human *telos* in God's six days of *energeia*; but this in turns leads him to the fathomless-but-knowable depths of God's essential seventh day. Moses himself, made to dwell in six days of labour, will see his own perfection as an always arriving, though never accomplished, rest.

However, it is when Philo begins to tell us how this gap is spanned that his project reaches its philosophical low point. When Moses discerns creation's Sabbath perfection, he 'did not so much conjecture as receive the impulse of divine inspiration under which he prophesied of the seventh day'. All prophecy is like this, and Moses only is prophetic when, as in the decoding of the manna, he 'No longer remained master of himself, but became inspired' (*Vit. Mos.* 2.46.250).[22] The question, so central to Plato and Aristotle, of how a human can share in divine perfection without being destroyed, is here surrendered by a return to prophetic metastasis. Philo can only bridge the religious gap by saying that Moses and the prophets

---

20 Colson (ed. and trans.), *Philo*, Vol. VII, p. 127.

21 See Bradshaw, *Aristotle*, pp. 59–64.

22 Yonge (trans.), *The Works*, p. 513.

no longer acted as humans when they perceived the true order of human perfection.

What does this mean for the human enterprise of *poesis*, which retains in Philo such an explicit linkage to divine creativity? The Law could only have been given, Philo says, in the desert, far away from cities. This is the case because Israel had to learn that the culture and laws made by humans are inventions that stand in stark contrast to the law of Moses, which comes as an oracle from God. Cities are full of 'mixed men' [μιγαδον] (*De Dec.* 2.10),[23] and their making is thus bound to be foreign to the making of God. Only the design of the tabernacle, received by inspiration far away from human creation, holds human *poesis* in participation with divine.

It is difficult to avoid the conclusion that the mixed men of Philo's bad cities are the inhabitants of Plato's good one. Philo sees the earthly path through cultic participation in God as problematic in that it risks reducing the transcendence of Yahweh to the ambiguities of human culture. It is not simply that humans become passive receivers of perfecting grace. Philo is aware that humans are agents, involved even in moments of 'pure' receptivity in action of some sort or another: like a man in a barber's chair, who is 'both *pasxein* and *poein*' as he 'cooperates receptively with the work of the barber' (*De cher.* 2.24.79). His arguments go beyond this easily spotted philosophical pitfall and in fact create a new one altogether: Philo's conception of the crossing of the human and divine in the character of the prophet ends in a fundamental undermining of his other assertions regarding human perfection. So, in receiving the divine, human prophets become something other than human. The prophet is 'called on the seventh day', and so no longer 'mixed' with the stuff of day six. He is of aether, not of earth.[24] The assembly of Israel are men and women made on the sixth day, mixed with aetherial inspirations only insofar as these are transmitted to them from Moses. The prophet alone can be perfected, and his perfection is in his exodus from the making-perfect of the six days to the made perfection of the seventh:

When the prophetic mind becomes divinely inspired and filled with God, it becomes like the monad, not being at all mixed with any of those things associated with duality. But he who is resolved into the nature of unity, is said to come near God in a kind of family relation, for having given up and left behind all moral kinds, he is changed into the divine, so that such men become kin to God and truly divine. (*Quaestiones et Solutiones in Exodum*, 2.29)[25]

---

23 Yonge (trans.), *The Works*, p. 518.
24 See Runia, *Philo in Early Christian Literature*, p. 70.
25 Philo, *Quaestiones et Solutiones in Exodus*, in Ralph Marcus (ed. and trans.), 1953, *Philo*, Supplement II, Loeb Classical Library no. 401, Cambridge, MA: Harvard University Press.

A new kind of deification announces itself here, albeit one with sources, as Goodenough rightly insisted, in the hermetic texts: a kinship with God that is no longer akin to humanity. Plato's account, once again, allows human cultic participation to direct itself towards godly transformation, 'so far as it was possible'. This is deification, in a sense, though it is not perfection, as the god or gods who share their being with us are imperfect. What Philo does, via Judaism, is to make God more perfect, but then suggest that human participation in God can either be cut off from God (by an essence/energy division, with the result that we share the perfection of a less than perfect God once again), or on the other hand cut off from humanity (by being alienated from the sixth day, with the result that the human is annihilated in divine perfection). Moses must either accept his imperfectibility with bold resignation (you can only know the *energeia* of my *dunameis*), or he must become divine in a cessation of the nature that existed before. Either way, perfection is defeated.

If Philo gives us a new analogical relation of human craft to the divine craftsman, and in such a way as to overcome the imperfection of the Platonic demiurge, he also highlights more effectively than any before him the *aporia* of human perfection. What we desire when we yearn for our perfection is something more than the possessing of all that we can name as objects of our desire. Perfection is necessarily beyond our ability to receive or even name: the very structure of desire teaches us this, as do the myths of Tantalus and Sisyphus. So then we are either called to become like the imperfect gods, without ceasing to be human (Platonism), or we are inspired by the perfect God without becoming Godlike (Judaism). Combining the two constructions, Philo says that divine inspiration makes us Godlike, but at the cost of making us less humanlike. If the early Christians improve upon Philo's theological and philosophical ideal, they do so not in spite of his account of posthuman deification, but rather by thoroughly immersing themselves within it. Further, the fact that they are eventually able to overcome the *aporia* is due in no small part to the promise of analogical *poesis* that guides the Philonic commentaries.

SECOND MOVEMENT

Emergence

4

The Gift of Fire:
Perfection in the New Testament

> I said, 'It's certain there is no fine thing.
> Since Adam's fall but needs much labouring.'
>
> William Butler Yeats

Blessed Transgression

The gods of Genesis find the daughters of men desirable, and thereby invite the deluge as a judgement on their improper boundary-crossing; Zeus falls for Io, and this time it is the desired one herself who incurs wrath. Hera's response curses an insolence implied by the human maiden's very existence: 'Do you hope to ascend,' Hera as much as demands of her, 'to the stature of a goddess, simply because an Olympian loves you? You will be a beast instead.' If Yahweh's heaven is too perfect to allow such transgressive affairs to stand, Olympus is too imperfect to follow them through to an untragic end. 'Never may one of the Gods descend for my love': this line could have been uttered by the daughters of Methuselah just as easily as by the chorus at the Caucasus.

The erotic transgression at the opening of the New Testament takes a rather different path: 'The angel said to her, "Do not be afraid, Mary, for you have found favour with God. And now, you will conceive in your womb and bear a son, and you will name him Jesus"' (Luke 1.30–31).[1] There are no Nephilim to curse, since Yahweh himself is now the one filled with longing. And this time the maiden receives a blessing for attracting the gaze of Israel's God; though soon enough a sword will pierce her soul, this will not come as a curse for bearing God's child, but rather as a fringe benefit of mothering a radical (2.34–35).

With this unprecedented opening, a body of literature composed along an eastern trade route of first-century Rome begins to craft a new account of the human end. How is our vision of the human *telos* altered, if a divine

---

1 Many thanks to Brent Driggers for lending me his expertise on the texts and ideas in this chapter.

transgression of the boundary between heaven and earth now brings blessings rather than curses? Building on the logic of the Annunciation, the New Testament writers no longer assume that the gods have their place in the heavens, while men and women belong naturally and finally to earth. The blessing of Mary the Favoured One invokes a new possibility for the lives, work and aim of human beings in relation to the life, work and aim of God.

Working on the Lord's Day: John's Gospel and the Epistle to the Hebrews

Linguistic form never entirely abstracts itself from conceptual content; when the New Testament uses variations of the term *telos*, the Aristotelian notion of an actualized maturation is always near the surface. Perfection is the energetic achievement of a dynamic potential: so Jesus' parents return to Galilee when the circumcision rite is perfected (τελειωσάντων) (Luke 2.39); the devil departs from Jesus when each of his tests has reached its perfection (συντελέσας) (Luke 4.13);[2] the single last word from the cross, reflecting a completed life's work, is *Tetelestai*, 'It is perfect' (John 19.30).

John's Gospel especially develops this notion that a person's end lies in the accomplishment of work. The 'it is perfect' that Christ utters implies also that 'I' – the worker of this work – 'am perfect'. Jesus can expire because his task, his lifecraft, is finished.[3] Immediately though we begin to wonder what has become of Aristotelian *eudaimonia* here, since crucifixion is a rather unlucky sort of ending. Two verses prior, the text draws the contrast for us: 'After this, when Jesus knew that all was now finished (παντα τετέλεσται), he said (in order to fulfil the Scripture), "I am thirsty."' What has happened to the project of a human life, if the central human of the New Testament can die thirsty, and yet still perfect?

A parallel text from early in the Gospel gives us the indicators we need to answer this question. Coming to a well in Samaria, Jesus requests from a woman there what he will one day ask of a Roman soldier: 'Give me a drink' (4.7). But then he tells her that his thirst has little to do with the project of his life, since the water he himself offers is the sort that overrides all

---

2 See David Peterson, 1982, *Hebrews and Perfection: An Examination of the Concept of Perfection*, Cambridge: Cambridge University Press, p. 33. I have benefited from conversations with Doug Travis regarding the use of *teleio* and its variants in the New Testament.

3 Hoskyns makes an appealing case that it is actually Psalm 22 that 'is finished' in Jesus' cry. The psalm opens with forsakenness by God, and John 19.24 references the eighteenth verse directly as the providential provision for the casting of lots. Verses 30–31 close the psalm with the proclamation of the one who 'has done it', that is, brought deliverance to the end of the earth. If his last days are following this psalm like a script, then 'it is finished' means, first, that the psalm itself has come to an end; secondly, that the psalmic deliverance is now finished, complete, perfected. Edwyn Clement Hoskyns, 1947, *The Fourth Gospel*, London: Faber and Faber, p. 531.

human thirst, just as the food that nourishes him is not the kind affected by bodily hunger. 'My food is to do the will of him who sent me and to complete (τελειώσω) his work' (4.34). His work is not his own, but the Father's, and the Son will be whole and nourished only when the Father's work is finished. The work he receives from his Father is to 'harvest' his Father's earthly fields:[4] to glorify the Father's name throughout the earth (17.4) and to prepare a place in heaven for those who share in his glory (14.2–4). It is also this work that will take him beyond the realm of Aristotelian fortune, since the Father sends him forth to come into an unreceptive land (1.11) and to receive the hatred of the world (15.18). This is the work he finishes on the cross, and that renders his life complete, actual, perfect, even as what looks like 'his own', his body and its need to live, breathe, drink and flourish, is so obviously incomplete. Like a carpenter's apprentice, Jesus has no work of his own beyond the completion of the master's craft.[5]

Because the work that Jesus does is a continuation of the Father's labours, John can recast Jesus' actions – and chiefly his work of healing – as a retelling of the creation story. So in the Sabbath day healing of a man born blind, Jesus spreads mud on the man's eyes, explaining to his disciples that 'we must work the works of him who sent me' (9.4). He is essentially perfecting the man's creation out of the dust of the earth,[6] the work of the sixth day, marking the temporary postponement of the seventh day's rest. An earlier Sabbath day healing account makes the same point: 'The Jews started persecuting Jesus, because he was doing such things on the Sabbath. But Jesus answered them, "My Father is still working, and I also am working" (5.16–17).

Jesus works on the Sabbath because his Father, Creator of heaven and earth, is still working. But why does the Father work on the Sabbath? Did

---

4 Both Raymond Brown and Ben Witherington III underline the parallels of misunderstood water (vv. 7–15) with misunderstood food (vv. 31–33), and they see both as leading to the 'metaphorical harvest': Christ offers living water; his food is his Father's work; thus he and his disciples will labor in the Father's fields, 'gathering fruit for eternal life' (v. 36). Raymond Brown, 1966, *The Gospel according to John (i–xii)*, Garden City, NY: Doubleday, pp. 178–82; Ben Witherington III, 1995, *John's Wisdom: A Commentary on the Fourth Gospel*, Louisville, KY: Westminster John Knox, pp. 119–25.

5 Brown, *The Gospel*, p. 218.

6 And this is perhaps a clue as well to what it means, from Chapter 3, to be 'born again'. See Wes Howard-Brook, 1994, *Becoming Children of God: John's Gospel and Radical Discipleship*, Maryknoll, NY: Orbis Books, pp. 216–18. A student in one of my classes in Austin made this suggestion about the mud. While many commentaries note that the making of a spittle-paste was a violation of Sabbath laws (Brown, *The Gospel*, p. 379; Witherington, *Wisdom*, p. 183; Herman N. Ridderbos, 1997, *The Gospel according to John: A Theological Commentary*, trans. John Vriend, Grand Rapids, MI: Eerdmans, pp. 335–7), none that I have found make the creation connection. However, in light of the Gospel's opening in the creation narrative and the presence here of a pool of water (9.7), I suspect that she was on to an important insight.

he not finish the work of creation long ago? For John he did not, and the Gospel demonstrates this with its characterization of the Logos as the one through whom 'all things came into being', who in turn 'came to what was his own, and his own people did not accept him' (1.3, 11). The work is not complete, since the material from which it is wrought has come estranged from its designer. A creation that does not know or reflect its creator is profoundly imperfect, and the creator of such a work of art will always be faced with a difficult decision: redeem the work or dump it and start over? From Genesis 3 onwards, the biblical God chooses the former over the latter, and now John's Gospel gives us a new interpretation of that choice. If creation is not yet *tetelestai*, then we are still within the six days of labour. In a sort of de facto revision of history, the Johannine theme proclaims that it is not Sabbath until God rests, and if God is still working, it is obviously not yet Sabbath.[7]

The Son, then, comes to complete the work of creating a world. But now, in a world of people who 'loved darkness rather than light', the Son must, in the great Johannine double entendre, 'be lifted up' (3.14; 8.28; 12.32, 34). Why is the crucifixion the ultimate act of the six days of creation, the point of history at which Christ can 'draw all people' to himself? John's Gospel leaves us with a kind of metaphorical hieroglyphic: to gaze upward at the suspended Son is to gaze upward at God, and thus to know our Creator for the first time. Drawn to the Logos, who was in the beginning with God, we find our end, and it is perfect.

What John's Gospel suggests in an image, the Epistle to the Hebrews works out in – surprisingly Philonic – theological detail.[8] Assuming the same relation of creation to the Son (1.2) as did John, Hebrews likewise argues that the work of the Father and Son together is the perfecting of creation. But here the Epistle plunges into the ontological mechanics of the task, and finds at the heart of the work the completion of the Levitical project: creation is perfected by Christ's work, because that work completes the atoning work begun by Yahweh in Israel's tabernacle.

Again like in John, the Sabbath ambiguity arises: God's 'works were finished at the foundation of the world. For in one place it speaks about the seventh day as follows, "And God rested on the seventh day from all his works"' (4.3–4). On the other hand, the sin that immediately marks

---

7 Ridderbos, *John*, p. 196, argues impressively that the issue of Sabbath work is 'incorporated into, and made serviceable to, the consummating and saving work of God in the Son'. Thus once we understand that God's work is to complete creation through Christ's saving work, the question of what is or is not permissible on the day of God's rest can disappear from the narrative: God is clearly not resting, if Jesus is still saving, so a postponed, eschatological rest collides completely and irreducibly with a life of saving labour.

8 The key text here is L. K. K. Dey, 1975, *The Intermediary World and Patterns of Perfection in Philo and Hebrews*, Missoula, MO: Scholars Press. Dey argues from several points, including linguistic patterns and theological imagery, that Hebrews is repeating or reinterpreting Philo.

created things in the Israelite chronicles reveals their unfinished natures, and so also we read, 'They shall not enter my rest' (4.5). Is the work finished, then, or still left to be perfected? The Epistle answers with a construction that indicates the future direction of theology in the age of Athanasius and beyond: an ontological distinction that separates the work of the Creator in the heavenly realms from his work in creation. The former is accomplished and complete; the latter continues on. Thus God rests, even while 'the promise of entering his rest is still open' (4.1).[9]

The liturgical work in the tabernacle forms the hinge of this distinction. When creation is made perfect (τελειῶσαι) (10.1) through atonement, it will enter into Yahweh's Sabbath rest. The Epistle rereads the history of Israel before God as a rhythm of ritual gift-giving intended to work toward this perfecting of creation.[10] 'Every high priest chosen from among mortals is put in charge of things pertaining to God on their behalf, to offer gifts and sacrifices for sins' (5.1). This gift-giving pries open the grip of Adam and Eve around the fruit, and renarrates Cain's quest for favour, the tower-builders for the heavens, and even the sons of God for the daughters of earth. Just as in Philo, Hebrews can recast the 'making of worship' as a type of the making of creation itself: the tabernacle of the wilderness is 'a sketch and shadow of the heavenly one' (8.5), and so functions on earth as a kind of secondary act of creation. The tabernacle stands between the imperfect people and the perfect Sabbath, and those who pass through it can enter Yahweh's rest (6.19), so perfecting the six-day work of the creating God.[11]

The new emphasis in the Epistle, beyond Philo, is the temporary and necessarily renewable character of the *poesis* of this tabernacle.[12] Precisely because it is a sketch, the sacrifices of this temple are incomplete, and must be sanctified and offered annually (9.7; 10.9–10). The author here echoes Philo's ratio between the creation of the world and the creation of the tabernacle within it, but adds a third, more basic kind of *poesis*. The heavenly making is not simply the act of creation now, but a 'begetting' inherent to the notion of Godhead itself. This is a making greater than the creation of

---

9 Harold W. Attridge, 1989, *The Epistle to the Hebrews*, Philadelphia: Fortress Press, pp. 123–8, points to the pattern of apocalyptic here, as Hebrews picks up from other sources in the genre the notion of a 'new Sabbath' in a 'new land', the 'new end' of a 'new creation'. He also notes the Philo parallels, without noting the important distinction traced in the paragraphs above. See also pp. 222–3.

10 Peterson, *Hebrews and Perfection*, pp. 168ff.; Attridge, *Hebrews*, p. 127; see also Norman Russell, 2005, *The Doctrine of Deification in the Greek Patristic Tradition*, Oxford: Oxford University Press, p. 85.

11 See the impressive study of Judith Hoch Wray, where the rhetorical use of 'rest', as a theological term distinct from land and Sabbath, allows her to identify Hebrews as a 'first century homily', inviting its audience to participate in God's work. Judith Hoch Wray, 1998, *Rest as a Theological Metaphor in the Epistle to the Hebrews and the Gospel of Truth: Early Christian Homiletics of Rest*, Atlanta: Scholars Press.

12 Peterson, *Hebrews*, pp. 126ff.

earth, since it occurs within a 'perfect tent (not made with hands, that is, not of this creation)' (9.11). This is indeed greater even than the making of the heavens, since 'to which of the angels did God ever say, "You are my Son; today I have begotten you"?' (1.5). The act of filial generation fills the Epistle's vision of God with a new kind of making, in which God eternally crafts a 'reflection of God's glory and the exact imprint of God's very being' (1.3).[13] The people of Israel invited to Sabbath can enter, through the representation of their high priest, but only ever imperfectly, not only 'because of unbelief' (3.19), but because the entire cultic *poesis* is suspended at such a great distance from the archetypal *poesis* of God.[14] Thus the Epistle makes its 'main point': 'We have such a high priest, one who is seated at the right hand of the throne of the Majesty in the heavens, a minister in the sanctuary and the true tent that the Lord, and not any mortal, has set up' (8.1–2).

A shadow image will always be incomplete, since only the offerings of the 'true tent' can be perfect. But the Christ story insists that the priest of this heavenly tent enters the shadow realms in order to perform his oblations there. The only perfect one comes to earth in the guise of an illegal priest: had he been earthly born, 'he would not be a priest at all, since there are priests who offer gifts according to the law' (8.4). Here, lifting himself up, as both priest and sacrifice, he completes on earth what was always already complete in God.[15] 'It is perfect' becomes true, in light of this invasion, in a way that was unimaginable before. Humans can enter God's seventh day now, though not in a 'naturally' human way, as this would entail hesitancy and the need for constant renewal. Now we slope upwards into Sabbath, working as a kind of divine resting, resting as a human work, sharing divinity even as we construct our humanity. Now that the work of the earthly temple has become the work of the heavenly tabernacle, sanctification has become perfect (10.14), and our entrance into Sabbath rest/work is complete.[16]

---

13 This theme of an intensified making caused by intensified proximity to God is brought out more sharply by Alan Mitchell than by either Attridge or Peterson. See Mitchell, 2007, *Hebrews*, Collegeville, MN: Liturgical Press, pp. 40–6.

14 Marie E. Isaacs, 1992, *Sacred Space: An Approach to the Theology of the Epistle to the Hebrews*, Sheffield: Sheffield Academic Press, p. 80, suggests that the opposition between Israel and the Church is not primarily a replacement of the former by the latter, as is often assumed. The guiding metaphor, she says, is God's household, and while Israel enters and enters again, always partially, Christ's followers are invited to enter fully and perfectly. Like Deuteronomy, she says, 'Hebrews addresses its readers as a generation standing on the brink of entry into the promised land.'

15 Attridge, *Hebrews*, pp. 210, 242–3, suggests a reading along these lines.

16 Peterson, *Hebrews and Perfection*, pp. 149–53, shows the highly important logic implicit in the text: since Christ's sacrifice is unique, the 'striving' of 12.14 and other passages is not towards a cleansing from sin, but is rather an incremental and dynamic journey into God's holy being. Humans are made sinless once, in Christ's priestly sacrifice; but they are sanctified constantly, as they come to enter, through the striving of life, this sacrificial act.

The Gift of Fire: Perfection in the New Testament

Here, though, we must begin to press upon the New Testament texts the philosophical question that has guided us throughout the present book. How is the 'completion' offered in Christ a perfection of the human form? If the perfect tent through which we make our entry into Sabbath rest is 'not of this creation', do we not emerge on the other side as no longer of this creation? How does Christ's priestly sacrifice perfect, rather than abolish, the temporal integrity of the human essence?

Both John and Hebrews indicate a common general trajectory, though without sculpting a vision with any philosophical rigour. The trajectory appears in the mixed pronouns of Christ's aside to his disciples, 'we must work the works of him who sent me.' It likewise appears in the Epistle's insistence that the perfect heavenly priest is 'made perfect' through his sufferings on earth (Heb. 2.10; 12.23), so that we can now 'go on toward perfection' (τελειότητα) (6.1). The Son who comes to make perfect the Father's work shares this work with us. 'Go on toward perfection' is not a call to us to take incremental steps toward moral flawlessness, as this is far from the Epistle's conception of the term. Rather it is a charge to take up the outlaw work of the heavenly priest, and make atonement for the sins of creation. Is this work a human one, or is it transferred extrinsically to us by sharing the work of the divine Son? This is our question, but not that of John and Hebrews: they insist only that we are called, invited, charged, to do this work. In the wake of the ascended Christ, the unfinished work of creating/atoning becomes the perfecting work of his disciples (Heb. 1.3; 10.12–13; John 17.11–13). We too may now 'be made one' with the Father, thus come to our human end having accomplished a divine work. We too may now die thirsty and perfect.

Justified by gift: Matthew's Gospel and Paul's Letters

If the moral dimension of perfection is understated in Hebrews and John, it is by no means absent from the New Testament. Indeed, a significant portion of these writings casts itself as a Midrash on Torah, and in that sense only intensifies attention to the Law. So, as Jesus comes teaching in the synagogues of Galilee and Judaea, he comes offering a 'new commandment' (John 13.34; 1 John 2.8), thus presenting himself as a new Moses in the 'new Moses tradition' of Jeremiah and the prophets. Luke's Gospel opens in a way reminiscent of Exodus: Israel is held captive by a powerful king, God's voice has gone silent and the identity of the tribes is so much in chaos that a direct descendant of David is a poor carpenter in a small country town.[17] Like Moses, Jesus comes to 'proclaim release to the captives' (4.18). Matthew's Gospel is in a sense a life of Moses, parallel in many ways to the text of his contemporary Philo, though now Jesus of Nazareth plays the role of the new Moses: thus he is rescued from geno-infanticide (2.13–14, 16–18), he is called out of Egypt back to the land of Canaan (2.15, 19–20), he is turned away by his own people (13.54–58).

---

17 See Josef Ratzinger/ Pope Benedict XVI, 2008, *Jesus of Nazareth: From the Baptism in the Jordan to the Transfiguration*, New York: Bloomsbury, p. 12.

This is especially the case when Matthew writes that Jesus 'went up the mountain' (5.1) with his disciples and the multitude that followed, and that he sat down and began to teach them. Here we first glimpse the novelty of this Moses and his Torah. The mountain is his Sinai and the crowds are his assembly of Israelites;[18] nowhere to be found, however, is the cloud of darkness, the cloud that increases in density in the proclamations of Jeremiah and Ezekiel. The tribes do not tremble at the mountain's foot; they gather at the top and hear how they are blessed.[19] *Makarios* here translates the Hebrew *barukh*, the term used throughout the Psalms in praise of Yahweh as well as for an attribute of Yahweh's people: those, that is, who receive blessing from their blessed God. Further, a strong sense of *eudaimonia* returns here, since the two terms often appear coupled pleonastically in Aristotle and Plato and have by this stage in the language become almost entirely synonymous.[20] From both the Greek and Hebrew, then, the blessed one is happy, but also a recipient of goodness from a benefactor: to be *makarios* is to be made happy by a good gift. These who are gathered upon the mountain receive as gifts the kingdom of heaven, comfort, the earth, righteousness, mercy, the vision of God, adoption as God's children and a reward in heaven (Matt. 5.1–12). Jesus then goes on to tell them of the excessive righteousness (5.20) that comprises his new Torah.

You have heard that it was said to those of ancient times, 'You shall not murder; and whoever murders shall be liable to judgment.' But I say to you that if you are angry with a brother of sister, you will be liable to judgment. (5.21–22)

You have heard that it was said, 'You shall not commit adultery.' But I say to you that everyone who looks at a woman with lust has already committed adultery with her in his heart. (5.27–28)

Again, you have heard that it was said to those of ancient times, 'You shall not swear falsely, but carry out the vows you have made to the Lord.' But I say to you, Do not swear at all . . . (5.33–34)

---

18 Ratzinger, *Jesus*, p. 66; Ulrich Luz, 2007, *Matthew 1–7: A Commentary (Hermeneia)*, trans. James E. Crouch, Minneapolis: Fortress Press, p. 182.

19 Though the second person formula in Luke demonstrates the intended reception of blessing more explicitly, this is not because Matthew's beatitudes should be read as less attentive to the crowd. Matthew is here following the older form of the 'Wisdom beatitude', such as Psalm 40: 'Happy are those who make the Lord their trust' (v. 4). Luke, by contrast, is developing this form rather more freely. See Luz, *Matthew*, pp. 187–8.

20 See Robert Spaemann, 2005, *Happiness and Benevolence*, London and New York: T&T Clark, pp. 57ff, for the point about classical Greek. For the new sense in Koine, see Luz, *Matthew*, p. 190: 'Μακάριος, in Greek originally a term reserved for the gods, in Koine can hardly be distinguished any longer from ευδαίμων and means "happy" in the fullest sense of the word.'

The trajectory of these early chapters in Matthew's Gospel is obvious enough. A new Moses has come, and he will walk the assembly of Israel up Sinai into the very midst of the divine presence. What they will encounter there will not be the abolition of the Torahs of Moses and the Prophets (5.17), but neither will they receive the Tablets in their old form. The prophet on the mountain proclaims an intensified ethic, corresponding to the radicalized proximity of the people to their once unapproachable God. Now they can see God, inherit his kingdom; they also must share his righteousness, which explains the admonition: 'Unless your righteousness exceeds that of the scribes and Pharisees, you will never enter the kingdom of heaven' (20).[21]

Paul of Tarsus is the New Testament's apostle to those peoples not immediately answerable to Israel's Law. Still, when he writes to the churches scattered throughout the Empire, the new law introduced by Christ is one of his stock images (Rom. 3.27; 8.2; Gal. 6.2). Where Matthew's Jesus, though, at least initially calls for a deepening and extending of Torah, Paul begins by unmasking a basic irony in the Torah itself: those who know Torah best know that it says that it cannot justify us, or make us righteous, before God. 'Now we know that whatever the law says, it speaks to those who are under the law' (Rom. 3.19), and what it says turns out to be, 'There is no one who is righteous, not even one' (3.10).[22] In fact, even if the texts themselves did not tell the readers of Torah that no one is righteous, the attempt to practice the *mitvot* would: 'If it had not been for the law, I would not have known sin. I would not have known what it is to covet if the law had not said, "You shall not covet." But sin, seizing an opportunity in the commandment, produced in me all kinds of covetousness' (7.7–8).

---

21 Ratzinger, *Jesus*, pp. 99ff.; Frank J. Matera, 1996, *New Testament Ethics: The Legacies of Jesus and Paul*, Louisville: Westminster John Knox Press, pp. 36–63. Matera summarizes the entire Matthaean ethic, with its account of an excessive command that is to be performed and embodied rather than simply observed by speech and tradition, in the phrase 'doing the greater righteousness'. See also Eduard Lohse, 1991, *Theological Ethics of the New Testament*, trans. M. Eugene Boring, Minneapolis: Fortress Press, pp. 67–73, for important references to similarly excessive beatitudes in the Talmudic literature of the Hellenistic world.

22 Stanley Stowers suggests with some persuasiveness that 'all have turned away' and 'all have sinned' of verses 12 and 23 are not universal in the abstract sense, but in a particular and apocalyptic sense: in these times, all have turned and are turning from God. Stanley Stowers, 1994, *A Re-reading of Romans: Justice, Jews, and Gentiles*, New Haven: Yale University Press, pp. 166–9, 194ff. Luise Schottroff corroborates this reading, pointing out that there is no reason to assume that Paul means 'the *will* to fulfill the law is sin', only that as it happens, humans fail to fulfil the law 'without exception'. The difference is important, and ties to the question of how much of his own Judaism Paul rejected. Luise Schottroff, 2004, '"Law-Free Gentile Christianity" – What about the Women? Feminist Analyses and Alternatives', trans. Barbara and Martin Rumscheidt, in Amy Jill Levine (ed.), *A Feminist Companion to Paul*, Cleveland: Pilgrim Press, pp. 183–94.

The project of a human life reaches completion then, not simply in the following of an earthbound law of human nature, but, as Christ says, only as we surpass this with an excessive righteousness that issues from the very presence of Yahweh. But is Paul not simply stating the obvious conclusion, in Romans 7? If humans fail to follow even Israel's earthy *deutero-nomos*, an excessive righteousness is beyond our scope entirely? How can we share the righteousness of an uncloudy Sinai when, as Paul ironically concludes, the only true *nomos* is this: 'when I want to do what is good, evil lies close at hand' (7.21)?

The apostle's own answer is that we do not become pleasing to God by contractually obligating God to call us righteous based on our performance of the human script. Our righteousness is given to us ahead of time by God, before any question of our deserts: 'since all have sinned and fall short of the glory of God; they are now justified by his grace as a gift' (3.23–4).[23] We are justified by gift. This is already the case for Abraham, who, Paul points out, receives the promise of blessing 430 years before the Sinai code arrives (Gal. 3.17), and who is declared righteous before he even receives the pre-Torah *mitvah* of circumcision (Rom. 4.10). If Abraham is not made righteous in God's eyes by following the law, neither, we may assume, is Moses, Elijah or Josiah. All are good not because they manage to avoid covetousness, but because they receive a grace that frees them from the evil that always 'lies close at hand'.

What is the content of this freeing gift? This question takes us to the very heart of Paul's theology. Abraham is given the promise of many descendants, and he believes that the promise will be fulfilled despite the condition of his own body, 'which was already as good as dead', or of Sarah's barren womb (Rom. 4.19–20). The faith of Abraham is not simply a trust that God will do what he says; it is implicitly more: a faith in the God who 'gives life to the dead and calls into existence the things that do not exist' (Rom. 4.17). The promise of a son is the promise of resurrection from the dead. He trusts, then, in the Christ who is only connoted, as it were, not denoted by the promise (Gal. 3.16). By trusting that he and his wife will return from the (mostly) dead and generate new life, he places his hope in the great event that Paul insists changes the make-up of humankind. Abraham is thus not justified by his conscious posture of assent to God's will, in the first place, but by Christ's resurrection, though he himself only believes in this event, as Paul says elsewhere, as 'in a mirror, dimly' (1 Cor. 13.12). As for Abraham, Paul says, so for us: we are justified by resurrection (Rom. 4.25).[24]

---

23 Stephen Westerholm and Douglas Harink help 'de-Protestantize' our reading of Pauline justification in the way compatible with what I am suggesting above. Stephen Westerholm, 2004, *Perspectives Old and New on Paul: The 'Lutheran Paul' and His Critics*, Grand Rapids: Eerdmans, pp. 352ff; Douglas Harink, 2003, *Paul among the Postliberals: Pauline Theology Beyond Christendom and Modernity*, Grand Rapids: Brazos, pp. 25–65.

24 Michael J. Gorman, 2004, *Apostle of the Crucified Lord: A Theological Introduction to Paul and His Letters*, Grand Rapids: Eerdmans, pp. 98ff.

We may be tempted here to rush Paul along to a conclusion, and say that since the gift of resurrection is what makes us holy and righteous, his new Torah of Christ actually amounts to the whole cloth abolition of the sort of ethic that governs life before death. This will not quite do though, since when he turns in Romans 9 to deal directly with the question of Israel, he begins by celebrating the oracles with which they are entrusted (3.2), and includes Torah in the list along with adoption, glory and worship, all of which are marks of his own preaching.[25] Further, Romans 12 commands the Christians of Rome to 'be transformed' so that they may come to know the 'good and acceptable and perfect' will of God, and this ends up launching him into a long train of imperatives that certainly have the ring of legal teachings on righteousness:

> Hate what is evil, hold fast to what is good; love one another with mutual affection; outdo one another in showing honour. Do not lag in zeal, be ardent in spirit, serve the Lord. Rejoice in hope, be patient in suffering, persevere in prayer. Contribute to the needs of saints; extend hospitality to strangers. Bless those who persecute you . . . (12.9–13)

A few verses later, he goes so far as to restate the second tablet of the Decalogue and calls it the content of the command to 'Love your neighbour as yourself' (13.9). So not only does Paul celebrate Israel for receiving the Law, but he extends, restates and summarizes that law for both Jew and Gentile Christians. Are we then not back to the problem of the unworkable excessive righteousness? What has happened here to the message that 'you are not under law but under grace' (6.14)?

Complicating things even further, 'having faith in Christ' is itself a command of sorts, a law that, even if it stands above all others, is still a law, and still calls the ones who seek perfection to obey it. So, as Paul acknowledges in Galatians, by calling us to make an 'effort to be justified in Christ, . . . I build up again the very things that I once tore down' (2.17–18).

The gospel of grace, then, is not a Not-Law, as if grace and law were equivocal and mutually exclusive ethics (Gal. 3.21). This new law, and the new commandments it entails, are distinct from Torah not by form, we might say, but by content.[26] They are *mitvot* still, but Paul has a new

---

25 A point that Badiou conveniently overlooks in characterizing Paul as 'against the Law'. Alain Badiou, 2003, *Saint Paul: The Foundation of Universalism*, trans. Ray Brassier, Stanford: Stanford University Press, 75ff. Luise Schottroff, 'Law-free', pp. 183–94, demonstrates how the very idea of a 'law-free Gentile Christianity' mischaracterizes both the early Christian movement and the Rabbinic environment that parented it. In addition, because of the close association of law with circumcision in Paul, the 'law-free' reading entails an inherent misogyny, as if the entire question of Christian freedom is whether or not boys need a *mohel*.

26 See Frank J. Matera, 1992, *Galatians (Sacra Pagina)*, Collegeville, MN: The Liturgical Press, pp. 97–100. This is the major flaw in Troels Engberg-Pedersen's argument for a Stoic Paul. Troels Engberg-Pedersen, 2000, *Paul and the Stoics*,

confidence that the resurrective power of Christ will make us perfectly law-abiding, and that the new law will not metastasize over the 'unfathomable depths' of Israel's God (Rom. 11.33). The pivotal point of Romans is the segue from Chapter 7, the Paul who discovers how to covet only when the Law tells him not to, to Chapter 8, where 'God has done what the law, weakened by the flesh', which is to say weakened by our inability to do good consistently, 'could not do' (8.3). The resurrection that he describes as the work of the Spirit in 8.11 is a direct response to the 'I died' of 7.10. Resurrection happens in him now, that is to say, just as it happened already in Abraham and Sarah, when the good-as-dead body and barren womb produced Isaac. Isaac is the risen Christ, as is Paul's newly discovered ability not to covet. 'The Spirit of him who raised Jesus from the dead' gives life even now to Paul's mortal body (8.11), so that when he puts on Christ (13.14), he will find that he can in fact do the works of the law.

This is why he says early on in Romans, surprisingly, that 'it is the do-ers of the Law who will be justified' (2.13).[27] Justification by faith does not exempt us from justification by works – here, the works of Paul's new Torah, which are like the commandments of Jesus' excessive Sinai. Rather, justification places us within the one who died and was raised, so that our Romans 7 identity does not simply die (or, more likely, kill us, as in 7.11), but dies with Christ, and rises up in Romans 8, prepared and enabled to seek out and embody God's perfect will. He is a new creature: 'so if anyone is in Christ, there is a new creation: everything old has passed away; see, everything has become new!' (2 Cor. 5.17) What Paul calls sanctification ('αγιασμον), taking over the Hebrew root *qds*[28] for the making holy of a priestly offering, is in fact synonymous with justification, since to become holy is to be 'reckoned as righteous' by God (Rom. 4.11; 6.19).[29] The gift of resurrection places a life in Christ: 'for you have died, and your life is hidden with Christ in God' (Col. 3.3). The gift then includes the sanctifying of the resurrected offering – now not only the first fruits of our labours, but our entire lives as first fruits of the world's resurrected life (2 Thess. 2.13).

Louisville, Westminster John Knox. By reducing Stoicism to a formula in which a transcendent object calls for a transformation in a subject, he notices a 'striking, for-mal similarity with Paul' (p. 67). Setting aside the question of whether there is any-thing about this formula that would keep Muhammad, Siddhartha and Confucius from being classified as Stoics as well, I repeat the observation above: Paul himself takes it to be the content of his gospel, not the form, that makes it distinct.

27 Following the view outlined and developed by Westerholm that 'Paul means what he says in Romans 2.13,' and is not simply adopting his opponents view as a rhetorical strategy. Westerholm, *Perspectives*, p. 154ff.

28 David P. Wright, 1992, 'Holiness (OT)', in *The Anchor Bible Dictionary*, Vol. III, New York: Doubleday, p. 237.

29 Gorman, *Apostle*, pp. 111–12, implies something close to this, by sketch-ing out the theopolitical character of sanctification. Righteousness is a distinctive lifestyle enabled by God and lived by a Christian community. Thus Christ is the 'believers' source of righteousness' (justification) and also the 'believer's holiness' (sanctification).

The justifying gift acts to make us holy, Paul suggests, primarily by re-calling our own weakness. So Paul's own frailties, he admits, are them-selves gifts from God that eat away at his charades of self-righteousness – his attempts, that is, to find himself self-justified, rather than made just through the gift of resurrection. An unbearable affliction in Asia (2 Cor. 1.8ff) brought Paul and Timothy to the point of death, but this in turn served as a reminder that only divine grace perfects our human lives, 'so that we should rely not on ourselves but on God who raises the dead' (1.9). Likewise, Paul's thorn in the flesh brought to him the comforting assurance from God, 'My grace is sufficient for you, for power (δύναμις) is made per-fect (τελεῖται) in weakness. . . . Therefore I am content with weakness . . . for whenever I am weak, then I am strong' (12.9–10).[30] All human weak-ness and strength is ultimately inscribed in Christ, who 'was crucified in weakness, but lives by the power of God' (13.4).

I have intentionally used two less common 'justification by . . .' phrases to this point, and avoided a third more common one. The meaning of Paul's 'justification by faith' (Rom. 3.28; 5.1; Gal. 2.16; 3.24) must be given in light of these two previous renditions, gift and resurrection. Faith itself might otherwise be taken as a 'work' in the Pauline grammar, a con-tractual obligation for which the reckoning of our righteousness is granted as an earned wage. It is not the work of believing that makes us righteous, for Paul, but rather a particular *pistis*, the posture of trust in the gift of the resurrecting work of God through Christ.[31] Faith justifies because it tells of how we will be transformed, in our resurrected bodies, into creatures who are able to keep covenant, avoid covetousness and be holy – faith in Christ justifies because the content of this faith sanctifies. Like Abraham, who was in the dark as to the ultimate expression of the promise's fulfilment, our resurrected and incorruptible bodies are still a mystery to us (1 Cor. 15.50–57). As 1 John puts it, 'What we will be has not yet been revealed' (1 John. 3.2); what we will do has, at least to a certain degree. We will do works of love, extend hospitality, contribute to the needs of saints, love our neighbours as ourselves. We will do the new law, because we are the new creatures able to perform these works.

So for the earliest Christian writers, human beings have the ability, if led by the Spirit who was active in the resurrection of Christ, to do the higher good. Where does this new Torah, and increased attention to moral possibil-ity, leave the enquiry into perfection – a term (or set of grammatically related terms) which Paul in fact uses only rarely? Recalling the metastatic resigna-tion of the prophets, it is not yet clear that this counts as a perfecting of the human form. Matthew teaches a greater righteousness, and Paul explains the theological warrant for hoping that we can fulfil it; John and Hebrews explain that this higher righteousness is founded on a transfer of tasks, so that the Christian vocation is actually a completing of the divine work. But this does not yet mean that we have stepped beyond the bound/unbound

---

30 See Gorman, *Apostle*, pp. 327–30.
31 Matera, *Galatians*, p. 138; Westerholm, *Perspectives*, pp. 352ff.

Prometheus *aporia*. New moral possibility and newly assigned labour does not immediately transfer into the metaphysics of *dunamis/energeia* or *phusis/ telos*. Could Paul, for instance, not be read as suggesting that the human nature is chronically imperfect and thus its only hope lies in standing down before the new nature introduced by resurrection? In that case, the suspended girdles remain severed, and the human form can fulfil all righteousness only in receiving the gift of a sublime and extrinsic divine perfection.

Holiness Perfected

The littleness of gods: Matthew's teleios tropes

Already, though, Matthew's Gospel has altered our image of a holiness that belongs at the foot of Sinai rather than the peak, simply by collapsing the distance between them. In fact, by referring to his new Torah on two separate occasions as the path to perfection, Matthew's Christ formulates the key shift that drives the plot and proclamation not only of the first Gospel, but of the *evangelion* presented throughout the New Testament.

The first perfection trope in Matthew comes in the midst of the Sermon on the Mount, after the 'you have heard . . . but I say . . .' anaphora discussed above. The concluding word of this new law of excessive righteousness is 'Be perfect (τέλιοι), therefore, as your heavenly Father is perfect' (τέλειός; 5.48). This is an imperative that must surely have sounded as startling to the ears of first-century Galilean Jews as it does to us now. It is, on one reading, simply a repetition of the Levitical theme as sounded within the Holiness School. If we draw clues as to Matthew's meaning from the second-century BCE translators of the Septuagint, however, we will note that the term they use to translate the Hebrew *qedosim* is *hagios*, rather than *teleios*: 'You shall be holy ('άγιοι) to me; for I the Lord am holy ('άγιος)' (Lev. 19.2).[32] Matthew's new Torah, in this case, offers a degree of participation in God that exceeds that of the Holiness Code, just as the 'greater righteousness' he installs exceeds that of the Pharisees. The writer tempers his construction with shades of another term, the Hebrew *tamim*, often rendered 'blameless' in English as in the NRSV's Psalm 18.25: 'with the blameless you show yourself blameless'.[33] *Tamim* is also sometimes rendered *teleios* in LXX.[34] This term bears a sense of fullness and completion in the Hebrew, and perhaps it appealed to the Evangelist as more

---

32 I am using Alfred Rahlfs's two-volume edition of the Septuagint, in the sixth edition: Alfred Rahlf (ed.), 1935, *Septuaginta*, Stuttgart : Privilegierte Württembergische Bibelanstalt.

33 Paul Nadim Tarazi, 1996, *The Old Testament: An Introduction*, Vol. III: *Psalms and Wisdom*, Crestwood, New York: St. Vladimir's Seminary Press, p. 65.

34 Botterweck et al. (eds), 2006, *The Theological Dictionary of the Old Testament*, trans. David E. Green, Grand Rapids, MI: Eerdman, Vol XV, s.v. *tamam*, p. 701.

readily compatible with the philosophically weighty *teleios*.[35] Whatever the case, Matthew seems to exceed the notion of a shared holiness here, suggesting that our ultimate end is deeply and inextricably connected with the ultimate end for God. Find a finished humanity in the 'finished divinity' of the Father, it seems to say. Holiness thus becomes perfection.

What is the real difference between 'be holy' and 'be perfect'? The greatest indicator is the other alteration that Jesus makes to the mitzvah, the exchange of the name Yahweh for Father. The excessive righteousness of the kingdom of heaven that has come near in Jesus (Matt. 4.17) is based upon a new relation of human actors to the God who commands. Yahweh is their Father, and they are his children. Whereas the scribes and prophets of the Hebrew text present familial images periodically as a descriptor of God's connection to Israel,[36] Jesus makes it the centre of his proclamation.

Like Paul, Matthew's Christ also offers summaries of the Law and Prophets, here grounded in the call to imitate the Father.[37] Sinai was not primarily imitative, but the excessive righteousness of this new Moses is. Therefore when he condenses the Decalogue into the commandment to 'do to others as you would have them do to you', or again to, 'love the Lord your God with all your heart, and with all your soul, and with all your mind, and . . . You shall love your neighbour as yourself' (22.37–40) or again simply to 'follow me', he is not merely providing them with simplified templates for Torah. He is instead 'completing' the Mosaic code, and insisting that its true prescription is not an order of human ethic, but essentially a human practicing of the divine ethic. God is the one who loves both God and neighbour: the first insofar as the Father proclaims his devotion to the Son,[38] and the Son's life centres on a prayerful devotion to the Father; the second insofar as the whole point of the proclaiming of the kingdom from the housetops, to lepers, Roman centurions, Canaanite women and (in Luke's Gospel) to strangers in ditches, is that the circle of beloved children is constantly expanding from the baptized Christ outwards, making

35 Albright and Mann make a case for a connection to *tamim*. They do so however by erasing any traces of the 'Greek' philosophical sense – that is, as moral and natural completion – from either term, even going so far as to render the line in English, 'Be true [alternatively, they suggest 'sincere'], just as your heavenly father is true.' W. F. Albright and C. S. Mann, 1971, *Matthew*, in *The Anchor Bible*, Garden City, NY: Doubleday, pp. 70–1. Cf. *Theological Dictionary* XV, p. 700, which shows the etymological traces of something strikingly similar to Greek philosophical perfection.

36 For instance, in Isaiah 9.6; 63.16; Jeremiah 3.19; 31.9; Malachi 1.6; 2.10.

37 Matera, *Ethics*, pp. 44ff.

38 Two or perhaps three times: At the baptism (3.17) and transfiguration (17.5), and in the voice of the centurion, whose words echo the Father's (27.54). 'Truly this man was God's Son!' seems to respond to both the chiding of the crowd, '. . . he said, "I am God's Son"' (v. 43) and Jesus' own cry of forsakenness, which suggests for a few brief verses that the blessing he received in the Jordan and on the high mountain is no longer his. In the centurion's cry, and in the resurrection which couples with it in the text (v. 53), the Father effectively announces that the blessing still holds.

neighbours out of the unrighteous enemies and 'my people' out of those 'who are not my people' (Rom. 9.25–26). This is the end of any *deutero-nomos*. The law commanded a holiness that, though from heaven, is 'not in heaven' (Deut. 30.11). Jesus insists that the fulfilment of the law is a holiness that can be done 'on earth as it is in heaven' (Matt. 6.10). Accordingly, he summarizes the law into actions that are commanded of people on earth because they are true of God in heaven.

The literary logic is, to be sure, apparent enough: Jesus, born of the 'blessed transgression' of the God who favours Mary, shares his divine heritage from atop the Galilean mountain, and those on whom he bestows this new line of kinship receive it as their new end. To be perfect like the Father is to be 'God with us' like the Son; the teaching on prayer which immediately follows 5.48 is, then, a kind of performative text: 'Pray then in this way: Our Father . . .' In doing so, you become children (5.45), living within the perfection that is the Father's, the Son's and, through the gift of familial expansion, yours as well.[39]

All good human deeds now register praise to the Father in heaven (5.16), a situation that would be impossible if the righteousness of human behaviour were not visibly connected to the righteousness of God. Likewise, the excessive command to love not only friends but enemies as well becomes a word of *patrimimesis*:

> You have heard that it was said, 'You shall love your neighbour and hate your enemy.' But I say to you, Love your enemies and pray for those who persecute you, so that you may be children of your Father in heaven; for he makes his sun rise on the evil and on the good, and sends rain on the righteous and on the unrighteous. For if you love those who love you, what reward do you have? Do not even the tax collectors do the same? And if you greet only your brothers and sisters, what more are you doing than others? Do not even the Gentiles do the same? Be perfect, therefore, as your heavenly Father is perfect. (Matt. 5.43–8)

Like Plato, Jesus does not condemn imitation itself here, but an imitation of the wrong crowd. There is a certain natural pagan ethic that offers itself as a pattern for social and civic life: Love friends and greet your kinsmen and -women with hospitality. Imitate these law abiders, Jesus says, and you will be Gentile-like, kin to the Roman taxman. But love even your enemies, and you will be imitating your heavenly Father. Here again we find Mary's son blending the heavenly ethic with an earthly charge. The falling of rain and the rising of the sun are themselves parables for the great event of enemy love that the whole of the Gospel narrates: the descent of the Son from

---

39 Luz notes that v. 48 is a *kelal*, an adaption from the Hillel principles of exegesis, which serves to summarize and transition. Thus 'love your enemies' in v. 46 is summarized in v. 48 as 'be perfect as your heavenly Father is perfect', and the reader/hearer is prepared to learn what sort of perfection the Father rewards, beginning in 6.1. See Luz, *Matthew*, pp. 6, 284.

heaven ends in crucifixion by even those he counts as friends; his resurrection opens the gates of heaven for all who follow him, including first of all an enemy who was 'keeping watch' over his execution (27.53–54). Thus perfection is the call to imitate the Father, who shows us his perfect love in the journey of the Son.

The law summary of 19.16–21 forms the second perfection trope in Matthew's Gospel.

> Then someone came to him and said, 'Teacher, what good deed must I do to have eternal life?' And he said to him, 'Why do you ask me about what is good? There is only one who is good. If you wish to enter into life, keep the commandments.' He said to him, 'Which ones?' And Jesus said, 'You shall not murder; You shall not commit adultery; You shall not steal; You shall not bear false witness; Honour your father and mother; also, You shall love your neighbour as yourself.' The young man said to him, 'I have kept all these; in what am I still deficient?'[40] Jesus said to him, 'If you wish to be perfect, go, sell your possessions, and give the money to the poor, and you will have treasure in heaven; then come, follow me.' When the young man heard this word, he went away grieving, for he had many possessions. (19.16–22)

In answer to the initial question, Jesus offers the Deuteronomistic teaching: God is the only one who is good; it is not for us to share in the goodness, but to keep the commandments. However, when the questioner asks what this ethic still lacks, Jesus, acknowledging the young man's theological perspicuity, responds with the excesses of the Sermon on the Mount: be merciful like your Father who knows how to give good gifts (7.11), imitate the wisdom of heaven rather than of earth (6.1–34) and follow me. The implication in Matthew 19 is explicated in Matthew 5: on the old ethic, God alone is good; for the new ethic, this is no longer true, since we are called to be perfect like he is.[41] The first answer, then, is 'holiness'; when the young man perceives that holiness is lacking, Jesus gives the new answer: 'perfection'.

Goodness and the keeping of commandments collide here, as does, once again, the old distinction between heaven and earth. Of course, as Jesus

---

40 Modifying the NRSV's 'what do I still lack' with Luz's translation, since, as he notes, the construction is genitive, not accusative. Ulrich Luz, 2001, *Matthew 8—20: A Commentary (Hermeneia)*, trans. James E. Crouch, Minneapolis: Fortress Press, p. 509.

41 Both Luz, *Matthew 8—20*, p. 514, and Matera, *Ethics*, p. 53, note the parallel injunction of Chapters 19 and 5: do the law excessively, and so be perfect by a greater righteousness. Neither, though, note what I take to be the added excess of 19.17. Just as the new law exceeds the old as a perfection, so the old theology according to which only God is good is now exceeded by the adoption of men and woman as perfect children. If this added excess is not implied, then it seems Jesus is suggesting that goodness is bifurcated into human and divine, while perfection is not; this though seems impossible after 5.43–48.

explains to his disciples when the young man leaves, being perfect is impossible for mortals (19.26), since without the gift of adoption by our Father we can never share his perfection. The most we can attempt is either the *polis*-sustaining ethic of the Gentiles (5.46–47) or the life-giving ethic of Moses (19.17).[42] But if the one who is good grants a share in his perfection, then he effectively reorders the proper human end as no longer merely mortal. Christ is the radical embodiment of divine otherness; on him the *ton agathon* descends, and in him humanity ascends to *ton agathon*.[43] Human nature is now renamed, through Mary's child, as Yahweh's offspring.[44]

In light of these two tropes, we must conclude that Matthew takes the *kerygma* of adoption to be also a *kerygma* of perfection. What sort of character do these newly elevated humans inherit? The sudden transition at the close of Chapter 5 juxtaposes perfection with a kind of smallness, and suggests that the two notions will ironically coincide. 'Be perfect, therefore, as your heavenly Father is perfect. Beware of practising your piety before others in order to be seen by them; for then you have no reward from your Father in heaven. So whenever you give alms, do not sound a trumpet before you . . .' (5.48 – 6.2). Jesus here installs humility as central to the practices of the new divine children. In doing so, as has often been noted, he sets up a contrast with the older heroic virtues of the Hellenistic traditions. However, this cannot be taken to mean that Christ calls his disciples to mind their station in the natural order of things, like the attunement to *hegemonikon* in the Stoicism of the first century.[45] Rather, in light of the placement of the discourse, we can only read the teaching on humility as a commentary on becoming like the Father. Do not sound trumpets when you go to give alms, becoming like actors (6.2–5), or flatter yourselves with verbal eloquence, becoming like Gentiles (6.7); rather become like birds and lilies, whose trust in the good governance of the Father is like that of a child who lives without fear of parental betrayal. This is indeed a call for humility, but of a tongue in cheek sort: by appealing to the praises of human observers, the almsgivers sell themselves short of the deifying praise of the Father; by appealing to the Father as if he were impressionable like a human observer, the Gentile wordsmiths also come up shy of their true and greater *telos*. Only the lilies live toward their true end; only they show awareness that the true good of creatures is deification in the way of the Son.

---

42 Jesus, in a sense, 'rejects the man's question' (see Luz, *Matthew 8–20*, p. 511) by dropping the 'eternal' out of his answer: Torah gives life; Torah completed in adoption gives *eternal* life, and thus perfection.

43 Luz, *Matthew 8–20*, p. 513.

44 This is why it is not the case that Matthew 'does not contain the sophisticated understanding of the human predicament found in Paul's letters'. Matera, *Ethics*, p. 59. The difference is that Jesus in Matthew is more ambivalent about the human ability to do the law: we may be able to, but this is not the ethics of the kingdom, so our ability is beside the point. The excessive righteousness is not simply 'lawful conduct' (p. 456), but the gift of adoption. Cf. Luz, *Matthew 1–7*, p. 290.

45 See Spaemann, *Happiness*, pp. 45ff.

Likewise, the later instruction to 'change and become like children' (18.3) emphasizes this smallness, and thus can only be read in the context of the perfection tropes, as well as the paradigmatic prayer of Chapter 6.[46] 'Whoever becomes humble like this child is the greatest in the kingdom of heaven' (18.4) because it is only in becoming children of the Father that we become great at all. 'Whoever welcomes one such child in my name welcomes me' (18.5), because Jesus is the true child of the Father, and only by welcoming childhood itself does one receive what he offers. The humility of children is the humility of the Son, which is the humility not of one who desires less than he might, but of one who refuses all ends that, though perhaps more easily attained, are subordinate to the one great end of being like God. The humility of the unclouded Sinai is one that ends all dabbling with golden calves, even the new calf of the Law itself, which has become a source, for the scribes and teachers, of a perversely self-deprecating pride.

The New Testament thus opens the way up Sinai and tells of the mysterious, counter-intuitive and even blasphemous truth that the newly unveiled mountain gives up. As in Plato, where our good is the contemplative embodiment of the form of the good, Israel's Yahweh is our Father, and our perfection is the embodied repetition of his. When the cloud evaporates, it reveals that humans are akin the God of Israel. That, surprisingly, is what the Sinai cloud was hiding all along.

Given theosis: 2 Peter

At this point we might find ourselves troubled by the kinship paradigm of the New Testament, wondering in an Aeschylian mode about the tension and proximity of our suspension from God's neck. Do the writers of the New Testament consider that this unveiled kinship abolishes the distinction between God and humans? This seems like a simple enough and obvious question to ask in light of the preceding account; the trouble is that to answer it is to lend a significance to it that is foreign to the New Testament itself. The Gospels and Epistles are prepared to tell their readers what Jews and Gentiles alike have received from the revelation of God in Christ. In light of this reception, the *telos* of life is changed, the finish line moved. So humans in Christ 'strain forward', they 'press on', attempting to 'take hold of that for which Christ took hold of' them (Phil. 3.12–13).[47] At no point do these texts stop to tell us what the limits of that reception are.

---

46 'Disciples who are like children are thus small, insignificant, and without power. Something of that sense is expressed in the following verses when for Matthew the "little" church members are caught in a snare (18.6–9), or when they lose their way and are as helpless as a lost sheep (vv. 12–13).' Luz, *Matthew 8–20*, p. 429.

47 While some have read these lines as an anti-perfection statement from Paul, Stephen Fowl argues that Paul is simply doing here what he does in places like Romans 7: that is, observing the imperfection in his own life and experience of the world, but not making any ontological statement about human possibility. Stephen Fowl, 2005, *Philippians*, Grand Rapids and Cambridge: Eerdmans, pp. 159ff.

Still, various New Testament passages use language suggesting that resurrecting grace preserves the human form, joining us to God without erasing the distinction. The Second Letter of Peter offers one rather simple
explanation of the distinction that holds in the new order of perfection:
God is the one who gives godliness, and the creature is the one who receives
it. 'His divine power has given us everything needed for life and godliness, through the knowledge of him who called us by his own glory and
goodness' (1.3). By structuring the relation of God to creatures as one of
gift-giving and gift-reception, the author creates a sort of Sinaitic reworking of Platonic participation.[48] As in Hellenism, we are made for godliness
and an order of glory and goodness that are ultimately the possession of
the divine; here, though, the gracious and unbounded Yahweh is the one
granting this gift, so he actually can, beyond Plato, offer us 'everything
needed' for godliness.

So the following verse, which initially sounds as if it could have come
from the *Theaetetus*, lands the reader in a very different space: 'Thus he
has given us, through these things, his precious and very great promises,
so that through them you may escape from the corruption that is in the
world because of lust, and may become participants of the divine nature'
(κοινωνοὶ φύσεως; 1.4). Recall the similar line from the dialogue: 'Therefore we ought to try to escape from earth to the dwelling of the gods as
quickly as possible; and to become like God so far as this is possible' (179C).
Like the Platonic text, which goes on, 'to become like God is to become
righteous and holy and wise', 2 Peter includes its own catalogue of mutually supporting virtues, all of which are the fruits born of a life that partici-
pates in God's nature: faith, goodness, knowledge, self-control endurance,
godliness, mutual affection and love (1.5–8).[49] Significantly however, the
qualifying phrase from Plato, 'so far as this is possible', has dropped out
here.[50] As it is not by our own human powers that we are summoned to
know and share in the divine being, there is no more reason to place these
limitations. The divine power (δυνάμεως) itself has made the gift of its
own glory (δόξη) and goodness (ἀρετή; 1.3). The recipient is not bound,
then, by the likeness that is accorded possibility. God's *dunamis* supplies
the new possibilities, and these gifts come to constitute our participation in

---

48 Or perhaps a Hellenistic reworking of Sinaitic revelation, in light of the schol-
arly consensus that Peter is here translating the gospel to a culturally Greek audience
who have little or no understanding of Israel's faith. F. Lapham, 2004, *Peter: The
Myth, the Man, and his Writings: A Study of Early Petrine Text and Tradition*,
London and New York: T&T Clark, pp. 161ff; David Horrell, 1998, *The Epistles of
Peter and Jude*, Peterborough: Epworth, pp. 142ff.

49 See Stephen Finlan, 2006, 'Second Peter's Notion of Divine Participation',
in Stephan Finlan and Vladimir Kharlamov (eds), *Theosis: Deification in Christian
Theology*, Eugene, OR: Pickwick Publications, pp. 32–50.

50 Finlan, 'Participation', pp. 33–6, notices the *Theaetetus* parallel, but not the
difference.

the divine nature. Further, God himself is not limited by the 'corruption of a lustful world', as he is for Plato, where the elements are constantly threatening to rebel against the Olympian order and revert to the Saturnine age. To be a participant in this unique divine nature is to receive a real hope of a perfectly peaceful end. The tragic overtones of Platonic *theosis* are entirely gone here. God has given the gift of divine participation; it is not our ability to 'escape', but the nameless forces of corruption and ungodliness, that are forever compromised.

Following this opening dynamic of unlimited *koinonia* in the divine *phusis*, the author names contrasting postures for the receiving of this gift, and this contrast marks an important stage in the growth of a non-Promethean perfection. On the one hand is the posture of Christ during the transfiguration, 'He received honour and glory from God the Father when that voice was conveyed to him by the Majestic Glory, saying, "This is my Son, my Beloved, with whom I am well pleased"' (1.17). This mode of reception, of which the author was a witness (1.18), becomes for him the paradigm of human *theosis*: God shares his eternal *doxa*, and it is the creature's greatest end to be made perfect in that *doxa*. Here he is like Saint Paul, whom he cites later as important though chronically opaque (3.15–16), in the suggestion that the divine *doxa* was not even for Christ something to be taken, not because it is not intended for human nature, but rather because taking the *doxa* by force will ruin its nature as gift (Phil. 2.6). The Messiah himself was deified by gift; this is our great hope as well. (In this respect, 2 Peter forms a corollary to Hebrews, where Christ's perfection through suffering becomes our perfection as well.)

In stark contrast to Christ's kenotic reception of glory are those who grasp at their own deification.[51] The antitype is supplied by the inhabitants of Sodom and Gomorrah in Genesis 19, though it could also be the tower-builders of 11, or the garden-dwellers of 3. By means of a word play, the author makes the angels into *doxas*, the glories or glorious ones (3.10). So while Christ graciously received the *doxa*, the men of Sodom and Gomorrah come under judgement for attempting to wrestle the *doxas* out of Lot's house, so they might 'know them' (Gen. 19.5). Peter does not condemn the men of Sodom for desiring the *doxas*,[52] but for desiring to take by force what was offered to them as gift. This then is the 'depraved lust' (2.10) of those cities: they attempt to rape God's glorious gift of *theosis*.

If 2 Peter does not fully answer the question Aristotle might have posed, 'how is *koinonia* with the divine a perfection of the human *phusis*?' it certainly indicates a trajectory that will be taken up by the Church in its early era, and perhaps most of all by Maximus the Confessor. The 'new

---

51 See Daniel Harrington, 2003, *2 Peter*, in *1 Peter, Jude and 2 Peter (Sacra Pagina)*, Collegeville, MN: The Liturgical Press, pp. 260, 263.

52 I am suggesting a parallel reading to what L. William Countryman argues as a 'complexity honoring' reading of Jude. William Countryman, 2003, *Interpreting the Truth: Changing the Paradigm of Biblical Studies*, Harrisburg, London, and New York: Trinity International Press, pp. 55ff.

creation' is not a foreign gift, the text implies, but a recapitulation of the original one, damaged to an almost unrecognizable degree by the likes of the men of Sodom. We were made to receive the *doxa*: the Christian doctrine of *theosis* sounds strange to us because creatures have gone strange, the Epistle suggests, not because Israel's God has. God has not, that is, decided at long last to wipe out his creatures and replace them with a 'new creation'. A proper understanding of perfection eludes us simply because a lusting world no longer recognizes its nature; fleeing Sodom with Lot, and so fleeing that part of ourselves that still feels at home there, we discover the ancient memory of a *phusis* made to rest in God.

You are our letter: 2 Corinthians

Perfection in the New Testament is, then, a non-tragic sharing in God's perfection, accomplished through a new order of kinship that is also the forgotten secret of our created nature. The Annunciation to Mary initiates this new narrative of human perfection, which does not so much negate the Athenian tragic cosmology as simply tell a different story. Prometheus simply does not appear, even by implication, as an archetypal myth in these writings. Jesus Christ is perfected as he perfects his Father's work; the Spirit of Christ leads his followers into that same end (1 John 4.13). Humans reach their perfection, for the New Testament authors, in endlessly repeating the words of Christ from the cross: 'I am thirsty; it is perfect.'

A final point regarding the literature of the New Testament bears adding. If, following the ascension, the work of God in Christ is handed over to those led by his Spirit, then the way in which the disciples go about perfecting that work suddenly takes on the greatest possible significance. In plain language: Christ is absent; those who long for a sabbatical from the work of atoning/creating can no longer hear his *tetelestai* from the cross, but must instead look to and listen to one another. The witness of the sufferings and joys of Christ's followers become for the Church a series of 'little last words' of Christ.

For this reason, it is not at all surprising that epistolary communication constitutes the majority of the New Testament.[53] Those who do not have Christ's perfected work before them have only each other, and so must 'be mutually encouraged by each other's faith' (Rom. 1.11). The call to

---

53 'If the gospel be the revealing or unveiling of a mystery hidden from ages and generations; if this mystery be the true constitution of humanity in Christ, so that a man believes and acts a lie who does not claim for himself union with Christ, we can understand why the deepest writings of the New Testament, instead of being digests of doctrine, are epistles, explaining to those who had been admitted in the Church of Christ their own position, bringing out that side of it which had reference to the circumstances in which they were placed or to their most besetting sin, and shewing what life was in consistence, what life at variance, with it.' F. D. Maurice, in *Kingdom of Christ*, in Jeremy Morris (ed.), 2007, *To Build Christ's Kingdom: F. D. Maurice and His Writings*, Norwich: Canterbury Press, p. 87.

'remember our labour and toil' (1 Thess. 2.9) is not simply a plea for recognition, but rather a calling to remember Christ's labours and toils. They must imitate Christ by imitating one another (1 Thess. 1.6–7; 2.14). Any hope for an immediacy of perfection has long since ascended into the clouds and disappeared with Christ; creation's end will now be mediated by the bread that the Thessalonians bake with their hands (3.6–13), the works of hospitality performed in Rome (Rom. 16.1–23), the tangible acts of love acted out among the Johannine community (1 John 3.18–24).

The economy of letter writing is thus the perfecting grace for the Christian diaspora. The churches left behind in Christ's wake become the absent Christ for one another. 'You are our glory and joy!' Paul says to the Thessalonians (1 Thess. 2.20). If there is 'any encouragement in Christ' or 'sharing in the Spirit,' he says to the church at Philippi, 'make my joy complete' through the life that you lead together (2.1–5). They suffer crucifixion in one another's afflictions (1 Thess. 5.9–11; Phil. 1.7, 29–30), they live the resurrected life in one another's joys (1 Thess. 3.8). They long to be together like they long to be with Christ (Phil. 1.23–26), and when they can no longer stand the separation, they write letters (1 Thess. 3.5).

A peculiar thing happens to the Platonic religious gap here. It seemed, for a time, to collapse entirely, when the Logos dwelt among them; then it opened again in dramatic fashion, as he ascended. Now the gap shifts, and God is both as close and as far as the adopted children are from one another. The gap of religious desire is not heaven to earth, but the difficult road from Corinth to Thessalonica, the risky seas separating Ephesus from Rome . . .

The harrowing Second Epistle to the Corinthians is perhaps the clearest expression of this pneumatic mediation of Christ's perfecting work. Paul writes to Corinth with the tone and expression of a love letter, but a love letter written in the midst of pain and misunderstanding.[54] 'I wanted to visit you on my way to Macedonia, and to come back to you from Macedonia' (1.15), but, in light of an unstated controversy between him and the Corinthians, 'I made up my mind not to make you another painful visit' (2.1). Thus, he insists, 'it was to spare you that I did not come again to Corinth' (1.23).

As he moves on, attempting to reconcile with his loved ones, Paul appeals to the intimacy and depth of friendship, which places them, as Aristotle might have said,[55] beyond the normal arrangements of civic justice. 'Surely we do not need, as some do, letters of recommendation to you or from you, do we?' (3.1)[56] Hoping that such formalities are moot between

---

54 Ben Witherington writes that if Cicero is right, and 'the ability to placate or reconcile' is a 'sign of true greatness in human character', then '2 Corinthians more than any of Paul's other letters reveals his largeness of soul'. Ben Witherington III, 1995, *Conflict and Community in Corinth: A Socio-Rhetorical Commentary on 1 and 2 Corinthians*, Grand Rapids: Eerdmans; Carlisle: Paternoster, pp. 327–8.

55 See Spaemann, *Happiness*, p. 109.

56 Such letters, Paul supposes, would be superfluous, not only because of the present friendship, but also because of their past history. Paul came to Corinth as a

those who have shared as much of themselves with one another as Paul, Timothy and the Corinthians have, he continues: 'You yourselves are our letter, written on our hearts, to be known and read by all; and you show that you are a letter of Christ, prepared by us, written not with ink but with the Spirit of the living God, not on tablets of stone but on tablets of human hearts' (3.2–3). Paul returns here to the new covenant passage from Jeremiah (31.31ff),[57] but gives it an altogether new twist: the writing is the Church itself, and the law will be inscribed not on 'our' own hearts, as in an immediate covenantal bond between God and his people, but now on hearts of friends. Yahweh promised to write a new law on the hearts of his beloved house of Israel; Paul here says that the church at Corinth is that law, carved into the flesh of his own heart.

As he carries out the image, he turns again to the familiar language of the *doxa* that was condemnation to Israel, but is life in Christ. This time, though, the reconciling work of Christ can be mediated only through reconciliation with the Corinthians. 'Now if the ministry of death, chiselled in letters on stone tablets, came in glory so that the people of Israel could not gaze at Moses' face because of the glory of his face, a glory now set aside, how much more will the ministry of the Spirit come in glory?' (3.7–8) It is the Spirit who makes them competent to be ministers of the new covenant's graces (3.6),[58] and it is only in the exchange of these graces that they can see what Moses' veil hid: 'And all of us, with unveiled faces, seeing the glory of the Lord as though reflected in a mirror, are being transformed into the same image from one degree of glory to another; for this comes from the Lord, the Spirit' (3.18). The mirror, for Paul, is the church at Corinth, and the unveiled access to the new Torah that Christ initiates, transforming his followers from glory to glory, is only possible through this ecclesial medium.[59] (This passage was perhaps not far from the mind of Thomas Aquinas when, centuries later, he wrote in his treatise on charity that life with friends is a *conveniencia* that perfects our love for God [*ST* II–II.23.1.])

As Paul draws his letter to a strained conclusion, it begins to sound like a tragi-comic love story. 'Here I am, ready to come to you this third time', yet not wanting his coming to induce dread, as this would obviously leave him feeling and looking foolish (12.11–14). 'If I love you more, am I to be loved less?' (12.15). It is Hosea, more than Jeremiah, that Paul now calls to

---

missionary, thus establishing the body that now accepts letters of recommendation when preachers and Christian travellers come through town. Since that is the origin of the congregation at Corinth, how could they need a letter for Paul? See Furnish, 1964, *II Corinthians (Anchor Bible)*, Garden City, NY: Doubleday, p. 193.

57 See Jan Lambrecht, SJ, 1999, *Second Corinthians (Sacra Pagina)*, Collegeville, MN: Liturgical Press, p. 41. Bultmann misses this connection entirely, suggesting that Paul's figure of a letter on hearts 'was evidently conceived by him on the spur'. Rudolf Bultmann, 1985, *The Second Letter to the Corinthians*, trans. Roy A. Harrisville, Minneapolis: Augsburg, p. 72.

58 See Bultmann, *Second Corinthians*, p. 77.

59 This fabric of intra-ecclesial communion justifies his request for the Jerusalem collection in chapters 8–9. See Witherington, *Conflict*, pp. 423–8.

mind: the lover who depends so entirely on the affirmation of the beloved that he will risk her scorn and ridicule.[60]

And then to the letter's closing: 'For we rejoice when we are weak and you are strong. That is what we pray for, that you may become perfect' (καταρτιοιν; 13.9).[61] Paul is suggesting that the entire body together is perfected, while the individual members may only experience portions of the completed work. More to the point, he is offering to be the weakness and the suffering, and enjoy the fruits of strength and power only as mediated through his beloved community in Corinth: *I will be the cross, you be the resurrection. Together we will constitute the perfect work of Christ for one another.* So, for Paul, if the churches can continue to be witnesses to one another of the work that is being perfected in them, the veil will one day come off the *doxa*, and all will see the words of the New Torah written on the hearts and faces of lovers and friends.

Beyond Stolen Fire

Perfection is, for these writers, the completion of God's task of creating the world. As such it is God's work, paradigmatically finished in six days and from which he rested in the 'perfect work' of the Sabbath. Though complete, however, the work is still to be done, and is finished only in the descending of the Son from on high, by his introduction of the greater unveiled righteousness of God, and by the sharing of this with the nations. And yet again, since by the time of his return to *doxa* all men and women were not yet drawn to him, the work is not yet finished. Thus, in Christ's wake, the world finds its perfection in the Spirit-led continuation of his work. The works of the New Torah are the fruits of a human life rooted in the re-creating work of Christ.

Several conclusions follow from this account of the New Testament sources. There is, first of all, no purely human perfection, since the great work of creation in which humans share is not a purely human work. The humility of the Gospels and Epistles is the ironic humility that refuses to take pride in human deeds, storing up treasure instead in heaven, the source and end of the new excessive righteousness. This new righteousness takes up the old and summarizes it into 'great commandments', which reconfigure the Law of earth as an *imitatio dei.*

---

60 See Rowan Williams, 'The Body's Grace', in Charles Hefling (ed.), 1996, *Our Selves, Our Souls and Bodies: Sexuality and the Household of God*, Cambridge: Cowley Publications, pp. 58–68.

61 The term suggests building to completion, and is similar in deployment to the word-family associated with τελειος, including connotations of building, maturing and flourishing. While this is the unique instance of it in the New Testament, a variant occurs in Ephesians, καταρτισμός, which the NRSV translates as '*to equip* the saints' (4.12). See Bultmann, *Second Corinthians*, p. 249.

Secondly, perfection is not first of all a moral state, although the fruits of these labours will in fact express a morality that incorporates and exceeds the morality of Israel. A moral code of any sort will always be a human end, a life oriented toward a certain laudable plane of virtue. That, though, is not what the New Testament envisions as perfect: the Father in heaven is perfect in a way that exceeds the performance of a scroll of virtues, and humans are called to exceed any such account as well. The New Testament no longer offers a holiness code, but instead a trajectory of human encodings of divine holiness.

For this reason the question of sinlessness is not in any respect at the centre of the New Testament's vision of perfection. The writer to the Hebrews is more concerned about sins after the sacrifice of Christ than the author of 1 John,[62] who makes the exchange of forgiveness more central to the fabric of the community. Paul, for his part, seems to assume that sin represents a lingering impulse – which he finds in himself – to self-justification, and this in turn is a sign that the work of resurrection has not entirely taken hold in him. For all, though, the abolition of sin is only a connotation of sharing in the *doxa* of Christ, not its goal. Humans are called to imitate God (Eph. 5.1) in completing the work of creation; resting content with the imperative of sinlessness simply sets the bar too low, rather like saying the point of an apple is to be without worms.

Further, and in light of these implications, perfection is a thoroughly communal project. Individual humans do not even become perfect at all except as a kind of side effect of a common project of participation in Christ's work. Christ is perfect because 'it is perfect'. Christ's followers are perfect only when the churches can pronounce together the completion of the creative work of God, in which suffering and rising plays the central dramatic role.

Finally, the command to love one another would seem to be the whole key to the finishing of the work (Rom. 13.9–10; 1 John 4.7–21), since the unveiling of the divine *doxa* on Matthew's mountain comes down to the light refracted off the faces of the church in Corinth. If the Spirit of love is perfected in humans (1 John 4.12), then they enter the house of the Father, where the love between Father and Son is repeated in an economy of letter writing, of longing for one another and the painful inscribing of names on hearts.

There are, to be sure, many questions unaddressed by the vision of perfection that emerges from the New Testament, including especially the philosophical implications of this new Torah. In spite of the radical novelty of 2 Peter's *theosis* language, for instance, the dialectic of giving and receiving retains a certain woodenness. How does a human, used to receiving gifts at the hands of other time- and space-bound creatures, receive the *doxa* of God in a way that does not reduce the gift to a merely human good? Human reception always involves an act of taking, and is not complete until a response is issued, a return gift of some sort. This is

---

62 Although see note 16, above, for the counter-argument.

what allows the ultimate human end, in Plato, to still be a *bios miktos*: we receive divine things as the active human 'numbers' that we are. Is this also true of our commerce with God in Christ? We receive the divine attributes, 2 Peter says, and with a fullness that eradicates the tone of resignation in *Theaetetus*. But the biblical text gives little guidance in sorting out the difficult questions of what it looks like to 'make' this reception.

In a related line of enquiry, Paul insists on the novelty of the new creation that we will become after resurrection. There is a strong rhetorical and homiletical appeal to this insistence, since, as I suggested above, this is part of his theology of justification by gift rather than by self. Philo's interpretation of the tabernacle instructions initiates an analogical structuring of human making as a repetition of God's creative work; the absence of any such analogy in Paul leaves the lingering question of how those who are reborn for works of righteousness in Romans 8 are the perfection of those who were entirely unable to do holy things in the Romans 7.

But this stands to reason. Bethsaida and Tarsus are not Athens and Alexandria, and Peter and Paul are not Plato and Philo. They are rather the preachers of a new perfection, and it will be left to later generations of Christian intellectuals to sort out the metaphysics of this sermon. They pass along the new idea, itself a reading of the descent and ascension of God's Son, that perfection comes to earth not as stolen fire but as extended gift. Perfection is God's gift to creation – the gift, in fact, of creating – and in sharing this creative work the divine nature opens itself entirely to creatures, extending to us the gift of our true and ultimate *telos*.

5

Distinguish to Unite:
Perfection in the Church Fathers, Part I

True loves are often sown, but seldom grow on ground.

Edmund Spenser

Symptoms of Withdrawal

The new faith in the Word made flesh might seem to make perfection, at last, a simple matter of *mimesis*. God the Father is perfect, Jesus Christ is that perfection performed in history; therefore human perfection is the embodied imitation of Christ's already embodied imitation of the Father's incorporeal perfection.

The trouble with this reading is not only that the acts of the Son on earth only ever indicate human perfections by means of parables, signs and secrecy. The even greater difficulty is the end of this history, when the incarnate Christ ascends to his Father, leaving behind no body and no new holiness code that would clarify the path of perfection. Instead, he sends out a Spirit 'who will lead you into all truth' (John 16.13). For the Johannine community this path was singularly cryptic, lined by accounts of all the beasts, numbers, riders and scrolls that John saw while 'in' this Spirit (Rev. 1.10). The slain lamb reigns as a distant lion, and his rule is mediated through the trials and tribulations of the seven churches and their angels. Similarly, Luke's literary sequel is an extended account of the Christian diaspora, which repeatedly makes us ask what it means to follow Christ through the strange new post-Ascension world, with all its military (Acts 12.1–23), economic (4.34 – 5.11) and cosmic (27.6–44) adversities.[1]

---

1 Rowan Williams's critique of Lukan pneumatology misses this dynamic, whereby the Pentecostal arrival of the Christ's Spirit on the young Church allows them to re-interpret the gospel as an event now happening to them: like him, they are baptized, driven into the wilderness and called to turn their faces toward martyrdom, trusting that the Spirit will raise them as it raised Christ. Williams, on the other hand, caricatures (rather uncharacteristically, as it happens) the Gospeller as seeing 'the Spirit as continuator of Christ's work, filling a space left by Christ's exaltation, manifest in the conviction of extraordinary experiences'. Rowan Williams, 2000, *On Christian Theology*, Oxford: Blackwell, p. 118.

Within a few generations, ironically, the followers of the one called 'God with us' were defending themselves against the charge of disbelief in a divine being as such. 'He, then, who is persuaded that God is omnipotent, and has learned the divine mysteries from His only-begotten Son, how can he be an atheist?' (Clement, *Stromata* 7.1)[2] The ritualization of divine absence, discernible in all Christian symbols and rites, left the 'new Gnostics' vulnerable to the supposition of a pure absence in place of a deity and, as Clement of Alexandria shows, in place of a morality as well. Without present, tangible gods and demigods to point toward goodness itself, how could this faith instruct its practitioners in the pursuit of goodness?[3]

The religious assertion of a divine withdrawal is not new. We have seen it in the priestly writings of the Torah and the metastatic resignation of the prophets, in the backing off of the Platonic gods from the chaos of the material order and in Philo, where Yahweh abstracts the Tetragrammaton from the arena of temporal participation. What is new in the Church Fathers is, first, the intensification of this withdrawal into a fundamental division within being, and, second, the affirmation of a positive vocational perfection inaugurated by means of this distinction.

The new ontological division appears in its sharpest form in the Nicene century, and especially in the rhetorical novelties of Athanasius. 'The Son of God is not a being made out of nothing, and . . . there is not the least affinity between Him and any created being whatsoever. Since He is God He cannot possibly be a creature, and it is the height of blasphemy to say that He is one' (*Contra Arianos* 2.1).[4] The withdrawal of God from the world is here no longer simply an affirmation of God's holiness, but has become the basic division within all being. Athanasius assumes, as the launching point of every line of theological reasoning that flows from his pen, that each and every nameable being is either a creature or a creator (*Ad Serapionem* 1.17).[5] Angels may be heavenly, immaterial beings who gather at God's

---

2 Alexander Roberts and James Donaldson (eds), 1893, *The Ante-Nicene Fathers, Vol. II: Fathers of the Second Century*, New York: The Christian Literature Publishing Co.

3 Clement builds up to this demonstrative question by arguing for the godliness (Θεοπρέπεια) of those who claim to have received knowledge of God through the Son.

4 Griffith et al. (eds), 1893, *The Orations of S. Athanasius Against the Arians*, London: Griffith, Farrar, Okeden and Welsh, p. 82. This is the central argument of Khaled Anatolios's 1998 book, *Athanasius: The Coherence of his Thought*, London: Routledge, especially pp. 7–27. See also John Behr, 2004, *The Formation of Christian Theology, Vol II: The Nicene Faith, Part 1: True God of True God*, Crestwood, NY: St Vladimir's Seminary Press, pp. 174–5, and 208ff.

5 C. R. B. Shapland (trans. and notes), 1951, *The Letters of Saint Athanasius Concerning the Holy Spirit*, London: Epworth Press, pp. 103–4. This line of reasoning is echoed later by Gregory of Nazianzus: 'If he is not from the beginning, he is in the same rank with myself, even though a little before me; for we are both parted from Godhead by time.' Edward Rochie Hardy (ed.), 1954, 'The Fifth Theological Oration. On the Spirit', in *Christology of the Later Fathers*, The Library of Christian Classics, Vol. 3, Philadelphia: The Westminster Press, p. 196.

throne and populate the various orders of existence from there to here; ontologically, however, they belong with us. The fault of Valentinus lay in 'ranking the angels with the Triad', whereas Moses already saw that 'angels are creatures' (*Ad Serap.* 1.10–12).

Thus, the old division between heaven and earth, teased apart in the New Testament, has dissolved by the fourth century; or rather, it has become a division no more radical than the categorical separations that hold within the earth itself. Angels are distinct from humans, just as humans are distinct from horses, horses from daffodils, and daffodils from dolomite. Creatures of heaven are higher than us in the great chain of being; relative to the Creator, though, they are still creatures, and this is the primary theological distinction.

Does this most basic separation not point directly to Shelley and company, and the modern bifurcation of perfection into the Olympian achievement of the divine will against the Titanic achievement of the human will? If there is 'not the least affinity' between Creator and creature, it would seem necessary to extrapolate from the distinction in natures a distinction in the perfection of those natures. Creaturely perfection would thus devolve already into its two modern variants: the obediential and the transgressive. If both types lead to the *aporias* traced in the beginning of this book, this would seem to be no more and no less than the inheritance of the distinctly Christian radicalization of the God–world divide.[6]

But a new logic is at work in the Fathers, advancing on the assumptions of the New Testament and marking out a path entirely distinct from the modern divide. As soon as Athanasius sets his basic distinction to work theologically, we find this new logic at work. 'As the Son, the living Word, is one, so must the vital activity and gift whereby he sanctifies and enlightens be one perfect and complete . . .' (*Ad Serap.* 1.20). The Son and Gift must share the perfection of the Father, who begets and gives, if in receiving them we are made holy. To 'reduce the Triad to imperfection' (1.20) is to condemn humans to everlasting imperfection, since we can only become what we receive. Ultimately, Arius and the Tropicoi are wrong not because of un-theological exegesis, or even philosophical errors, but because they name God in a way that defeats the god-making that is always the primary assumption for Athanasius.[7] Regarding both Son and Spirit, then, he can demand that his opponents meet him on the newly assumed platform of *theo-poesis*; if they do, his argument is flawless: the Spirit, 'therefore, who

---

6 As Gauchet argues it is. See Marcel Gauchet, 1997, *The Disenchantment of the World: A Political History of Religion*, trans. Oscar Burge, Princeton: Princeton University Press, pp. 47ff.

7 Norman Russell, 2005, *The Doctrine of Deification in the Greek Patristic Tradition*, Oxford: Oxford University Press, pp. 167–86. Russell's careful research into terminology and development makes this now the authoritative text on the subject. His over-reliance on rather anachronistic distinctions, however, causes him to come to some unwarranted conclusions, such as the claim, pp. 184–6, that Athanasius sees Antony as imitating Christ ethically, rather than as participating in the Logos ontologically.

is not sanctified by another, nor a partaker of sanctification, but who is himself partaken, and in whom all the creatures are sanctified, how can he be one from among all . . . those who partake of him?' (*Ad Serap.* 1.23).

The logic of god-making, of withdrawal-for-perfection, is admittedly counterintuitive, and it will take us some pages to sort out. It is, however, the same logic evident already in the Johannine reassurance, 'it is to your advantage that I go away' (John 16.7). As Logos, he is 'in the beginning with God', and so 'lives' on the Creator side of Athanasius' divide; as incarnate he 'lived among us' (1.2, 14). John's Logos descends for ascension, thus setting into motion a journey that serves the end of an ever greater sharing of divinity with creation. It is, after all, only his own journey from the Father and back again that allows Jesus to pray, 'The glory that you have given me I have given them, so that they may be one, as we are one, I in them and you in me, that they may become completely one' (John 17.22–3).

The Creator/creature distinction is a radicalization of the prophetic metastasis; it also, and through this radicalization, marks an ontological thaw, a springtime in which the frozen liturgical alphabet mobilizes into a boundary-crossing fluidity. Christ's going away is to our advantage, and the sending of the Spirit ensures that our longing for a lost God will finally be something other than either a tragic yearning or a resignation to noncontemplative obedience. The Fathers effectively recast the priestly/prophetic withdrawal of God as the super-Sinaitic ascent of Christ. No longer is God's presence simply to be feared, nor God's ascending absence simply to be lamented. As in Philippians 2, the presence of Christ in the form of a servant is a sign of loving condescension; likewise, his absence acts as a summons to glorification of all who strive to imitate him (vv. 2.5). These verses form the backbone of Augustine's entire Christology, wherein we are invited to stretch out from the humbled and emptied *forma servi* to the exalted fullness of the *forma dei* (*de Trinitate* II). Likewise, Clement's pneumatology originates in the motion that imitates Christ's journey into divinity: the Spirit seals our 'perfect adoption' as children like the Son, inviting 'assimilation to God, then, so that as far as possible a man becomes righteous and holy with wisdom . . .' (*Strom.* 2.22).[8] If God's Son is also the true human, then the Platonic 'so far as possible' is no longer just a mystical speculation on sublime boundaries, but now is a biographical description of Christ's own journey into God.

In the pages below, I will argue that the pan-Nicene tradition[9] consistently maintains something of this sort as a new paradigm of creaturely

---

8 Rowan Williams, 2001, *Arius: Heresy and Tradition*, rev. edn, Grand Rapids: Eerdmans, pp. 124–31.

9 I am adapting Lewis Ayres's term, 'pro-Nicaea', which describes a Nicene school of theology, between 360 and 390, and common to both Greek and Latin Fathers. I mean to suggest, in addition to this, that prior to the Nicene century a common heritage can be found among the Greek and Latin Fathers which invites, though does not necessitate, the fourth-century developments. See Lewis Ayres, 2004, *Nicaea and its Legacy: An Approach to Fourth-Century Trinitarian Theology*, Oxford: Oxford University Press, pp. 6–7.

perfection. The uniquely Christian separation of Creator and creature is not an impermeable ontological divide, intended to keep the heavenly Father and the earthbound creatures in their respective places. Rather, it is a new sort of religious gap that installs the grounds for a more radical union of creatures with the Creator than one finds in either Judaism or Hellenism. This installation unfolds only gradually, as Trinity and Christology begin to bear fruit in a theological anthropology. Ultimately, as I will show, the Fathers receive and radicalize – partially through a further incorporation of Plato and Aristotle – the teaching of the New Testament that union with God is a perfection of *energeia*. God's work becomes the perfecting activity of the working human creature: like Christ's own end, our perfection lies in working the works of the Father to whom we, with Christ, ascend.

Erotic Hypostases

I said above that Athanasius's key division is a novelty, and this is certainly true in terms of both the consistent naming of the divide between Creator and creature, as well as in the degree to which his rhetoric relies upon it.[10] Still, the theological motivation for this division originates in what was already a fruitful tradition before him. Christian ontology separates beings from God in order to give all beings a *telos* in God; this dynamic appears first of all in the distinctions within the divine being itself.

When Origen of Alexandria insists that Christ, 'the wisdom of God', is not 'without hypostatic existence' (*De principiis* 1.2.2)[11] he initiates a grammar that entails several scriptural intersections. First, he fills out 1 Corinthians 1.24, 'Christ, the power of God and the Wisdom of God', with the contents from Proverbs as well as from the Wisdom of Solomon (*De princ.* 1.2.9 –13):[12]

> For she is a breath of the power of God,
>> and a pure emanation of the glory of the Almighty;
>> therefore nothing defiled gains entrance into her.
> For she is a reflection of eternal light,
>> a spotless mirror of the working of God,
>> and an image of his goodness. (Wisd. 7.25 –6)

---

10 A point that comes through clearly in Williams, *Arius*, pp. 110ff.

11 Origen, *On First Principles. Koetschau's Text of De Principiis Translated into English*, trans. G. W. Butterworth, 1973, Gloucester, MA: Peter Smith, p. 15.

12 See Williams, *Arius*, p. 134. The 'excellent name' of Christ in Hebrews 1 and the 'holding together of all things' in Christ in Colossians 1 already resonate with the language of Wisdom 7–8. 1 Corinthians certainly echoes this passage, with its crucified Christ as true Wisdom. though perhaps even more it recalls Proverbs 7–9 and the contrast of Lady Wisdom with Lady Folly.

Lady Wisdom, in the Hebrew texts, 'has her subsistence nowhere else but in him who is the beginning of all things, from whom also she took her birth' (*De princ.* 1.2.5). She emanates from this divine source by nature, and is not related to it by adoption (*De princ.* 1.2.4). As image, she 'preserves the unity of nature and substance common to a father and a son' (*De princ.* 1.2.6). In short, 'she' is the one we also call 'the Son'. In aligning Christ with Wisdom, Origen insists that the distinction between the characters of the Father and Son is only the distinction between a font and the 'pure emanation' that flows from it.

Unwilling, however, to leave the Son emanating in a flow of substantial indifference, Origen reasons that 'an act of the Father's will ought to be sufficient to ensure the existence of what he wills' (*De princ.* 1.2.6). Existence implies a degree of separation and autonomy, just as the image of a parent is not that same parent again, but a child (*De princ.* 1.2.6). Alongside this intersection of Corinthians and Wisdom, then, Origen reads Hebrews 1.3, 'He is the reflection of God's glory and the exact imprint of God's very being [ὑπόστασις].' Christ is thus not wisdom as a character attribute of the Father, or a name for the Father seen twice; rather he is Wisdom as a character in and for herself, with integrity and existential identity: 'God's wisdom hypostatically existing' (*De princ.* 1.2.1).

Why does Origen insist on the rather aporetic language of pure emanation plus hypostatic distinction, an *aporia* that stretches third-century theological grammar beyond its capacity, and indeed, as we shall see, stretches his own grammar to its limits as well? The reasons are exegetical, operating at both the literal and spiritual levels. For the literal, the point is a rather obvious one: how else could a reader of Scripture handle the character differentiations in the Gospels? A Christ who can refer to God as 'the Father who sent me' (John 8.18) is certainly 'from', perhaps even from as 'breath' or 'pure emanation'. He is 'from', though, in such a way as to distinguish his presence from the absent Father in a sharper manner than the Wisdom passages allow.[13]

More profoundly, though, the spiritual reading insists upon this distinction, and it is this, I suggest, more than anything else, that provides the fabric for Nicene Christology. Only if Christ is distinct from the Father can he show us the way to the Father: 'Our Saviour is therefore the image of the invisible God . . . when considered in relation to the Father himself, and the image, when considered in relation to us, to whom he reveals the Father' (*De princ.* 1.2.6). The 'reflection of eternal light' is therefore not simply a mirror in which the Father sees his own face, nor is the emanation a ray of light shooting out of the sun into a void. Instead, Christ is the light that enlightens the created world (*De princ.* 1.2.7).

---

13 See John Behr, 2001, *The Formation of Christian Theology, Vol. I: The Way to Nicaea*, Crestwood, NY: St Vladimir's Seminary Press, p. 185. Behr's treatment, pp. 184ff, of the complex issues of Origen's Trinitarianism is both charitable and precise. See also Henri Crouzel, 1989, *Origen*, trans. A. S. Worrell, San Francisco: Harper & Row, pp. 186ff.

We find a basis for this reading in yet another scriptural intersection in Origen's language. If Hebrews refers directly only to a hypostasis of the Father, and Christ as *eikon* of this hypostasis, Origen finds a warrant for an extension of the term in the Johannine prologue (*De princ.* 1.2.6): 'The true light, which enlightens everyone, was coming into the world' (John 1.9). To be enlightened, for Origen, is to receive the light of the Son, and so the knowledge of the Father, since 'no one knows the Son except the Father, and no one knows the Father except the Son and anyone to whom the Son chooses to reveal him' (*De princ.* 1.2.6, quoting Matt. 11.27). The one who mediates this knowledge to us must be more than an emanation, like a stream of water or a ray of light. He must be a hypostatic centre of knowledge: and not just any knowledge, but knowledge of the one who sent him.[14] He is thus like a stream that flows in both directions, a ray of light that turns back contemplatively on the sun which gives it subsistence. As a hypostatic emanation, he can become the site of a new deifying career for God's creatures. 'For at that time those who have come to God because of the Word which is with him will have the contemplation of God as their only activity, that, having been accurately formed in the knowledge of the Father, they may all thus become a sign, since now the Son alone has known the Father' (*In Jn.* 1.92).[15] The Word/Son must be the sort of emanation that can contemplate its Father, if he is to be the site of our divine contemplation as well.

This language finds a very near parallel in the religious philosophy of Plotinus who, in view of their common teacher, could be considered Origen's pagan little brother.[16] In explaining 'how life was purveyed to the universe of things' (*Enneads* 5.1.2),[17] the philosopher suggests that a principle of 'unapproachable wisdom' (*Enn.* 5.1.4) governs the divine soul in which all individual souls share. This Intellectual Principle, the *nous*, 'knows that it can of itself beget an hypostasis', the Soul (*psuche*) it governs, but also sees itself as a hypostasis begotten by the One (*Henas*); *nous* 'can determine its own Being by the virtue emanating from its prior' (*Enn.* 5.1.7). *Henas*, its emanating *nous*, and *nous*'s emanating *psuche* are therefore the hypostases that provide the font of all life.

---

14 See Williams, *Arius*, p. 139. Crouzel (pp. 188–90) rightly emphasizes Origen's consistent use of *epinoia* as a term for the various titles accrued by Christ, but he oddly neglects the importance of *hypostasis* in his Christology. cf. Williams, *Arius*, p. 132, and Behr, who notes the centrality of the son's hypostatic existence in Origen's system not only for Christian spirituality, but for all exegesis as well. *Formation*, p. 169.

15 Origen, *Commentary on the Gospel According to John*, vol. I, trans. Ronald E. Heine, 1989, Washington: Catholic University of America Press. See Behr, *Formation*, p. 185, Williams, *Arius*, p. 139, and Ayres, *Nicaea*, pp. 50, 83, who though he challenges Williams's defence, still agrees on this basic construction.

16 'Origen was certainly already head of the catechetical school when he began to attend the lectures of Ammonius Saccas . . . Ammonius, a few years later, would be the teacher of Plotinus, the founder of neo-platonism, who was twenty years junior to Origen.' Crouzel, *Origen*, p. 10.

17 Plotinus, *The Enneads*, trans. Stephen MacKenna, 1991, London: Penguin.

These hypostases are, for Plotinus, differentiated by their degree of participation in the One, or, in the case of the One, by being simple and unparticipating. *nous* is like 'reason stored within' the One (*Enn.* 5.1.3)[18], while *psuche* is like 'reason uttered', sent forth to create further multiplicity on beings' journey toward materiality. Both see and know, but *nous* sees and knows itself, while *psuche* sees and knows only what is exterior to it (*Enn.* 5.3.8). The first hypostasis, however, does not see and know at all, since even self-perception is 'dual to itself' (*Enn.* 5.3.10). In an act of self-contemplation, I must be both the one seeing and knowing and the one seen and known. The One admits no duality though and thus admits no knowledge: 'if this had intellection it would no longer transcend the Intellectual-Principle but be it, and at once be a multiple' (*Enn.* 5.3.11).[19] *nous* is the knowing of the One, and stands as an icon of the One's transcendent hypostasis. It points toward its transcendent source 'as the sun's rays tell of the sun' (*Enn.* 5.1.7).

Most importantly for Plotinus, *nous* seeks and loves the One, as 'the offspring must seek and love the begetter' (*Enn.* 5.1.6), and *psuche* seeks and loves the Oneness it sees in *nous*. The differentiation of hypostases serves the ultimate purpose of allowing individual souls who have forgotten their God and Father – and, in this forgetting, forgotten also themselves (*Enn.* 5.1.1) – to return, through *psuche* and *nous*, to the One, turning their own souls to it in knowledge, love and prayer. 'Admiring the world of sense . . . let us mount to its archetype, to the yet more authentic sphere: there we are to contemplate all things as members of the Intellectual-Principle – eternal in their own right, vested with a self-springing consciousness and life – and, presiding over all these, the unsoiled Intelligence and the unapproachable wisdom' (*Enn.* 5.1.4).[20]

For Origen, the hypostatic separation of Father and Son serves a similar end. Learning to pronounce the name of the Son is a matter of ascending in him to loving contemplation of the Father, and those who 'do not give him substance nor . . . elucidate his essence' take away the site of their own deifying contemplation of the Father (*In. Jn.* 1.151).[21]

Here, however, an importance difference emerges in Origen's account of the hypostases. If the Son is 'beloved' of the Father, as the New Testament

---

18 Georgios Lekkas demonstrates how Plotinus distinguishes One and *Nous* almost entirely by describing one in terms of the other. This, as we shall see below, installs the dyadic tension that Origen must leave behind. Lekkas, 2005, 'Plotinus: Towards an Ontology of Likeness (On the One and Nous)', *International Journal of Philosophical Studies* 13 (1), pp. 53–68.

19 See Lekkas, 'Towards', p. 58.

20 See Sara Rappe, 1996, 'Self-Knowledge and Subjectivity in the *Enneads*', in Lloyd P. Gerson (ed.), *The Cambridge Companion to Plotinus*, Cambridge: Cambridge University Press, pp. 250–74.

21 See Behr, *Formation* I, pp. 184–5; Williams, *Arius*, pp. 137–40; Rowan Williams, 1999, 'Origen: Between Orthodoxy and Heresy', in W. A. Bienhart and U. Kuhneweg (eds), *Origeniana Septima: Origenes in den Auseinandersetzungen des 4. Jahrhunderts*, Leuven: Leuven University Press, pp. 12ff.

suggests, then the First Hypostasis is not a supreme unity in the Plotinian sense of a One above the powers of knowledge and love. If for Plotinus the One's 'perfection entails' also 'the offspring', simply because 'a power so vast could not remain unfruitful' (*Enn.* 5.1.7), for Origen 'this Son was begotten of the Father's will' (*De princ.* 4.4.1) and the Son's turning in contemplation on the Father is a response to the charitable turning of the Father's face towards his own.

This allows Origen to move beyond the tragic element that remains a consistent thread in the Athenian tradition.[22] This element reappears in Plotinus's One, who generates *Nous* without looking, thus reifying a tension between unbroken unity and unresolved multiplicity. In fact, a dyadic element appears in a tension that inserts itself not only between the strata of being, but also within each. So the 'highest phases' of *Psuche* reside in an 'unbroken transcendence' with *Nous*, while the 'lower power' is characterized by penetration into the material (*Enn.* 4.8.2).[23] The same is true of *Nous*, so that there is a higher phase that never really descends from the preceding hypostasis, presenting instead a remainder with the One, which even 'is' the One in virtue of its unity.[24] At the same time a lower phase of *Nous* has in a sense always already descended to *Psuche* and is constituted as potential multiplicity, so that, under this dyadic strain, the hypostases are at one and the same time all that is above and below, and also nothing at all: more or less empty sets, consisting only of brackets that distinguish them from the other hypostases. This dyadic arrangement allows Plotinus to offer a pathway to union that counters the old Platonic notion of a departure from materiality, because in a sense the individual souls have never been mixed with matter at all: 'even our human Soul has not sunk entire; something of it is continuously in the Intellectual Realm, though if that part, which is in this sphere of sense, hold the mastery, or rather be mastered here and troubled, it keeps us blind to what the upper phase holds in contemplation' (*Enn.* 4.8.8). But this is no true ascent: Plotinian mysticism is a frozen stability within the soul that is countered by a frozen stability above it. Union with the divine will always be partial, imperfect and unnatural, since it fights against the bifurcation of a soul that is permanently inscribed on the grid of the dyadic hypostases.

Origen's teaching of the unity of charitable will between Father and Son allows him to conceive of the hypostases non-dyadically, and thus to open the path for participation in the divine that, like 2 Peter, has jettisoned the tragic remainder. Does he not though, in altering this structure, lose the simplicity of divine being that Plotinian transcendence guards against?

---

22 This general point is argued cogently in Mark Julien Edwards, 2002, *Origen Against Plato*, Burlington: Ashgate.

23 Denis O'Brien, 1999, '*La* Matière *Chez* Plotin: *Son Origine, Sa Nature*', *Phronesis* 44 (1), pp. 45–71.

24 Gregory Shaw describes with great clarity the contrast between Plotinus and Iamblichus on this point in Shaw, 1995, *Theurgy and the Soul: The Neoplatonism of Iamblichus*, University Park, PA: Pennsylvania State University Press, pp. 25ff.

How can a loving Father avoid becoming more explicitly dyadic, doubling his character in directing his will to an extrinsic other?

In fact, this question brings us to the limits of Origen's hypostatic language. Lacking a metaphysical structure to answer this question, his account of God reads the New Testament's loving Father through the lens of a Middle Platonic stratified divinity.[25] Closely related is the problem of creation itself, which for Origen exists eternally as other to the eternal Creator. Salvation is ultimately a return to this extrinsic relation to the Father that the unfallen world enjoyed from before all time, and Christ is the fitting mediator, since he himself exists eternally as multiplicity-tending object of the simple Father's love.[26]

Fourth- and fifth-century Trinitarianism, however, does not reject Origen, but rather extends and clarifies his language of separation.[27] In arguing that any uncreated being is the simple and self-unifying God, Athanasius simply resituates the Mediator and Comforter within the divine being as a preservation of divine simplicity, since 'the holy and blessed Triad is indivisible and one in itself . . .' (*Ad Serap.* 1.14.93).[28] The hypostatic differences must be negotiated within a common being, and this is because 'divine nature', as Gregory of Nyssa puts it, 'does not admit of an opposite' (*De Vita Moysis* 1.7).[29] Neither, though, does it admit of degrees, and so Gregory of Nazianzus can negotiate a gap between divine simplicity and creaturely complexity that is unspannable by any mid-range being: 'For anything between these two, whether having nothing in common with either or a compound of both, not even they who invented the goat-stag could imagine' (*Oration* 31.6).

This new ontological language in turn prepares the ground, as we shall see below, for a theology of perfection that opens out in a rigorous philosophical language the 'homiletical' indications of the New Testament. In effect, the Nicene-era language for the Trinity, in shifting the site of the central ontological division, shifts the site of the central theological question of creation's *telos*. Origen asks, *how does the Spirit allow us to share in the Son's hypostasis in such a way as to participate in the Son's eternal*

---

25 See Illaria L. E. Ramelli, 2009, 'Origen, Patristic Philosophy, and Christian Platonism: Re-Thinking the Christianization of Hellenism', *Vigilae Christianae* 63, pp. 226–7. It is perhaps enough here to cite the importance of Numenius in Plotinus as a way to suggesting that Middle Platonism formed a sort of fall back for Origenism as well. For this, see 'Porphyry: On the *Life of Plotinus and His Work*', in Plotinus, *The Enneads*, p. cxii n. 12; Dillon, 1996, *The Middle Platonists, 80 B.C. to 220 A.D.*, Ithaca: Cornell University Press, p. 366. Denis O'Brien qualifies Plotinus's dependence on the Middle Platonists by pointing out the great novelty of the doctrine of generation from the One. O'Brien, 'La matière', pp. 45–71.

26 Williams, *Arius*, pp. 145–6.

27 Ayres, *Nicaea*, pp. 21ff.

28 See Ayres, *Nicaea*, p. 47. See also Augustine, *Civitas Dei* 18.43.

29 Gregory of Nyssa, *The Life of Moses*, trans., intro, and notes Abraham J. Malherbe and Everett Ferguson, 1978, Mahwah, NJ: Paulist Press.

contemplation of the Father? Athanasius, Augustine and Nyssen will leap from Origenism to a deeper question: *how does this participation, which is the unified work of the simple Creator, constitute the perfection of complex and fragmentary creatures?*

One of the remarkable aspects of this development is the retention of the Origenian language for the distinct members of the Godhead, even as the name 'Origen' itself becomes an increasingly unpopular citation. Athanasius is more than hesitant about the term hypostasis, as its philosophical heritage seems prone to reduce its subjects to beings that are 'foreign and strange, and alien in essence from one another'. Though he never fully embraces the term in his own writings, Athanasius is willing to accept that those who favour the term mean to say that God is 'not just a trinity in name only, but existing and subsisting in truth' (*Antiochene Tome*).[30] Augustine too, and for the same reason, admits that the Greek term to him remains 'rather obscure' (*De Trin.* 5.2.10).[31] But by this time the term has retained purchase, and the Council at Chalcedon incorporates it, apparently as the most fitting way of suggesting that 'the difference . . . of their mutual relations one to another has caused the difference of their names' (Nazianzus, *Orat.* 31.9). That it returns suggests that Origen's scheme of differentiation-for-deifying-participation remains internal to Nicene Christianity, even if Origen himself does not. 'Hypostasis' in Nazianzus and others means something like a distinct character-in-relation within a single flow of being, who can turn and look in love on an other to whom it relates. If this is accurate, then so is Gregory's famous quip: 'Origen is the whetstone of us all.'[32]

Christ the Wedge

The Church Fathers construct a new distinction between Creator and creature, then, in order to give place to the exchange of desire with God that forms the human *telos*. Like the Father's beloved Son, the creature has as her perfection a commerce of love with her Father in heaven.

At this point though, as we trace an emerging perfection, the now familiar philosophical challenge inserts itself. If ontological division is now primary, how can this participation be construed as perfection? If we are made in the likeness of the Beloved, and yet the Beloved is of a different order entirely than we are, it seems that arriving at our end will always be just that – a termination, a dissolution of creaturehood. Although Athanasius and others install the division in order to protect *theosis*, have they not, precisely in the installation, severed the Danaan belts that hold time-bound beings in suspension from the eternal God?

---

30 Antiochene Tome, quoted in Ayres, *Nicaea*, p. 174.

31 *On the Trinity*, trans., intro, and notes Edmund Hill, ed. John E. Rotelle, 1991, Hyde Park, NY: New City Press.

32 Quoted in Behr, *Formation* I, p. 201.

In one important sense, the revisions of the Nicene era do exactly that. In radicalizing the mediating work of Christ, they both construct and respond to a new religious gap between humanity's divine goal and its creaturely existence. As Augustine puts it: 'The Son of God, who is himself the Truth, took manhood without abandoning his godhead, and thus established and founded this faith, so that man might have a path to man's God through the man who was God. For this is "the mediator between God and men, the man Christ Jesus."' The distance is inconceivably great, and so God must provide for us 'a way'. The way must be a human way, if it is not to destroy humanity, and so 'as man he is our Mediator; as man he is our way'. As this pathway, though, Christ constructs the ontological gap even as he spans it: 'For there is hope to attain a journey's end when there is a path which stretches between the traveler and his goal. But if there is no path, or if a man does not know which way to go, there is little use in knowing the destination.' Christ is the road to heaven paved in human flesh and ordered to human modes of discovery; his very existence radicalizes the distinction of natures, even as he performs in his own hypostasis their harmonic coincidence (*De Trin.* 4.1.4–5). The natures must remain separate, like the origin and destination of a journey, if the path itself is to perform their unification.[33] '. . . And this road is provided by the one who is himself both God and man. As God, he is the goal; as man, he is the way' (*Civ. Dei,* 11.2).[34]

Thus radical mediation installs and assumes a radical gap, and for Patristic Christology neither the gap nor its mediation entirely precedes the other: 'For in speaking of the appearance of the Savior amongst us, we must needs speak also of the origin of men, that you may know the reason of his coming down was because of us . . .' (*De Incarnatione* 4.2).[35] The separation of Creator and creation allows Athanasius to call the encounter with Christ a deifying encounter (God becoming human, humans becoming gods), and, reciprocally, the deifying work of Christ allows him to keep creation and Creator separate. Just as in Origen there can only be love by crossing a hypostatic distinction, here there can only be union by the crossing of an eternity–time boundary.

A Christian revision of classical virtues follows upon this distinction between path and end. If temporal justice no longer hangs suspended from

---

33 Like a sign I once saw while driving through the Texas Hill Country: 'We're sorry this road is so long, but if it were any shorter it wouldn't reach.'

34 See Peter Brown, 2000, *Augustine of Hippo: A Biography*, Berkeley: University of California Press, p. 145. Brown describes how the image of the *iter* came gradually to replace the Plotinian image of an ascent in Augustine. He, though, reads this too much as a rejection of the 'quest for perfection' (p. 153) that characterizes Pelagius and other contemporaries. In short, Brown reads Augustine/Pelagius too much as a distinction of tragedy/comedy, resigned sinner/ heroic demigod, or perhaps even Prometheus Bound/Prometheus Unbound.

35 Athanasius, *Incarnation of the Word*, in Philip Schaff and Henry Wace (eds), 1893, *A Select Library of Nicene and Post-Nicene Fathers of the Christian Church*, Vol. IV, New York: The Christian Literature Co., p. 38. See Anatolios, *Coherence*, pp. 26ff.

eternal, but is now marked by a break within being, then a generic depth-dive into humanity will no longer suffice for the human determination of an eternal good. Morality must become surgically Christocentric, since only this humanity offers a reliable path to divinity. So when a novice writes to enquire of Gregory of Nyssa 'how anyone can become perfect through a life of virtue', his response is that Christian perfection is a 'partnership' in the name of Christ, a sharing signified in our bearing the name 'Christian'. To become perfect means only 'to become what the name implies' (*De perfectione* 97–8).[36] Pride of place among these implied characteristics must go to humility, as Maximus says, since the path toward perfection lies on the outside of our human hypostases, and is found only in the human life of the divine hypostasis (*Ambiguum* 10.1205c).[37] This is why Augustine can insist, echoing the Magnificat, that human pride is self-defeating:

> But what good does it do a man who is so proud that he is ashamed to climb aboard [a raft of] wood, what good does it do him to gaze afar on the home country across the sea? And what harm does it do a humble man if he cannot see it from such a distance, but is coming to it nonetheless on the wood the other disdains to be carried by? (*De Trin.* 4.4.20)

Trust in the mediation of Christ, and the 'wood upon which' he bears us to God, is vocationally more significant to us than a vision of our teleological homeland. Indeed, since only he can show us this end, all perfection must now take the form of a 'believing in order to understand'.[38]

Even trust in Christ can function metastatically though, since one can honour Christ's humanity without receiving his mediated divinity. It is only as giver of our deifying end that he provides for us a way to our 'country across the sea'. So, under the tutelage of Ambrose and the formative influence of Catholic liturgy, Augustine 'acknowledged Christ to be the perfect man', fully actualized in body and intellectual soul. 'Yet I held that this same man was to be preferred to others not because he was Truth in person, but on account of the outstanding excellence of his human nature and his more perfect participation in Wisdom' (*Confessiones* 7.19.25).[39] Such an acknowledgement, as he later came to see, is not salvific. Trust in Christ, unless it is trust in his performance of the eternal Logos, is trust in a

---

36 Virginia Woods Callahan (trans.), 1967, *Ascetical Works*, Washington, DC: Catholic University of America Press.

37 Andrew Louth (trans. and ed.), 1996, *Maximus the Confessor*, London: Routledge.

38 See Susan Mennel, 1994, 'Augustine's "I": The "Knowing Subject" and the "Self"', *Journal of Early Christian Studies* 2, pp. 291–324, for a careful treatment of the dynamics of pride and alterity in Confessions. Also, more broadly attending to the question of transformation in the human will, see Michael Hanby, 2003, *Augustine and Modernity*, London: Routledge, pp. 90ff.

39 John E. Rotelle (ed.), 1997, trans. Maria Boulding, Hyde Park, NY: New City Press.

creature, and so cannot train us for union with God. This is to know Christ as the human road, but not to contemplate him as the divine end; this is why for Augustine, Christ at the last judgement will appear in the form of the servant, since if he were to come in the form of God, those who do not know his divinity could not see him or hear his decrees (*De Trin* XIII).[40]

We are now prepared to restate the problem in a clearer way. The gap between creation and its Creator seems to suggest, more profoundly than the Aristotelian *deutero agathon*, that creatures are either ordered to union with their creator, which must annihilate them as creatures, or towards perfection of their created nature, a perfection which must remain immanent to createdness itself. Christ, indeed, seems to drive a wedge into the pre-Christian religious gap. Now: either deification or perfection, but never both.

Perhaps, though, this is a false problem. Is this gap between perfection and deification not simply the result of the fall? In Eden, surely, the Danaan belts held true? The quotation from Athanasius above seems to indicate this conclusion.

> For in speaking of the appearance of the Savior amongst us, we must needs speak also of the origin of men, that you may know the reason of his coming down was because of us, and that our transgression called for the loving-kindness of the Word, that the Lord should both make haste to help us and appear among men. (*De Inc.* 4.2)

If it was the transgression that called for the mediating word, then it is only in the exile from Eden that perfection becomes problematic. In our unfallen createdness, our calling to union with God was also a summons toward our perfection as human beings.

Athanasius, however, cannot provide such a simple solution to our problem, for the simple reason that *theopoesis*, being made a god, is for him at heart a relation of dependence. It thus requires a 'further gift' (*De Inc.* 3.3), regardless of whether or not the journey has become compromised in a fall from the true Logic in which we were created. True, in Eden we refuse the gift; this fall does not actually separate us from God, however, since God's act of creating already accomplishes this. The fall simply allows us, or partially allows us, to turn back to a kind of 'false natural' – 'natural' because it is a conversion back to the nothing from which we were made, 'false' because we turn toward nothing as if it were possible to exist gift-lessly, as if our existence itself were not already a gift. 'For transgression of the commandment was turning them back to their natural state, so that just as they have had their being out of nothing, so also, as might be expected, they might look for corruption into nothing in the course of time' (*De Inc.*

---

40 This is consistent with Origen's argument that deification is impossible if Christ is only seen as the flesh, and not as the enfleshed Logos. *Homilies on Leviticus* 1.1, as quoted in Behr, *Formation* I, pp. 174–6.

4.4).[41] We are formed to become Godlike in a human way, through the mediations of time; it is our attempt to become Godlike in a Godlike way, immediately, that brings about our exile from the garden. Ironically, post-Edenic humanity continues the 'positive' sin of the garden in a new negative form, since attempting to annihilate ourselves in giftlessness is just as God-usurping as trying to deify ourselves by stealing the 'further gift' of deification.[42] So the fall does not install the gap and necessitate a mediator; the rebellion rather refuses the gap that always separates us from our Creator. In paradise, receiving the further gift that mediates our end to us is a sort of cultural habit; east of Eden, the mediation can only come in the flesh.

Augustine is even clearer on this point. 'Being omnipotent, he is able to make out of nothing . . . because he is just, he did not make the things he made out of nothing to be equal to him whom he begat of himself' (*De Natura Boni* 1).[43] It is out of justice that God installs and preserves the gap between the eternally begotten image and the temporal images of that image. Thus, created unequally, we are subject to change, and will always struggle within our createdness to know and love the God who is not so created (*Conf.* 4.15.26).[44] 'That I exist' is 'your gift to me' (*Conf.* 1.20.31), and as a gift it is also the radical font of my creatureliness that I can never peer into. In a sinful world, my attempts to negotiate this gap take the shape of self-disintegration,[45] but in a broader sense, 'I' was always to have been a disintegration, since a being passing through time is only ever a passing. To be temporal is not only to be locked in a present that is shut off from past and future, but it is to be without a present as well, since the moment dissolves as soon as I reach for it (*Conf.* 10.15.20). A creature thus exists without any purchase on the temporal landscape that could provide sure footing for an allegorical journey to our heavenly home.[46] This very captivity is graced, however, since living within inexperienceable time can make us fit for the super-experience of eternity. Similarly, the lapsed world may be overgrown with thorn and thistle, but these very thorns and thistles have measure, form and order and thus are just as aesthetically suited to our fallen human condition as

---

41 See Russell, *Deification*, pp. 169–72.

42 Athanasian original sin is not, as is sometimes said, simply a matter of corruption of flesh, but it is also of a super-volitional continuation of Edenic fall in a way that makes us helpless to overcome it. See Behr's account of this dynamic, *Formation* II.1, pp. 189ff., which helps to distinguish the fourth-century Greek from the late medieval Latin accounts of volition, sin and nature.

43 J. H. S. Burleigh (ed.), 1953, *Augustine: Earlier Writings*, Philadelphia: The Westminster Press.

44 Hanby's account, *Augustine*, pp. 55ff., of Christ as the temporal pathway into eternity in Augustine's theology is unsurpassed.

45 See Mennel, 'Augustine's "I"', and E. Zum Brunn, 1988, *St. Augustine: Being and Nothingness*, trans. R. Namad, New York: Paragon House Publishers.

46 Ayres, *Nicaea*, pp. 335–43, with extreme insight, hinges his account of Augustine's 'pro-Nicene' theology on the latter's analogical ascent through language, initially and primarily in the reading of Scripture.

the tree of life was to our Edenic labours. The tree was there in order to share eternal good with time-bound creatures, and the thorns and painful growths that follow are this same offering, translated into the new dialect of exile. Said differently, the garden itself is already crowded with the material mediations of thorn and thistle. They are gift: we require such mediations for contemplation of our Creator, since this act for which we were created must continually draw us beyond ourselves (*Sermon* 2.16).[47] Like a briar along a path, which produces a wince from a hiker as she scrapes up against it, or a web of weedy vines, which a frustrated gardener must spend an entire day disentangling from fragile vegetables, nature's intrusions coax us ecstatically outside ourselves. As such, they are fitting channels for mediating our union with God.

This reciprocal construction – tree as thorn, thorn as tree – should make clear that the ontological divide in no way suggests a Manichaean remainder in Augustine, nor a generally anti-somatic register in Athanasius.[48] Any notion that creation is a fall is entirely overcome by the end of the Nicene century. The materialization of *logoi* beyond God is a witness to the Logos within God (Athanasius, *De Inc.* 1.3). The human creature is for Augustine more than the crafted being of the sixth day; with its reason and skill, our nature is light and dark, rising and falling, a 'teeming life of every conceivable kind, and exceeding vast', revealing 'measureless plains and vaults and caves of my memory', marked by 'no boundary anywhere' (*Conf.* 10.17.24). In short, human nature is the whole creation in miniature, the work of all six days in one, all of which hymns praises to the invisible God in the very fabric of its createdness.

What remains unclear to this point, however, is how perfection can retain any significance as the completion of a nature, given the location of our *telos* on the far side of a division in being. Even prior to the Athanasian divide, Origen and Irenaeus both to a certain extent recognize this problem and respond by more or less underscoring it. So Origen supposes that our created nature, which is always shrouded by sinful multiplicity, will be overcome, and we will change eschatologically into angels (*De princ.* 1.64). Irenaeus's slightly more interesting solution is that radical changes of nature are in fact natural to us: we were made from dust into men and women, so it should come as no real surprise when one day we are changed

---

47 Philip Schaff (ed.), 1888, *Nicene and Post-Nicene Fathers*, First Series, Vol. VI, trans. R. G. MacMullen, Buffalo, NY: Christian Literature Publishing Co.

48 In spite of James O'Donnell, who claims, without any substantial textual support, that Augustine's anti-Pelagian polemic enacts a return of the repressed Mani. O'Donnell, 2005, *Augustine: A New Biography*, New York: HarperCollins, pp. 292ff. Cf. Mennell's attention to embodiment in the *Confessions* and Hanby's attention to creation's inherent beauty and desirability (*Augustine*, pp. 82–90). For Athanasius's part, the reading of his Christology as fundamentally a Logocentric intrumentalization of the flesh has been dismantled and repaired by Anatolios (*Coherence* pp. 72ff) and Behr (*Formation II.1*, pp. 215ff). For the instrumental view, see Aloys Grillmeier, 1975, *Christ in Christian Tradition*, Philadelphia: Westminster John Knox Press, pp. 317ff.

from men and women into gods (*Adversus haereses* 5.3.2–3).[49] Even this line, in the end, proceeds by abandoning the Aristotelian construction of a *phusis* with its *telos*, and assumes that deification will establish us firmly within new a nature. Are humans made, precisely as human creatures, for union with God? If we are, then union must be conceivable as our perfection. But how can this be?

To return briefly to the Christological amplification of this problem: Chalcedon's tension between two natures within a single *ousia* does not dissolve this conundrum, but only intensifies it. In one Person, two natures that are foreign to one another are joined. Does this conjoining introduce human nature to a union that is exotic to its own intrinsic and natural end? In this case human nature has a perfection outside of Christ, and a deifying exaltation within Christ, but this is impossible to square with Paul's letter to the Colossians, where he insists that it is in Christ alone that 'all things hold together' (Col. 1.17). Or perhaps human nature is perfected only as it is hypostatically united to the divine nature? In this case, human perfection is possible only for God incarnate, and we were fashioned with natures that were naturally deficient, since Adam and Eve were not the Word made flesh. But this only reinserts a new Gnostic remainder, construing creation as a fall into disorder that can only be 'perfected' by having its created integrity dissolved. How then is Christ our perfection?

We must trace the solution to this problem in two stages, for reasons that I will explicate along the way: first the divine gift of a perfecting participation, then, in the following chapter, the human reception of this gift.

Wisdom on Pilgrimage

Chalcedon teaches 'two natures, without confusion, without change, without division . . .' This, though, should not be taken to imply that the Church Fathers envisioned the Person of Christ as the unity of two generically separable natures, like a centaur or a goat-stag. The unity is first of all a unity established by and in God, and his is a different sort of nature than any that can be combined with it. Only by taking account of the radical unicity of the hypostatic union can we come to see how human *theosis* is also the human *telos*.

Augustine, like Origen, appeals often to the Wisdom of Solomon as the beginning of his account of the Logos. As God's 'spotless mirror', Wisdom is filled not only with the goodness and order of God, but of creation as well: 'She reaches mightily from one end of the earth to the other, and she orders all things well' (Wisd. 8.1). Explicating this fullness, Augustine can say that 'The whole series of all times is timelessly contained in God's

---

49 Alexander Roberts and James Donaldson (ed.), 1885, *The Ante-Nicene Fathers*, Vol. I: *The Apostolic Fathers with Justin Martyr and Irenaeus*, New York: The Christian Literature Publishing Co.

eternal Wisdom' (*De Trin.* 2.2.9).[50] The incarnation is in this respect not something entirely new, since one of those times timelessly contained is 'that time in which that Wisdom was to appear in the flesh' (*De Trin.* 2.2.9).[51] There is then a structural parallel between the *logos asarkos* and the Word made flesh, since the latter is a particular – or the particular – instance of the former. Augustine speaks of this parallel, still using the language of Wisdom, as movement: 'because he is a certain pure outflow of the glory of almighty God' (*De Trin.* 4.5.27), the Son can appear within time as an extension of this outflow. The movement from the Father that describes his eternal being gives shape to his movement from eternity into time.

Never one to fear taking words back once he has offered them, Augustine second guesses the tradition he has already begun following in calling the Son 'Wisdom'. 'The Son is not Word in the same way as he is Wisdom' (*De Trin.* 7.1.3) since the former term names the distinct *non est* that differentiates one Person from the other two, while Wisdom, like being, is common to all three. Wisdom is less a relational name, then, and more properly a name of God's substance or nature. If we link this reasoning with his exegesis of Wisdom 7 and 8, we find Augustine suggesting that the divine nature contains all things, including all forms and all time of creation. Divine nature, then, has a certain affinity for becoming created, since this nature is also the Wisdom that 'reaches mightily from one end of the earth to the other'. Wisdom bears an eternal likeness to the forms that eternally and simply inhere within it and so also to the temporal forms that mirror them *ad extra*.[52]

Irenaeus suggests, on this same logic, that 'in becoming man he recapitulates his own handiwork' (*Adv. haer.* 3.16.6).[53] In this very literal sense then, he 'came to that which was his own': Christ redeems by 'restoring to His own handiwork what was said of it in the beginning, that man was made after the image and likeness of God; not snatching away by stratagem the property of another, but taking possession of His own in a righteous and gracious manner' (*Adv. haer.* 5.2.1). Christ's dwelling with creatures for their salvation is therefore nothing like a Jovian colonization of another god's property; it is the creation of the one God that stands in need of that same God's redemption.

The Alexandrians link the incarnation to the *Logos asarkos* simply by noting that the life and sufferings of the former show something inherent in

---

50 See Ayres, *Nicaea*, pp. 317ff.

51 See Rowan Williams, 1993, '*Sapientia* and the Trinity: Reflections on the De Trinitate', in B. Bruning, M. Lamberigts and J. van Houten (eds), *Collecteana Augustiniana: Melanges T. J. von Bavel*, Leuven: Leuven University Press, pp. 317–32.

52 Augustine will eventually solve the question of Wisdom's being both Person and nature by saying that the Son is 'principally' called Wisdom, since he is the manifestation of God's Wisdom to us. Yes, all are Wisdom, but Wisdom is an outflowing of being, and so most like the Son who has his being as the outpouring of the Father's. *De Trin.* 15.5.28–9.

53 As quoted in Behr, *Formation* I, p. 128.

the eternal life of the latter. So Clement takes up Philo's allegorical reading of Aaron's vestment in the tabernacle, now echoing the key Wisdom passage: the robe's hermetic symbols show in a concealed sense 'the agreement which from heaven reaches down to earth'. They are thus a fitting allegory for Christ, 'who is said to be the Father's face, being the revealer of the Father's character to the five senses by clothing Himself with flesh'. Within the veil of priestly flesh is hidden the superhuman priestly work of the Logos, as within the rhythms of his life is hidden 'a kind of divine music' (*Strom.* 5.6). Origen manages to take this repetition one significant step further, suggesting that the crucifixion reveals the essential goodness of the Logos more fully than remaining in unkenotic glory could have (*In Jn* 1.231).[54]

Similarly in Denys the Areopagite: because the Logos is eternally given in the Godhead, its outward extension into the sphere of multiplicity can be differentiated from its being in divine unity, but still figured as a type of this eternal being. This relation of figuration is possible because both the eternal begetting and the temporal birth tell the same story, and name the Logos in the same way. He is God's generosity, and the incarnation demonstrates his personality in a way that 'befits its generosity' in eternity. So he is called a Light that comes to us but 'never abandons its own proper nature, or its own interior unity' (*De coelesti hierarchia* 121B),[55] in that as the incarnate one, he is doing and being what he has 'always' done and been.

Christ is in this sense not really 'two things' at all, but rather a single Person on pilgrimage into 'that which was his own' – even, we might say, into that nature which was his own. For Augustine, the pilgrimage of the Son is a kenosis into himself, which in turns provides a pathway for the ascending of all the forms that inhere within his divine nature. This is the basis for his 'canonical rule', whereby what is said of Christ in Scripture is either said of him in view of his descent, thus in what the Epistle calls the 'form of a servant' (*De Trin.* 1.4.24) or in view of his Personal identity, the 'form of God' (*De Trin.* 2.1.2). He uses this scheme to solve the problem of divine-sounding and human-sounding attributes of Christ in the New Testament. This will appear to us as a wooden, extrinsic lens for interpretation only if we misread him to suggest that there are two kinds of subjects in Christ, so that where one subject does not fit a passage, the other must.[56] Actually, Augustine is surely right in arguing that the biblical texts themselves construct Christ's character differently, according to whether they show him as the Lord who set out from his glorious home and returns there, or as the pilgrim who 'has no place to lay his head' (Luke 9.58). The most

---

54 See Behr, *Formation* I, p. 173.

55 Colm Luibheid (trans.), 1997, *The Complete Works*, Mahwah, NJ: Paulist Press. I am influenced in this reading by Ysabel De Andia, whose emphasis on the centrality of Christology in Denys's account of deification is revolutionary in Areopagite studies. See Ysabel de Andia, 1996, *Henosis*, Leiden: Brill.

56 As Catherine Mowry Lacugna reads him. Catherine Mowry La Cugna, 1991, *God for Us: The Trinity and Christian Life*, San Francisco: HarperCollins, pp. 84–5.

significant implication of his rule, though, comes when Augustine shows that in many cases the same text can be read either way: 'For example, *My teaching is not mine, but his who sent me* (John 7.16); it can be understood by the form-of-a-servant rule, which is how we treated it in the previous book; and also by the form-of-God rule, of his being equal to the Father and yet from the Father.'[57] The key point is that Christ can make his journey through time because he is eternally the 'Beautiful' pilgrim who sets out from his 'Source', and is brought back by the 'Delight' of that home which never forsakes him (*De Trin.* 6.2.12).

When the Fathers develop the language for Christ's humanity as enhypostatically joined to his divinity, it is out of an attempt to insist that Christ has no human narrative other than that of the Divine Pilgrim. Christ cannot have a human Person, since this would grant a teleological integrity to his human nature, and leave us too securely within the realm of Aristotelian metaphysics.[58] How does the human nature of Christ receive this hypostatic union as a perfection? The point must be not that his human nature is amalgamated to a divine nature in a competitive space, but rather the divine nature descends in Person into existence as a human nature, granting to the human nature the end it has always desired, since it is the end for which humanity was created. The form of all creation descends into himself, personifying a created nature, allowing it to share in his own divine end, which is also his humanity's proper end. In this way Christ's humanity is deified, and this deification is also its perfection, since, unlike a union of, say, hydrangeas and tulips, Christ unites in his Person two natures that are fit to one another. The Logos is already the human, though simply and eternally; the human is already the Logos, though multiply and temporally.[59] The incarnate one never ceases to be the divine one, not because the divinity is packed away inside in a secret compartment of his human personality, but because Christ in the body is like his own eternal divinity, telling the same story in his flesh that his personality tells in eternity.

The human Christ is divine then in the same sense that a king disguised as a swineherd is still the king, as in the Saxon legend of Alfred and the burnt cakes. This story, which could only originate in a culture whose imagination was fixed on the Christian narrative of God dwelling with his people,[60] tells of a king who one day appears at the door of a peasant woman in his kingdom, tired and famished after a defeat on the battlefield. Not realizing who he is, the woman agrees to feed him if he will watch the cakes in the oven. When, overcome with care and fatigue, he lets the cakes

---

57 Lacugna, *God for Us*, p. 99.

58 As Sergeii Bulgakov, 2008 [1933], *The Lamb of God*, trans. Boris Jakim, Grand Rapids: Eerdmans, pp. 1–50, demonstrates.

59 My reading of the Fathers has been shaped, in this respect at least, by Bulgakov's. See Sergei Bulgakov, 2004 [1936], *The Comforter*, trans. Boris Jakim, Grand Rapids: Eerdmans, pp. 1–40; and *The Lamb of God*, pp. 1–88.

60 I am indebted to Alan Gregory for discussions of this legend and its theological implications.

burn, he earns a scolding and beating from the woman. Later, when she discovers his identity, the peasant tries to apologize, but he refuses to accept, claiming that her actions were just. His humility is a true humility, in that he takes the beating not out of an excess of self-abnegation, but rather because it is in a very basic way deserved. He has burned his cakes, and they are doubly his, since she gives them to him as he stands before her, in the form of a beggar, while in the form of the king the cakes, the oven, the kitchen, the cottage, the grains fields and even the peasant herself are all his. Presumably, he would not have taken this beating in a Norman or Spanish peasant's cottage, since there he would either be a king in a foreign kitchen, or a hungry peasant who does not understand the regional language. Neither should be beaten, as a general rule. But because he comes to the kitchen as his own, he can 'be' the hungry cake-watching peasant analogously to the way that he is the satisfied cake-watching king. In fact, if by burning the cakes he behaves un-kinglike, not caring for his own properly, by taking the beating he behaves in a kingly fashion once again, recognizing and championing the cause of justice. At that precise moment when he is being beaten without retaliation, he is perfectly peasant-like and perfectly kingly at the same time.[61] Like Christ, again, who is most perfectly divine precisely in his condescension to human form (Origen, *In Jn.* 1. 231).

If Christ can, in the *forma servi*, live enhypostatically as the Beloved lover of the Father just as he lives in the *forma dei*, then his humanity receives this union with God as a new end, beyond its nature, that is also the completion of its nature. Jesus of Nazareth does in his flesh the work of the Eternal Son, and so is this Son, and has the same *telos* as the Son. 'For us he became a road or way in time by his humility,' while never ceasing thereby to be 'for us an eternal abode by his divinity' (*De Trin.* 7.2.5). The hypostatic union would be meaningless if we could not discern Son-like qualities in the human words and acts of Christ, just as it would no longer be true that Alfred was king, if he had entirely ceased to embody the virtues of kings when he came as a peasant. That he does not cease to be kingly, that Christ does not cease to be Sonly, shows that the latter can, in his kenotic form, still allow the hypostatic gap between Father and Son to unite him in love to the Father, even when he appears on the far side of the great ontological division.

Moreover, because Christ is eternal Wisdom spoken in time – that Wisdom who stretches from one side of the cosmos to the other – his descent gives a new end to all created forms that is at once both natural and transcendent (Col. 1.15–17). As the Spirit gathers all things into Christ, all things are given the gift of a union with God that is also each form's proper perfection. As Maximus says, deified creatures 'cleave to the logoi' that defines them, as unique participations in the Logos that created them (*Ambiguum*

---

61 My version of the tale gathers elements of several retellings, collected and analysed in David Horspool, 2006, *King Alfred: Burnt Cakes and Other Legends*, London: Profile Books Ltd, pp. 8off.

7.1084b).[62] And if the human nature assumed by the Logos can live divine participation as its own perfection, then so can the forms of all things that inhere within him. Like the gods in Genesis, who are ultimately caught up in and judged by Yahweh's long journey, all creatures – kings and peasants, hydrangeas and tulips – are destined for the embrace of Wisdom, whose pilgrimage through her own creation re-establishes the wise end for which all these things were originally fashioned.

---

62 Paul M. Blowers and Robert Louis Wilken (trans.), 2003, *On the Cosmic Mystery of Jesus Christ*, Crestwood: St Vladimir's Seminary Press.

6

Saving the Form:
Perfection in the Church Fathers, Part II

'What kind of human being is anyone who is human and nothing more?'

Augustine of Hippo

So creatures are the Logos's own, and his pilgrimage to reclaim us as such unites created nature to its deifying end.

But will our natures bear his claim? If the union of all things with the Beloved Hypostasis had happened in sheer immediacy, at the scene of the Nativity perhaps, or the cross, or the empty tomb, or in the Upper Room at Pentecost, then all the forms of creation would dissolve into their founding Logos, and the *logoi*, essentially temporal mediations of the Logos, would be no more. Even if we delay this incursion of immediacy to the *eschaton*, this remains the point at which created form is lost, and perfection rolls over into a deifying destruction. Can creatures, as creatures, enact their union with Christ, in whom 'all things hold together' (Col. 1.17), without dissolving into the eternally simple union of the Beloved, through Love, with the Lover? Can human nature, or any created nature for that matter, bear the weight of this deification without crumbling under it?

If the Church Fathers answer this question hesitatingly, they nevertheless answer affirmatively, and so commit themselves and Christian thought ever after, to a rigorous philosophical heritage. If the human must be saved, then so must human bodies, human reason, human desire. The natural machinations of the human creature, so 'recently created' (Irenaeus, *Adversus Haereses* IV.38.2) must mediate the supernatural gift of deification, rather than stand down in preparation for an immediate and therefore inhuman reception. In answering this way, the Church Fathers insist that *theosis* will also be a perfection.

This chapter will trace five key steps toward this philosophical rigour in the Fathers' developing account of perfection. I arrange them more or less chronologically, and intend to suggest that they build on one another. I do not mean by this that the earlier stages are simply overcome in the writings that come after, since in fact much of what is accomplished in the beginning stages remains, and on occasion even surpasses the later constructions. Even so, there is, as I will attempt to demonstrate, a clear crescendo of perfection theology in the early centuries of Christianity.

Irenaeus and the Potter's Wheel

The Irenaean ascent

Irenaeus of Lyons sets the problem up with precision by insisting, against the Gnostics, that there is nothing wrong about being made with material and temporal limitations. The irony of sin, in fact, is that the time-bound creature's attempt at self-deification ruins the only true path to deification. The animals in Eden 'bring no charge against God for not having made them men; but each one, just as he has been created, gives thanks that he has been created'. Human beings, however, 'cast blame upon Him, because we have not been made gods from the beginning, but at first merely men, then at length gods'. And in bringing this charge against our mediated deification, we blame the God who 'has adopted this course out of His pure benevolence' (*Adv. Haer.* IV.33.4).

In this case the real question of perfection is not *how Godlike can a creature become?*, since this seems almost to fail to register with Irenaeus as a possible conundrum. 'Only the Uncreated is perfect, that is, God' (*Adv. Haer.* IV.38.1). It is nonsensical to ask if creatures could have been made perfect with God's perfection, since that is the same as asking whether the creature could have been created as uncreated. Deification never implies for him – or for any of the Church Fathers – that creatures cease to be creatures in their union with the Creator. Creaturely perfection is rather in 'approximating the uncreated' (*Adv. Haer.* IV.38.3). The provision of this increase is the goodness of creation's very fabric, so that the temporal beings who, even had they been offered immediate perfection, 'could not possibly have received . . . contained, or . . . retained it' (*Adv. Haer.* IV.38.2), might experience this lack as a calling to Godlikeness.[1]

The real question of perfection then is how a creature, meant to become Godlike, can continue this progression after short-circuiting the very path that stretches beyond creaturely limits. 'How . . . can he be immortal, who in his mortal nature did not obey his maker?' (*Adv. Haer.* IV.39.2) Human mediacy is the pathway towards assimilation to the Father's perfection, and we sunder this assimilation precisely by grasping for immediacy, by attempting to be Godlike in a Godlike way, rather than in a human way (*Adv. Haer.* V.1.1).[2] Rehearsing Jeremiah's metaphor of the potter's wheel, Irenaeus says that human perfection is deification 'in due time', like the moist clay that must remain moist if is to receive perfect form in the potter's hands. The crafted one refuses this perfection only by claiming it, like clay that hardens into self-made form before the hands have finished the crafting (*Adv. Haer.* IV.39.2).

---

1 Norman Russell, 2005, *The Doctrine of Deification in the Greek Patristic Tradition*, Oxford: Oxford University Press, pp. 107–8.

2 See Denis Minns, 2006, 'Truth and tradition: Irenaeus', in Margaret M. Mitchell and Frances Young (eds), *The Cambridge History of Christianity* vol. 1, Cambridge: Cambridge University Press, pp. 270–1.

Does the potter's wheel not, though, simply rehearse the problem of a human who must cease human activity, in order to receive perfect form from beyond (which is therefore only perfection in an ironic sense)? It does not, because for him staying moist means being human in the fullest sense of our created nature. We are designed to be human, and in being human we become gods. This means that there is an 'ancient law of human liberty' (*Adv. Haer.* IV.38.1) according to which God generously bestows his good upon us, and our reception of it comes through wilfully and actively performing the good. Because he assumes that perfection is a participation, Irenaeus does not construe active performing in opposition to passive accepting, but rather always sees performance as a way of accepting the gift: 'God therefore has given that which is good, as the apostle tells us in this Epistle [Romans], and they who work it shall receive glory and honour, because they have done that which is good . . .' (*Adv. Haer.* IV.38.1). Human agency is therefore, at its most perfect, the reception of grace. Pure passivity, on the other hand, aligns ironically with the impatience of Adam and Eve in Eden, insofar as it marks an attempt to stop acting like humans and receive one's *telos* immediately. But this attempt at pure reception destroys both nature and its perfection; it would have, that is, had not God recapitulated humanity in the perfect mediation of his Son (*Adv. Haer.* III.18.7).[3]

The Irenaean plateau

Are moist natures, however, fit for immortality, or must nature itself in some sense be overcome in the supernatural gift of the Logos? There is, for Irenaeus, an element within the clay that will always resist deification. The quotation cited above, 'God therefore has given that which is good, as the apostle tells us in this Epistle [Romans], and they who work it shall receive glory and honour', continues: 'because they have done that which is good when they had it in their power not to do it' (*Adv. Haer.* IV.38.1). The negative construction here builds upon Paul's argument in Romans 2 by suggesting that the gifts of God resulting in deification are gifts that we must 'justly possess'. If God gave these gifts out of mercy alone, God would be acting unjustly. Had Adam and Eve, though, entered the world aligned to goodness alone, God's gifts would not be a just response to a just action. Rather, the right acts of creatures must always entail a choosing of good over evil. Alternatively, those who do evil, or rather passively refuse to do the good, also justly possess their inherited condemnation.

Does the Genesis account, though, not insist that knowledge of good and evil is forbidden to the natural man and woman? For Irenaeus, the

---

3 See Steenberg's excellent account of the Trinitarian and Christological mediation of the human form in Matthew Craig Steenberg, 2009, *Of God and Man: Theology as Anthropology from Irenaeus to Athanasius*, London: T & T Clark, pp. 16–54.

prohibition of the fruit already entails the consequences of eating it: 'Since God therefore, gave to man such mental power, man knew both the good of obedience and the evil of disobedience . . . that he may never become indolent or negligent of God's command' (*Adv. Haer.* IV.39.1). Thus the human creature, limited and infantile, depends on the life God bestows in order to continue to work and act; and this dependence is also a knowledge of good and evil, so that the acts we do can be justly called good, and justly share in the perfecting goodness of God. If Irenaeus wins ground against the Gnostic rendering of creation as a fall (and in this limited sense at least, Origen is still Gnostic),[4] he saves created goodness only by preserving a Gnostic remainder: we can be called good, and God can justly reward our goodness, only if the knowledge of good and evil is inherent to the human creation. For Irenaeus, we are born eating the fruit.

Perfection in this case, though always a temporal mediation, is also a movement past this mediation, since our final reward will continue to be just, even when the doing of evil is no longer possible. We were created knowing good and evil, but this created nature will have as its perfection a knowledge of the good alone. If this reward is still just, it must be because grace in some sense overcomes not only our fallenness, but also even 'the substance of created nature' (*Adv. Haer.* IV.33.4). This does not mean, as in Origen, that the deified human becomes a different species altogether, but still that our nature is destined for a radical change, when the mortal body that knows good and evil puts on the immortality that knows only the good. Irenaeus saves the coherence of his eschatological account by suggesting that radical changes of nature are in fact natural for us, as 'we ought to perceive from our origin, inasmuch as God, taking dust from the earth, formed man' (*Adv. Haer.* V.3.2). Receiving the power of immortality is still a fitting end for our nature, but only because radical transformations of nature are natural for us: dust to sinews, sinews to mortal human, mortal human to a god. But does this radical change give us any structure for talking about the enjoyment of human life, the fulfilment of desire or the knowing of God? All of this language assumes that eternal life meets a human creature who operates in mortality by means of enjoyment, desire and knowledge, a creature who will receive this eternal life as an end that she can experience as an end. What Irenaeus lacks is a language that can mediate the final baked hardness of the pot to the moist clay on the wheel, so that it can be a useful pot, but somehow without losing its created moisture. For this, further developments are necessary.

---

4 In spite of the rigorous and important defence of Origen against this critique in M. J. Edwards, 2002, *Origen against Plato*, Aldershot: Ashgate. On Irenaeus and Gnostic deification, see Jeffrey Finch, 2006, 'Athanasius on the Deifying Work of the Redeemer', in Stephen Finlan and Vladimir Kharlamov (eds), *Theōsis: Deification in Christian Theology*, Princeton Theological Monograph Series 52, Eugene, OR: Pickwick Publications, pp. 92ff.

Gregory on the Purple Attributes

The Nyssan ascent

Perfection in Gregory of Nyssa is less a reward for a righteous life than a fitting end to God's creative act. He 'creates man for no other reason than that He is good', and since 'He would not exhibit the power of His goodness in an imperfect form, giving our nature some one of the things at His disposal, and grudging it a share in another', he fittingly shares with us 'all goods' (*De hominis opificio*, 16.10).[5] As we are created for this share in unmixed goodness, the knowledge of evil has no place within the human form. The prohibition on the tree did not include an offer of evil that the humans were called to resist, since they could neither have recognized nor been drawn to any opposition to goodness. In order to entice them to sin, the serpent had to test the limits of his own craftiness: a simple suggestion to 'do evil' would be far too blatant for these gardeners. His plan to reorder the image of divinity as the image of vanity required 'a fruit blended and mixed with opposite qualities' (*De hom.* 19.5), so that Eve, knowing only goodness, might assume that a fruit good for the eye was also good for the soul. She did not know of good and evil, then, but only the good, which is always a proportionate kind of knowing. By manipulating her attraction to a particular good, the serpent enticed her to desire it out of its own proportion, so that the goodness of a piece of fruit overtook the goodness of her friendship with God. For one fashioned as *eikon Theou*, what other path to corruption could there be? No opposition is possible in the form, and therefore none is necessary in order to reveal human perfection: 'the beauty of the form' is enough (*De hom.* 18.9).[6]

Having posited a nature fashioned without any trace of evil, Gregory avoids the Irenaean shortfall. His eschatology is consistent with his protology: 'if nothing comes from above to hinder its upward thrust (for the nature of the Good attracts to itself those who look at it), the soul rises ever higher . . .' (*vit. Moys.* 2.225). We can now see the entire human career as an ascent toward perfective union, without the lingering question of what happens to our nature when evil disappears from our vision.[7] There is thus a philosophical coherence to Gregory's famous adaptation of the Pauline

---

5 *On the Making of Man*, in Philip Schaff (ed.), 1888, *Nicene and Post-Nicene Fathers*, Second Series, Vol. V, trans. R. G. MacMullen, Buffalo, NY: Christian Literature Publishing Co. Translating in this final phrase ἀγαθά as 'goods', rather than, with *NPNF*, 'good gifts', since the later translation implies a reference to the Epistle to James, δόσις ἀγαθή, whereas with the ἀγαθά alone, Gregory seems to be invoking Plato's form of the Good as source of all goods.

6 Hans Urs von Balthasar, 1988, *Presence and Thought: Essays on the Religious Philosophy of Gregory of Nyssa*, trans. Mark Sebanc, San Francisco: Ignatius Press, pp. 57–63.

7 Von Balthasar identifies here a distinction between gift and participation: God gives the entire human form, and then invites the human to participate in this creative act through its own practical career. Balthasar, *Presence*, pp. 65–9.

epekteinomenos (Phil. 3.13): '... the soul rises ever higher and will always make its flight yet higher – by its desire of the heavenly things *straining ahead for what is still to come*' (*vit. Moys.* 2.225). A nature made to know and share in the limitless Good becomes perfect in a limitless passage into this knowledge. 'For the perfection of human nature consists perhaps in its very growth in goodness' (*vit. Moys.* 1.31).[8]

Does Gregory, then, suggest that only an unfallen creature is perfectible? No, since for him, as for all the Fathers, the fall does not annihilate created goodness, but rather complicates the ascent. This is due, first of all, to the way in which God created us. Like an artist 'painting the portrait to resemble his beauty' (*De hom.* 5.1), the Creator brushes us in with the royal purple of his own attributes, embodied in created things as virtues. For one so fashioned, ascending towards the good means developing these virtues through embodied life. This might have been as simple a matter as climbing Jacob's ladder, rung over rung, towards the limitless good; now, challenged and tempted by evil, ascending towards the good is the journey up a mountain, with the lurking dangers of beasts, darkness and avalanches. For Gregory, though, Moses' journey up Sinai is always still Jacob's journey up the ladder, since sin has no licence to change the landscape of perfection (*De hom.* 18.9).[9]

Tying the notion of ascent closely to the reflecting capacity as God's image, Gregory can further give us language to understand creaturely perfection as sharing in the eternal reflecting of the Father in the Son. So perfection, he says, is 'partnership' in the name of Christ, and the essence of this vocation is 'to become what the name implies' (*De perfectione*, 97–8). To become Christian is to become Sonlike, and thus to assimilate to the divine nature. So

[w]hen Christ is called 'rock,' this word assists us in the firmness and permanence of our virtuous life, that is, in the steadfastness of our endurance of suffering, and in our soul's opposition and inaccessibility to the assaults of sin. Through these and such things, we also will be a rock imitating, as far as is possible in our changing nature, the unchanging and permanent nature of the Master. (*De perf.* 108)

Here Gregory repeats the Platonic 'as far as is possible', but with a note that carries his construction beyond Plato as well as Irenaeus. The creature bears a fittingness for this assimilation in Gregory that she could not have

---

8 Hart's account of the Gregory's doctrine of God and its relationship to his account of the perfection of the *imago dei* is in many respects unsurpassed. See David Bentley Hart, 2002, 'The Mirror of the Infinite: Gregory of Nyssa on the Vestigia Trinitatis', *Modern Theology* 18(4), pp. 542–56.

9 See Farmer's insightful reading of Gregory, with special attention to the intermingling of the pure and mixed praise, in Tamin Jones Farmer, 2005, 'Revealing the Invisible: Gregory of Nyssa on the Gift of Revelation', *Modern Theology* 21, pp. 72–4.

born in either of these authors. This fittingness appears in both a Christo-logical and Trinitarian register.

First, in his Christology, Gregory paves the way for human participa-tion by reading Christ as the divine Word written in human artistry.[10] The original Sinai tablets were human nature, 'unbroken and immortal', 'fash-ioned by divine hands'. In turning away, creatures caused the tablets to be broken. (Did we break them? Or, in a more Irenaean fashion, did God break them to spare us? Gregory does not tell us which.) This transgres-sion was met, however, with a more radical accommodation: 'The true Lawgiver, of whom Moses was a type, cut the tablets of human nature for himself from our earth.' Thus while God is still the author of the second draft of the tablets, Christ 'became the stonecutter of his own flesh' (*vit. Moys.* 2.216). Christ's work then is 'to imitate in material construction that immaterial creation' (*vit. Moys.* 1.49). Christ's own labours were con-jectural, in the sense that his striving toward the infinite was always a kind of 'giving birth to himself' (*vit. Moys.* 2.3), guessing at the ratios of mate-riality that would best ascend into harmony with the divine.[11] Ultimately, the lesson of the ascension of the bodily Christ is that 'no difference of any kind can be perceived – for whatever one sees in the Son is Godhead' (*Ad Theophilium*).[12]

If this is Christ's work, it is also ours. So, echoing Philo, Gregory says that 'after his descent from the mountain', Moses/Christ employs work-men to build the tabernacle 'according to the pattern shown to him' (*vit. Moys.*1.51). Human nature, 'made to desire and not to abandon the tran-scendent height' (*vit. Moys.* 2.226), is reconnected with its true end in Christ, and so the contingent conjectures of material life can be construed so as to bear the weight of eternal likeness. Our hands assist us in this, not only as the body's principle means of carving and fastening, but also in that they are the mark par excellence of a linguistically oriented creature who can thus learn to speak the divine language: if we lacked hands, not only could we not write our language down, we would not be able to speak it either, as we would then require snouts adapted for gathering food rather than for articulating diverse syllables (*De hom.* 8.2, 8). Our hands then are doubly adapted for creatures made to fashion divinity within space and time. 'You, as a sculptor, carve in your own heart the divine oracles which you receive from God' (*vit. Moys.* 2.320). In Christ, we become scribes of the New Law, writing with human fingers and constructing with hu-man culture the Words imagined from before creation itself in the divine Logos.

---

10 For accounts of Gregory's Christology as foundational to his understanding of human excellence, see Werner Jaeger, 1961, *Early Christianity and Greek Paideia*, Cambridge. MA: Harvard University Press, pp. 86–102; and Brian E. Daley, SJ, 2002, 'Divine Transcendence and Human Transformation: Gregory of Nyssa's Anti-Apollinarian Christology', *Modern Theology* 18 (4), pp. 497–506.

11 Russell, *Deification*, pp. 229–30.

12 Translation is from Daley, 'Divine Transcendence', p. 499.

Though Gregory is not so deliberate about connecting the human image with the inner life of the Trinity as Augustine, he still is concerned to show that, if we are made in Christ's image, then the entire Trinity is somehow evident in our nature. The fact that God takes counsel with himself prior to the fashioning of humans suggests that there is a singularity of purpose in the work of the Godhead, and thus a singularity of vocation traceable in the human form that God creates. So the unity of human perfection is not only a testimony to the unity of Christ's Person, but to the unity of the entire Trinity as well. At the same time, just as in creatures various powers can co-operate in this unified pursuit, God can be one while still being various, since along with an all-knowing source there is an all-obedient Son and a Spirit who 'searches everything, even the depths of God' (1 Cor. 2.20): 'The Deity beholds and hears all things, and searches all things out: you too have the power of apprehension of things by means of sight and hearing, and the understanding that inquires into things and searches them out' (*De hom.* 5.2).[13]

In Gregory then, perfection takes a major step beyond the Platonic limitations. Created out of nothing but divine attributes, our nature knows no other perfection than these attributes. Unfallen materiality can never stand in the way of this advance, since, in Adam, human nature is inscribed with divine Law. Neither, though, can fallen nature finally compromise the advance, since Christ performs this reinscription, inviting us to overcome vice and sin on the path to the assimilation for which we were first crafted by God's hand.

The Nyssan plateau

Does the human modality of *straining ahead for what is still to come* ultimately comprise a comic or tragic anthropology? If this drama ends in a marriage rather than a death scene, then it must be that temporal creatures are suited not only for the ascent up Sinai, but also for the consummation of their journey, in the 'dazzling darkness' of the cloud at the mountaintop.[14]

Here we come to the limits of the Nyssan account of perfection. When he asks how the temporal is like the eternal, his initial answer echoes Athanasius. The ontological distinction between Creator and creature keeps time from collapsing into its source; further, because the creature is the image of the Creator, its difference and distinctiveness is also its path to analogical harmony. This, however, remains a view 'from above'. When he looks out from the eyes of the one ascending the temporal mountain, he oddly exchanges the imaging distinction of Creator/creature for the more polarized infinity/finitude. 'We hold the divine nature to be unlimited and infinite', therefore the best end of a created nature will be an unboundaried perpetuity: 'Since, then, those who know what is good by nature desire participation in it, and since this good has no limit,

---

13 See Hart, 'Mirror', pp. 542–56; Lewis Ayres, 2004, *Nicaea and its Legacy: An Approach to Fourth-Century Trinitarian Theology*, Oxford: Oxford University Press, pp. 345–63.

14 Farmer, 'Revealing', p. 77.

the participant's desire itself necessarily has no stopping place but stretches out with the limitless' (*vit. Moys.* 1.7).

Aware of the tragic implications of this construal, Gregory responds with pastoral encouragement:

> It is therefore undoubtedly impossible to attain perfection, since, as I have said, perfection is not marked off by limits: The one limit of virtue is the absence of a limit. How then would one arrive at the sought-for boundary when he can find no boundary?
>
> Although on the whole my argument has shown that what is sought for is unattainable, one should not disregard the commandment of the Lord which says, *Therefore be perfect, just as your heavenly father is perfect.* For in the case of those things which are good by nature, even if men of understanding were not able to attain to everything, by attaining even a part they could yet gain a great deal. (*vit. Moys.* 1.8–9)

It would be easy to make too much of this concession in Gregory. His *Life of Moses*, like his *On Perfection*, is written as a spiritual guidebook rather than an ontological treatise on the completion of created natures. He has a keen sense of the movement that is basic to created nature, and wants to insist to his neophyte readers that a *telos* in God does not 'promise any cessation or satiety of desire' (*vit. Moys.* 2.232),[15] as that would imply a destructive perfection. He wants, then, to urge them not to seek passive stillness, but to turn their natural restlessness toward the boundless journey into the divine nature.

For all that, however, his notion of divine infinity is strangely flat, as if God's boundlessness were, despite Gregory's insistence to the contrary (*vit. Moys.* 1.7),[16] opposed to our finitude. Perfection is the boundless God, finitude is limitation, and therefore finite beings are chronically imperfect. He even suggests that the divine acts by which we know the unity of the Godhead (θεότης) are fitted for finite understanding, and therefore 'under' the true divine infinity. So he argues, with an almost Ockhamist surgical logic: 'In order to mark the constancy of our conception of infinity in the case of the Divine nature, we say that the Deity is above every name: and "Godhead" is a name. Now it cannot be that the same thing should at once be a name and be accounted as above every name' (*Ad Ablabius, NPNF* p. 335).[17] Thus the elliptical conclusion: infinity is the cloud of darkness

---

15 See Balthasar, *Presence*, p. 153, on this point: 'Through the Incarnation we learn that all the unsatisfied movement of becoming is itself only repose and fixity when compared to that immense movement of love inside of God: Being is Super-Becoming.'

16 Hart's reading, though an important corrective to the boring typology of east-starts-with-triplicity, west-starts-with-unicity, winds up taking Gregory in too Augustinian a direction, inserting an 'analogical interval' (Hart's wonderfully rich phrase) between the infinite and finite that simply does not operate in the bulk of Gregory's spiritual writings. See 'Mirror', especially pp. 544–5.

17 See Ayres, *Nicaea*, pp. 345–63; and John Behr, 2004, *The Formation of Christian Theology*, Vol. II: *The Nicene Faith, Part 2*, Crestwood, NY: St Vladimir's Seminary Press, pp. 427–35.

beyond the discernibly simple unity of the Godhead. Finite nature can only know the acts of the infinite, but not the infinite nature itself. 'The name of deity signifies activity and not nature' (*Ad Ab.* p. 154),[18] since we name God according to act, not according to the nature which, 'in all respects infinite' (*Ad Ab.* p. 335),[19] is technically unknowable.

Understanding is left off, then, in the cloud, and desire for the unknowable and unattainable is the ultimate expression of creaturely holiness. But this compromises our nature by truncating the cognitive powers not with a perfection, but with a disappearance. Gregory is aware of this, and seems to accept it as the tragic end of humanity. Like Moses in the darkness, our end is 'beyond nature' (*vit. Moys.* 1.58). We are not fit to know the infinite, although we are fit to desire it. For that reason, human existence is a constant day of preparation for Sabbath, a ceaseless toiling up the mountain, never coming to rest in the knowledge which it desires, but which finitude is not given to know (*vit. Moys.* 2.144).

What does this endless labour signify, finally, for Gregory's Christology? Christ can 'imitate in material construction that immaterial creation', and does so in such a way that his humanity goes transparent to – but without dissolving into – his divinity. This is human perfection. But does this not point in the direction of the later Scotist doctrine of the primacy of the incarnation? If only a hypostatic union to the divine achieves perfection, then Christ alone is the true human, and cannot share with us that true humanity that realigns perfection with our nature. Finite personhood is, in this case, only a barrier to perfection, and Christ becomes the divinized humanity that we can never be, because it is a humanity we were never created to be. Only the hypostatically divine human can move beyond the tragic face of *epectasis*. In this respect, Augustine represents a step beyond Gregory of Nyssa.

Augustine on the Roundness of Nuts

The Augustinian ascent

Just as concerned with perpetual human progress as Gregory, Augustine cites the key Philippians passage at several key points in his writings.[20]

---

18 William G. Rusch (ed.), 1980, *The Trinitarian Controversy*, Minneapolis: Fortress, p. 154.

19 Ayres falls short here, in overlooking the centrality of 'infinity' as more than just one among the divine names, but the super-name than relativizes all others. When Ayres does treat the term, he assumes it means simply 'incomprehensibility', and thus can use it, similarly to Hart, as an opening for anagogical ascent. But if it is above the field of names, it is also above the field of participation, and therefore useless for our journey into God. See *Nicaea*, pp. 352–61.

20 For instance: when noting that his life, 'but a scattering', is ultimately only 'established in you' (*Conf.* 11.29.39), from the Sheed translation, 1970, Indianapolis: Hackett Publishing Co. pp. 230–1; after the 'failure' of the *caritas* image, when he cites Philippians 3.13 as that text which 'above all' teaches us how our desire for God becomes our godliness: 'Perfection in this life, he is saying, is nothing but

His conversion to Catholicism from Manichaeism was motivated almost entirely by the growing awareness that the latter installed a rigid dogmatism that threatened to shut down human development: 'I could make no progress in it' (*Conf.* 5.10.18).[21] But it is exactly this insistence on advancement towards the good that leads him to argue that understanding is not entirely left behind in our union with God. We experience this union as the perfection not only of our will, but of our reasoning powers as well. Thus one who does not understand the incomprehensible God of whom Scripture speaks 'should sorrow that he comprehends it not, and find out whereby he is hindered from comprehending, and remove those hindrances, and, himself changed from worse to better, aspire after the perception of the unchangeable Word' (*Sermon* 117.3).[22]

How does he allow a union with God that does not compromise God's infinity? Augustine is more purely Athanasian here than Gregory, since for him the distinction between Creator and creature is always primary and spanned not merely by the being of Christ, but by his movement: by kenotic descent and deifying ascent (*De Trin.* I.21).[23] God is an eternal movement that, in Christ, comes to entail creation; by naming the divine in this way, Augustine limits, as it were, the attribute of infinity: 'God is not even infinity, if by that we mean limitless expansiveness' (*De Trin.* VIII.3). In fact, the human mind is more properly called infinite in this respect, since there seems to be no traceable horizon to what we can expect, remember or know (*De Trin.* X.2). God's infinity is of a different sort altogether: indeed, by turning inward and exhausting the potential of the infinite *mentis* to

---

forgetting what lies behind and stretching out to what lies ahead intently' (*de Trin.* 9.1); see also where the pilgrim's 'way is rendered beautiful by the wisdom he longs to reach' (*de Libero Arbitrio* 2.17.45).

21 The translation of the phrase is quoted in Peter Brown, 1992, *Augustine of Hippo: A Biography*, Berkeley: University of California Press, p. 48. Brown's treatment of the conversion especially emphasizes the lack of human growth as 'the definitive condemnation of the Manicheean system', and, reciprocally, the defining characteristic of catholic faith. See also pp. 48–9 as well as 143–4.

22 Sermon 117 in the Benedictine numbering, Sermon 67 on the New Testament in the *NPNF* edition. This translation is taken: Philip Schaff (ed.), 1888, in *NPNF* VI, trans R.G. MacMullen, Buffalo, NY: Christian Literature Publishing Company.

23 Catherine Mowry LaCugna, 1992, *God for Us: Trinity and Christian Life*, San Francisco: HarperCollins, pp. 87–8, notes the importance of the Philippians 2 for his Christological hermeneutic. She sees this, however, as a bifurcation of Christ's humanity and divinity that protects God's being from cosmic interaction, thus missing the key to the entire reading. Christ is in the form of a servant as the one who moves from heaven to earth in love, and in the form of God as the one who ascends into heaven after conquering death. Thus LaCugna's claim on p. 99 that Augustine 'formalizes in Latin theology the breach between oikonomia and theologia' does not hold. See Michael Hanby, 2003, *Augustine and Modernity*, London: Routledge, pp. 13–18.

image the super-infinite God, Augustine installs a more properly analogical gap between creation and Creator. Even the infinite is unequal to the task of naming God (*De Trin.* VIII.2–4).

Simplicity plays the role for Augustine that infinity plays for Gregory, as the attribute that unifies all the divine perfections in which we share. Certainly Gregory makes use of simplicity as well, arguing that the unity of divine action is our clue to the simplicity of the divine being (*Ad Ab.* *NPNF* p. 154). But for Gregory, since in saying that God is one we are naming the act and not the nature (because to name God's nature we must be beyond ours), simplicity is really an attribute that fails to adhere to the divine essence. His appeal to infinity in this way unifies the divine essence in a setting that is beyond our participation. For Augustine, however, the attributes coincide in God's simplicity, rather than God's infinity. So, while for a human soul it is 'one thing to be ingenious, another to be unskillful, another to be sharp . . .', God can be called various names like 'great, good, wise, blessed, and true', that yet do not signify a change from one characteristic to another, since 'his greatness is identical with his wisdom . . . and his goodness is identical with his wisdom and greatness, and his truth is identical with them all; and with him being blessed is not one thing, and being great or wise or true or good, or just simply being, another' (*De Trin.* VI.8). In simply being, that is in being simply, God is also all the things that he is: great, wise, good, true and blessed.

Does simplicity, though, really allow us to advance toward perfection any more fully than infinity? For Augustine it does, since the coinciding of names is not only an ontological site beyond our createdness but also the primary summons upon that createdness. Following Aristotle, he notes that people who are equal 'in courage are also equal in sagacity and justice' (*De Trin.* VI.6), since a courage that is lacking in either of these two traits is ultimately a lesser sort of courage. So while it is true that what is 'multiple is in no way simple' (*De Trin.* VI.8), it is also the case that the saints, truly virtuous foci of created multiplicity, can bear witness to divine simplicity through partial simplicities on earth. In noting this, Augustine can say what Gregory could not: human existence can provide true, if still shaded, knowledge of the divine nature.[24]

This move to simplicity through analogy allows Augustine to avoid the Philonic *aporia* according to which God as Being is beyond God as Creator, and to do so without falling prey to the Origenian solution that assumes an eternally existing creation. God is not Creator in a way that is secondary to his existence, because creating, whether we conceive of it as a giving birth or as a speaking things into existence, is an analogue for the begetting-of-the-Son/speaking-of-the Word that happens eternally. So God is Creator *ad extra* in such a way as to mirror his own Fatherhood *ad intra*.[25] 'Thus in that Word who is coeternal with yourself you speak all

---

24 See Hanby, *Augustine*, pp. 67–8.

25 Hanby, *Augustine*, pp. 68–71; Ayres, *Nicaea*, pp. 375–83 and Rowan Williams, 1993, '*Sapientia* and the Trinity: Reflections on the De Trinitate', in B. Bruning, M.

that you speak simultaneously and eternally, and whatever you say shall be comes into being. Your creative act is in no way different from your speaking' (*Conf.* XI.7.9).

If God's creativity is now unified with God's being, then human participation in this creativity can be deifying in a more profound manner. As labouring creations of a labouring God, humans hang more securely from the divine neck than the Athenians could have imagined. Human making appears as the soul's 'power to cultivate itself' (*De libero arbitrio* II.20.56) and is, for Augustine, simply what humans do: making a home, making a friendship, making meaning. This work, which always occurs in the *ad extra* space of multiplicity, can yet become a pathway towards sharing in the divinity. It is in fact the original gift to humans and so the 'beginning of their perfecting' (*De lib.* II.20.56), since it allows us not only to acquire the virtues, but also to acquire a deep understanding of our dependence on God:

> So by that very difficulty [the soul] is admonished to implore for its perfecting the aid of him whom it believes to be the author of its beginning. Hence he becomes dearer to it, because it has its existence not from its own resources but from his goodness, and by his mercy it is raised to happiness. (*De lib.* III.22.65)

Fallen humanity retains this structure, so that we continue to strive, but now against God, whereas we were created striving towards him. Hell itself still bears the marks of this perfecting order, since it is only as those beings made to strive for God that we can experience the brokenness of the analogical bond as a torment. Thus 'even the eternal fire will be proportioned' according to God's justice (*De civitate Dei* XXI.16). Whether humans are labouring to name animals and pick ripened fruit, labouring to bear children and till the earth or labouring against the tormenting fires of judgement, their very struggle is at very least a spectre of the girdle that suspends them from God's creative work.

When Augustine says that 'the universe is always complete and perfect' (*De lib.* III.9.23), he is not appealing to some sort of proto-Leibnizian theodicy, but marking creation as essentially a perfecting gift. The universe is perfect not as a snapshot of all things as they ought to be, but as a cosmic drama that invites us to exist within it in our particularly human way: to develop preferences for one thing or experience over another, to move from simpler to more complex forms of knowledge, and in so doing to ascend within its orders, and even to perfect the cosmic perfection. If, in noticing the many imperfections of the cosmos, we blame the Creator for shoddy workmanship, we become like the one who, because he 'understood perfect rotundity, should be annoyed that he did not observe it in a

Lamberigts and J. van Houten (eds), *Collecteana Augustiniana: Melanges T. J. von Bavel*, Leuven: Leuven University Press, pp. 317–32.

nut' (*De lib.* III.5.14). Such judgements misconstrue cosmic perfection as a piece of plastic art detachable from its Creator, rather than as a ladder that beckons us to ascend to the Maker himself. If this nearly repeats the observation of Irenaeus, that a rejection of our mediacy is a rejection of the gift, is also goes beyond Irenaeus, in showing that it is the very moistness of the created clay that mediates our ascension into the divine being.

Augustine carries the logic even further, arguing that the imperfections of time, like the imperfections of a nut, are an aspect of the perfect cosmos. If every moment is a passing away, every present a lament for an absence, this only invites the gathering of the past in human memory, and the presenting of the future in human hope (*Conf.* IV.8–9.14). Time is, in fact, immeasurable without human participation, and our stretching out from one moment to the next becomes for him a kind of icon of the stretching of time itself toward eternity (*Conf.* XI.23.29ff). Time itself – and not just the pilgrim's journey within it – is thus an *epectasis*. I progress forward, 'forgetting the past and stretching undistracted not to future things doomed to pass away, but to my eternal goal' (*Conf.* XI.29.39). Our duration within it is useless as a means of grasping material objects or even particular moments, since the fate of temporality is to pass away. Ironically, this leads Augustine to the opposite conclusion of Gregory: if we are created on the fabric of time, then God is the only thing that we can possess. By contrast, to sin is 'to pursue, as if they were great and wonderful, temporal things which . . . can never be possessed with complete certainty' (*De lib.* I.16.34).

We are, in these chapters, tracing the emergence of a Christian *telos* that stands free from the Promethean *mythopoesis* that later imposes itself upon it. But have we really found that here? Does Augustinian perfection, in its reaching up analogously into the heavens, not simply coincide with a Titanism of the very sort that made Barth weep and Shelley cheer?

Perhaps, but for the fact that the mediating way of Christ is the way of humility:

> First we had to be persuaded how much God loves us, in case out of sheer despair we lacked the courage to reach up to him. Also we had to be shown what sort of people we are that he loves, in case we should take pride in our own worth, and so bounce even further away from him and sink even more under our own strength. So he dealt with us in such a way that we could progress rather in his strength; he arranged it so that the power of charity would be brought to perfection in the weakness of humility. (*De Trin.* IV.2)

By following the route of Christ's humility, we retell our own journeys through time as Wisdom's pilgrimage, and 'make Christ', we might even say, by embodying his kenotic narrative with the account of our own lives. So Augustine establishes Christ's narrative as a journey through time to eternity, and then casts himself in the role of the Prodigal, attempting to make the same journey back to the Eternal Father: 'But I am struggling to return from this far country by the road he has made in the humanity of the divinity of his only Son . . . ' (*de Trin.* IV.1). The *Confessions*, in this light, is essentially a re-membering of the fragmentations and dislocations of his past as advancements along this road, even, or especially, when he does not realize where these steps are taking him. He memorializes his own brokenness as a sharing in Christ's brokenness. Through this act of renarration, the pilgrim gathers memories and desires into the humble Christ, placing herself also thereby in the ascending Christ. Eternity is our eternal home; but we arrive in this home by passing time in Christ. 'Come down, that you may ascend, ascend even to God, for you have fallen in your attempts to ascend in defiance of God' (*Conf.* IV.12.18).

Augustinian deification is not 'Titanic', then, in the modern sense; but neither is Augustinian humility anti-Titanic:

> There is no effrontery in burning to know, out of faithful piety, the divine and inexpressible truth that is above us, provided the mind is fired by the grace of our creator and saviour, and not inflated by arrogant confidence in its own powers. (*De Trin.* V.2)

The desire to know heavenly things is not here a Faustian rebellion against the natural cosmic orders. Moreover, we have moved beyond the foundations of Graeco-Roman Titanism as well, in which participation in God is tragically limited by temporality. Thus, for instance, Augustine can offer a subtle critique of the Icarus mythology, in which the child and his father improperly attempt to fly toward the heavens with the wings they have fashioned. Whereas for Ovid the attempt to achieve Godlikeness offends the eternal ones by encroaching upon their territory (*Metamorphoses* VIII.183–234),[26] for Augustine the sin is not in the attempt to soar toward the heavens, but in doing so before our human understanding has a chance to catch up:

> So then, brethren, it were better if we could keep silence, and say, 'This the faith contains; so we believe; you are not able to receive it, you are but a babe; you must patiently endure till your wings be grown, lest when you would fly without wings, it should not be the free course of liberty, but the fall of temerity' (*Serm.* 67.7)

To fly without wings, or with wings held together with wax, will certainly destroy an earthly being. The divine fire is more than babes of earth can bear, and Icarus and Prometheus alike would do better at this stage to remain earthbound. But babes are meant to grow up, and Augustine revises the myth's end accordingly: through time and formation our wings will

---

26 Ovid, *Metamorphoses*, trans. Charles Martin, 2004, New York and London: W. W. Norton and Company.

grow, till we can make the journey that the Titans and child-heroes could not.

In order to maintain that human knowing is not only useful along the journey, but also perfected in the end, Augustine relies upon a tight connectivity of understanding and desire as partnered for deification.[27] The famous question 'how can I love what I do not know?' leads him to the conclusion that in order to know God as the one he most truly desires, he must in some sense already have known him. 'I have discovered nothing about you that I did not remember' (*Conf.* X.24.35). But how can he remember God, when, as he shows in great detail, his earliest memories are godless? It can only be, he says, that I 'remember' according to an order of memory that transcends my active rehearsing of details and events. For Plato, he notes, this implies a belief in the transmigration of souls: the servant can be led to 'discover' the Pythagorean theorem because his soul has learned it through different embodiments in the past. But for Augustine,

> the conclusion we should rather draw is that the nature of the intellectual mind has been so established by the disposition of its creator that it is subjoined to intelligible things in the order of nature, and so it sees such truth in a kind of non-bodily light, just as our eyes of flesh see all these things that lie around us in this bodily light, a light they were created to be receptive of and to match. (*De Trin.* XII.24)[28]

Thus there is a way of knowing that is written into our beings from the beginning, a pre-established structure for understanding that allows all knowing to occur. This is key to human perfection, since it allows for an illuminated and mystical knowledge that reaches back to our origin, and thus forward to our perfection. Even if we see God now only in a glass darkly, this kind of seeing anticipates the face-to-face knowing. This eschatological knowing will not destroy our temporal nature, since even now, every act of knowing is an illumination, relying as it does on the craft of the Creator. Deification perfects the temporal form of humanity, because the form itself originates in this gift, proceeds through life by means of it, and ends its days resting in the Sabbath of divine light.

The Augustinian plateau

If the human mind is always illuminated by memory of the divine, how does the illuminating gift itself work to perfect the active thinking, remembering and desiring of the human? Augustine does not suggest that cognitive activity goes dormant in the vision of God, since this would amount to a compromise of the creature's createdness. But does illumination avoid

---

27 See Michael Hanby, 2005, 'These Three Abide: Augustine and the Eschatological Non-Obsolescence of Faith', *Pro Ecclesia* 14 (3), pp. 340–60.

28 See Williams, '*Sapientia*', pp. 326ff.

this difficulty too simply, by positing a consubstantiated divinity in the human form, alongside the human per se?

Illumination is a perfection problem in Augustine, or, rather, it is his response to the problem deification poses for perfection. Humans think and reason by analogy, and so the perfected human must know God by means of this same human skill. But how can this be? 'From what likeness or comparisons of things known to us are we able to believe, so that we may know the as yet unknown God?' (*De Trin.* VIII.8). Even limiting the line of questioning to a single attribute does not help, since the one who loves God's justice must herself be just, if only minimally, in order to recognize it. 'How can someone ever wish to be just who is not so yet?' (*De Trin.* VIII.9)[29] So deification seems to freeze the human being into the same dialectic that we saw earlier infecting the Plotinian system: either I have always known justice, and therefore been just, or I have never known justice, and can therefore never be just. Or, as in Plotinus, the higher part of my soul will always be just, while the lower part never will be.

Augustine attempts to escape this *aporia* by suggesting that we know the withdrawn God and God's attributes differently than we know absent objects in the world around us. To use his example: when, in Hippo, he hears someone speak of Carthage, he is able to recall from memory the streets and buildings of the city. When, on the other hand, he hears someone speak of Alexandria, where he has never been, he fabricates an image in his mind from bits and pieces of his memories of Carthage, Rome and other cities, as well as from reports he has heard from others about Alexandria. However, when he thinks about goodness and justice and love, 'I am not recalling something absent like Carthage, or fabricating it as best I can like Alexandria, whether it is like my fabrication or not like it; but I am perceiving something that is present to me, and it is present to me even if I am not what I perceive . . .' (*De Trin.* VIII.9). The 'form and truth' (*De Trin.* VIII.9) of justice are found in my own mind, which is lit up with this knowledge, before I ever acquire memories gathered through the body or fabrications made by my imagination.

If this were all Augustine had to say on the issue of human memory and knowledge, he would leave us with a seriously deficient anthropology. Recollection and fabrication would be activities of a humanity truncated by a superior form, one illuminated by a preternatural memory of God. This is, again, a Plotinian solution, since the analogical mode of knowing belongs in effect to a lower soul that is trumped by the superhuman knowing of the higher.

This is not, in fact, all that Augustine has to say on the matter. The very project of recalling and fabricating, he says, relies on an elusive aesthetic that guides our mental processes. 'Thus when I call to mind the ramparts of Carthage which I have seen, and also form a picture of those of Alexandria which I have not seen, I prefer some of these forms in my imagination to others' (*De Trin.* IX.10). I appeal to a set of rules about what makes a thing

---

29 See Hanby, *Augustine*, pp. 49–50, 90–105.

beautiful and memorable and praiseworthy, even if I am not entirely aware of this appeal. So the form of truth that lies in the depths of our recognition of and desire for love and goodness and justice lies also in our recollection and mental fabrication of the walls of Carthage and Alexandria. Even fabrication can share in illumination, since a man 'fabricates in his consciousness some imaginary form which will stir him to love . . .' (*De Trin.* X.4).

Still, what does illumination really imply? Humans are temporal beings, Augustine constantly reminds us, and so we experience being as a stretching out between moments of our own existence. The temporal making of ideas can stir us to love, and so stir us to love God, but only because a timeless recollection of truth underwrites this making. So humans can be united with God through knowing and loving, but only because human ways of knowing and loving are prescripted onto a non-human knowing and loving. Fabrication of ideas is deifying because it is a kind of not-fabricating; but illuminated knowing continues to be of a different order than the analogical path. How do humans experience this prefabricated truth as the perfection of their fabricating lives? This is the question that Augustine cannot answer.

Can the illuminated and the fabricated ever meet? Is it possible to see in the building of ideas from bodily experience in the world the opening up of transcendent journey into God? In order to make this claim, theology has too become more 'religious' than the faith of Saint Augustine. It must, that is, re-envision every aspect of the natural as an analogous opening to the divine. For such a vision, we turn to the writings of Denys the Areopagite.

Denys and the Elusive Philanthropist

The Dionysian ascent

Denys makes use of the stock images of Christian perfection present in many of the texts we have treated above. The Trinity guides us in 'the wisdom of heaven', and, as 'the brilliant darkness of a hidden silence', will 'lead us up beyond unknowing and light' (*De mystica theologia* 1.997A–B). Moses' ascent up Sinai continues to be the icon of perfection par excellence, and it is still into a cloud of unknowing that he progresses:

> He sees the many lights, pure and with rays streaming abundantly. Then, standing apart from the crowds and accompanied by chosen priests, he pushes ahead to the summit of the divine ascents. And yet he does not meet God himself, but contemplates, not him who is invisible, but rather where he dwells. This means, I presume, that the holiest and highest of the things perceived with the eye of the body or the mind are but the rationale which presupposes all that lies below the Transcendent One. (*De myst.* 3.1000D)

When Moses passes through all the knowable and perceivable gifts, there will always be more to know. Thus when he 'plunges into the truly mysterious darkness of unknowing', he will be engulfed not only in the unity of the divine act, as in Gregory, but also into a share in the essence, in a way that is at once more 'positive' and more 'negative' than in the Cappadocian teaching: Moses is 'supremely united to the completely unknown' (*De myst.* 3.1001A).

These constructions may scarcely seem to help the argument along, since a uniting to 'the completely unknown' must surely shut off human rational powers. Subtly, though, the images and phrases become intensified in these writings, deepening a sense that the deified human is also the human brought to its perfection. This is due in part to a new structure of pagan religious philosophy upon which Denys operates.

In the third century CE, the Syrian philosopher Iamblichus approached the Platonic corpus with a new guiding logic: if union with God is the end of our existence, then our materiality and temporality are suited for this end.[30] In other words, time and bodies are not a qualification on our perfection, but perfection's appropriate pathway. Like the New Testament, Iamblichus and his student Proclus argue that any essential resistance need not qualify a truly gift-giving God; thus, a new emphasis on divine generosity overrules the Plotinian dyad. A metaphysical hierarchy still issues from the One, but is now constituted by 'the gift of the same essence and power imparted by the primary to the secondary Gods' (*De mysteriis*, 1.19).[31] Because the One is not simply excessive, as in Plotinus, but also philanthropic, it can establish subordinate strata prior to any bi-polar attractions, and thus guarantee a unity beyond the dyad.[32]

In place of Plotinus's intrinsically stratified polarity, theurgy positions a hierarchical mediation. So Proclus explains, 'For the transition from the transcendent to the participating should not be immediate, but there should be as media those essences which are combined with things that participate'.[33] Each layer of being is a *bios miktos*, consisting of essences given from above, for a new existence at further remove from its source.[34]

---

30 Gregory Shaw, 1995, *Theurgy and the Soul: The Neoplatonism of Iamblichus*. University Park: Pennsylvania State University Press, pp. 45ff.

31 *On the Mysteries*, trans. T. Taylor, 1999, Frome: Somerset. See Diadochus Proclus, *Elements of Theology*, trans E. R. Dodds, 1963, Oxford: Clarendon Press.

32 Though Iamblichus retains the notion of the dyad, it loses the sense of a fundamentally negative relation of resistance between strata, and becomes instead a 'frontier' [*metaíkmion*] between the one and the many, at once internal and external to both. 'The dyad possesses the characteristics of both' the one and the many, and holds the two together in a participatory relation. (Iamblichus, *Theologoumena Arithmeticae* 10, quoted in Shaw, *Theurgy and the Soul*, p. 66.) It is, in other words, that which distinguishes the gift from the giver, without marking any opposition between the two. There is thus nothing more than an intrinsic frontier between the one and the *pleroma*, distinguishing the latter without essential separation (*De mysteriis* 10.7).

33 *In Timaeus*, quoted in Shaw, *Theurgy and the Soul*, p. 66.

34 See Jean Trouillard, 1972, *L'Un et L'Ame selon Proclos*, Paris: L'Association Guillaume Budé, pp. 91–109.

Each 'above' mediates *henads*, or traces of the One, to its 'below'. Each layer is, in this sense, pure mediation. The lower remains intrinsic to the higher, and thus subordinately 'akin' to the higher (*Elementatio theologica*, Prop. 34). This kinship in turn generates reversion, *epistrophe*, since 'all things desire the Good, and each attains it through the mediation of its own proximate cause: therefore each has appetition of its own cause also' (*Elem. theo.* Prop. 31). In desiring the One, the many in fact desire themselves, the ultimate *Henas* of their own henadicity, since they could not desire the One at all if it were not as cause of their being and generator of this very desire.

Even while connecting the One and the multitude so intimately, though, Proclus insists that the One is *amethekton*, unparticipated. While this may seem to erect again a rigid boundary between absolute divinity and all that comes from it, in fact in the theurgist we find it functioning exactly in the opposite way, similarly to the Creator/creation distinction in Athanasius. Here the One is unparticipated in the sense of an excess of donation that is irreducible to the reception, not in the sense of an ontologically quarantined 'beyond'. The situation is perhaps like the tides, which can donate the ocean's activity to the land, thus creating beaches, though without ever actually 'sharing the ocean' with the land. The difference between land and sea only highlights the generosity of the latter: tides are the ocean's way of giving itself to land, and beaches are the land's way of become as ocean-like as possible.

This transcendent generosity of the One in this way implies the priestly arts. An initiate can invoke the One liturgically, Iamblichus argues, because the very power of invocation is a gift of the God which she seeks. God gives his own invocation: 'This power is never drawn down to its participants either in the production of the worlds, or in the providential inspection of the reams of generation, or in predicting concerning it. For it imparts all things good, and renders all things similar to itself' (*De mysteriis*. 3.17). The invocations of a priest, using water and barley in sacred rites to appeal to the divine, do not 'impress' upon the gods, as if the gods were passible; rather, they perform the ascent of the soul as a response to the unwavering beckoning of the gods (*De mysteriis* 1.12, 41).[35] Prayer, assisted by symbols as channels of divine manifestation, awakens the trajectory of divine participation in the worshiper, awakens, that is, a 'habit of good' (*De mysteriis* 1.5,15)[36] that takes its essence from the good itself; once aroused, the soul 'longs vehemently for its counterpart, and becomes united to the absolute perfection' (*De mysteriis* 1.15, 46).[37]

In this liturgical tampering with grains and liquids, the theurgist operates on the assumption that materiality is not in opposition to the One.

---

35 This is Porphyry's objection: see *Letter to Anebo* 12–21, in Stephan Ronan (ed.), 1989, *Iamblichus of Chalcis, On the Mysteries (De Mysteriis Aegyptiorum)*, parallel trans. Thomas Taylor and Alexander Wilder, London: Chthonius Books.
36 This line comes from Wilder's translation.
37 Shaw, *Theurgy and the Soul*, pp. 129–42.

If this assumption is correct, then the soul of the theurgist herself will no longer be qualified by division, but will instead become a unit of mediation, the transport of the body toward its union with the divine. 'Every particular soul, when it descends into temporal process, descends entire' (*Elem. theo.* Prop. 211). In turn, the ascent is equally entire. At this point we can observe a certain theurgical populism asserting itself against the elitism of the Academy: for the Plato of *Theaetetus*, it is only Thales and his disciples who can remove themselves from the realm of appearances sufficiently to ascend into Godlikeness. Likewise for Plotinus, due to the errancy of the fallen part of the soul from its unfallen part, only the philosopher, who can afford the time and effort to leave matter behind, will ascend toward union with the One.[38] The theurgists, on the other hand, insist that the ratios performed in the rite are actually native to materiality itself, since the unparticipated One is the donator even of the barley leaves on the altar. There is indeed a transformation that occurs in the rite, a conversion of priest and offering alike; this conversion, however, marks a turning of matter back to a god-directedness that is not foreign to it, but from which it has become alienated (*De mysteriis* 1.21).[39] In this way the priest performs explicitly what the artisan performs implicitly: the conversion of matter towards divine perfection. The soul of the theurgists, that is, attunes itself to divine, and thus receives the manifestation of its own original givenness, the 'frontier' which constitutes it that has never ceased to exist eternally in *nous* (*De mysteriis* 3.9). In this way, matter, which in all Platonisms is capable of seducing the soul to its own destruction by turning it away from *nous*, is here also sacramental, and so uniquely endowed as its own antidote.[40] Perfection for Iamblichus and Proclus is therefore the 'becoming divine ratio' of an embodied soul (*De mysteriis* 10.6). The 'perfect body' is numeric, which is to say its *eidon* transcends the material even as it holds the material within itself. Matter's perfection is its true and ultimate existence not simply in *nous*, but in the one itself: a consummation of the temporally embodied forms with the eternally perfect *pleroma*.

Leaping off from the theurgical texts, Denys argues, more directly than any before him, that the unlimited generosity of God correlates with a created nature that does not in any way hinder us from union with the divine.[41]

---

38 Shaw, *Theurgy and the Soul*, p. 12.

39 In Wilder's translation: 'The Rite both copies the order of the gods, both that of the gods of the world of Mind and that of the gods in the sky, and contains the eternal metres of things that are, and wonderful spectacles which were sent down from the Creator and Father of All, by which also the things of Silence are represented by arcane symbols, the things without form are held firmly in forms, the things which are superior to any likeness are represented unshapen, and everything is accomplished by a sole Divine Cause, which is so far remote from passive conditions that no reasoning faculty can reach to it'.

40 Shaw, *Theurgy and the Soul*, p. 46.

41 Russell, *Deification*, pp. 248–62.

'Every Good endowment and every perfect gift is from above, coming down from the father of lights'. But there is something more. Inspired by the Father, each procession of the Light spreads itself generously toward us, and, in its power to unify, it stirs us by lifting us up. It returns us back to the oneness and deifying simplicity of the Father who gathers us in. (*De coelesti hierarchia* 1.120B)

This 'something more' is the Augustinian linkage between kenosis and ascension. Now, though, the Platonic 'so far as it is possible' is not simply a negatively qualifying effect of our spatial and temporal limitations, but rather a positively qualifying marker for the 'limits' of God's generosity: the divine is the 'Source of perfection for those being made perfect', and so 'generously and as far as may be, it gives out a share of what is hidden' (*De divinis nominibus* 589C).[42]

This reversal, however subtle, is remarkable: if Argos had to plummet the depths of human *phusis* and *polis* in order to discern the extent to which foreign asylum seekers share in the justice of the Gods, Denys suggests that we must plummet the inscrutable depths of the Trinity in order to discern how fully the divine being shares itself with all the sons and daughters of earth. Indeed, the Trinity itself is this sharing, since Fatherhood is eternally the giver of a Sonship that the Spirit manifests; this entire dynamic is shared outward, thus linking the economy to the intrinsic life of the triune God: 'Godlike minds come to be and be named "Gods" or "Sons of Gods" or Father of Gods. Fatherhood and Sonship of this kind are brought to perfection in a spiritual fashion, that is incorporeally, immaterially, and in the domain of the mind, and this is the work of the divine Spirit . . .' (*div. nom.* 645C). Thus the deeper we progress into the dynamics of the Godhead, the deeper the generosity goes, and so the more divine the human gift shows itself to be.

Why then does he continue to insist that Moses' ascent up Sinai culminates in an unknowing, and that the rays of the illuminating gift proceed from beyond being, even beyond the being of divinity? Denys is here adapting the Procline *amethekton* to ensure divine transcendence even in the very reception of divine grace (*div. nom.* 645C).[43] Our Godlikeness is an assimilation to the one who is 'beyond all divinization'. This assimilation comes via the issue of a call (*div. nom.* 592A), and responding to the call requires an ontological gap, like Origen's hypostatic *eros*. God's

---

42 See Ysabel de Andia, 2006, *Denys l'Aréopagite: Tradition et Métamorphoses*, Paris: Vrin, pp. 290ff.

43 See also how excess rather than lack informs the well known *triplex via* of divine naming, in *De mystica* 2.1000B. For the use of the Procline *amethekton* in Denys, see Paul Rorem, 1984, *Biblical and Liturgical Symbols within the Pseudo-Dionysian Synthesis,* Toronto: Pontifical Institute of Medieval Studies, pp. 106–10. Cf. Andrew Louth, 1989, *Denys the Areopagite,* Wilton, CT: Morehouse, pp. 83–4, whose critique of Proclus is not sufficiently attuned to the differences between Plotinian and theurgic worlds.

withdrawal is therefore a beckoning, now more fully conceivable as a display of divine philanthropy: 'He who surpasses everything also transcends the source of divinity . . . if by divinity and goodness you mean the substance of that gift which makes us good and divine . . .' (*Epistolae* 2 1068A). God is not the substance of the gift, but rather appears in the substance as the always excessive Donator. This denial is no longer dyadic, but 'a denial in the sense of a superabundance' (*div. nom.* 640B). 'Beyond being' (ὑπερουσίου), simply means for Denys 'ungiven', and while the entire substance of the Father is donated to the Son and Spirit, and through the Son and Spirit analogously to creation, the Person of the Father, he insists, is not. The Father alone is in this sense beyond being (*div. nom.* 641D).[44] Indeed, if excessive gift-giving has its own source in the eternal Trinity, then God's Sinaitic withdrawal is no longer a distancing at all, but a movement of deeper intimacy: here Moses is granted a share in the withdrawal of Persons that characterizes the interchange of gifts within God's very self.[45]

This sharing is evidenced within our theological language and our liturgy. In terms of the former Denys explains, in the *Divine Names* and *Mystical Theology*, that Spirit-guided negation must always reopen Christ–centred affirmation. So of Christ 'there is conception, reason, understanding, touch, perception, opinion, imagination, name, and many other things. On the other hand he cannot be understood, words cannot contain him, and no name can lay hold of him' (*div. nom.* 872A).[46] Similarly, in liturgy, a given order incarnates the divine among the worshipping body, but this is only deifying if it gives itself to spiritual contemplation. By tying *theoria* to the doctrine of the Trinity, Denys is able to navigate the analogical relation between our movement into God and God's motionless, self-contemplative movement into himself. Because the gift of *theoria* is the mission of the Spirit, deification is a matter of intrinsic assimilation, rather than any external imposition of an alien righteousness: 'For it is not from without that God stirs them toward the divine. Rather he does so via the intellect and from within and he willingly enlightens them with a ray that is pure and immaterial' (*De ecclesiastica hierarchia* 376B). The *paideia* of the Church, for Denys, can be a seamless movement into the divine because even the most mundane instantiation of *theoria* partakes of divine *theoria*, and can therefore rise into union with God.

In this way, finally, naming God is a kind of fabrication, as Augustine struggled and eventually failed to say. Though 'our minds will be like those in the heavens above . . . for now . . . we use whatever appropriate symbols we can

---

44 Thus Denys does not lend himself to an Arian reading, since οὐσία does not mean 'nature' here, but 'having a source of donation', as in the parable of the Prodigal Son (Luke 15.12).

45 Rorem, *Biblical and Liturgical*, pp. 194–5.

46 See Ysabel de Andia, 1996, *Henosis: L'union à Dieu chez Denys L'Aréopagite*, E. J. Brill, Leiden, New York. De Andia has turned scholarly attention to the centrality of Christology in Denys's account of deification. See also *Tradition et Métamorphoses*, pp. 292 and Russell, *Deification*, pp. 254–5.

for the things of God' (*div. nom.* 592C). The form of every created thing is a longing for God, differentiated by the appropriate kind of longing for each creature; accordingly, 'the intelligent and rational long for it by way of knowledge' (*div. nom.* 593D). We use the human paths of knowing to arrive at a divine destination, and we do this by fashioning analogies with which 'we are raised up' (*div. nom.* 592C) to the unity of our mind's truly desired knowledge. In order to praise the divine Giver, 'you must turn to all of creation'. So the uncaused Source is 'sun, star, fire water, wind, dew'. It is 'rightly nameless and yet has the names of everything that is . . . hence the songs of praise and the names for it are fittingly derived from the sum total of creation' (*div. nom.* 596C–D). We make the divine names just as we make all ideas, abstracting from particulars to universals. In doing so, we ascend that ladder on which God has placed all things, a truly perfect universe, as Augustine said. It is all perfect, Denys says, completing the Augustinian doctrine, because all things are arranged as a hierarchical ladder constructed for our nature's ascent. The divine, in fact, 'has bestowed hierarchy as a gift' (*eccl. hier.* 162A).[47]

Creators fabricate the name of God: though this originates in Denys as an epistemological linking of knowing-God with knowing-the-world, it ultimately becomes a way of describing the vocation of human beings as such. We are made to fashion divinity in the world. Here Denys is most fully both a theurgist and a Trinitarian theologian.[48] With his construction of an ascentive hierarchy as the materialization of gift, we are ever nearer a metaphysical structure that can fit the bill of New Testament perfection. There, as we saw, to be perfect is to share in the completing of God's work. This work, for Denys, is the ultimate goal of our ascent. Hierarchy is not simply 'an order' of creation, but also 'an activity for divine approximation' (*coel. hier.* 165A). It is the 'perfect arrangement, an image of the beauty of God which sacredly works out the mysteries' (*coel. hier.* 165B). To find ourselves within an ordered, active assembly of gifts is to find ourselves as summoned to work within this structure to allow the divine gifts to materialize within it (*coel. hier.* 165B–C). So 'for every member of the hierarchy, perfection consists in this, that it is uplifted to imitate God as far as possible and, more wonderful still, that it becomes what Scripture calls a "fellow workman for God" and a reflection of the works of God' (*coel. hier.* 165A–B).

The Dionysian plateau

Our work shares in God's work, as the New Testament says, and thus our perfection is the *tetelestai* of the divine operation in the created order. But how can this work still be ours, if it is accomplished by the eternal God? A philosophically complete answer to this question only emerges gradually, as we

---

47 De Andia, *Tradition et Métamorphoses*, pp. 288ff.

48 De Andia, 2001, 'Symbole et mystére selon Denys l'Aréopagite', *Studia Patristica* 37, pp. 434–45; de Andia, 1997, 'La theologie trinitaire de Denys l'Aréopagite', *Studia Patristica* 32, pp. 290–5.

have seen. In Irenaeus, the human receives permission to go on being human, and is warned against any immediate self-baking. But where does this situate us eschatologically? Gregory helps us press further; the eternal passage of soft clay into the divine kiln need never destroy our humanity, since that nature itself is created from nothing but the divine attributes. Christ is the human God-maker, allowing us to 'imitate in material construction the immaterial creation'. Is this, though, ultimately a tragic endgame? Augustine advances another step, aligning human creativity with the divine nature, so that our analogously creative work will also be deifying. The cosmos is a ladder, lifting us toward a pan-perfection. But why, then, does he compromise the analogy of human creative work at the point of language where it should bleed through with positive deifying content? In Denys, the pathways of human knowing open more fully to this deifying transcendence. Illumination is no longer a proto-deposit of grace-for-transcendence, but the divine excess of all human activity, primarily that of contemplative name-making. So by naming God with the crafted names of creation, we actually climb the cosmic ladder, perfecting the world while passing into union with God.

If Denys insists that our perfection is in contemplating the benevolent Giver, he never for a moment allows his focus to shift from giver to gifts. If he ponders 'sun, star, fire, water, wind, and dew', he does so only as a means of asking how these things are signs, pointing toward the uncaused Cause. *What is the human?* is a question only interesting to him as a indicator of the ascent into sign; thus the perfecting of human nature is not yet entirely discernible within this dynamic deification. How does the ascent up the hierarchical ladder perfect the form given to the ascenders? The material for a reply is here, since both the knowing and the desiring of the *eidos* is preserved in the ascent; yet Denys is interested only in the ladder itself, and in leading us up into union with our Benefactor. How is the ascent our perfection? For this, the doctrine must enter the final stage of its Patristic emergence.

Maximus and the Sabbath for Perfection

It belongs to creatures to be moved towards that end which is without beginning, and to come to rest in the perfect end which is without end, and to experience that which is without definition, but not to *be* such or to *become* such in essence. (*Ambiguum* 7.1073B)

Through this interplay of motion and rest, Maximus the Confessor articulates a theology of creaturely perfection as a sharing in God that is also the completion of creation. If Denys, we might say, learns God only by looking up the ladder, Maximus insists that we learn God also by looking down: unifying ascent is also the perfection of each unique and specific icon of the divine buried in created things.[49]

---

49 See Hans Urs von Balthasar, 1988, *Cosmic Liturgy: The Universe according to Maximus the Confessor*, trans. Brian E. Daly, SJ, San Francisco: Ignatius Press,

Maximus begins from Gregory's teaching on the trajectory of the saint – 'by constant straining towards God, he becomes God' (*Amb.* 7.1080C),[50] and asks, beyond Gregory, how one might conceive of this straining itself as a union with God. All created things come to be as a movement towards an end, and 'nothing that comes into being is its own end, since it is not self-caused' (*Amb.* 7.1072B). Created being is motion, and this distinguishes it from the being of the Creator, which does not strive for any *telos*.

And yet this motion does not simply strive toward; it also strives within, and is thus a name for the very essence internal to each thing. 'A *logos* of angels preceded their creation . . . a *logos* preceded the creation of human beings, a *logos* preceded everything that receives its becoming from God . . .' Each logos defines and differentiates the pathway by which it travels toward God; but 'beyond the idea of difference and distinction' stands the Logos itself, in whom all these various strivings take place:

> Through this Logos there came to be both being and continuing to be, for from him the things that were made came to be in a certain way and for a certain reason, and by continuing to be and by moving, they participate in God. (*Amb.* 7.1080B)

Motion, then, is nature. All motion is God-directed, so all things naturally tend toward God.[51] For the human, made not simply for passive union, but beyond this for an active knowing and loving, perfection requires a supernatural gift. This is why, for Maximus, deification can never be the activization of a potency. 'Deification does not belong to what lies within our potentiality to bring about naturally . . . For no logos of that which transcends nature lies within it.' Humans are the unique creatures 'logicked' by – defined, distinguished as – an active and intentional straining ahead for an internal share in the Logos of God. Only the 'liberality of the Creator' could ever grant this perfection to creatures. Yet this liberality is not a sheer and radical *novum*, since it meets and names the tacit desire that forms human nature itself. Perhaps only the Creator knows the true desire that gives humanity its nature; still, this is our nature, and the gift is our perfection. 'I therefore did not abolish the natural activity of those who will experience this', as if this activity might 'naturally cease'. Instead, I 'simply indicated the supernatural power that brings about deification and produces what it does for the sake of the person deified' (*Opusculum* 1.33A–36A).[52]

So, while the gift of perfection lies solely within the divine power and initiative, 'we are not permitted to say that grace alone brings about, in the

---

pp. 49–58. Notice the great though subtle difference between this and the sort of perfection that follows the nominalist turn: here one can learn God only by looking to creation; there one can learn creation without looking to God.

50 See George Berthold, 1980, 'The Cappadocian Roots of Maximus the Confessor', *Paradosis*, pp. 51–9.

51 Von Balthasar, *Cosmic*, pp. 137ff.

52 This translation is from Russell, *Deification*, p. 276.

saints, insight into the divine mysteries without any contribution from the natural capacity to receive knowledge.' If we did say this, it would be as much as saying grace destroys, rather than perfects, our nature. Instead, just as the Logos 'accomplished divine work in the flesh', through the co-operation of Christ's body, so also 'the Holy Spirit accomplishes in the saints the ability to understand the mysteries, but not without the exercise of their natural abilities or without their seeking and careful searching for knowledge' (*Quaestiones ad Thalassium* 59).[53] With this insight, the Patristic account of perfection ascends to a new height, achieving for the first time the philosophical rigour necessary to show that union with God is also a perfecting of the human form.

Armed with this new account of human ends, Maximus can shed new light on Christology as well. In Christ, humanity shows itself for the first time to be something other than an opponent of God. The deification of Christ's humanity is also the perfection of the human form, since both a human will and 'energy' remain discernible at all times within the incarnation.[54] Something of the old Antiochene Christianity returns here, as Maximus fights for the integrity of a human order of action in Christ as essential for the salving of wholesale human action.[55] While Tabor is certainly the site of the great unveiling of Christ's divinity, where the human lover of perfect wisdom shows himself to be the divinely perfect lover of wisdom (*Amb.* 10), it is at Gethsemane that we see his deified humanity most clearly as also a human perfection:

> *Not what I will* – absolutely precludes opposition and instead demonstrates harmony between the human will of the saviour and the divine will shared by him and his Father, given that the Logos assumed our nature in its entirely and deified his human will in the assumption.

This is Maximus's great insight into the controversial matter of the two wills in Christ: he had neither a single divine will operating upon his human body, nor a divine and human that operate gnomically, in necessary opposition, as in lapsed Adam. Rather, there are two only in performing a dance of unity, with the divine leading and the human mirroring at each step.

> It follows, then that having become like us for our sake, he was calling on his God and Father in a human manner (ἀνθρωποπρεπως)when he said, *Let not what I will, but what you will prevail*, inasmuch as, being

---

53 This translation is from von Balthasar, *Cosmic*, p. 72.

54 Russell is thus wrong to say that Maximus abandons the Christological reference of *theosis* out of a fear of Apollonarianism (*Deification*, p. 237). See Ian A. McFarland, 2005, 'Fleshing Out Christ', *St. Vladimir's Theological Quarterly* 49, pp. 417–36; and Adam G. Cooper, 2005, *The Body in Maximus the Confessor: Holy Flesh, Wholly Deified*, New York and Oxford: Oxford University Press.

55 Von Balthasar, *Cosmic*, p. 55.

God by nature, he also in his humanity has, as his human volition, the fulfillment of the will of the Father. (*Opusc. 6.*68C)

The human will of Christ is not abolished by the prayer; rather, his human nature finds its perfection in humanly recapitulating the divinity which is its origin and end.

By insisting on natural human motion as intrinsic to deification, Maximus gives both the Platonic *bios miktos* and the Aristotelian *deutero-telos* its ultimate expression.[56] We are made perfect in a human way and not ever-defeated by a quest for an end that eludes us. Yet in Christ, this human end situates itself within the divine perfection, fully and finally exorcizing any tragic remainder. Our 'God-formed mind' is 'mingled with divine reason' just as Christ's was (*Amb.* 7.1077B), so that a newly perfect *anthropos* emerges from the alchemists' cauldron.

Moreover, Christ is at once the holiness 'very near you' of Torah, but also the holiness of heaven that Moses refused. The proximate perfection Moses offers is no longer simply a human destination, but is now the mediation of God at 'either end' of our human temporality:

> for giving us existence he has constituted [our existence] as being, well being and eternal being – and the two ways of being at the extremes are God's alone, as the cause, while the other one in the middle, depending on our inclination and motion, through itself makes the extremes what they are ... (*Amb.* 10.1116B)[57]

'Well being' is the Augustinian road, mapped on Christ's journey, from our protological 'being' to our eschatological 'being eternal'. By being human well, Moses becomes 'like a picture preserving beautifully the copy of the archetype', thus fashioning eternal being in the midst of his own temporality (*Amb.* 10.1117C). Perfection is thus the mediation itself, the appearance of divine perfection within the craft of human life, what Nicholas Cusanus later calls the *ratio* of creation to Creator, discernible with an utter uniqueness in each existential form (*De docta ignorantia* 2.4).

Perfection of this sort, read through the garden prayer of Christ, instantiates a new account of humility. Humility (ταπείνωσιν) is the logos of all the virtues (*Amb.* 10.1205A), but does not signify a refusal of *theosis*. Rather, it is the character of one who comes to *theosis* via the Irenaean

---

56 Von Balthasar makes the important point about Maximus's taking up of Aristotelian teleology. He sees this too much, though as an anti-Platonism, suggesting wrongly that *kinesis* in a Platonic mode is 'a sinful falling way', whereas for Aristotle and Maximus it is 'the good ontological activity of a developing nature' (Balthasar, *Cosmic*, p. 135).

57 Bradshaw reads Maximus too much as a proto-Palamite and thus misses the importance of the preservation and perfection of human knowledge in the divine essence itself. David Bradshaw, 2004, *Aristotle East and West: Metaphysics and the Division of Christendom*, Cambridge: Cambridge University Press, pp. 193, 203–6.

route, refusing self-glorification, even the self-glorification that can come to be associated with voluntary dishonour and poverty (*Amb.* 10.1205C), and receives glory instead as the far greater gift of a supernatural perfection of created nature. 'Therefore they are rightly judged to be blessed both by God and by men, because, by the grace of the great gift of God, they have become manifest images of the radiant, ineffable and evident glory' (*Amb.* 10.1205C).

Our work becomes God's work, then, because our being mediates God's eternity. If, however, our motion is our life, are we not still Sisyphus, all at once desperate for the labours to cease, and terrified of their cessation? Is there a Sabbath for perfection?

To recapitulate the Logos is to receive the Spirit, and so to receive the gift of desire that allows the incarnate Christ to seek union with God in the first place. For Maximus, our perfection is not in a sempiternal attempt to accommodate a perfection for which we are not fit, but rather a striving to rest our appetites in the only 'dwelling place' (*Amb.* 7.1077B) for which they are fit: the eternal excessive unity of God.[58] This movement is thus not simply human, but involves a mingling of our natural motion with the movement of Persons internal to the Godhead. The 'Sabbath rest' of God is eternally a rapturous motion of embrace and exchange, and to be embraced by the embracing God is to exchange a 'natural' mode of knowing and desiring with a supernatural, 'to know God even as we are known' (*Amb.* 7.1077B). In this inversion of the natural relation, in which a mobile creation 'stretches out' toward a motionless God, the creaturely stretching itself comes to rest within the *ad intra* erotic strivings of God. The creature's rest then, along with the perfections of all creaturely movement, remains a gift, as Christ himself said (Matt. 11.28–30). Beyond the iconic rest of sleep and death lies the eternal Sabbath of the absolute perfection, a Sabbath beyond both motion and rest, of the Triune God (*Amb.* 7.1073B; 10.1113B–D).[59] So if a *perichoresis* with the divine is our perfection, this is only because the divine itself is also a *perichoresis*, and the Logos that recapitulates us through the interpreting work of the Spirit is itself eternally striving in the Spirit for union with the Father. This work accelerates even to the point of God-making, since the saint's vocation lies in 'wholly imprinting and forming God alone in himself' (*Amb.* 7.1084C). If Christ performs this interpenetration uniquely on the cross, perfecting in his work the work of the Father, our own actions perform it as well, revealing a diagonalized kinship with the divine that is more basic than our disinheritance: 'Through the abundant grace of the Spirit it will be shown

---

58 Jean-Claude Larchet, 1996, *La divinisation de l'homme selon saint Maxime le Confesseur*, Paris: Cerf, esp. pp. 383–97; Russell, *Deification*, pp. 277ff.

59 'Peace is not simply confirmation but at the same time a transcendence of motion' (Balthasar, *Cosmic*, p. 142). Balthasar argues that this is, in spite of its more immediate critique of Gregory, ultimately more Nyssan than Augustinian. But he relies, oddly, on a reading of Augustinian 'rest in God' as self-annihilating. In fact, as we have seen, the difference is minimal.

that God alone is at work . . .' Just as the two wills in Christ can intersect in one harmonious Person without dissolving the integrity of the human form, so too in this work 'there will be only one activity, that of God and of those worthy of kinship with God. God will be all in all wholly penetrating all who are his in a way that is appropriate to each' (*Amb.* 7.1076C). In a way, that is, that perfects, rather than destroys, the unique intensity of divine action that defines the nature of all created things. There is one activity, and that activity slants upward into God even as it reaches out into the materiality of created nature.

In Maximus then, Origen's hypostatic separation comes home to roost, his insistence that the greatest end of any creature lies in finding itself to be loved by the Creator. *Theosis* could never be the desire for more than is due, since *theosis* is also perfection. Creatures do not want to be *homousian to patri*; they want to be in love with the Father's *ousia*. The perfecting that emerges in the Church Fathers originates in this desire, and develops in stages, as the Fathers generate a vocabulary capable of defining creation as that dependent being which receives God without destroying itself. This is the end of all things, 'the rest of the loving heart in eternal motion around the beloved' (*Quaest. ad Thal.* 59).[60]

---

60 Von Balthasar, *Cosmic*, p. 170.

THIRD MOVEMENT

Distortion

7

God's Lost Acreage:
The Disjunction of Perfection in the
Middle Ages

What is so strange and extraordinary is not that God really exists but
that such a thought – the very idea of the necessity of a God – should
have occurred to a vicious wild animal like man, for that concept is so
holy, so touching, and so wise that it does man too much honour.

Ivan, in Dostoevsky's *The Brothers Karamazov*

Flapping without Feathers

In the fourteenth century, a Franciscan whose name has not survived the
erosions of textual tradition wrote a poem on Ovid's *Metamorphoses*.[1] The
poem is nearly six times the length of the original and consists of allegorical
interpretations of the many transformations that make up the classic. His
purpose, as a later librarian would explain by marginalia in his own copy
of the *Ovide moralisé*, was to 'transform the fables into a morality play of
the death of Jesus Christ'.[2]

The poet proceeds, first, by retelling each legend, and then by reading it
as a Christian cautionary tale. So for instance he writes of Daedalus, the
architect imprisoned on an island, who attempts to escape, *contre nature
humain* (*Ovide moralisé*, 1599), by flying through the high heavens. He
covers himself and his son with feathers till they are like 'ancient wildmen',
or simply like birds (*Ov. mor.* 1607–9). They fly and Daedalus gives his
son the warning: *ne voles trop hautement/ ne trop bas* (*Ov. mor.* 1635–6).
Inevitably, the boy flies to the high heavens and the heat of the sun melts

---

1 C. de Boer (ed.), 1966, *Ovide moralisé: Poème du commencement du quator-
zième siècle, publié d'après tous les manuscrits connus*, vol. 3 (books 7–9), Wiesba-
den: Sändig. I have benefited from conversations with Nunzio D'Allessio about this
text, and about scholarship on the Middle Ages more generally.

2 In Robert Levine, 1989, 'Exploiting Ovid: Medieval Allegorizations of the
Metamorphoses', *Medioevo Romanzo* 14, p. 198. My translation.

the wax that holds the feathers to his arms. He waves his arms anyway, but, alas, humans cannot fly (*Ov. mor.* 1684).

In extrapolating a moral to the fable, the fourteenth-century poem returns to an account of human ends very nearly identical to the original pagan vision. Ovid's anthropology shows through clearly in his own text, in Daedalus's warning to his son:

> Listen to me: keep to the middle course,
> dear Icarus, for if you fly too low,
> the waves will weight your wings down with their moisture;
> and if you fly too high, flames will consume them;
> stay in the middle and don't set your course
> by gazing at the stars . . . (*Metamorphoses* 8.281–6)

A similar imperative appears in the story of Arachne, 'who (it was said) accepted praise that set her/ above the goddess in the art of weaving' (*Met.* 6.9–10), and also, though in reverse, in the human Io's 'crime' of appealing to the divine Jupiter: 'O maiden worthy of almighty Jove . . .' (*Met.* 1.816). For the Romans, Jupiter acts justly, on some level anyway, in cursing Io with the body of an animal, since her original divine beauty was already transgressive of the human form.

In chastising Daedalus for a sin against nature, a sin which, in this case, bears fruit only in the journey of his son, who 'suffers because he desires more and more' (*Ov. mor.* 1879), the Christian allegory reverts to tragic, Hellenistic anthropology. At the same time, though, by introducing a Christological element to each myth, the author leaves tragedy behind, and makes the 'middle course' into a simplified moral injunction that it never was for the ancient authors. The Greeks, as we have seen, maintain a view of humans as imperfectible, in that the divine desire that is undeniably within us can never be fulfilled. But Christ, Christian hope maintains, completes all unfilled longing; for our poet, that means that any remaining desires for the heavens after the work of redemption must simply be negated. The way of the sea and land are cut off from us, and humans cannot fly: the only path that might free us from our human prison is the path that God wilfully forges for us, beyond and even against our nature. In flying to us from the heavens, God performed 'the incarnation for human redemption'. This is the true flight, the flight of the divine Son to the womb of a virgin, a gracious act that, though still *contre humain nature* (*Ov. mor.* 1814), takes place out of God's inscrutable love for his fallen human child. The only flight ordained for human nature is 'the love of God' (*Ov. mor.* 1823), and in this love we follow the middle human path of the incarnate redeemer, not looking toward the heavens from which he descended. The desire for glorification, even glorying in the gifts of God (*Ov. mor.* 1844), always leads to an Icaran fall. God became human because humans could not – ought not – become divine.

In the Franciscan telling, a new account of a grace that contradicts nature, rather than perfecting it, begins to emerge. The celestial heights belong to God alone, and to desire these heights at all is to desire inordinately, a new Promethean raid of heaven.[3] By reading this ancient anthropology alongside the narrative of Christ coming to earth from heaven, the poet alters both the pagan and the Christian accounts, creating a new version of human ends. God is now a gracious transgressor whose transgression we are not to imitate: we follow the human career of Christ, but his origin in the heavens in closed off to us, as it always was. It is now creation, rather than sin, that bars us from union with God. The incarnation is the only true union of God and humanity, the only deification, and it is therefore decidedly not a perfection of human nature. Deification itself is *contre nature humain*, and that nature has no perfection, in the philosophical sense of a completion, but only a vocation to a perfectly obediential resignation.[4] God breaks the rules once, by untraceable gift, but nature still reigns and limits: wave our unfeathered arms as we might, humans cannot fly.

This is, as the current chapter will argue, the eventual trajectory that perfection takes in the late Middle Ages. The New Testament vision of a *koinonia* in the divine *phusis* comes to be rewritten as a resignation to an ordained 'middle course' of undeifiable humanity.

Lady Philosophy Makes an Addition

How does perfection become a resignation rather than a deification? In order to trace the distorted vision of human ends that takes hold from the fourteenth century onwards, and which captivates still our modern and postmodern imaginations, we must first attend to the new heights that perfection attained during the period known as the scholastic era.

The beginnings, to be sure, were not impressive. Centuries passed before any Latin Christian could approach the clarity of Maximus on human ends, and the primary reason for this is that centuries passed before any school for classical education existed in the West that approached the schools at Alexandria, Constantinople or the Syrian Nisibis.[5] Maximus can ponder the passage from Aristotle's *Physics* which reads, 'I call perfect what is disposed according to its nature,'[6] and, in bringing this line to bear on the Christology of Fathers, can formulate with ease an account of human *theosis* which takes full measure of the nature which such an end perfects: 'God will be all in all wholly penetrating all who are his in a way that is appropriate to each' (*Ambiguum* 7.1076C). After the collapse of

---

3 R. Baldwin, 1986, 'Peasant Imagery and Bruegel's "Fall of Icarus"', *Konsthistorisk Tidskrift* 55 (3), 101–14, p. 104, esp. notes 42 and 43.

4 I am building off the idea of 'obedientiary perfection' in John Passmore, 1972, *The Perfectibility of Man*, London: Duckworth, p. 14. See 'Exposition', above.

5 Josef Pieper, 1960, *Scholasticism: Personalities and Problems of Medieval Philosophy*, trans. Richard and Clara Winston, South Bend, IN: St. Augustine's Press, pp. 41–2.

6 I quote it as it appears in Thomas's *Summa*, at I–II.110.3, resp.

the Roman Empire and the erosion of its educational network, it would be another 700 years before a Latin writer could ponder that passage from Aristotle. It would be this long, too, before a Latin theologian could write of deifying perfection with such precision.

Still though, a Latinized perfection does not emerge *ex nihilo*, when the universities of Paris, Milan and Cologne finally receive Aristotle from his Arabic translators. In fact, the impulse to formulate a Christian teaching on human ends in many ways names the basic drive of scholasticism itself, the drive to register the 'divine teachings' of Scripture and the Fathers within the developing language of the human sciences, so that human students could learn them and move freely and critically within them.[7] When Boethius, in the sixth century, concludes a brief and very Augustinian letter on the distinction of substance and relation in the Godhead with the brief and very Augustinian line, *fidem si poterit rationemque coniunge*, he is giving the charge which the following centuries will attempt to fulfil: 'as far as you are able, join faith and reason' (*Utrum Pater et Filius* 71).[8] Simply receiving faith and passing it along as an uninterpreted collection of imperatives would be evidence of an inadequate anthropology, as it would bear the implication that reason itself is imperfectible. Human *ratio* too has its perfection, for Boethius, and this it finds most of all when it is employed in the *intelligere* of faith. When a network of schools finally develops in the West, these schools dedicate themselves to reasoning about everything that populates the human world, from constellations to musical fifths (Albert, *Metaphysicorum* I.1.1);[9] the fact that they also enquire about Genesis and theories of eternal causality stands as a witness to the long attempt to join deifying faith to human reason.

It is worth noting here the difference between Boethius's *si poterit* and Plato's *kata to dunaton*. When Socrates says 'we ought . . . to become like God so far as this is possible' (*Theaet.* 176b–c), he is bemoaning the tragic remainder that hovers over a material cosmos, inherited from its pre-Olympian disorder. To become like God as far as possible is to escape materiality as far as possible, even if, as we have seen, we only ever accomplish this through the ritualized mediations of matter itself. For Boethius, however, becoming gods 'by participation' (*Philosophiae consolationis* 3.10.89–90) requires not a divorce of divine things from earthly, but rather their conjunction: *fidem si poterit rationemque coniunge*. Christian deification is not a matter of escaping the material, since the Catholic faith begins in the teaching that 'Christ grew after the flesh' (*De fide catholica* 216).

---

7 Pieper, *Scholasticism*, 23ff; G. R. Evans, 1980, *Old Arts and New Theology*, Oxford: Oxford University Press, pp. 224ff; Philipp W. Rosemann, 2007, *The Story of a Great Medieval Book: Peter Lombard's Sentences*, Peterborough, Ontario: Broadview Press, p. 83.

8 *Theological Tractates, The Consolation of Philosophy*, trans. E. K. Rand, H. F. Stewart, and S. J. Tester, 1973, Loeb Classical Library no. 74, Cambridge, MA: Harvard University Press. Translation from Pieper, *Scholasticism*, p. 37.

9 Albertus Magnus, in A. Borgnet, J. Quétif, Ê. Borgnet (eds), 1890, *Alberti Magni, Opera omnia*, Vol. 6, Paris: Apud Ludovicum Vivès.

Just the opposite, in fact: to conjoin faith to reason is actively to pursue the materialization of the supernatural into the discursive language in which humans live and move and make their world.

Of course, by linking the human end and its pursuit to Christ, Boethius is not only 'humanizing the divinity'[10] more profoundly than Hellenism could have, but he is also more spectacularly divinizing the human. So, when he tells Lady Philosophy that 'true and perfect happiness' is that which 'makes a man sufficient, powerful, respected, famous, and joyful' (*Phil. cons.* 3.9.80–2) she replies, first, in a way that Socrates, Aristotle or Seneca might have: 'Do you think there is any among these mortal and impermanent things which could produce a happiness of this kind?' (*Phil. cons.* 3.9.89). Unlike Socrates and Aristotle, though, who make our desire for permanence in an impermanent cosmos a mark of the tragic nature of existence, and unlike Seneca, who makes the disparity into an imperative to rein in our desires so that we want nothing that cannot be taken from us,[11] Boethius's sage calls him to desire this happiness and more: 'Oh my pupil . . . I should call you happy in this opinion, if you but added this' (*Phil. cons.* 3.9.86–7).

As she introduces her addition, her logic shows the lover of wisdom just how to join faith to reason: the pursuit of permanence, she argues, is at base a pursuing of goodness. Further, if God is the ultimate Good, then what we are in fact seeking, as we pursue these materializations of happiness, is God. Finally, since God is 'ungrudging' of this Good, so as to share it with us as a 'heavenly pattern' (*Phil. cons.* 3.9b.6–7), then 'every happy man is a god', though, to be sure, 'by nature God is one only: but nothing prevents there being as many as you like by participation' (*Phil. cons.* 3.10.89–90). Joining the earthly to the heavenly, reason to faith, Boethius thus follows the indicators of the New Testament and the Fathers in outlining an account of human ends that moves beyond the tragic to the evangelic: 'For you know the generous act of our Lord Jesus Christ, that though he was rich, yet for your sakes he became poor, so that by his poverty you might become rich' (2 Cor. 8.9).

Is this to say that universities were required in order to produce a fully developed, theological account of human perfection? In fact, yes, at least looking backwards at the way thought developed through these centuries. While the monasteries preserved the theological and philosophical texts, and developed traditions of *glossa* and commentary, they were not well equipped for the intense challenges and defences that characterized the exploration of

---

10 The phrase is Chesterton's, in the context of a comparison of 'two Friars', Thomas and Francis: 'The humanizing of divinity is actually the strangest and starkest and most incredible dogma in the Creed.' G. K. Chesterton, 1986, *St. Thomas Aquinas*, in *The Collected Works of G. K. Chesterton*, Vol. II, San Francisco: Ignatius Press, p. 433.

11 See for instance Letter XII: 'To live under constraint is a misfortune, but there is no constraint to live under constraint' Robin Campbell (trans.), 1969, *Letters from a Stoic*, London: Penguin, p. 59.

human virtues and political orders in the ancient Academy. If theology was to open itself to discursive reasoning practices, and thereby demonstrate that an end in God is simultaneously a perfection of the human form, it would have to give account of itself before a community of 'universal' inquiry,[12] and this means in part supplying a university community with a unifying rationale of theology itself as a discipline. Boethius's own account of the Catholic faith follows an 'order of discourse' (*De fide* 97) that is chiefly narratival, moving through the biblical accounts of creation and the crossing of the Red Sea to the Virgin Birth (*De fide* 98–187). Does this not, by its very structure, suggest that faith is simply a matter of 'what happened', what is revealed in sacred text, and is therefore not open to any *ordo* than the *ordo revelatus*? This was the pedagogy of Christian educators until the twelfth century, when the question of theology's relation to the disciplines of the liberal arts begins to generate reflection on the unity and order of Christian teaching.[13] In this respect, a tenth-century Benedictine novice, for whom faith was an assumed point of initiation, could afford to ignore questions of rational ordering of doctrine; a theology student at the later universities, where one encountered not only Jews, Muslims and pagans but also algebra, physics and medicine, could not. But precisely for this reason, the university student could give an account of the Christian doctrine of union with God as also the proper end of the *humanum*; the novice cannot.

Poking at horses

But even while the scholastic centres of the high Middle Ages were centuries into the future, the monasteries of Europe began contorting themselves so as to allow speculation on human perfection to develop. It was after all among the Benedictines of Le Bec, in the late eleventh century, that Anselm wrote his treatises *Proslogion* and *Monologion*, works which together attempt to demonstrate the intellectual power of Christian teachings.[14] Anselm's writings make this step by preserving and developing the Augustinian language of *eros*, a theme that, partly on his account, will remain intrinsic to the perfection language of the entire scholastic era.

In his *De grammatico*, written also at Le Bec, Anselm invents a distinction between appellation and signification proper that he puts to use implicitly in his theological discourses. A spoken or written word, he notes, always occupies a particular intersection of a linguistic network. In view of this occupancy, the word can potentially refer to – or call to mind, appellate – more than its definition points to. For instance, we normally think of the term 'white' as either an accident of a substance or as an abstract noun. As a noun, though, the term can imply nothing concrete and particular:

---

12 Evans, *Old Arts*, pp. 53ff. See Alasdair MacIntyre, 2009, *God, Philosophy, Universities: A Selective History of the Catholic Philosophical Tradition*, Lanham, MD: Rowman and Littlefield Publishers.

13 Evans, *Old Arts*, pp. 91–5.

14 Pieper, *Scholasticism*, pp. 56ff.

'Suppose that without your knowing about it a white horse has been shut up in a building. And suppose someone says to you: "In this building there is whiteness." . . . Would you thereby know that a horse is in that building?' (*De grammatico* 14).[15] You would not of course. However,

> Teacher: What if you saw a white horse and a black ox standing beside each other, and someone said to you with regard to the horse, 'Poke it', but did not indicate by a gesture which one he was speaking of. Would you know that he was speaking of the horse?
>
> Student: No.
>
> Teacher: But if in reply to you – who do not know, and who have asked 'Which one?' – he were to say 'white,'[16] would you discern which one he was talking about?
>
> Student: On the basis of the name 'white' I would understand that the horse was meant. (*De gram.* 14)

Thus 'white' signifies only an accident of the horse, but, if the substance of the horse has already entered the field of signification, 'white' can also name (or be appellative of) the whole horse. White is here 'appellative of that which it does not signify' (*De gram.* 15).

This innovation in logic allows words to say more than they say, or to call to mind more than they signify, and this is essential for one who is primarily interested in speaking of God. For an epoch that is discovering the inescapability of language for human existence, Anselm rescues theology: with his innovation, the task of theologizing is not ruled out from the start, as it would be if words were locked into prefabricated definitions.[17] When he turns to theology, famously in the long prayer of the *Proslogion*, this same added weight-bearing dimension of language both undergirds and frustrates his logic. God is *aliquid quo majus cogitari non potest*, 'that than which no greater can be thought' (*Proslogion* 3),[18] and Anselm tries to magnify his cogitations sufficiently to conceptualize this being. Near the

---

15 Trans. Jasper Hopkins and Herbert Richardson, http://jasper-hopkins.info/ (accessed 5 November 2010). I have also consulted the Latin, Francis Salesius Schmitt (ed.), 1946, 'De grammatico', in *Opera Omnia*, Vol. 1, Edinburgi: Apud Thomam Nelson et Filios, pp. 159–61.

16 I have altered Hopkins's translation here, who says 'the white one', since the point seems to me to hinge on the irregularly substantive use of the single term *album*: 'Magister: Si vero nescienti tibi et interrogant: quem? Respondet: album: intelligis de quo dicit?'

17 Alain de Libera, 1995, *La philosophie médiévale*, Paris: Presses Universitaires de France, pp. 292ff.

18 S. N. Deane (trans.), 2003, *St. Anselm: Basic Writings*, Chicago: Open Court, pp. 54–5.

end, however, having worked out and defended what we have all learned to call his ontological proof for God's existence, he admits a sort of defeat:

> My soul, have you found that which You were seeking? You were seeking God, and you have found that He is something highest of all – than which nothing better can be thought. And you have found that this [Being] is life itself, light, wisdom, goodness, eternal blessedness, and blessed eternity and that this [Being] exists everywhere and always. Now, if you have not found your God, then how is He this [Being] which you have found and which with such certain truth and true certainty you have understood Him to be? On the other hand, if you have found [Him], then why is it that you do not experience what you have found? O Lord God, why does my soul not experience You if it has found You? (*Pros.* 14)[19]

More than just a standard pre-modern show of humility, this admission is, I believe, enormously significant for Anselm's understanding of his own theological task. The *magis esse* of God cannot in fact be thought, and so we might say that the appellation 'God' lies beyond the concept signified by a list of superlative terms. This term occupies a particular linguistic intersection, where liturgically and scripturally trained desires cross intellectual discursion, that winds up loading the name with more than its definition can handle. Reason thus arrives at a satisfactory proof of the concept 'God'; desire, though, unseats the definition, and insists that the term God calls to mind more than it can signify, like the term 'white' does when I am poking a horse. So context, for the distinction between appellation and signification, is everything: in the context of Christian faith, 'God' is significant not just of the greatest *res* that can be thought, but of a greatness that is defined by its very retreat from thought, and thus by its escape from its own concept (*Pros.* 15).

It is *eros*, then, that both drives and disturbs Anselm's correlation of faith and reason and thus of the supernatural and natural.[20] The same holds true in his *Monologion*, where he attempts a meditation on the teachings of Scripture not 'urged on the authority of Scripture itself' but rather 'enforced by the cogency of reason'. The enforcing, he says, could proceed in many ways, but 'I shall adopt one which I consider easiest' for the enquirer who has no knowledge of the Scriptures: 'For since all desire to enjoy only those things which they suppose to be good, it is natural that this man should, at some time, turn his mind's eye to the examination of that cause by which

---

19 This 'soul-experience' is certainly not a 'concept' in the Scotist sense, but might be seen as a precursor to it. See Olivier Boulnois, 1999, *Être et Représentation: Une généalogie de la méthaphysique moderne à l'époque de Duns Scot*, Paris: Presses Universitaires de France.

20 Pieper misses this, and so reads Anselm as a precursor to modern rationality (*Scholasticism*, p. 72). Cf. the insightful reading by Barth, who sees that the human *ratio* is constituted by a desire to 'participate in the *ratio Dei*'. Karl Barth, 1960, *Anselm: Fides Quaerens Intellectum*, trans. Ian W. Robertson, London: SCM Press, pp. 44ff.

these things are good . . .' (*Monologion* 1). He extrapolates the entire edi-
fice, including an account of the tri-unity of the supreme good, from this
beginning point, the basic assumption that all humans desire the good,
and also to know the good we desire. Anselm maintains throughout all his
writings this profound assertion that the teachings of Christianity cannot
be different from the demonstrations of human reason, and his confidence
in this is in tune with the dictum of Boethius. For Anselm though, the hinge
is always *eros*, for it is finally only the desire that wells up out of our souls
that can push us to see the horse when the words only say 'white'.

What Anselm gestures toward in this line of his theology will become
a key to scholastic anthropology, especially for the thirteenth century: humans are characterized by a natural desire for the supernatural. At the
same time, though, a certain hesitation begins to emerge here, and we will
see this hesitation bear fruit in the fourteenth century. If the intellect is satisfied with a conceptual ascription ('white' is a colour; 'God' is that being
than which no greater can be thought), but the desire unseats the signification by calling up contextually excessive content ('white' is the horse; 'God'
is beyond any thinkable being), then are we left to say that the intellect has
a perfection that is separable from the will's? Anselm, as we have seen,
partially cuts off this line of questioning by insisting that the intellect itself
follows the will, and attempts to understand God (if not whiteness) anew
in light of his excessive desire. Still though, the possibility of two perfections will remain in the medieval air, and eventually will receive explicit
elaboration.

The insides of eels

The natural desire for the supernatural is perhaps the chief expression of
the excess of appellation over signification, since in this construction the
desired object is excessive of our natural ability to signify it. So for Albertus
Magnus, the Dominican whose life spans the thirteenth century and whose
teachings were in their day even more influential than those of his student
Thomas Aquinas, the desire to understand God as the cause of all being is
no more 'unnatural' than the beekeeper's desire to understand pollination
or the anatomist's desire to acquire an intimate knowledge of the digestive
tract of an eel. (Aristotle was mistaken, as it happens, to say it ate only
mud, since 'I myself have seen it eat frogs, worms, and pieces of fish' [*De
animalibus* VII].)[21] A natural desire to know begins with particulars, and
ends only in an encounter with the gracious benefactor of universal being.

For Albert, following Boethius, human enquiry falls into three basic
tracks. Because our minds inhabit bodies that are located in space and time,
knowing about specific spatial and temporal beings – bees and eels – is part
of human perfection. At the same time, we seek not only knowledge of the
specifics, but the formulas and ratios that hold beyond temporal locatedness:

---

21 Quoted in Pieper, *Scholasticism*, p. 114.

thus a mathematical science is also part of our perfection. Finally though, we are governed by a third kind of knowledge: 'the transphysic', or divine science, 'which perfects the intellect insofar as it is something divine within us, just as natural science perfects the intellect insofar as it is in time, and the mathematical science insofar as it inclines toward the infinite' (*Metaphys.* 1.3).[22] The transphysic is the basis and origin of the two others. So the natural scientist finds that her science rests on the presumption of mobile bodies. Likewise the mathematical scientist presumes the constancy of quantity and relation. Both 'posit a being whose being itself they cannot, from their own principles, demonstrate' (*Metaphys.* 1.3). The divine science is the path of enquiry into this *esse ipsum*.

Thus for those beings who seek the source of enquiry itself, to stop short of the ungrounded divine would be to deny themselves the perfection of their built-in desire for the transphysical, transmathematical encounter. The desire for the good is the signature of creation, insofar as all things long for their own good ends (*Summa theol.* 1.6.26.2).[23] Humans are born desiring goodness itself, the donative source of all being, and so find their particular end in deification: our perfection lies in becoming, ultimately and eschatologically, the good we desire.

The intimate discipline

Once the desire for the supernatural comes into view as a natural aspect of the human form, faith becomes a sort of excess of reason whose pursuit is thoroughly reasonable: we are imperfect if we come to rest in natural objects alone, perfect only as we rest in God. Does this conjunction of faith with reasonable demonstration, though, not generate a rationalism that marks the death of mysticism and spirituality? This remains, to be sure, a common reading of the scholastic inheritance, and one can see such critique growing already in, to take a famous example, the charges brought against Abelard by Bernard.

However, even in the controversial methodologies of Abelard himself we can hear a note of mystical perfection. The desire to subject the teachings of the faith to dialectical disputation is at heart a desire to give the faith universal appeal, and thus is characteristic of a particularly acute missionary fervour.[24] If at times this fervour leads to a hyperbolic rationalization of the mystery, this hyperbole is not always implied by the task. So for Boethius, theology is a *disciplina*, a field whose mode of enquiry follows its own

---

22 Translation is by Alan Gregory and myself, with reference to de Libera's French in Alain de Libera, 2005, *Métaphysique et noétique: Albert le Grand*, Paris: Librairie Philosophique J. Vrin, pp. 367–70.

23 See de Libera, *Métaphysique*, pp. 184–9.

24 See, for instance, *Theologia Christiana*, Book 2, in James Ramsay McCallum (trans.), 1948, *Abelard's Christian Theology*, Oxford: Blackwell. This characterization of the era follows Gillian Evans's account of the twelfth century: see *Old Arts*, pp. 118ff.

internal rules,[25] both parallel to and divergent from other disciplines. Parallel, in that the theologian can establish the rules for theological discourse, as a science pursuant of 'the abstract and separable . . . without matter or motion', just as the physicist can establish the rules for her discourse as that science dealing 'with motion . . . not abstract or separable; for [physics] is concerned with the forms of bodies together with their constituent matter' (*De Trinitate* 2.5–16). Theology at the same time diverges from these other sciences, in that its ideas have a special intimacy[26] due to its particular end. Theological enquiry pursues 'the source of being' (*De Trin.* 2.19–20), including even the source of my 'being' interested in theology. To find God is not to find a particular object, but to find the being itself in which all pursued objects coincide (*De Trin.* 4). Like Augustine, Boethius insists that we can pursue justice out of a desire for justice and we can pursue mercy out of a desire for mercy; when we begin to get a glimpse of the place where they coincide, so that justice is merciful and mercy is just, we find that our own internal desires and pursuits have shifted. To find this place is to find God, and to find oneself changed by the encounter is to be made like God.

Similarly, later writers like Alan of Lille, picking up on the Anselmian innovation in grammar, insist that the theologian can borrow vocabulary from the liberal arts, not because the terms apply univocally between, say, physics and Christology, but precisely because they do not. Each name must be 'transferred from its proper signification',[27] so that its ascription to God will both point us toward the divine being, and also inform us of the excessive gaps between Creator and creation. Read theologically, the various disciplinary divisions of the university are tracks pursuing attributes of being; the theologian knows and assumes at every point that these attributes, which occur in the created order *via divisim*, are all synonymous *sub specie aeternitatis*. Thus to conjoin faith and reason is not, in the high scholastic method, to replace spirituality with logic, but rather to show the higher, 'spiritual logic' at work in the *transphysic*. The desire for union with God, these scholars argue, is not entirely separate from the desire to know what the inside of an eel looks like, or what path Saturn will take through the heavens. It exceeds these desires, like the horse exceeds its signifying whiteness; yet the only path to 'that horse' is through poking at its whiteness, and the only path to our supernatural end is through poking at the natural discoveries of time, space and relation.

Grace: The Ladder Descends

When Thomas Aquinas arrived in Rome in 1265, he came with the charge to found a Dominican house of study that would address the lack of theological

---

25 Evans, *Old Arts*, p. 96.

26 Evans, *Old Arts*, p. 105, commenting on Boethius but quoting Gilbert of Poitiers.

27 Alan of Lille's *Regulae Theologica*, as quoted in Evans, *Old Arts*, pp. 113–14.

formation among the Friars of the Roman Province.[28] This charge, to which
the *Summa Theologiae* is his ultimate response, allowed him to formulate
certain ideas about theological study, and in particular about the intersection of our intellectual pathways of natural reason with our ultimate goal
of union with God, that had been welling up to the surface of his intellect
for quite some time. His *Summa*, which for many centuries seemed to have
been a creative though failed experiment,[29] marks the high-water mark of
Christian teaching on perfection in Latin theology. This claim generates a
series of questions that will carry us through the remainder of this chapter:
How did he come to make this experiment? What does he say? Why does
it 'fail'? What are the implications of this failure for the schools of the late
Middle Ages?

Thomas wrote his *Summa* in the tradition of theological instruction already well developed by the middle of the thirteenth century. Peter Lombard's *Book of Sentences*, compiled and composed at the cathedral school
of Notre Dame 100 years earlier,[30] had inaugurated the method of theological teaching that would still be in use by the time of the Reformation.
What Lombard manages to accomplish, in his four volumes, is the first real
systematizing of Christian ideas. For a generation for whom the writings
of the Fathers seemed an impenetrable wall of manuscripts locked away
in the scriptoria of countryside abbeys, far removed from the intellectual
pursuits of Paris, Naples and Cologne, Lombard reformulated the theological inheritance into a coherent and teachable whole. Though he learned
from important early *summas* like Hugh of Saint Victor's *De sacramentis*,
nevertheless those earlier texts answer questions that belong more to the
monasteries: what does Scripture say? What do we believe on account of
its testimony? How do we live according to its teachings? In the intellectual climate that would soon blossom into the great early universities of
Europe, the questions needed a more 'universal' shape: What are humans
for? How does the revelation of God in Scripture revise this end without ignoring or replacing it? How can we understand this revelation with minds
that function by means of rational inquiry, classification and discursive
thought? The novelty of the *Sentences* lay primarily in reformulating the
monks' questions for the humanist intellectuals of the city.[31]

In making this shift, Lombard is still following the injunction of Boethius:
'as far as you are able, join faith and reason'. Both are driven by the concern that without this conjunction, revealed theology and reasoned liberal
arts might arrive at two separate ends for the being known as human – a

---

28 Rosemann, *Lombard's Sentences*, p. 80; Jean-Pierre Torrell, 2005, *Saint
Thomas Aquinas*, Vol. 1: *The Person and His Work*, trans. Robert Royal, Washington, DC: Catholic University Press, p. 142.

29 Rosemann, *Lombard's Sentences*, pp. 80–2; Torrell, *Saint Thomas*, pp. 158–9:
'To imagine that this innovative project was accepted with enthusiasm, even by the
Dominican confreres of our author, would be an error' (p. 158).

30 Rosemann, *Lombard's Sentences*, p. 24.

31 Rosemann, *Lombard's Sentences*, pp. 23–4.

concern that would re-emerge with such drastic consequences at the end of the thirteenth century. Humans have only one end, for Lombard, and this end is the one revealed to us in Scripture: 'then we shall be like him, for we shall see him as he is' (1 John 3.2). We arrive at this end, though, not by denying our humanity – or even 'the humanities' – but rather by receiving the words of Scripture and the Fathers as a discipline that we can teach and learn just as we teach and learn jurisprudence or medicine.[32] Indeed, if the Christian account of things begins with the incarnation, then it begins with God inhabiting a humanly studiable form of life (*Sententiae* III). Grace perfects nature, it does not destroy: this is what the scholastic era assumed, and it is why Lombard attempted, 'with the poor widow', to place a reasoned mite in the treasury of faith. The conjunctive work of the theologian is certainly 'a work beyond our strength', but, like Nyssan's ascent up Sinai, 'the desire to make progress spurs us on' even as 'the weakness of failure' pulls us back (*Sent.* I, Prologue 1).

The book itself, for all that, is rather cobbled together, and famously unsystematic, and it is chiefly for this reason that the commentaries born from it would have fewer and fewer points of contact with the Master's book as the centuries progress.[33] This is already apparent in the very first sentence, as Thomas points out (*Summa Theologiae* I.1.7) when Lombard makes an excerpt from Augustine into the basis of his entire scheme: 'All teaching concerns things or signs.' This becomes for him a basic division in theology, which further divides into things usable and things enjoyable (*Sent.* 1.1.1). Roughly, the four books deal with things to be enjoyed (God, Book 1), things to be enjoyed and used (rational creatures, Book 2, as well as Christ, Book 3), things to be used only (the rest of creation, Book 2) and signs (sacraments, Book 4).[34] How unifying, though, is a plan of study that begins with a bifurcation? Biology is about life; cosmology about the order of the world. How is theology about signs and things? More importantly, for our purposes, what is the logical unity of usable and enjoyable things? Does this not leave open the charge that there are different sorts of objects jammed under a common disciplinary heading and that perhaps the end of a human as ordered to an enjoyed thing (God) will be different from the end as ordered to a usable thing (eels and white horses)?

Divine excess

In his *Summa contra Gentiles*, a theological textbook intended for missionaries on the Iberian frontier of the Christian world,[35] Thomas senses the urgency of improving upon Lombard. If creation informs us of a human

---

32 Giulio Silano, 2007, 'Introduction', in *Peter Lombard, The Sentences*, Book 1: *The Mystery of the Trinity*, trans. Giulio Silano, Toronto: Pontifical Institute of Medieval Studies, pp. xix–xxvi.

33 Rosemann, *Lombard's Sentences*, pp. 82ff.

34 Rosemann, *Lombard's Sentences*, p. 25.

35 Torrell, *Saint Thomas*, pp. 105–7.

end that is different than the one revealed through Scripture in Jesus Christ, then those who study the order of nature without beginning in Scripture will reject the Christian revelation as being contrary to reason. If, on the other hand, the human end produced by natural philosophy is identical to the human end produced by revealed theology, the student of philosophy will still reject the latter, now from the observation that revelation is superfluous, like a pen that can write two identical pages, when one has a copy machine that can make three. Thomas overcomes this dilemma by appealing to divine excess.

Excess generates a participatory perfection in two ways. First, in his account of creation, Thomas argues from Aristotle's theory of agency to a direct linking of divine perfection and the perfection of creation. All agents have two kinds of operations: one that remains within and one that is expressed without. It is always in virtue of the latter that other agents can discern the former (*Summa contra Gentiles* 2.1.2).[36] I can know what another person is thinking or feeling, to the extent that I know it, because of what she writes or says, the way she raises an eyebrow, shakes her head, or simply stares at me unblinkingly. I can know the psychological activity of my Labrador, to the extent that I can, by observing his tail, his posture, his eyes and his gait.

God, like a Labrador, is active both *ad intra*, in knowing, loving, willing and rejoicing, and *ad extra*, in creating, preserving and governing. God is an operator, and so is known in his works. Far from having its own autonomous end, then, creation exists only as the *opera ad extra* of the divine agent. This answers Lombard's original division: theology is not about things and signs, or enjoyed things and used things, or even God and everything else; theology is about God. It is not about God in isolation, however, because as an agent God is not an isolated object, and to treat him as such would be to study him outside of his current environment. God's activity *ad intra* generates an account of the divine attributes, while God's activity *ad extra* generates an account of creation as the divine craft. Divine perfection and cosmic perfection, understood in this way, are but two kinds of divine perfection, the perfection of God's being and the perfection of God's making, with the former existing as the ground of the latter (*ScG* 2.1.3).

The second way in which God's excessive being generates a participatory account of perfection is linked to the first: because creation is the teleologically oriented expression of divine perfection, rational agents within the created order can know the divine being in the trajectories of their own natures. Philosophy is thus possible, and is even a truth-filled enterprise, because the wisdom of God flows outward from the wisdom discernible in the things he makes, preserves and governs (*ScG* 1.2.1).[37] The graced location of the human being within this order is as that creature 'to which it

---

36 James F. Anderson (trans.), 1955, *Summa contra Gentiles*, Book 2: *Creation*, Notre Dame: University of Notre Dame, p. 29.

37 Anton C. Pegis (trans.), 1955, *Summa contra Gentiles*, Book 1: *God*, Notre Dame: University of Notre Dame, p. 61.

is connatural to derive its knowledge from sensible things', and yet whose 'perfect good is that he somehow know God' (*ScG* 4.1.1).[38] If the believer qua believer does this by beginning with God's revelation in Scripture and descending into material things, the philosopher qua discursive reasoner proceeds on the same ladder, simply ascending where the believer descends (*ScG* 2.4.5). Both intellectual journeys traverse the same scale, since the sensible world is nothing but divinity exceeding being into action.

At the same time, we can consider the excess in the opposite direction as well: the creative act exceeds the natural disposition of the divine being; the being yet remains ever-excessive of the act. Just as the being of my Labrador exceeds his expressed character, there is more to God than I am able to know and name by studying his outward activity. 'Men are ordained by the divine Providence towards a higher good than human fragility can experience in the present life' (*ScG* 1.5.2). The *Summa contra Gentiles* revolves around this problem. How can creatures, who know and love through senses and steps, and yet whose good is to know and love the eternal and supersensory cause, ever come to their perfect end?

Thomas's solution is elegant in its very simplicity: it is a joy, and even a morally formative joy (*ScG* 1.2.1, 1.5.3), to strive for that which exceeds us, and God ultimately grants the end we cannot reach. Significantly, he builds this argument not on Scripture initially, but on Aristotle's story of Simonides, who said that humans should only ever attempt to know human things. Aristotle's own answer is that, paraphrasing only slightly, such a life would be boring: 'although what we know of the higher substance is very little, yet that little is loved and desired more than all the knowledge that we have about less noble substances' (*ScG* 1.5.5). From this, Thomas draws the conclusion that 'even the most imperfect knowledge about the most noble realities brings the greatest perfection to the soul' (*ScG* 1.5.5). The 'chief duty of my life' is also the activity which brings the greatest joy, 'even though this may surpass my powers' (*ScG* 1.2.2).

Imperfect knowing brings perfection: Thomas is not saying here that we ought to overlook our imperfection as we await 'something else' that will allow us to achieve our end. Instead, the joy-bringing pursuit of the God who lies beyond our own comprehension is itself the gift that makes us perfect.

Yet, because man's perfect good is that he somehow know God, lest such a noble creature might seem to be created to no purpose, as being unable to reach its own end, there is given to man a certain way through which he can rise to the knowledge of God: so that, since the perfections of things descend in a certain order from the highest summit of things – God – man may progress in the knowledge of God by beginning with lower things and gradually ascending. (*ScG* 4.1.1)

---

38 Charles J. O'Neil (trans.), 1955, *Summa contra Gentiles*, Book 4: *Salvation*, Notre Dame: University of Notre Dame, p. 61.

The 'certain way' that is given is the way of human knowledge itself: the descending gift supplies the ascending perfection. The senses and the natural philosophy that they inform give us 'certain likenesses of what belongs to faith and certain preambles to it, as nature is a preamble to grace'.[39] The first gift of grace, we might say, is nature, and for humans that means that our desire to know and love what is beyond us is itself a gift that supplies the most basic shape of our very natural longings.

How, though, do we acquire knowledge not just of the pathway, but of the gifted character of our journey upon it? That is to say, as humans gain knowledge of God through his *ad extra* expressions, how does his excess enter their cognitive field, so that it can 'strengthen in man the view that God is something above what he can think' (*ScG* 1.5.3)? At this point a certain formalized separation of doctrines fights against Thomas's great insight, that the top of the ladder is the excessive source of its base. 'Some truths about God exceed all the ability of human reason. Such is the truth that God is triune. But there are some truths that the natural reason also is able to reach. Such are that God exists, that he is one, and the like' (*ScG*, 1.3.2). He does, in fact, separate out 'some truths' from others, even placing them in separate books, so that Books I—III deal with those things available to natural reason and Book IV with the Trinity and salvation, 'those divine things that have been divinely revealed to us to be believed, since they transcend the human intellect' (*ScG* 4.1.9). His method of argument changes as well, so that his proofs begin in Book IV from sacred text rather than philosophical tradition: 'When all things are carefully considered, it is clear and manifest that sacred Scripture proposes this for belief about the divine generation . . .' (*ScG* 4.1.10).

By proceeding in this way, Thomas attempts to preserve divine excess, and especially our way of experiencing divine excess, by disentangling revelation from reason. Apparently aware of the risk involved here, in the short step from a reason–revelation divide into an account of two truths, and from there to a double account of perfection – perfected in nature, perfected in grace – Thomas admits, 'I am speaking of a "twofold truth of divine things",' but insists that this holds 'not on the part of God Himself, Who is truth one and simple, but from the point of view of our knowledge, which is variously related to the knowledge of divine things' (*ScG* 1.9.1). But if the ascent through nature is the very material of the gift of grace, if indeed this is the content of the miracle of perfection itself (*ScG* 1.6.1), then is this formalized separation of natural knowledge from graced knowledge not the wrong approach to a Christian understanding of the human form?

---

39 From his commentary on Boethius's *de Trinitate*, quoted in Pegis's Introduction to *ScG* 1, p. 25. See also Thomas's insistence in his commentary on Job that Job's own contrition and conversion occur 'without doing violence to the unity of his person'. Cited and quoted in Torrell, *Saint Thomas*, p. 121.

The insides of humans

So when Thomas came to Rome to begin teaching theology, it was not simply the condition of the students that drove him to write a new *summa*, nor the state of theological pedagogy in general, though both of these were clearly factors. In regards to the latter, he states famously in his new prologue that 'We have considered that students in this science have not seldom been hampered by what they have found written by other authors', in which the piling up of questions and the path through them shows no clear unifying logic. The risk is the loss of theology as a science, and hence the loss of a perfecting relationship of faith to reason. In such pedagogy, reason is replaced by 'repetition', 'weariness' and 'confusion' (*ST* Prologue).

The conditions of education in the Dominican *studia* also initiate Thomas's new project. The primary method of theological education for these schools consisted in the close study of morality manuals, such as Raymond of Penafort's *summa de casibus*, a thick text of instruction on virtues and disciplines from which Thomas borrows a good deal in the second part of his own *Summa*.[40] But manuals of this sort proceed by way of the same 'multiplication of useless questions' that Thomas criticizes in his Prologue. Theology is not about God and all the things that humans must do if they are to be moral; it is still only about God, and God's perfections *ad intra* are displayed in God's perfections *ad extra*. The exemplar, the human who is *imago dei*, does not have its own list of perfections, but becomes perfect through a timely repetition of eternal agency. So Thomas must begin his own treatise of morality not with a groundless imperative on right action, but with the analogical link between divine and human perfection: 'We have treated the exemplar and those things that come forth from him; now we treat the image, and those things that come forth from him' (*ST* Prologue to II–I).

Even beyond these two occasions, though, Thomas revises his theology because he senses a gap in his own system. Why should the doctrine of the Trinity belong to the final part, with the things revealed only to faith, while the doctrine of God's existence and attributes goes up front, in Volume I? Should theology and philosophy come so entirely unhinged? Similarly, do the sacraments teach and form us in a way completely different from other participatory pedagogies of human sciences? If faith begins in the reading of Scripture, what sorts of human efforts can we bring to bear on this reading?

These questions and others motivate Thomas to overhaul the 'Sentences Commentary' tradition yet again. To begin with, he moves the material on the Trinity up into the first volume, following immediately the treatise on 'God and the Divine Attributes'. No hard break occurs in the text, as that would suggest that whereas we were first in the realm of reason, we have now crossed over into the fortress of faith. He does, to be sure, lead his arguments more often with Scripture here than before: 'Divine Scripture uses,

---

40 Torrell, *Saint Thomas*, pp. 119–20.

in relation to God, names which signify procession . . .' (*ST* I.27.1, *resp.*). But he just as often links the logic of the Trinity to the logic defined in the earlier sections: 'Thus, as the divine intelligence is the very supreme perfection of God (*ST* I.14.2), the divine Word is of necessity perfectly one with the source whence He proceeds, without any kind of diversity' (*ST* I.27.1, *ad.* 2). By doing both, that is, by making arguments for the Trinity based in Scripture as well as philosophy, he is able to re-establish the relation of faith and reason as one of excess, of 'certain likenesses' and 'preambles'.

Still though, his treatise on the divine unity comes first, and the Trinity later: does this not imply that natural reason can know God in one way, revealed faith in another? Here too, the difference is excessive rather than disjunctive. Human beings, he says in the famous 'Five Ways', know causes by means of their effects, since causes properly traced inhere in their effects.[41] Following the trail left through causality in various ways, Thomas thus comes to assert the existence of an ultimate cause, 'and this everyone understands to be God' (*ST* I.2.3, *resp.*). In beginning his doctrine of God in this way, though, Thomas is simply following the Aristotelian/Patristic rule of identity: *opera ad extra indivisa sunt*. According to the Fathers, as we have seen, the unity of God is discernible primarily in the unity of God's agency in the world. The contemplative, then, can never reason to the inter-Personal distinctions in any straightforward epistemological sense. For this reason, divine unity always comes first, even in the East.

What is never entirely clear in the Fathers, however, is how the logic of revealed tri-unity can be viewed as an unfolding of metaphysical uni-unity. For instance, from Gregory's insistence, 'every operation which extends from God to the Creation . . . has its origin from the Father, and proceeds through the Son, and is perfected in the Holy Spirit', and 'for this reason the name derived from the operation is not divided with regard to the number of those who fulfil it' (*Ad Ab. NPNF* p. 334), we discern that the three Persons are substantially one. For evidence that they are three, however, Gregory can only appeal to Scripture, which is to say revelation, as a kind of sublime backdrop to his argument. In effect, metaphysics is able to serve theology in the naming of divine unity, but not in the naming of tri-unity.[42] This is a deficiency, since being 'hidden with Christ in God' (Col. 3.3) implies the possibility of contemplating the Persons in their hypostatic distinctions. Thomas goes further here than Gregory, arguing that 'relation really existing in God is really the same as His essence; and only differs in its mode of intelligibility' (*ST* 1.28.2, *resp.*). The Persons within God are not post-metaphysical distinctions within a single metaphysically discerned substance, but in fact are themselves as substantial as the divine *essentia* itself. Therefore, if divine unity can actually be discerned in the *unus actus* of God, and unity of act leads to the discernment of unity of *substantia*, then the *substantia* itself must in turn always be manifesting its internal

---

41 Rudi Te Velde, 2006, *Aquinas on God: The 'Divine Science' of the* Summa Theologiae, Aldershot: Ashgate Publishing Company, pp. 37ff.

42 See Bradshaw, *Aristotle*, pp. 158–60, 215–17.

relationality.[43] Every effect of God in the world is, as Augustine saw, both one work of God and a *vestigia trinitatum*.

So, in Question 27, the 'ultimate cause' of Question 2 is given content. The unity of God is revealed in the unity of a first cause; but if that first cause is in fact given, and given so as to generate the fullness of all things that inhere within it, then this cause is not only a unity but also a relation, a relation that manifests the cause outwardly as 'giving' and 'fullness'. Further, if we can discern 'procession' outwardly in the cause, we can also discern procession within, since 'As there is an outward procession corresponding to the act tending to external matter, so there must be an inward procession corresponding to the act remaining within the agent' (*ST* I.27.1, *resp.*). The effects of a cause provide a trace of that cause; thus in God there must be, first, an *ad intra* expression of reason, since the cause issues *ad extra* as an expression fit for our understanding (I.27.2, *resp.*). Secondly, donation must proceed *ad intra*, since the cause issues forth into creation as a donating will (I.27.3, *resp.*). To see God as ultimate cause then is to see God as Trinity, though the Trinity only through a glass darkly: as Logos, since understandable effects imply Understanding in the cause; also as *Donum*, since these effects must express the Will of one who causes/gives them. Thus, although the treatise on the divine unity comes before the question of divine Persons, once we come to the latter, we see that metaphysically discernible unity is already Trinitarian, since causality unfolds as the inner Word with the propensity to be given as the desirable Gift.

The Trinity then is discernible for metaphysics, precisely because metaphysical reason can never find its ultimate object without the constant prodding and beckoning of revelation. Metaphysical knowledge has always been Trinitarian, though even Adam and Even would never have discerned this had they not been given the grace to see the theophanic appearances of God, which were themselves, as Augustine says, types of the mission of the Logos and *Donum* to unfallen world (*De Trin.* V.6 and 16). We bring all preambles and analogies of natural knowing along with us when we go out to meet revelation, and what we find there is what we have always known, because what we find is the incomprehensible Donator of the knowledge that we have been crafting and fashioning all along. Natural knowing relies on grace for its perfection, and just for this reason it must correspond to revealed knowledge, even if it does not yet know the *ratio* of correspondence. Natural vision is thoroughly flooded with the supernatural: so for Thomas it is wrong-headed to look at a tree and not see it, at some level, to be clapping its hands.[44]

Thomas makes similar adjustments in his appeals to the revelation of first principles and the material of faith, or Scripture and sacrament. It is fitting, he says, that Scripture uses poetic figures and corporeal metaphors,

---

43 This follows Ayres's treatment of Nicene theology in general, and Augustine in particular. See Lewis Ayres, 2004, *Nicaea and its Legacy: An Approach to Fourth-Century Trinitarian Theology*, Oxford: Oxford University Press, pp. 286ff.

44 Thanks to Alan Gregory for this way of putting things.

because we are embodied creatures whose intellects function by encountering material bodies and who desire precisely in and through these encounters. 'The ray of divine revelation is not extinguished by the sensible imagery wherewith it is veiled', as Dionysius says (*Coel. Hier.* i); and its truth so far remains that it does not allow the minds of those to whom the revelation has been made, to rest in the metaphors, but raises them to the knowledge of truths' (*ST* I.1.9, *ad* 1). If we are to receive grace in a human way, that is, in a way that does not destroy our sensitive intellect and appetite, then revelation must come mediated through a material text that attracts our receptivity through poetics and figures. We make our deifying ascent not in spite of the earthy poetics of the text, but by locating our own earthy *poesis* in the midst of it, and rising into God through the metaphors of human existence.[45]

This in turn leads Thomas to affirm the possibility of many senses to a single text, and in particular of the fourfold interpretation of Scripture. The things spoken of 'literally' in Scripture themselves act as signs, and this provokes the imagination to construct new layers of spiritual meaning (*ST* I.1.10, *resp.*). Traces of Augustine and Denys are obvious here. If poetry and metaphor can draw our natures to receive the grace that completes them, this encounter with Scripture will not be solely a reception, but will spawn its own graceful metaphor-making, through the imaginative crafting of allegories and figures from the written text. After all, *auctor sacerae Scripturae est Deus*, who is infinitely meaningful, and thus the divinely provoked desire can encounter and create countless images of Christ and the eternal glory from the *sensus literalis* of the text (*ST* I.1.10, *resp.*).[46] A single sense of Scripture, on the other hand, would collapse the participatory order of the temporal many and the eternal one, since it would imply that God makes meaning in time in a one-to-one correlation of sign and signified. Instead, our natural mode of comprehending metaphors and interpreting poems is fitted to the task of receiving revelation. The many meanings are one, 'insofar as this is possible' for the many. Scripture's manifold participation in the divine unity of the literal sense in which God intended it is, we might say, its own deification, as well as being the ladder for ours.[47]

We find a corresponding appeal to the sacraments as material causes of faith, in the *Tertia Pars*, where Thomas asks whether sacraments are necessarily sensible, and whether they need to entail words. He answers both affirmatively, and hinges his reply, as he does through so much of the final part, on an appeal to *conveniencia*. 'The sacraments . . . are signs for man's sanctification. Consequently they can be considered in three ways: and in each way it is fitting for words to be added to the sensible signs' (*ST*

---

45 Gilbert Dahan, 1992, 'Saint Thomas d'Aquin at la metaphore', in *Medioevo* 18, pp. 85–118. Thanks to Olivier Boulnois for bringing this text to my attention.

46 See Rowan Williams, 2000, 'The Discipline of Scripture', in *On Christian Theology*, Oxford: Blackwell, pp. 44–60.

47 Peter M. Candler Jr., 2006, *Theology, Rhetoric, Manuduction, or Reading Scripture Together on the Path to God*, Grand Rapids: Eerdmans, pp. 86, 151ff.

III.60.6, *resp.*). It is humans who are joined to God by means of these gifts, and so it is convenient to the form that these gifts be shared in a way that humans can receive them. The same ears that learn to discern bird songs learn to discern God's calling in the liturgy; the same tongue that acquires a taste for savoury foods acquires a taste for redemption, even when the transformed substance of the bread and wine exceeds our sensory receptors.[48] Grace perfects, and spiritual sensation does not replace or destroy our natural *animus*.

How does grace perfect, though, without either superseding nature, or reducing itself to nature's quality enhancement programme? In his account of grace as both operative and co-operative, Thomas takes the student of theology to the very heart of the question of perfection. Just as the entire cosmos is ordered to God, but some things are led to God by other things, the human creature is led to God both by God and by other things, other humans, words, signs or anything that we encounter in creation that can serve to point us toward God. Being ordered in this way means that we receive actively: we who 'take in' Scripture by means of creative metaphors and poetic extravagancies also take in grace by means of habit-forming co - operation. Grace, Thomas says, can be conceived in two ways: 'as divine help, whereby God moves us to will and to act; secondly, as a habitual gift divinely bestowed'. Either way there is a 'double effect' of grace. According to the first, we are helped, passively, when we begin to desire God, actively. So, as he quotes Augustine, 'he operates that we may will; and when we will, He co-operates that we may perfect' (*ST* I–II.111.2, *resp.*). As a habitual act too there is a double effect, since the habit itself makes us holy, but the power by which the habit justifies and heals originates in God.

For habitual action, then, the second doubling, Thomas does not envision simply a human side of grace, but a grace that is both humanly received and freely embodied, and given by God with the sort of character that allows it to be received and freely embodied. Just as 'the work of heat is to make its subject hot', the work of God is to make us Godlike. The existence of the habit of grace within us is thus always dependent on God's will to establish us as en-graced. But a fire is not simply a hot thing, but a thing that works to 'give heat outwardly', so the operating of the habit is the activity of the graced one, like the being-hot of a fire is an operation that accords with its gifted being (*ST* I–II.111.2, *resp.*). Thus the human habit of grace is both a divine gift and human activity.

This is why the theological virtues, by which humans can enjoy the end that exceeds their nature, even as their nature is convenient to this end, are 'infused' by God. The natural virtues anticipate this reception, so we make friends and we tend fields, Thomas says, and this prepares a natural site for the receiving of divine gift (I–II.109.5). Further, even the act of infusing occurs through human modes of reception: the seeing of miracles, hearing of sermons, reading of Scriptures, the experience of charitable acts from one's

---

48 See John Milbank and Catherine Pickstock, 2001, *Truth in Aquinas*, London: Routledge, pp. 74–5.

friends . . . (*ST* II–II.6.1, *arg.* 2, *ad* 2). Just as in Aristotle's rhetoric, where the truth has always to be mediated persuasively through various accommodations, Christian faith itself in Thomas passes through these various 'external causes' of human embodiment and temporality. Yet, beyond Aristotle, the faith which these persuasions induce exceeds the natural aims of those persuasive ends themselves, since 'man, by assenting to matters of faith, is raised above his nature' (*ST* II–II.6.1, *resp.*). So faith, hope and love are infused within us as humanly–divinely caused ways of being humanly divine. The 'human side of grace' is only a perfect way of living because these habits are given by God as our fitting ways of receiving God's own perfection.[49]

Operation and co-operation are thus inextricable for Thomas under both the 'habitual' and 'divine help' headings. This is the case most of all because, as he insists, grace is a single gift of the unified Godhead. Its essence is divine work, and the oneness of grace shares in the unity of God (*ST* I–II.110.1, *resp.*). This unity, however, is not a univocity, as a choice between an uncreated and created agency would imply. Who causes the perfecting of the created order? God, in the first place, as 'the gift of grace surpasses every capability of created nature, since it is nothing short of a partaking of the Divine nature . . . For it is as necessary that God alone should deify, bestowing a partaking of the Divine Nature by a participated likeness, as it is impossible that anything save fire should enkindle' (*ST* I–II.112.1, *resp.*). But grace also 'signifies a temporal effect' (I–II.111.3, *ad* 1)[50] that in turn generates a temporal field of creaturely causality, since God's habitual way of causing is to cause causes. So the angelic beings are 'graces' who contemplate the various levels of cause and effect within the created order, and are themselves causes at a sublevel to the divine as well as to the hierarchical choirs above them. Thomas shows no more compulsion to choose between a human and divine causality than he does between an isolation of cause in archangel, throne or cherub. All is divine operation, and all is thoroughly mediated through creaturely co-operation.[51] Supernatural perfection is in this way like the 'good graces' that a soldier receives from his king: to stand receptive to the grace is not really to receive; when the soldier returns gratitude for the gift (*gratias beneficiorum*), then he truly receives the grace, and is thus perfected by the excessive gift (*ST* I–II.110.1, *resp.*).

The deifying light

Does the *Summa Theologiae* solve the problem of perfection? There is certainly no text in the philosophical or theological tradition that gives a fuller

---

49 Te Velde, *Aquinas on God,* pp. 160ff.

50 Te Velde, *Aquinas on God,* pp. 150–5.

51 Bernard Lonergan, 2000, *Grace and Freedom: Operative Grace in the Thought of St Thomas Aquinas,* Toronto: University of Toronto, p. 87. See also Etienne Gilson, 1937, *The Philosophy of St. Thomas Aquinas,* trans. Edward Bullough, Freeport, NY: Books for Libraries Press, pp. 167–203.

and more rigorous answer to the question of how human beings can find their fulfilment in that which exceeds them. At the same time, though, the Condemnations of 1277 reject the Thomistic solution, reading it as too closely aligned with the 'double verity' doctrine of Siger of Brabant: reason leads to natural truth, including the natural truth about human ends, while faith leads to supernatural truth and the supernatural human ends. The Condemnations revolve on the critique of this idea that 'certain things are true according to philosophy that are not true according to the Catholic faith, as if there were two contrary truths, as if the truth of Holy Scriptures could be contradicted by the truth of the pagans whom God condemned'.[52]

As we have seen, Thomas is motivated primarily by a desire to say just the opposite of this, and there is peculiar thickness to the interpretation of the panel that collapses the two solutions into one. Thomas's controversial response to the eternity of the world question in particular, which drew such heavy fire from the Parisian readers, is in fact a theologically sound argument hingeing on the notion that the very reasoning by which we demonstrate the world's existence belongs to the world itself. Thus 'by no demonstration can it be proved, that the world did not always exist' (*ST* I.46.2, *resp.*). This logical gap, however, does not indicate a 'natural truth' that is contradicted by a doctrine of *creatio ex nihilo*. 'The newness of the world cannot be demonstrated on the part of the world itself' (*ST* I.46.2, *resp.*) any more than geometry can prove the existence of geometry. The human sciences do not have their own ends, parallel to or contradictory of the divine science; rather, the divine exceeds the human and supplies the protological and eschatological margins which mundane thinking can gesture toward but never achieve.

Still, there are gaps in the texture of Thomas's work which point in the direction of double verity, even if the reasonableness of an eternal creation is not one of them. Most significant in this regard is a collection of issues surrounding the illumination of the soul.[53] For Augustine, as we have seen, the divine light infuses the human form from its origin, and so ought never to be extractable from it, even though it exceeds the human form at every point. Augustine never entirely manages a theology of human making that allows for the mediation of this divine light and so is forced at points to say that the divine light operates only where human fabrication does not (see Second Movement, above). Thomas's account is essentially the same: 'The faculty of seeing God, however, does not belong to the created intellect naturally, but is given to it by the light of glory, which establishes the intellect in a kind of "deiformity"' (*ST* I.12.6, *resp.*). The human, destined to see God as he is (1 John 2.2, quoted in *ST* I.12.4, *resp.*), must receive this *lumen gloria*, since otherwise we would see God merely as *we* are.

52 Quoted in Alain de Libera, 1991, *Penser au Moyen Âge*, Paris: Éditions du Seuil, p. 122. My translation is from his French. Chesterton, *St. Thomas*, pp. 473–4, discusses the potential for confusion between Thomas and Siger.

53 I owe my development of this line of critique to a verbal hint from Olivier Boulnois.

What happens to the human powers, though, in this reception of the light of glory? From all we have seen already from the *Summa*, we would expect a relation of excess, whereby natural reason anticipates illuminated reason without reducing its grand discoveries, like studying a map of the Appalachian Trail anticipates non-reductively the actual hike. What Thomas appeals to, though, is a kind of super-reason, which corresponds to infused virtue analogously to the way that natural reason corresponds to acquired virtue: 'For as the acquired virtues enable a man to walk, in accordance with the natural light of reason, so do the infused virtues enable a man to walk as befits the light of grace' (*ST* I–II.110.3, *resp.*). When he attempts to persuade us that a deification of this sort is also a perfection, all our earlier protests about the destruction of nature return:

> Human understanding has a form, viz., intelligible light, which of itself is sufficient for knowing certain intelligible things, viz., those we can come to know through the senses. Higher intelligible things the human intellect cannot know, unless it be perfected by a stronger light, viz., the light of faith or prophecy which is called the *light of grace*, inasmuch as it is added to nature. (*ST* I–II.109.1, *resp.*)

So rather than a human way of experiencing the world, the divine light provides a superhuman way of experiencing, that then allows us to leave off reasoning in our native discursive mode so that we can reason in a deiform mode. Does this not leave the unilluminated human understanding to find its way to a 'natural truth' unaided by grace? The new reasoning that he introduces thus struggles against Thomas's plan of the *Summa*, a plan to conjoin faith, excessively, to natural reason. Rather than an experience of the mountains that perfects-by-transcending the reading of a map, this account of illumination is like the granting of 3-D glasses for the creatures dwelling in Flatland. In that case what we receive may improve us, but it cannot perfect our nature.

Post-Metaphysical Deluge

Let us say then, without overemphasis, that Thomas's *Summa* largely succeeds in conjoining faith and reason on the grid of grace and nature. Let us say also that the points at which it does not manage to carry this conjunction through with consistency open its author up to the charges which led to the *Summa*'s dismissal, for so many centuries, as a theological failure. The great worry of the 'post-Aristotelian' culture at the end of the thirteenth century was that Christians might suppose human happiness can find its 'end' before it ever receives the supernatural gift:[54] that humans

---

54 Pieper, *Scholasticism*, pp. 129–33; Andrea A. Robiglio, 2004, 'Breaking the Great Chain of Being. A note on the Paris condemnations of 1277, Thomas Aquinas and the proper subject of metaphysics', *Verbum* 6, pp. 51–9.

might be complete prior to the resting of their hearts in God. In this, they found Thomas's experimental answer to be lacking.

But it is precisely this pietistic worry that led to the very breakdown of scholasticism itself, if we take this term to signify the attempt of the schools to demonstrate a logic of perfection through the conjunction of the natural and graceful ends. After 1277, natural reason precedes revealed theology, as the setting of a table for a meal must precede the meal itself. A well-ordered table will allow for the commencement of the meal, but the food will come or will not come, based entirely on the will and mood of the chef. In effect, as we shall see, the Condemnations created an environment in which Thomas's methodology was outdated before it ever really hit the schools. The future would belong to the rising Franciscan school, which would bear such remarkable fruit in John Duns Scotus.[55]

Ironically, although it was Aristotelian Christianity that came under attack, the separation of these disciplines resulted in a more 'purely' Aristotelian academy: first, simply because natures and sciences were more clearly categorized and kept from bleeding over into one another, and in this way tended to create, via curricular divisions, a potential for manifold truths that had really never manifested itself before.[56] Secondly, whereas earlier theologies like that of Boethius were structured upon the order of Scripture, and later, as in Thomas, by a followable ordering of revealed doctrines, the new separation of revealed theology from metaphysical theology allowed the latter to come fully under the governance of the syllogism. Once the erotic yearnings of the Psalter and the *Confessions* were replaced by a strictly unbroken middle,[57] it became impossible to 'stretch' the logic of human perfection in the way that the Fathers and Thomas had done.

In order to see how Scotus's teaching on human perfection differs from Thomas's, we must first of all see how his metaphysics 'sets the table' for revelation. He begins in the apparently benign claim that the first object of metaphysics is being: not a particular existing being, but the being of the very possibility of existing, the bare and neutral *esse essentia*. While not empty, in that it contains all things that can exist,[58] it contains them indeterminately, as pure *potentia*. 'For whatever is of itself intelligible either includes essentially the notion of "being" or is contained virtually or essentially in something else which does include "being" essentially. For all genera, species, individuals, and the essential parts of genera, and the

---

55 Olivier Boulnois, 1998, *Duns Scot, la rigueur de la charité*, Paris: Les Éditions du Cerf, pp. 16ff.

56 As de Libera has argued, *Penser au Moyen Âge*, pp. 14–18, 122–9. See also Roger French and Andrew Cunningham, 1996, *Before Science: The Invention of the Friars' Natural Philosophy*, Aldershot: Scholar Press.

57 Boulnois, *Etre et représentation*, pp. 223–5, 243–4, 259–65.

58 Olivier Boulnois, 1988, *Sur la connaissance de Dieu et l'univocité de l'étant*, Paris: Presses Universitaires de France, pp. 54–6.

Uncreated Being all include being quidditatively' (*Ordinatio* 1.3.137),[59] that is, as the first answer to the question *what is it?* The concept of being is thus attributable to God, just as it is attributable to any thing that bears in its *rationis* the actuality or possibility of existence.

So God is 'being'; in addition, there are three kinds of attributes that metaphysics can ascribe to God. Simple perfections (*perfectiones simpliciter*; *Ord.* 1.3.38; 1.8.185; *Reportatio* I–A, Prol.1.3.55) are God's proper attributes, we might say, as they are by their *forma* infinitely actualizable, and thus formally attributable to the *purus actus*. Being is not a simple perfection, since it is commonly and univocally attributable to all, created, uncreated, finite, infinite.[60] Being is simple *quidditas*, pure 'what-ness', but not a perfection of any rational idea. Wisdom, however, is an actualization within being that, while it can be mixed with *potentia* in finite manifestations, does not imply neutrality in its formal notion in the way that *esse essentia* does. Wisdom is a 'perfection simply'. Though we attribute wisdom to finite creatures, the very concept 'wants' to be attributed, so to speak, to an infinite being, since as a character trait it is simple and unmixed (*Ord.* 1.3.39). So 'wisdom in the divine is not according to that notion by which in us it is formally an accident but in a more perfect way . . .' (*Rep.* I–A, 8.2.2.27).

The *perfectiones simpliciter* retain the emphasis of the Dionysian *via negativa* through a distinction that Scotus calls 'intrinsic modes': without splitting divine and human wisdom into separate concepts, since we know God's wisdom only through knowing our own, this single concept can be attributed in one of two modes, or magnitudes: the infinite and the finite (*Ord.* 1.8.138–40). Infinite wisdom is a perfection of being, while finite wisdom is an imperfection: 'In creatures these perfections are imperfect' (*Rep.* I–A, Prol.1.3.55). To the extent that the perfect mode transcends the imperfect, and that extent is 'infinite', to the same extent does God, to whom alone infinite wisdom is attributed, transcend creation. So when ascribing a trait to God, 'the formal notion of something is considered; the imperfection associated with this notion in creatures is removed, and then, retaining this same formal notion, we ascribe to it the ultimate degree of perfection and then attribute it to God' (*Ord.* 1.3.39). That God 'owns' the term in an ultimate way means that our use of it is both univocal and equivocal all at once: univocal in that the 'middle' must hold, so the wisdom

---

59 Citations from the *Ordinatio* and *Lectura* are from the Vatican Edition, 1950–, *Opera omnia*, Civitas Vaticana: Typis Polyglottis Vaticanis. The translation of this passage, and others unless noted, is Allan Wolter's, here taken from Wolter (trans. and ed.), 1962, *Philosophical Writings: A Selection*, Indianapolis: Bobbs–Merrill Hackett, p. 5.

60 Although note the contradiction between *Ordinatio* and *Reportatio* I–A, Prol.1.3.92. See Boulnois, *Sur la connaissance*, p. 33. All *Reportatio* references, unless otherwise noted, are to the bilingual edition, Allan B. Wolter and Oleg V. Bychkov (trans. and ed.), 2004, *Reportatio I–A: The Examined Report of the Paris Lectures*, St. Bonaventure, NY: Franciscan Institute.

attributable to God must be conceptually identically to the wisdom of creatures; equivocal, in that God retains the attribute according to an infinite
modality, and so divine wisdom is separated from the wisdom ordained
to creatures by an ontological disjunction. Thus, where Thomas locates
an ontological excess that gives the term 'wisdom' an analogical character
when humans use it, Scotus refers to a dual aspect of divine power: God in
his *potentia absoluta* is infinitely wise; God in his *potentia ordinata* grants
finite wisdom to his creation.[61]

All perfections of God are pure; but besides *esse essentia* and these attributes which apply to God perfectly, there is a third category of concepts,
attributable to God 'by comparison with what is outside' (*comparatione ad
extra*; *Rep.* I–A, Prol.1.3.92). These are the convertible attributes, named
as such because, while they add content to the conceptualization of a being, they are logically 'convertible with it' (*Lectura* 1.8.109).[62] They are
attributes rather than perfections, since 'a concept that includes a relationship to what is outside is not the per se concept of a pure or unqualified
perfection' (*Rep.* I–A, Prol.1.3.107). While the difference between, say,
'good' and 'wisdom' may seem slight, the path toward attribution reveals
the distinction. Wisdom is formally infinite, and so a pure perfection. To
say, however, that God is good is not to appeal in the first instance to a
positive characteristic of the divine *in se*, but primarily to relate him to
his gifts. 'God is wise', faith asserts, even though the way in which this is
true in an absolute sense in God is unapparent to us; 'God is good', on the
other hand, is a matter of experiencing the graces of God and responding
to them in thanksgiving. We attribute goodness to God by comparing God
with subjects outside of his being, and calling him the efficient and final
cause, or simply 'Good'. Goodness, truth and unity are connected to creation by means of causality, and thus are not pure or simple perfections,
but complex and relative attributes, even while they are metaphysically
interchangeable with 'wise' and 'being' (see *Rep.* I–A, Prol. 1.3.92).

But Scotus faces a new sort of problem with this typology of attribution. 'A *distinctio rationis*', he insists, is always 'modelled upon some
distinctio realis that corresponds to it' (*Rep.* I–A, Prol. 1.3.62). If God
is named according to these three types of attribution, and these corresponding attributes, like all names, must link up with a distinct reality of
some sort, how does the naming of God not lead to a breakdown of divine
simplicity? That is, if 'the Good', 'Wisdom' and 'Being' are all said of God,
and each is not only a different kind of attribution, but has a separate

---

61 See this distinction in *Ord.*, 1.44. Amos Funkenstein treats the development
from Thomas to Scotus in Amos Funkenstein, 1986, *Theology and the Scientific
Imagination from the Middle Ages to the Seventeenth Century*, Princeton: Princeton
University Press, pp. 131–3.

62 Translation in Wolter, *Philosophical Writings*, p. 4. But he translates *conver-
tuntur* as 'co-extensive', which loses the important Scholastic notion of interchangeable names. See Antonie Vos, 2006, *The Philosophy of John Duns Scotus*, Edinburgh:
Edinburgh University Press, pp. 289ff.

correlating reality in God, then how is it meaningful to ascribe unity to the divine being?

The Augustinian/Thomistic solution that the perfections are distinct only according to our *modus significandi*, and to the extent that we experience union with God we also experience the union of the attributes, is not available, since Scotus considers this to be simply a bit of nominalist sophistry.[63] Instead, he avoids compromising divine simplicity by means of his introduction of a fourth and final kind of attribution, which is the most basic distinction within being. We have in fact already seen this distinction operating, above, in the language of 'intrinsic modes'. Scotus gives the name 'transcendental disjunctives' (*passiones transcendentes disiunctae*) to a set of divisions that split the field of *esse essentia* prior to any particularization through actual existence: infinite/finite is the most basic, as we have seen, but the disjunctives include also necessity/contingency and actuality/possibility (*Lect.* I.8.109; *Rep.* I–A, 8.2.5.143). Of these pairs, while both terms are transcendental, meaning 'they are not contained under any genus' (*Lect.* 1.1.8.109),[64] one half of each is an attribute of God, in light of that attribute's infinite magnitude. If God's being is delimited from neutral *esse essentia* first by the ascription of the transcendental disjunctive 'infinity', then no composition can be ascribed to it, since composition applies only in finitude, the other half of the disjunctive. God has wisdom, love, freedom, actuality, necessity, etc.; but God also has being and all his perfections infinitely, which means that there is no composite separation between what God has and what God is. God is wisdom, love, freedom, actuality, necessity, etc., as *unum deum*, precisely because God is infinite. Infinity is thus the ultimate divine attribute, since it unifies all the others by including them 'virtually' within itself (*Ord.* 1.3.59).

Does this mean, then, that all of God's non-relative attributes collide and dissolve, ultimately, in the infinite sea of God's existence? They cannot, since 'a conceptual distinction' must always be 'modelled upon some real distinction that corresponds to it'. The primary disjunctive of infinite/finite thus paves the way for Scotus's invention of the 'formal distinction'.[65] Even in the infinite, he says, the attributes remain formally distinct. They retain their proper *rationes*, so can correspond to our concepts, even if, modified to the asymptotic infinite, they are not 'really' isolatable from one another.

Therefore when we name God, all of our ascriptions, whether transcendental disjunctives, relative attributes, pure perfections or simple 'being' attach themselves to the one God by virtue of the infinite magnitude they all share (*Ord.* 1.3.58–59).

---

63 See the discussion of real and formal distinctions, especially relevant to Scotus's reading of Henry of Ghent, in Boulnois, *Sur la connaissance*, pp. 60–1.

64 See Boulnois, *Sur la connaissance*, pp. 57–8, and Vos, *Philosophy*, pp. 289–90.

65 See Catherine Pickstock, 1998, *After Writing: On the Liturgical Consummation of Philosophy*, Oxford: Blackwell Publishers, pp. 64, 122ff.

By this solution, though, Scotus creates the very problem that will inaugurate a new narrative of human perfection. Infinity is, like all the disjunctives, an attribute of God that is not shared *ad extra*: a pure perfection like wisdom is shared with creatures in imperfect magnitude, but 'infinity, as God possesses it, is not' (*Ord.* 1.3.60). God is infinite, creatures are not-infinite, or simply finite. However, because this primary disjunction modifies all of the names, it ensures that, effectively, none of them are shared, since all the attributes become 'pure perfections under the aspect of infinity' (*Ord.* 1.3.59). Creatures can only know God's *perfectiones simplicites* by their negations. We can share in a wisdom that is conceptually univocal to God's, but we can share in it not as a perfection, but only as an imperfection. Similarly for the relative attributes, to know God by his effects is to know him by a causality that is, in fact, identical to God's being. Is God *in quid* what he is *in quale*? Is he, that is, essentially identical with what he is relatively/qualitatively? Logically, yes, since the concept of God itself must be univocal, and therefore 'God is good' and 'God causes things to be good' must operate with an identical subject. Epistemologically, though, for the wayfarer, they are not identical (*Ord.* 1.3.59), since this identification occurs on the wrong side of the metaphysical fence to ever become known to us. Even being itself, which is univocal, and so prior even to the Creator–creature distinction, self-modifies through the disjunction of magnitudes. Our being is conceptually identical to God's, but we are no closer to sharing in it as human agents than if it were utterly equivocal to ours.[66] So God is one, but this unity 'occurs' in a space beyond human participation, since God's attributes intersect in the lost acreage of his infinity.

For this reason, the metaphysical attribution of divine names and perfections will not be perfecting for human nature, since the creature will always remain within the magnitude transcendentally disjoined from God. But this is not an oversight by the subtle doctor. He most certainly intends this scenario, since it is precisely our natural imperfection that invokes the transgressive gift of the divine will. That is to say, at the end of metaphysics, within revealed theology, we are encountered by the knowledge that we desire but for which we are naturally unfit (*Rep.* I–A, Prol. 1.1.14).[67]

We see this breach, for instance, in his account of charity. Since Lombard's original book, a great debate had ensued on the question of whether charity was a synonym for the Holy Spirit, a debate that centred especially around Romans 5.5: 'God's love has been poured into our hearts through the Holy Spirit that has been given to us' (see *ST* I–II.109.3, *arg.* 1). Lombard himself initiates the controversy by making the equation.[68] Thomas, as we might expect, says that charity *in God* is the Holy Spirit, while our habituation of charity is a participation in God which is nonetheless anticipated by natural love (*ST* II–II.23.2, *resp.*). For Scotus, this way of sorting the matter out is still far too ambiguous. Charity in God is, indeed, plainly

---

66 See Pickstock, *After Writing*, 122–23.
67 Boulnois, *La rigueur*, pp. 66–72.
68 Rosemann, *Lombard's Sentences*, p. 30.

and simply the Spirit (*Rep.* I–A, 17.1.1.44), but this makes charity itself unfit for human habitude. Natural love is the humanly appropriate act, and this act does not win any merit in regards to the divine will. Charity alone is meritorious. But if all that humans can achieve is a love that accords to their nature, then how will they ever find favour with God? His answer is that the act is essentially the same, but that charity itself, the divine will, chooses to take one act of loving as charity, and another simply as natural. In this sense, 'the natural act of love, as we speak of it here, is properly potential as regards the meritorious act' (*Rep.* I–A, 17.1.1.16). Charity is thus not mediated through human loves, but immediately descriptive of an act of the divine will that bears no intrinsic connection to the human act. 'Putting it another way, we could say that the meritorious is not a specifying and completing factor in the moral order, because it does not indicate some intrinsic goodness or rectitude in the agent but it only presupposes such and bespeaks in addition a relationship to the accepting will' (*Quodlibet* 17.20).[69] Not a perfection then, but the gift of a new actuality.[70]

What holds for the distinction 'love/charity' holds also for nature/grace and metaphysics/faith. In this Scotus takes up the Anselmian version of the natural desire for the supernatural, and the hesitation implied within it. Even if we cannot know the God we seek until revelation introduces us to an order of knowing beyond our human finitude, still Scotus argues that this revealing God is the one we were seeking. Thus desire for revelation is embedded in our natural paths of knowing: 'There is a natural desire in one knowing an effect to know the cause, and in knowing the effect distinctly to know the cause distinctly. But such a desire is not quieted by only knowing God in equivocal effect . . .' (*Rep.* I–A, Prol. 3.2.223). God can be known distinctly only through revelation; thus natural desire cannot remain satisfied with a natural perfection. The intellect indeed achieves a sub-perfection of knowledge in metaphysics, but it is the restlessness of this natural desire for distinct and particular knowledge that refuses to allow this metaphysical perfection any ultimacy. While metaphysical knowledge is satiated in finding the ultimate cause, supernatural knowledge (revelation) alone can respond to our natural desire. So the full perfection of the creature hinges entirely upon the will of God to respond to our desire for knowledge of God in himself (*Ord.* Prol. 57).

The trouble, Scotus says, invoking Thomas's distinction in *Summa contra Gentiles*, is that 'some truths about God can be known naturally and some cannot' (*Ord.* Prol. 227). Metaphysics can arrive at the former, only revelation can get us to the latter. For this reason, metaphysics is 'a science of the simple fact', and, though complete in itself, is subsequently qualified as lacking in relation to revealed theology, in which the volitional supergift of God lets us know him as 'reasoned fact' (*Rep.* I–A, Prol. 3.1.235).

---

69 Felix Alluntis and Allan B. Wolter (trans. and ed.), 1975, *John Duns Scotus. God and Creatures: The Quodlibetal Questions*, Princeton, Princeton University Press, p. 394.
70 See Boulnois, *La rigueur*, pp. 91–100.

Metaphysics has its own perfection, then, though the human agent who engages in this science will ultimately see its conclusion as qualified (*Rep.* I–A, Prol. 3.1.236), because her desire will refuse to rest in this science as a whole. Metaphysics, or natural knowledge, is perfectible in itself, though it will subsequently be rejected by desire. It is as if Anselm's whiteness were metaphysically a colour, but erotically a horse. For Scotus, it is not that a human being as such has dual perfections, but more that intellect and desire have separate perfections, and it is only the ultimate and untraceable victory of desire over intellect that brings the two together.[71]

But this means that the natural way of knowing is not perfected in revelation, but ignored, set aside in response to desire's beckoning. If knowledge of effects cannot be always already ordered toward the knowledge of distinct cause we desire, if metaphysics can be only 'foundational theology' and not an inchoate beginning of revelation, then the human who is placed in the world with a desire for understanding has no perfection. If our way of knowing cannot be blended, as in Maximus, with divine knowing, then humans are not made holy by a salvaging and renewing, but by a radically new beginning: revelation comes as flooding of the natural order, without an ark for the preservation of a metaphysical remnant.

Icarus Falls (A Second Time)

Thus at the end of Scotus's metaphysics we encounter a new vision of human perfection. If it comes only in light of the Parisian Condemnations, and so obviously has sources in earlier attempts to sort out the links and distinctions between metaphysics and revealed knowledge, it is here, in these series of lectures at Oxford and Paris at the turn of the fourteenth century, that these earlier attempts receive full and rigorous organization. From this point forward, human reason can neither discern nor share in divine perfection. This represents a radical break with the *opera ad extra* tradition, and thus even with Aristotle, since indentifying an agent's unity was always before this a matter of identifying the unity of that agent's activity in the world. For Scotus it is not the activity of God that denotes the unity, but only the formal priority of infinity, and this magnitude never appears to finite knowers. Said otherwise: the conjoining of revelation to natural knowledge ensures that *gratia perfecit naturam, non tollit*, for Thomas; in Scotus, the disjunction means that God's perfection is unshared, and thus grace passes from God to a negative space in creation that is naturally unfit for it. Far from a doubling of human perfection, in Scotus there is no perfection at all.

Prior to this disjunction, and prior to Paris, 1277, Thomas's writings can imply, like Anselm's, that God's perfections are more than a formal

---

71 This is why de Lubac's groundbreaking account of the 'two perfections' in modern theology does not give a sufficient framework for understanding the differences between Thomas and Scotus: "*Voila un Duns Scot bien thomiste!*" Henri de Lubac, 1946, *Surnaturel; études historiques*, Aubier: Editions Montaigne, p. 265.

magnitude, as they are bound intimately to the bettering of all finite being. We are divine perfection *ad extra*, for Thomas: we are crafted divinity. When a creaturely *intelligere* conceives of God, no transcendental disjunction breaks the truth of the attribution into a pure apophasis for human nature. Instead, since we are always 'united to God as to one unknown' (*ST* I.12.13, *ad* 1), the concept itself stretches analogically from the mundane toward the transcendent. Divine perfection is shared in such a way as to form, like in Denys, a ladder for human perfection. Thus for Thomas there is no perfection but that vision of God which we encounter, habitually, through the natural processes of human knowing:

> Consequently the perfection of a rational creature consists not only in what belongs to it in respect of its nature, but also in that which it acquires through a supernatural participation of Divine goodness. Hence it is said above (I–II, Q. 3, A. 8) that man's ultimate happiness consists in a supernatural vision of God: to which vision man cannot attain this vision unless he be taught by God, according to [John 6.45]: *Every one that hath heard of the Father and hath learned cometh to Me.* Now man acquires a share of this learning, not indeed all at once, but little by little, according to the mode of his nature. And everyone who learns thus must needs believe, in order that he may acquire science in a perfect degree ... (*ST* II–II.2.3)

If it is humans who acquire this knowledge, little by little, then our 'supernatural sharing in divine goodness' is also the perfecting of our nature.

The line of division between metaphysics and theology becomes, in the High Middle Ages, the point at which a theology of Christian perfection stands or falls. If natural knowing is disjoined from graced knowing, then perfection is no longer an ascent through human knowledge, but an abrupt intrusion by intuitive revelation into the fabric of discursive and natural knowing. The naming of God is no longer an ascending language, and thus cannot, with any real consistency, be seen as perfective. A creature whose *forma* not only awaits revelation, but in fact constitutes an illuminated desire for revelation, can be perfected by a transcendent gift; a creature whose knowing and loving is metaphysically complete on its own, and still imperfect and non-deifying, cannot become perfect at all. She can be 'taken as' meritorious by the hidden will of a sovereign God, but this is not a Sabbath rest for her natural activity, only a new and alien righteousness.

This thread of perfection instructs the trails of divergence of Thomas and Scotus. In Christology, for instance, Thomas gives us an incarnation fit for the recapitulating not only of our sinful condition but of our bodily nature (*ST* III.1.2, *resp.*), and so a revelation that, like Scripture, comes to us through bodily metaphors and poetics. Scotus offers a union of natures in Christ that confronts a humanity not suited for divine union at all, and so in fact Christ is deified in humanity's place (*Rep.* III, 7 [Wadding VII, pp. 450–511]).[72] This is why for Scotus, Christ does not receive grace in a naturally human way, and his true baptism is not the one in the Jordan, but the one that occurs in the immaculate womb of Mary (*Opus Oxoniense*, 3.1 [W. VII, pp. 91–3]). For Thomas, there can be no question of Christ's needing to be baptized in the Jordan in order to be cleansed, but he undergoes the rite in order to 'plunge the Old Adam entirely in the water', and so to open the path for all humanity to sinless eternal life (*ST* III.2.39). Thomas's Christ recapitulates human nature through time; Scotus's Christ is immediately human in a way that resists fallen human participation. Indeed, even unfallen: for Scotus, Adam in the garden can not offer God proper praise, since he is confined by the metaphysical limitations of a creaturehood closed in on itself in all but its will. Christ, on the other hand, can offer right praise, and so can be deified, Christ alone, as hypostatically atemporal, can achieve perfection (*Rep.* III.7 [W. VII, pp. 450–1]).[73]

We can see here, finally, the formula which our Franciscan allegorist will take up. The human creature is Icarus: we are guilty of impiety if we consider deification a gift that Christ might share with us. Entrapped on our island, we are separated from God by a multi-elemental disjunction, a disjunction which can be overcome only by the transgressive grace of the hypostatic union, not by an excessive completion of our nature.

The emergent perfection of the Fathers was in this way distorted in the latter Middle Ages, and all the more so as Thomas became an increasingly isolated figure after the Condemnations.[74] And what is lost is, to repeat, a

---

72 The following citations are from the Wadding edition: Lucae Waddingi (ed.), 1639, *Joannis Duns Scoti Doctoris Subtilis Ordinis Minorum Opera omnia, Vol. VII*, Lugduni (Lyons): Sumptibus L. Durand, pp. 91–3; See Boulnois, 2005, 'Duns Scotus, John' in Jean-Yves Lacoste (ed.), *Encyclopedia of Christian Theology, Vol. I*, London: Routledge, pp. 460–1.

73 Boulnois, 'Duns Scotus, John', p. 460.

74 Robiglio, 'Breaking', p. 57. Though I have dealt in this chapter with the Latin Middle Ages only, the developments in the East bear some striking similarities. The Councils at Constantinople in 1341 insert a break between natural 'Aristotelian' knowledge of God and the knowledge given only by the will of God. Palamas, similar to Scotus, emerges as a leading theological voice after these disputes because he inserts his own disjunction within the divine being, with the result that our deification is qualified as a sharing in the given activities of God, and not in the ungiven essence. See John Meyendorff, 1964, *A Study of Gregory Palamas*, trans. George Lawrence, London, Faith Press. Palamas's opponent, Akindynsos, plays an important role here, worthy of more scholarly exploration, since he argues that the desire for deification is the gift of Lucifer to Adam. See Russell, *Deification*, p. 307. Palamas never explicitly disagrees with this, and indeed his qualification of our end as sharing the energies alone is in part a response to this challenge. Palamas, in other words, implies that Lucifer and Adam fell by trying to share the essence, the inaccessible 'lost forty' of the divine being, when only the activities are suited for created things. Meyendorff sees this, recognizes the anti-Thomism, but does see the theological problem (pp. 6, 162ff). Anna Wilson minimizes this divergence in stressing, quite importantly, the continuities in between the two. A. N. Wilson, 1999, *The Ground*

vision of perfection in which a rational being receives the grace of revelation as the constant completion of her own natural orders of loving and knowing. A perfection of this sort cannot quite isolate the point at which metamorphosis occurs, since deifying grace has been tangled up in our bodies and metaphors and metaphysics from the first desire that we ever expressed and the first idea that ever illuminated our minds. This vision requires a truly Christian Icarus, who finds that the gift of wings allows him to take such a journey through the heavens that he might soar even beyond Apollo without being destroyed, since such heights belong naturally to his supernaturally ordered perfection.

Perfection, on the other hand, is lost when God's infinity becomes a hidden plain of untraversable acreage. Still though, a theological discourse on the subject continues; indeed, perfection receives more rather than less discussion after the Middle Ages. How does this new loss manifest itself? How do early modern theologies coordinate the new disjunction with the Patristic ideal of life as an existential journey into God? Can immediate revelation be construed as perfecting grace for creatures whose live are spread through time? We turn now to a literary tradition that inherited these theological problems.

of Union: Deification in Aquinas and Palamas, New York and Oxford: Oxford University Press, pp. 120–2, 160–1, 173–4.

8

The Vanishing Grail:
The Denial of Perfection
in English Literature

Inter poena et tormenta
Vivit anima contenta.

Antonio Vivaldi

Sinning Like Pagans

When Christopher Marlowe first lent his pen to the story of Doctor Faustus and the already infamous 'devil's pact', a familiar classical figure seemed the obvious place to begin. 'This man that in his study sits', the chorus tells us (*Prol.* 28),[1] so progressed in his studies of theology,

> Till swoln with cunning, of a self-conceit,
> His waxen wings did mount above his reach,
> And, melting, heavens conspir'd his overthrow. (*Prol.* 20–3)

The doctor is a new Icarus, who tosses aside the 'middle course' of liberal arts in favour of the atmospheric realms of the 'damned book' of necromancy. Significantly though, Faust's downfall is not primarily caused by wizardry. Mephistopheles's arrival is brought on not so much because of the spell with which Faustus has summoned him ('That was the cause, but yet per accidens', [III.48]), but rather because the devil and his master have heard Faustus 'rack the name of God, abjure the Scriptures and his Saviour Christ' and 'abjure the Trinity' (III.49–50, 55). The chorus tells us that Faustus has attempted to mount above his reach, and the dialogue tells us that he has renounced the Christian faith; Marlowe never suggests any interpretive gap here, and we are left to assume that the two sins are really synonymous.

---

1 John D. Jump (ed.), 1962, *Doctor Faustus*, Cambridge, MA: Harvard University Press.

This late medieval riff on the morality play moves with such indecorous immediacy between the two mythic structures that the reader is likely to take the reference as nothing more than a classical flourish on the play's surface, thus missing the theological subversion underway in the depths. The Triune God is offended by the wings of Icarus. By extension we can also count on God to reject the transcendent beauty of Io, the divine aspirations of Arachne and the celestial designs of Prometheus. Faustus is guilty before the Christian God for straining against the chains that bound pagan humanity. Thus in Marlowe's drama we find 'the beginning of what we may call the Promethean setup, the sympathetic picture of the sad, proud sufferer defying omnipotence'.[2] But this set-up depends upon the tacit imposition of one perfection narrative onto another: how do we come to the assumption that the Triune God will be offended by these lofty human desires?

In the literature of the late Middle Ages and early modernity, the pagan *mythopoesis* gradually imposes itself on the perfection of the Church Fathers. This imposition, as we have seen, is already underway in the *Ovide moralisé*, with the added ingredient of a kind of Christological fatalism. What is new here, in both the literature and the theological prose, becomes in time the autograph of the new perfectionism: namely, the celebration of humility as chief of all virtues. *Humilitas* means following the middle course of Icarus and avoiding the Titanic lusts that disrupt the Jovian order.[3] In some cases this new humility translates into an option for deification rather than perfection, that is, into the suggestion that humans are united to God as the naturally imperfectible to the naturally perfect. In other cases humility means abandoning both projects at once, since in this reading humans of the middle course are destined to run that course to the end, and any quest for either perfection or divine union is cast as an Icaran trespass.

What happens to the Fathers' alignment of divine and human perfection under the simplistic imperative of humility? How does the Christian *telos* shift, distort and languish in the late medieval and early modern world?

Tossing Coins to the Devil

If our route turns now from the Cappadocians and Thomas to the *Canterbury Tales*, *The Faerie Queene* and *Paradise Lost*, the shift in genre will inevitably cause some ripples in the pavement. All the same, the shift itself is important, since these later medieval and modern authors use poems and stories to communicate the complex of ideas surrounding Christian perfection. Even as the theologians of the late Middle Ages continue to write *summas* and commentaries on the *Sentences*, it is Dante, Chaucer and

---

2 Dorothy Sayers, 1978, *The Whimsical Christian: 18 Essays*, New York: Mac-Millan Publishing Company, p. 267.

3 See Carlo Ginzburg, 1976, 'High and Low: The Theme of Forbidden Knowledge in the Sixteenth and Seventeenth Centuries', *Past and Present* 73, pp. 28–41.

Malory who begin to appear in the rhetoric of preachers and parishioners in quest of holiness.[4] Why is this?

The literature itself gives us the most important answer. For a host of reasons that scholars continue to sort out, the medieval poets invented a language of interiority that captured the imagination of the age and forever changed the way humans understand their passage through the world.[5] The Wife of Bath's Prologue 'offers readers one of the most detailed and persuasive narratives in medieval literature of what the textured experience of living in the world feels like';[6] and in so doing she gives us cause to wonder for the first time what it 'feels like' to seek holiness. When Christian the Pilgrim finds himself mired in the Slough of Despond,[7] he becomes for us a figure of the changing moods and inconstant resolve that challenge our own pursuit of perfection.

In an important sense, though, this invention was far from new. Augustine's passage into soul and Scripture in the *Confessions* certainly offers us a figure of internal turmoil and mutability. Gregory, likewise, gives us Moses explicitly as an icon of our pursuit of perfection. Both Moses and the narrated self of Augustine's book give us precisely what Bunyan would later allegorize as Christian's passage toward the Celestial City. Indeed, even the scholastic tradition engages an interiority of sorts. Thomas's *Summa* is in many ways a *Confessions* on a different register. Like Augustine's narration of his own quest, Thomas's text unfolds as a literary performance of the divine being in which the reader, the babe craving pure milk, is invited to participate (*Prol.*).[8] So the reader of the *Summa* pursues a pathway from the metaphysical edges of divine causality to the intrinsic relations

---

4 The popularizing and laicizing of religion during the Renaissance found a great resource in this popular literature: see Marvin B. Becker, 'Aspects of Lay Piety in Renaissance Florence', in Charles Trinkaus and Heiko Oberman (eds), 1974, *The Pursuit of Holiness in Late Medieval and Renaissance Religion*, Leiden: E. J. Brill, pp. 177–99; also John W. O'Malley,'Preaching for the Popes', in the same volume, pp. 408–40, which traces the way that popular images replaced high scholastic reasoning even in more formal homilies. For later uses, see Velma Bourgeois Richmond's exploration of the employment of the *Tales* in the nineteenth century as moral guides for young children: Velma Bourgeois Richmond, 2004, *Chaucer as Children's Literature: Retellings from the Victorian and Edwardian Eras*, Jefferson, North Carolina and London: McFarland and Company.

5 For an insightful account of this, see Elizabeth Fowler, 2003, *Literary Character: The Human Figure in Early English Writing*, Ithaca and London: Cornell University Press. See also John C. Hirsh, *Chaucer and the Canterbury Tales: A Short Introduction*, Malden, MA: Blackwell Publishing, pp. 82ff; R. James Goldstein, 2007, 'Future Perfect: The Augustinian Theology of Perfection and the *Canterbury Tales*', *Studies in the Age of Chaucer* 29, pp. 87–140, and C. S. Lewis's account of 'real changes in human sentiment' in C. S. Lewis, 1958, *The Allegory of Love*, New York: Oxford University Press, pp. 11, 45ff.

6 Goldstein, 'Future Perfect', p. 127.

7 John Bunyan's *The Pilgrim's Progress*, W. R. Owens (ed.), 2003, Oxford and New York: Oxford University Press, p. 17.

8 In reading the *Summa* in this way, I have been influenced by David Burrell and Mark Jordan.

of the Three Persons, and then to the human perfection that images these relations. From here, as in Dante, we follow the course of the fall within creation that violates this intended end, until, as in the Mass, we finally approach Christ, as the very gift that the entire journey has taught us to desire. Without asking how the pilgrim feels about becoming holy, and without prescribing the sorts of emotive responses and experiences that might count as evidence to her, Thomas simply lays out his text as a pathway into God, a metaphysical–mystical ladder, complete with excurses on desire, temptation and the vices that offer themselves as footholds along the way.[9] Is it so far a reach to imagine Thomas rearranging his language in the shape of the coming allegories? *Having exited the house owned by Love,* he might have written, *we enter a clearing in which there is a great table, and at it is seated a voluminous man whom a plaque identifies as Lord Gluttony. 'Does this man,' my companion asks me, 'employ the faculty of reason, or is he ruled entirely by desire?'* . . .

But even if it is not quite as novel to the age as some have assumed, 'invented interiority' still manages to startle us by its submersion into the fabric of human existence. If Augustine, Gregory and Thomas give us texts as a road for our pilgrimage, they do not give us a Beatrice or Virgil to take our hand and walk us down it. So in the *Commedia*, instead of following a fabric of logically interconnecting questions that lead us deeper into God, here the reader follows the 'author' and his companions through the ascents and descents of the illuminative, purgative and unitive dimensions of the Christian pilgrimage.[10] Every encouraging smile from Beatrice invites a further movement of our will and understanding into participation in God, and so the entire metaphor of the journey constructs our passage as a still very Thomistic event of a grace that perfects, rather than destroys, nature.[11] We experience God in human existence similar to the way that we experience a strange land on a long journey: by passing through its surprising and unpredictable changes, its dangerous ravines, mountain vistas, and familiar and unfamiliar inhabitants. Ultimately, of course, the journey into God will transcend all these analogical repetitions: 'it cannot be explained *per verba*, so let this example serve until God's grace grants the experience'. What Dante discovers is that the experience will indeed be granted, but in a way that 'trans-humanizes' the itinerant (*Paradiso* I.70–72).[12] Human

---

9 See Peter M. Candler Jr., 2006, *Theology, Rhetoric, Manuduction, or Reading Scripture Together on the Path to God*, Grand Rapids: Eerdmans, pp 94ff.

10 See E. G. Gardner, 1913, *Dante and the Mystics: A Study of the Mystical Aspect of the Divina Commedia and its Relations with Some of its Mediaeval Sources*, London: J. M. Dent and New York: E. P. Dutton.

11 'Beatrice's smile *is* the way that Dante journeys toward the beatific vision of God'. Peter Hawkins, 'All Smiles', in Vittorio Montemaggi and Matthew Treherne (eds), 2010, *Dante's* Commedia: *Theology as Poetry*, Notre Dame, Indiana: University of Notre Dame Press, p. 47.

12 Mark Musa (trans. and ed.), 1995, *The Portable Dante*, New York and London: Penguin Books.

vision will remain human, even as it shares in the beatification which perfects only by deifying.[13]

In claiming that the texts that give us the richest accounts of perfection also engage an explicit or implied dynamic of interiority, I perhaps make clear that I do not take the language of interiority itself to be philosophically or theologically bankrupt.[14] The inwardness of Augustine, the attention to individual holiness in Gregory and Maximus, Thomas's road signs for the mind that seeks vision and insight, the Wife of Bath's tortured will: these are various inflections of an interior attention that ought not to be read as proto-Cartesian *res cogitans*, whatever our evaluation of the latter.[15] Only by allowing them to speak on their own, and refusing to lock them into the back history of a now too-familiar account of the rise of modern subjectivity, will we manage to hear them speak at all. When we do so, in fact, we find a familiar patristic resonance in much of the medieval literature, even as the later writers begin introducing new elements and imperatives.

Following Dante and especially the fourteenth-century tale-teller Giovanni Boccaccio, Chaucer employs the journey theme as a kind of literary foil, staging his vulgar tales within the ironic setting of a pilgrimage to the shrine of Becket. His *Tales* are often the most profound theologically where the clowning is at its best, which is to say that Chaucer follows a cycle of holiness in spite of his best efforts at sacrilege (see 'Retraction' 3–6).[16] As each tale unfolds, it becomes obvious that these are not simply good stories competing for the prize of a free dinner, but stories that carry within themselves the character of their various tellers.

---

13 Douglas Hedley, 'Neoplatonic Metaphysics and Imagination in Dante's *Commedia*', in Montemaggi and Treherne (eds), *Dante's* Commedia pp. 245–66.

14 This is the weakest point of the arguments in Charles Taylor's otherwise brilliant accounts of the religious dimensions of modernity. See Charles Taylor, 1989, *Sources of the Self: The Making of Modern Identity*, Cambridge, MA: Harvard University Press; Charles Taylor, 2007, *A Secular Age*, Cambridge, MA and London: Harvard University Press. Interested primarily in sorting out the back-history of the modern subject, Taylor pays lip service to the corruptions of Christian theology that lead to it, but without attending to the radicality of these corruptions. The result is a narrative that allows us to note, for instance, the self-assertion of the Good Samaritan over against 'the demands of sacred social boundaries' and the subsequent corruption of such self-assertion in modern 'disciplined society in which categorical relations have primacy' over familial and social bonds (*Secular*, p. 158). In the end though, we risk closing his book and assuming (in spite of his caveats) that the road from Samaria leads to Herbert Hoover's White House.

15 See Michael Hanby, 2003, *Augustine and Modernity*, London: Routledge, pp. 8–12.

16 'Crist have mercy on me' for 'the Tales of Caunterbury, thilke that sounen into sinnen', in V. A. Kolve and Glending Olson (eds), 1989, *The Canterbury Tales: Nine Tales and the General Prologue*, Norton Critical Edition, New York and London: W. W. Norton and Company, p. 258. Unless otherwise noted, all the references and citations from the *Tales* are from this collection.

So the knight tells of the competing virtues that haunt the chivalry code like warring gods, and the rude and drunken Miller an ironically self-deprecating tale of fools and libertines which ends up offering no moral at all, but only derision, a broken arm and a rod of hot iron 'amid the ers' ('Miller's Tale', 707). Similarly, the Wife of Bath's long prologue is a ramp into an Arthurian displacement of her own difficulties in marriage: she is boxed on the ear by a husband who loves to read tales of foolish women ('Wife of Bath's Tale', 669–70, 795–96), and she explains her own need to have a husband at all times, whose body and 'instrument' is ever under her control (132, 193–277). She then tells her tale of a lusty young knight, 'in th'olde dayes of the King Arthour' (857), whose rape of a virgin results in a quest that sends him, for the customary year and a day, out in search of womanhood (904–10). What he discovers, with the guidance of a fairy maiden in the forest, is that he is not capable of knowing a woman at all, and his true quest becomes one for the virtue, honour and forgiveness that he lacks. His journey unsettles his lust for control and immediate self-gratification because of a simple and entirely unmanageable event: he falls in love. In this way, the Wife's Tale gives an account of herself that she is as yet unable to tell, simply because her own life's tale is still unfolding.[17]

Alysoun of Bath, that is to say, is not yet to Canterbury, where her own quest ends, and so we should not be surprised to hear her explicit refusal of perfection:

Virginitee is greet perfeccioun,
And continence eek with devocious.
But Crist, that of perfeccioun is welle
Bad nat every wight he sholde go selle
All that he hadde and give it to the pore,
And in swich wyse folwe him and his fore.
He spak to hem that wolde live parfitly,
And lordinges, by youre leve, that am nat I.
I would bistowe the flour of al myn age
In the actes and in fruit of marriage. (105–14)

Christ invites the devotion of those who 'wolde live parfitly', and, she informs us, 'that am nat I'. What then, we might wonder, is she doing on the Canterbury road, telling tales of profound spiritual discovery and redemption? Though commentaries on her tale have often read in these lines an

---

17 George L. Kittredge was among the first to develop this notion of interweavings of tales and tellers: George Lyman Kittredge, 1927, *Chaucer and His Poetry*, Cambridge, MA: Harvard University Press. See Glending Olson, 'Chaucer's Idea of a Canterbury Game', in James M. Dean and Christian K. Zacher (eds), 1992, *The Idea of Medieval Literature: New Essays on Chaucer and Medieval Culture in Honor of Donald R. Howard*, Newark: University of Delaware Press, and London: Associated University Presses, pp 72–3.

ironic staging of Chaucer's own critique of the monastic professionaliza-
tion of perfection, the literary construct of the wife herself disallows any
direct interpretation of the author's convictions.[18] The Wife is not a static
character, but a wayfarer on a journey, and the pairing of prologue with
tale and of her tale with the others suggests a subtly crafted literary texture
to all of her dialogue. Her anti-perfectionism is echoed in a later tale in
the character of Melibee, who also hastily exclaims that he should not be
asked to aim for perfection, only to be challenged on the point by his wife
Prudence. 'Pacience', Prudence says there, citing both Seneca and Saint
James (and implicitly invoking Irenaeus), 'is a greet vertu of perfeccioun'
('The Tale of Melibee', 46.2706).[19] And we, Chaucer implies, ought to
have patience with Melibee, with the Wife of Bath, with all the pilgrims, as
also with our friends, fellow wayfarers and with ourselves. Perfection, after
all, even the desire to seek perfection, is not the attainment of a moment, a
single afternoon or even a year-and-a-day.

So the telling of the Tales becomes a way of placing the tellers themselves
on pilgrimage. They often express rich images of repentance and atonement,
even where 'holiness' would appear to be the furthest thing from their minds.
It is not only the Wife, the Miller, the Knight, the Reeve and the Parson who
travel the holy road, it is also Arcite and Palamon, Nicholas and Alison,
and the *lusty bacheler* ('Wife's Tale', 126). The pilgrims are the stories they
tell; the tales proper are commentaries on the biographical prologues which
frame them. Indeed, is there any other way to 'make pilgrimage', to sanctify
the journey, than to tell themselves onto the road in this way? A 'self' for
Chaucer is a disparate collection of desires, unifiable primarily by a singular
quest for holiness; it is not yet the inward gazing spirit of rational manage-
ment that it will become thereafter. The Canterbury lyrics construct their
characters through a publicly presented, outwardly narrated collection of
memories, encounters, virtues and vices.[20] The Wife of Bath, like any pilgrim
seeking holiness, is all of these intersections at once. And she places her 'self'
on a path that slopes upward, from her narrative imperfection to the teleological holiness of the martyr's shrine.

This fabric begins to unravel already in the fifteenth-century Lollard writings: 'Examine who so ever will twentie of thes pilgremis, and she shall not

---

18 See Goldstein, 'Future Perfect'. pp. 121–5; also Geoffrey W. Gust, 2009, *Constructing Chaucer: Author and Auto-Fiction in the Critical Tradition*, New York:
Palgrave Macmillan, pp. 28ff. Gust renders great insight into the ironic distances
between the narrators and their stories, but then, oddly, seems to assume that he
can unite both tale and narrator into a single ideal author, Chaucer the Poet/Pilgrim,
who apparently was gay.

19 In Alfred W. Pollard (ed.) 1929, *The Works of Geoffrey Chaucer: The Canterbury Tales (Text)*, Oxford: Basil Blackwell, p. 226. See Goldstein, 'Future Perfect',
pp. 130–2.

20 Olson, 'Chaucer's Idea', pp. 79–88; Hirsh, *Chaucer and the Canterbury Tales*,
p. 82: 'Chaucer constructs the pilgrims as knowing travelers, though their destination is barely in sight as their tales come to an end. They live somewhere in between
Babylon and Jerusalem, and turn sometimes to one, sometimes to the other.'

fynde thre men or women that knowe surely a commaundment of God, nor can say their Pater Noster and Ave Maria nor their Credo redely, in ony maner of langage' (Thorpe, *Examinacion*).[21] Sir William Thorpe, in his own account of his trial defence, complains that these pilgrims undertake the journey 'more for the helthe of their bodies than of the soules', and 'more to have here wordlely and flescheley frendship than for to have frendshep of God and of his seintis in heven' (*Exam.*). The very possibility of this comparison implies the birth of a new bifurcation of alternatives: one must opt for either healthy bodies or healthy souls, friendship with fellow travellers or friendship with God, *foolisch* or *trew* pilgrimage.[22] For Chaucer, the absurdity of a drunken miller telling bawdy and adulterous tales on the path to the most sacred shrine in England is in no sense anti-religious, in the dichotomous sense that we now use the term. In fact, these scenes are anti- or super-religious in the older sense of the term: if imperfect wives and millers can go out seeking perfection in spite of themselves, then monasteries can no longer lay claim to the 'councils of perfection' as their own theological property. The world of the Tales is the world of Carnival, where the excess of personae that inhabits each teller breaks out onto the narrated surface in accounts of the murders, deceptions, loyalties and loves that human lives tend to gather as thy progress. The tales, together with the unifying trope of pilgrimage, thus constitute a celebration of the unreserved deterritorializing of hell by the powers of Becket and the saints of God. Given enough road, the theological virtues will conquer the deadly sins: this eschatological imperative is so obvious and unqualified to Chaucer that he goes on insisting that even these *foolisch* stories, and these *foolisch* pilgrims, belong on this sacred path.[23]

---

21 From Kolve and Olson (eds), *The Canterbury Tales*, pp. 260–1.

22 From Kolve and Olson (eds), *The Canterbury Tales*, p. 259. On this point, see Taylor, *Secular*, p. 39. Chaucer is not immune to the sway of the Lollards. See his 'Retractions', cited above, which make a sharp distinction between his sinful writings and his moral writings and translations. See also Andrew Cole, 2008, *Literature and Heresy in the Age of Chaucer*, Cambridge, UK and New York: Cambridge University Press, especially Chapter 4.

23 Taylor, *Secular*, pp. 46–9, 87, 124, notes with his usual dexterity the way in which 'the world turned upside down' of Carnival moves from being celebrated in the Middle Ages as a kind of self-mockery of human hierarchy to being rejected in early modernity as a simple 'invitation to sin', 'a denial of ambiguity and complexity in an unmixed condemnation . . . (we are witnessing the birth of what will become in our day p.c.)' (p. 87). By suggesting, however, that the earlier mode of festal baccanalia is an indication of the 'complementarity, the mutual necessity of opposites' (p. 47), he weakens his interpretation with a kind of Taoist slant. It would be more in the spirit of the Middle Ages to see this rather as a recognition that there is no ultimate opposition to the divine attributes and that the vices themselves are only relative and privative forms of the virtues, to be kept in check by a civic order that is itself only temporary. In the feast of the beatified saints, no true desire shall be unfulfilled, no truly pleasurable dish shall grow cold on the table. This, surely, comes more to the point of what the 'counter-festivals' of the Middle Ages were actually celebrating.

The morality plays of the late fifteenth and early sixteenth centuries carry on this practice of the Carnivalizing of everyday life. The gospel, they suggest, has so illuminated the pathway towards perfection that it can expose all those devils and vices that tempt us as fools and asses whose tricks are no more than juvenile clowning. So *Mankind*, for instance, stages an orgy of the demonic, with a host of demons dancing around the hero, ridiculing his trust in God, singing him the astonishingly perverse 'Christmas Song', attempting to trip him up in a mocking game of football (325–36, 723).[24] They rhyme to him in mock liturgical Latin, as when they find him digging in the soil, and shout, salvation 'is in *spadibus*! Christ's curse come on your *headibus*!' (391).

In spite of the foolishness, though, we are drawn in, as to the 'Miller's Tale', and find ourselves laughing and enjoying the demons' act. This is in fact the principal 'trap' of the morality plays, a manipulated complicity of the audience in the vicious behaviour of the players.[25] *Mankind* even presents us with the first known account of an audience paying for public theatre.[26] In lines 454–74, the demons leave the stage and move through the audience, calling out the threat that unless they raise enough money, no one shall see the demon with the unnaturally large head that they are about to unleash on Mankind. And of course, playing our prescribed role, we reach into pocket and purse to ensure the demonic spectacle.

In the end, though, the demonic Carnival is just that: the Shrovetide exuberance that comes before the greater comedy of Lent. So, in contrast with absurd rhyming of the demons, we begin to hear the thicker phrasing of the liturgy when the character Mercy comes onstage.[27] Once Mercy ministers to Mankind and helps him expel the demons, she can refer to the greater play that takes place in Mankind's glorification:

Mankind is wretched, he hath sufficient proof.
Therefore God grant you all *per suam misericordiam*
That ye may be playferes with the angels above
And have to your portion *vitam aeternam*. Amen! (911–14)

The morality plays dramatize the very Chaucerian point that imperfection and perfection are not polarities in human existence. If they were, there would be no pilgrimage at all, since our failings would always keep us from beginning the journey. Further, by enticing us to play along, they play out the psychomachic battle[28] between perfection and imperfection not only within the souls of the players and narrators, but within the souls of the watchers and readers as well. Are we leaning forward to see the demon,

24 Douglas Bruster and Eric Rasmussen (eds), 2009, *Everyman and Mankind*, London: Arden Shakespeare.

25 Bruster and Rasmussen, 'Introduction' to *Everyman and Mankind*, pp. 13–14.

26 Bruster and Rasmussen, 'Introduction', p. 13.

27 Bruster and Rasmussen, 'Introduction', pp. 10, 17.

28 Bruster and Rasmussen, 'Introduction'. p. 15.

whose voice we hear off stage? Then we are effectively dropping money into the hat, rejecting Mercy and waging the devils' war on Mankind. Are we grinning as we read the perverse exegesis of Alysoun of Bath? Then we are identifying with her rejection of the vocation to be perfect as our Father in heaven is perfect. The point though, and one that was so largely lost on the Lollard imagination, is that we are expected to play along, to laugh and pay our shillings, just as we are expected to cry 'crucify' on Good Friday. Our route into God's holiness overlays Christ's incarnate route to deification; it is always *per suam misericordiam* that we are made playmates of the angels in heaven. We never stall in our temporal transience, never freeze into a stature that is perfectly free of temptation or even fallenness. It is the crucified Christ who has made perfect the human form, and so our laughter during Mardi Gras will continue, but as a kind of self-mocking anticipation of the laughter on Easter Sunday. The imperfections of human existence, even our attempts to desire imperfection as such, are no match for the perfection performed historically and eschatologically by Christ.

This body of literature continues, then, to locate perfection on a Thomistic grid. The operations of grace entrench themselves in human habit so that human nature, and all that it entails, is perfected rather than destroyed. The literary form itself accomplishes this, as these writers assume that an allegory should be, first of all, a well-told tale. They draw us in with the appeal of a particular narrative loop, but then call us to pause a bit and reflect on the universality of their play. The tales of page and stage call us to perfection diachronically, so to speak.[29] They catch us up in the action without waiting for us to process mentally what they are asking of us. We drop in our coins because we want the demons to keep it up and only later wonder what this says about our character. We get annoyed by the fellow onstage who abandons Everyman (287–88)[30] and only later ponder what it means that the friend's name was not Geoffrey or Cynthia, but 'Fellowship'. The allegory moves us along from the particularity of the literal sense (that friend leaves that man, this man imitates these lyrics rather than those) to the universal (that fellow is Fellowship, and fellowship abandons everyman; this man is Mankind, and mankind parrots the songs of mischief rather than those of mercy). When the loop closes, we are back to the particularity of the reader or hearer who finds this story to be his own: Do I not daily abandon everyman and parrot the songs of mischief? Throughout this movement, the mythopoetical temporality is essential, since this is what informs the audience that we travel into God's presence something like we travel into town, and we make friends with Doctrine and Sacrament something like the friendships we build throughout our own communities. Hence Knowledge's blessing on Everyman: 'Eueryman, God gyue you tyme and space!' (608).

The time and space for making pilgrimage is the time and space for human incompleteness to journey into the Easter faith. This, again, is missed

---

29 Rowan Williams, 1999, *On Christian Theology*, Oxford: Blackwell, pp. 44–7.
30 Referencing the edition in Bruster and Rasmussen, *Everyman and Mankind*.

entirely when public theologians such as Thorpe argue that *trew pilgrimages* 'ought to be interpreted gostely' (*Exam.*). There is no spiritual journey that does not involve the body and no universal truth that does originate and return to narrated particularity. Thus humans can experience perfection by advancing through the relay of particularity and universality that the very term 'perfection' implies: we who are only ever here in part are called to become complete.[31] Only a growing confidence in humanity's ability to reason free of the realm of *foolisch* contingencies and common folklore would suggest that we skip the mediations of human incompleteness, and opt directly for a *gostely* perfection.[32] By arguing for such a revision, the early modern theological tradition begins to break down the mediating cycles of liturgical and Christological tradition, and in doing so loses the ability to trace the trail of the complex and disjointed human into its perfect end in God.

Green Meadows, White Bulls

In Sir Thomas Malory's late fifteenth-century version of the French *Queste del Saint Graal*, this breakdown of mediated perfection is especially evident. As Arthur's knights prepare to leave Camelot in search of the cup of Christ, the text draws a stark distinction for us between Lancelot, 'most mervayloust man of the worlde, and most adventurest' (p. 537)[33] and Galahad, 'passynge fayre and well made, that unneth in the worlde men myght nat fine hys macche' (p. 497). The latter, though actually Lancelot's son, is more properly 'Sonne of the Hyghe Fadir' (p. 516). When Galahad manages to pull from the floating stone the sword whose hilt Lancelot humbly refuses to try, we see all too clearly how the quest for the grail will proceed. The son will eclipse the father, and the apotheosis of Galahad will give way to Lancelot's forlorn return to the Round Table.

The reasons for his lack of success are a secret to neither the reader nor to Lancelot himself. 'My synne and my wyckednes hath brought me unto grete dishounre' (p. 518), he laments, before confessing to a holy hermit 'how he had loved a queen unmesurabely and oute of mesure longe' (p. 519). Twenty-four years of love-making with Guinevere stand between Lancelot and his quest's end, so that even in his moments of grace and revelation he remains 'a man of eville wycked fayth and poore beleve' (p. 536). His lips will never touch the sacred cup.

---

31 See Exposition, above.

32 See also Hans Frei, 1974, *The Eclipse of Bibilical Narrative: A Study in Eighteenth and Nineteenth Century Hermeneutics*, New Haven: Yale University Press, pp. 1–17. As Sayers, *Whimsical*, p. 207, puts it, allegory, like a parable or fable, 'tells a literal story that is complete in itself, but which also presents a likeness to some spiritual or psychological experience so that it can be used to signify and interpret that experience'.

33 All citations are from Stephen H. A. Shepherd (ed.), 2004, *Le Morte Darthur*, Norton Critical Edition, New York and London: W. W. Norton and Company.

Lancelot is the tragic hero of Malory's *Le Morte Darthur*, and especially of the *Tale of the Sankgreal*. If Galahad is wholly attuned to the sacred, and knights like Gawain more or less in search of secular adventure, Lancelot is 'torn between the two worlds'.[34] He is a hero of tournaments and jousts in the field, and his deeds are everywhere celebrated; yet they are also the source of the pride that makes him unfit for his true desires. Even his love for Guinevere is ambiguous, as if Malory is perhaps giving us permission to admire the knight for this passion and chivalrous worship, even while we recognize it as his spiritual undoing.[35] He is 'nat stable' (p. 543), and but for this instability he would be next in line after Galahad to drink from the cup. Lancelot, who wishes only to be among the knights of heaven, is destined ever to be *erthly* (p. 537). Though he desires the heavenly attributes, he must satisfy himself with a more mundane display of virtues: beauty, bounty, seemliness and strength (p. 584). His quest is always already destined to fail; thus his less than inspirational cry as the quest begins: 'Go we to seke that we shall nat fynde' (p. 539).

How is Lancelot supposed to feel about being 'the most merveloust man of the worlde', yet for all that a man of earth rather than of heaven? His character arcs through the Tale from a kind of 'bad infinity' of hopelessness, to an over-reaching zeal, to an ultimate satisfaction with his own lot. An important clue for the reader's navigation of this complex curve comes in Ector's dream of Lancelot as Tantalus, the Homeric hero cursed by Hades to thirst for an undrinkable draft:

And so he rode tylle that he cam unto the fayryst welle that eve he saw, and there Sir Launcelot alyght and wolde have dronke of that welle; and whan he stowped to drynke of that water, the water sanke from hym. And whan Sir Launcelot saw that, he turned and wente thidir as he com fro. (p. 539)

The well is not simply the Grail itself, as the ubiquitous hermit Nacien explains. 'The welle betokenyth the hyghe grace of God, for the more men desire hit to take hit, the more shall be their desire' (p. 542).[36] But Lancelot does not take it, and so, we must assume, he desires it less, to the extent that he is even able to walk away without having drunk of this grace of God at all. Lancelot drinks of earthly cups, and receives earthly grace.

---

34 Catherine Batt, 2002, *Malory's* Morte Darthur: *Re-making Arthurian Tradition*, New York: Palgrave, p. 135.

35 Lewis, *Allegory*, pp. 21ff., explores this complex literary and theological motif by which a knight exchanges devotion to God with devotion to a landed, married lady.

36 It is significant that Malory never uses the *Queste*'s phrase *grâce del graal*, always substituting for it 'grace of God', thus further distancing the *telos* of a human adventure from the *telos* in God. See Ann Marie D'Arcy, 2000, *Wisdom and the Grail: The Image of the Vessel in the* Queste del Saint Graal *and Malory's* Tale of Sankgreal, Dublin: Four Courts, p. 339.

Eventually, when he ends his failed quest for these high graces, he will find peace with his lot in life, and express this peace in a curiously self-laudatory appraisal: 'No man has lyved better than I have done to enchyeve that I have done' (p. 578).

With Malory's Lancelot then, we return to an Aristotelian deutero-perfection, though now, with perfection aligned with sinlessness (especially chastity in the bedroom, though also mercy on the battlefield), the second-ary achievement is cast as a kind of happy imperfection. Tantalus tries a few times to get the water that keeps sinking down as he stoops, and then ultimately shrugs it off with the remark that he is not all that thirsty anyhow. Lancelot's arc is in this sense exactly the opposite of Alysoun of Bath: she refuses perfection only to have the very refusal caught up into her pilgrimage toward sanctity; he quests for perfection for many months, before finally returning in peace to his fellows of the Round Table, as much as acknowledging to them that Christ 'spak to hem that wolde live parfitly, /And lordinges, by youre leve, that am nat I'.

This transition is made possible, at least partially, by the new position that Malory gives to humility in his moral drama. When Gawain has a dream of 153 bulls in a meadow, Nacien interprets it thus: 'By the medow oughte to be undirstoode humilité and paciens; tho be the thynges which bene allwey grene and quyk', and the bulls he should take to be the knights of the Table. The Round Table itself was founded so that 'men mowe no tyme overcom humilité and paciens' (p. 541). There are three white bulls, though one turns out later to have spots: Galahad, Percivale and Bors (who 'trespassed but onys in hys virginité' [p. 542]). These three occupy the same meadow as the 150 black bulls, though the latter are too proud to stay and graze there: 'For if they had, their hartes shoulde have bene sette in hu-milité and paciens' (p. 541). Their wicked desire to go seek other pastures does not represent their decision to leave Camelot and go in search of the Grail, Nacien explains, but rather their decision to depart prior to receiv-ing confession: thus the unchaste knights leave the meadow of humility in order to seek the grail. The conclusion of the vision foresees the fate of all three Grail finders: the rapture of Galahad, Percivale's monastic retirement and Bors' eventual return to Camelot.

What does it mean that all the bulls, Galahad and Bors, Lancelot and Gawain, occupy the same space? Only that they could all have gone on quest, black, white, spotted alike, without ever leaving the meadow, since the attainment of the Grail depends entirely on the sinlessness of the knight, while the ability to quest depends on humility alone. Lancelot and his en-tire herd could have stayed in the meadow, with hearts 'sette in humilité and paciens', and quested 'perfectly' as humble and patient sinners, at home in their imperfection. Patience here is not the gradual sanctification that it is for Irenaeus and Chaucer, but more like a Stoic long-suffering, a virtue by which one graciously receives whatever limited ends she is allot-ted. Galahad, meanwhile, is no less humble, but is still granted a higher end: something like *theosis* in fact, in view of his perfect life and perfect faith. Humility thus trumps the other virtues, like faithfulness and chastity, since whether one is chaste is secondary to the matter of whether one is humbly chaste or humbly unchaste, humbly merciful or humbly violent. Indeed, humility trumps even perfection itself, since the black and spotted bulls will retire one day in their pasture as pleasantly unperfected. Even the speckled Bors can live at ease in a state of semi-*theosis*, with hind legs in Camelot, forelegs in heaven and all four hooves planted firmly in the meadow of humility.

To understand Gawain's meadow as a post-Christian image of humility, we only have to return to Thomas, who argued that humility is a second-ary virtue, since it is a disposition rather than a true perfection of hu-man character. Charity, the form of all virtues, is also their highest good, since it names our unsurpassable participation in the caritas of God (*ST* II–II.23.6). Like lovers who are distant from one another, we practice a host of virtues in order to remain in communion with God; when the lov-ers come together again, they experience, at least for fleeting moments, an evaporation of all the faithfulness, trust, hope, patience and kindness that sustained them for so long. All these virtues fade behind the backdrop now, and are upstaged by the single great virtue of union with the beloved. Charity is in this sense the eschatological perfection of all other virtues. In the midst of sin, death and a constant temptation to self-reliance, humil-ity is the only path towards this charitable union with God. But just as those who mourn will be comforted, those who humble themselves will be exalted (*ST* II–II.161.5, *ad* 3–4). To celebrate humility as more ultimate than its own perfection in charity is to celebrate the cup of Christ's blood divorced from its liturgical narration of our entry in his resurrection and glorification; indeed, these two distortions go hand in hand in Malory, and he is certainly not alone in this.[37]

Malory, in fact, dismantles much of the theological structure of the French text, carrying out what comes to look at points like a clumsy hatchet job.[38] Allegories rich and full in the source become in his text spliced and unfollowable even for the questers, as when Gawain is surprised to find that the seven knights he has just finished slaying were the Deadly Sins, and then he is surprised again to hear that he must do penance for slay-ing them, since slaying men is a wicked thing to do (p. 516). We feel the literary jolt with Gawain: are they real men, or are they allegorical sins? Surely the answer to this question will help the knight determine the right the thing to do with his sword. But no clarity is coming, and we leave the castle as snookered as the luckless Gawain. Or, to take another example, the text is filled with archetypal relationships between fathers and sons, but they are too convoluted to allow a theology of adoption like we find in the New Testament.[39] Lancelot prays to 'Swete Fadir, Jesu Cryste' as the same addressee, and Christ calls Galahad and his companions 'My sunnes'

---

37 See D'Arcy, *Wisdom*, pp. 328–30, 362; also Taylor, *Secular*, pp. 64ff.

38 Batt, *Re-making*, pp. 32–34, 150–8; D'Arcy, *Wisdom*, pp. 325ff.

39 This also represents a revision of the French text: see Batt, *Re-making*, pp. 149–50.

(pp. 574, 584). The divine being is thus entirely Father, and even the title 'sons' now marks not our participation in, but solely our subordination to the Triune Creator. In all, Malory's Arthur narrative is in many ways simply a poorly told tale, since he changes names, omits important plot points and breaks the storyline into dissociated fragments, leaving the reader to invent connections missing from the pages.[40] Such fragmentation is itself theologically important, since, as I suggested above, the cohesiveness of a revelatory play, poem or allegory is a testament to our ability as human reasoners to journey into the true. Alternatively, a story that comes in fits, starts and interruptions seems designed to make us 'ponder our distance from, rather than access to, revelation'.[41]

Perhaps, in the end, this is part of Malory's point. A sense of mourning pervades his entire manuscript, as in the much debated 'May passage', where he laments the love of men and women for one other that is, in his time, without wisdom or stability, an eroticism that comes to self-expression in a world of feeble natures and 'grete disworship'. Just as winter 'allway arace and deface grene summer', so this breakdown of nature and love follows a greener age: 'But the olde love was nat so' (p. 624).[42] The textual fragmentation may simply be a literary sign of the world the poetry describes: we readers encounter the age of chivalry like we encounter the ruins of a castle on a hilltop. The knights have all left the fellowship, Arthur is dead, and the age of true love and true worship has come to an end. At Galahad's death, while angels usher his soul to heaven, a hand reaches down and takes the cup as well, 'and sythen was there never man so hardy to sey that he had seyn the Sankgreal' (p. 586). 'Hardy' is a near synonym for 'perfect' or 'holy' here,[43] and the point is clear: the grail is gone, and there will be no more Galahads, no more sisters of Percivale (pp. 559–60),[44] and no more 'perfait beleve'. The limited good of the *erthly* Lancelot is now the best that we can achieve. If the writer of the following lines misses the mournful tone of the narrative as a whole, she sees quite clearly the implications for human perfection: 'From a completely allegorical work whose adventures are a means to a partial discovery of a higher truth, [Malory] has fashioned a tale whose final goal becomes an excuse for the discovery, through adventure, of the good to which man can attain on earth.'[45] Malory is thus the first writer to recognize how perfection languishes

---

40 See Batt, *Re-making*, pp. xviii, 32, 148, 158.

41 Batt, *Re-making*, p. 34.

42 See Batt, *Re-making*, p. xiii, for a treatment of this passage, and her entire book for a careful treatment of the 'ruins of chivalry' theme.

43 See also the term in the 'Ship of Faythe' passage, p. 561.

44 She, along with Galahad, is the key Christ-type in the tale. See Batt, *Re-making*, p. 135.

45 The line is from Sandra Ness Ihle's *Malory's Grail Quest*, and quoted in Helen Cooper, 'The *Lancelot-Grail Cycle* in England: Malory and his Predecessors', in Carol Dover (ed.), 2003, *A Companion to the Lancelot–Grail Cycle*, Cambridge: D. S. Brewer, p. 158.

in the ruins of the medieval world, and also the first to recommend that we soldier on like Sisyphus on his hill, or rather like Tantalus at the well, until the thirst for union with God leaves our throats on its own accord. The daylight of perfect endings has passed: now comes the night in which all bulls are grey.

A Sabbath for Elves

The mourning of Malory notwithstanding, the fifteenth and sixteenth centuries are not principally centuries of tragic recollections of the perfection possible in lost ages. They are the centuries of intellectual and cultural rebirth, and of the rise of a humanism that is, in its origins, thoroughly theological. With important headwaters in Eckhart and the Rhineland mystics, a new stream of theological productivity begins to flow, traceable on the Continent through the writings of Nicholas of Cusa, Pico de Mirandola, Marcilio Ficino and Pierre de Berulle. For these authors, the human pilgrimage is more than a resignation to what the fates or fortunes allow.[46] In Cusanus in particular we encounter a creative and foundationless naming of a new human form, which is itself a corollary to creative acts of naming the divine being. 'The oneness of the human mind', he says, 'is the being of its own conjectures.' As its conjectures are its reasoned attempt to 'enumerate' the divine mind, guessing at God's perfection is always simultaneously a poetic divinizing of the human *telos* (*de Coniectures* I.5–6).[47] If Edmund Spenser's *The Faerie Queen* inherits this swell of theological humanism, it does not, as we shall see, manage to hold entirely at bay the new anti-Titanic forces that still swirl within.

Spenser's epic poem opens with the tale of 'tall clownishe younge man' ('Letter to Raleigh'),[48] a holy fool, perhaps,[49] wandering errantly and erringly

---

46 See C. S. Lewis, 1954, *English Literature in the Sixteenth Century Excluding Drama*, Oxford: Clarendon Press, pp. 1–20, 50.

47 The translation is from Jasper Hopkins, from the text at http://jasper-hopkins.info/, accessed 15 October, 2010. I've transliterated 'coniectures' rather than opting for Hopkins's 'surmises', which might carry more a sense of straightforward deduction than Nicholas's Latin term denotes. 'Coniectura igitur est positiva assertio, in alteritate veritatem, uti est, participans'. (I.11.57.) See again Taylor's simplistic account, in *Secular*, p. 113, which misses the excessive funding of the human by the divine: The 'introduction of a stance of *poiesis* into the domain of praxis' in Nicholas and others creates 'a science in which truth is confirmed by instrumental efficacy'.

48 Spenser's 'Letter' prefaces the Penguin edition, to which all the following citations of Spenser refer: Thomas P. Roche, Jr. and C. Patrick O'Donnell, Jr. (eds), 1978, London: Penguin Books. The citation above is to p. 17.

49 See Christopher Bond, 'The "Legend of Holinesse" and the Fall of Man: Spenser's *Faerie Queene* 1 as Milton's Original for *Paradise Lost* 9 and 10', pp. 208–09, in Charles W. Durham and Kristin A. Pruitt (eds), 2008, *Uncircumscribed Mind: Reading Milton Deeply*, Selinsgrove, PA: Susquehanna University Press. Bond cites Nohrnberg's *The Analogy of the Fairie Queene* on this point.

across a fantasy-scape of dragons, giants and witches. From the outset, he takes us deeper into the lost world of courtesy and adventure than Malory. If the latter gives us a world fragmented by the ruins of chivalry, Spenser plunges immediately into this lost age. Does his construction of human ends deepen and extend Malory's? Finding our 'Gentle Knight' . . . pricking on the plaine/ Y cladd in mightie armes and siluer shielde' (I.i.1-2.), we might expect another perfection *du Lac*: a morality of the earthly sort, that is, in which our hero's humility gives us cause not just to overlook, but even to expect the occasional burst of wrath or surrender to lust.

To be sure, the untried young clown, the Red Crosse Knight, is by the story's end no stranger to the deadly sins. He makes his way into the House of Pride and, even while disgusted by the parade of sins he sees before him, finds himself 'mongst the middest crowd' (I.iv.15), caught in their thrall in ways that seem to undermine his very will to resist. In fact, from his first bout in Errour's den to his climactic battle with the great dragon, his behaviour is always virtuous in only an ambiguous sense. Reminiscent of Gawain's quandry with the seven sins/knights, Red Crosse's armour and sword are the Pauline weapons of righteousness, but also 'instruments of wrath and heavinesse'. He fights with Sansfoy, and though the latter fights for wrong while Red Crosse 'strives for right', (I.v.9) their methods remain identical: 'with greedy force each other doth assayle' (v.6); 'each to deadly shame would drive his foe' (v.9).[50] He falls in with the false Duessa, forsaking his pledge to the true Una, but does so, ironically, through a bit of witchcraft in which his very chastity betrays him. In all of this, Spenser reaches further than Malory to show us the limitations of earthly heroes: it is not simply that we are unable to hold to the virtuous life, but that even our best intentions land us in the mire.

> What man so wise, what earthly wit so ware,
> As to discry the crafty cunning traine,
> By which deceipt doth maske in visour faire,
> And cast her coulours died deepe in graine,
> To seeme like truth, whose shape she well can faine,
> And fitting gestures to her purpose frame;
> The guiltlesse man with guile to entertaine? (vii.1)

At the poem's thematic centre, however, is a kind of double excess of perfection that that makes a surprisingly Thomistic point. For the first excess, the all-too-limited knights errant do not have the final say on the *telos* of human pursuits, since the poem is not about them at all, but about 'Arthure, before he was king, the image of a braue knight, perfected in the twelue priuate morall vertues, as Aristotle hath deuised' ('Letter', p. 15). Arthur enters each of the six books with a knightly display of the very

---

50 See Darryl J. Gless, 1994, *Interpretation and Theology in Spenser*, Cambridge and New York: Cambridge University Press, pp. 66, 93.

virtue that each knight lacks (holiness, temperance, chastity, friendship, justice and courtesy). When Calidore, Book Six's Knight of Courtesy, falls prey to Disdayne, Arthur not only vanquishes the foe, but waits upon Calidore's Lady to determine Disdayne's fate, thus defeating the enemy and schooling Calidore in the virtue of courtesy all at once (VI.vi). The titular hero must fight the final enemy, as in all the books: Arthur departs, leaving Disdayne to Calidore, thereby demonstrating that the lesson in virtue is learned. In this way, all the wanderings, errings and unwitting failures of the knights become a kind of engraced crafting of a perfect life: Arthur provides the *traditio*, and the schooled knights engage in a piece of virtue-poesis, making perfection out of the fragments and contingencies of their respective journeys.

The Book of Holinesse is the first to demonstrate this pattern. Arthur appears just when Red Crosse strays from the holy path. For Spenser, as for Thomas, holiness is nearly identical to 'religion', the devotion of all virtues to God.[51] Courage can be holy or unholy, depending on the end to which it is devoted; courage tempered with religion is the sort that makes one holy. By allegorizing holiness with a knight's allegiance to his lady, Spenser retreats from the late sixteenth century, as Malory retreats from the fifteenth, to the increasingly foreign landscape of courtly love.[52] Red Crosse loses, albeit through the best intentions, his holy devotion to Una; Arthur must enter, swear his services to her, rescue the errant one from prison, and then ride off in time for the latter to finish his sworn service to his Lady (I.ix.20).

Red Crosse is the first Reformed knight of epic fantasy; he is also of that unique brand of early Protestantism in which co-operating grace was never imagined to be a threat to divine initiative.[53] These knights 'don't need maps', as one commentator puts it, since their journeys are not chartable paths to a gaugeable perfection. Like Israel in the wilderness, the point is to move in and among the challenges and obstacles that come along, growing closer to their goal in character and faith though not in geography.[54] So 'Faery Court' is an elusive place that cannot appear at all in the stanzas of the poem until a thick latticework of virtue has formed. Perfection is not a movement in space but in time, and we still today retain this dimension in figures of speech which mark temporal development by means of spatial allegories: we 'pass through' phases, our projects are not finished yet but are 'getting there' . . .

---

51 See Gerald Morgan, 2004, '"Add Faith vnto Your Force": The Perfecting of Spenser's Knight of Holiness in Faith and Humility', *Renaissance Studies* 18 (3), pp. 452–3.

52 See Sayers, *Whimsical*, p. 221.

53 See Gless, *Interpretation and Theology*, pp. 33ff.

54 Joanne Woolway Grenfell, 'Do real knights need maps?', in Andrew Gordon and Bernhard Klein (eds), 2001, *Literature, Mapping, and the Politics of Space in Early Modern Britain*, New York: Cambridge University Press, pp. 224–38.

In fact, since he is free of the notion that Red Crosse, and the rest will ever get there (unless perhaps via what another commentator calls 'the *et cetera* principle'),[55] Spenser is free to tell a good story. Red Crosse can become perfect poetically, through *poesis*, without ever threatening to estrange himself from his naturally human readers. If Lancelot is an all-too-familiar human, resigned to imperfection, Galahad is not really recognizable as a human at all. Red Crosse rides halfway between these, swerving now toward one, now toward the other, but never colliding with either. He sounds notes of perfection with occasional clarity which then quickly fade, only to ring out again more brilliantly at some later point. Spenser is thus a Renaissance inheritor of Chaucerian subjectivity: his pilgrim knights slowly gather the full complex array of human will and agency, and from these fragments they fashion selves capable of true virtue and perfect devotion.[56]

At the same time, because it is a more successful drama, it is a still more successful allegory. We now can fear the seduction of the maiden Du'essa simply as a conniving sorceress, and only then begin to notice the pairing of her name with Una, the truthful maiden. Is she perhaps not only a shape-changing witch in our particular plot, but also duplicity itself, in the universal plot we share with Red Crosse?[57] High adventure poetry can become a drama of holiness more powerful even than the morality plays, since these invite us to lose ourselves more completely in their landscapes, just prior to the reminder, which may only come by a nudge or gesture, of what the true land is that we inhabit. The *mythopoesis* of Middle Earth, Narnia, Earthsea, Prydain and Hogwarts are still, in this sense, Spenserian allegory.[58]

What sort of perfection, though, is the Aristotelian excellence of Arthur? We are left to guesswork here, as the arc of the poem is but half complete, the second part never begun. Certainly, though, we have enough of the story to note a lack of full *eudaimonia*. Arthur identifies himself as a type of tragic Fisher King, with a 'fresh bleeding wound, which day and night/ Whilome doth rankcle in my riven brest' (I.ix.7). The wound is his longing for the Faery Queene herself, a pang he has carried with him since their erotic and ghostly encounter in the forest: 'When I awoke, and found her place devoyd,/ And nought but pressed gras where she had lyen/ I sorroed all so much, as earst I joyd,/ And washed all her place with watry eyen' (I.ix.15). Arthur is then a kind of 'higher' Lancelot, seeking in vain for his elusive Grail, and Una's remark nearly repeats Nacien's to Lancelot: 'For onlely worthie you through prowes preife/ Yf living man mote worthie be, to be her liefe' (I.ix.17).

Should we then take Arthur's verdict to be the pronouncement of the poet: 'Deepe written in my heart with yron pen,/ That blisse may not abide

55 Gless, *Interpretation and Theology*, p. 172.
56 Gless, *Interpretation and Theology*, pp. 70ff.
57 Lewis, *Allegory*, pp. 314ff.
58 See John Milbank, 2005, 'Fictioning Things: Gift and Narrative', *Religion and Literature*, 37 (3), pp. 1–37.

in state of mortall men' (I.xiii.44)? We should not, I suspect, and this its because of the second excess of Spenserian perfection. With Arthur 'on his way/ to seeke his love', Red Crosse and Una have one more important stop to make before the final battle with the dragon who holds her royal parents captive. They go to the House of Holiness, kept by 'Dame Caelia . . . thought/ from heaven to come, thither to rise' (I.x.4–5). This serves as a sort of hospital and training ground for the weakened knight, as Caelia's three daughters, Fidelia, Speranza and Charissa, attend to him during his stay. The Pauline voice sounds as unmistakably in Spenser as in Thomas: the public and private virtues are naturally perfecting, but beyond them 'these three remain', the theological virtues that link the pilgrim knight with the supernatural grace of true perfection. Through disciplines of faithfulness, hopefulness and works of charity,

> [s]hortly therein so perfect he became,
> That from the first unto the last degree,
> His mortall life he learned had to frame
> In holy righteousnesse, without rebuke or blame. (I.x.45)

Equally Thomistic is the doorkeeper of Caelia's house: Humiltá, the 'aged syre' (I.x.5), opens the way for them, because if charity is the perfecting of all virtues, humility is the human path toward his divine end.[59]

Arthur embodies a perfection that exceeds Red Crosse, and yet Red Crosse learns a perfection that exceeds Arthur and so transcends the tragedy of mortal impermanence.[60] So while still in the House of Holiness, Red Crosse begins a Sinai-like ascent (x.53) with Mercy the deputized nurse to visit the sage Contemplation. When the latter sees them coming, he gives Mercy the opportunity to express this excessive perfection. He

> [a]sked to what end they clomb that tedious hight.
> 'What end' (quoth she) 'should cause us take such paine,
> But that same end, which every living wight
> Should make his marke, high heaven to attain?'

Through the care of faith, hope and charity, then, Red Crosse climbs to the place from which he can contemplate/ascend into the high heavens.

The scene atop the mountain overlooking the new Jerusalem is a deification scene more reminiscent of Cicero's *Somnium Scipionis* than of Sinai or Nyssan's *Vita Moysis*. Red Crosse is able to see atop the mountain clearly enough to remark that the city's towers far outshine his memories of Faery

---

59 See Morgan, 'Perfecting', pp. 463–74.

60 Philip Rollinson, 1987, 'Arthur, Maleger, and the Interpretation of *The Faerie Queene*', *Spenser Studies* VII, pp. 103–21, makes the point that Arthur stands not for 'grace', but for a 'magnificence' that undoes the misrule caused by the vice of intemperance.

Court.[61] At this point, Contemplation discloses Red Crosse's own birthright: the belaboured knight is actually 'of Faery', kidnapped in his infancy, only to be found later and raised by a human ploughman. The kidnapping, the sage explains, altered the child's nature: 'Such men do Chaungelings call, so chaungd by Faeries theft' (65). Though this is news to Red Crosse, the reader has already received hints to this effect when the poet repeatedly calls him 'Elfin Knight' (for example x.44), and compares him during his battle with Sansjoy to a griffen (v.8).[62] The hideous giant Orgoglio, an anti-typical projection of Red Crosse's own imperfection, is himself a kind of negative changeling, since '[t]he greatest Earth his uncouth mother was/ and blustering Aoelus his boasted syre' (vii.9). The creature is literally swollen with 'arrogant delight' of his doubly regal nature, even though in fact he is merely 'puft up with emptie wynd, and fild with sinfull cryme' (vii.9–10).[63]

In what sense, then, does Spenser embrace a post-medieval Titanism (or anti-Titanism: see Exposition)? We begin to see hints of a distortion when the poet suggests that only a primordial alteration of our nature makes us fit for deification. Red Crosse is 'a man of earth' (I.x.52), Contemplation says, raised by a ploughman and christened 'George', which means tiller of soil.[64] In this, he is Lancelot, the *erthly* knight. But he is elfin as well, and suited for a heavenly end. Red Crosse is a griffen and an elf-man, just as his alter ego is an earth-wind. When the knight asks, on Contemplation's mountain, 'How dare I thinke such glory to attaine?' (x.62), Spenser hopes we can work out the answer for ourselves: he would not be eschatologically fit for deification unless he were protologically fit for it as well. The man of earth is earthbound, while faerie lineage is immortal and superlunar, belonging naturally in the heavenly city; only the one who is both can travel from the earthly forest to the celestial Hierusalem. But does this slight twist on Thomas's 'natural desire for the supernatural' not take us to a rather different destination? If we are fit for deification only because we never left heaven, then deification marks an intrusion upon, not a perfection of, the earthly creature.

This reading of a naturalized deification in *The Faerie Queene* helps make sense of the incomplete and otherwise tangential finale, the beautifully strange 'Cantos of Mutabilitie'. No longer wandering freely in a landscape of quests and virtues, we arrive here in allegory of the classic type,

---

61 '"Calm yourself Scipio, Do not be afraid. But remember carefully the things I am about to tell you. Do you see that city there?" . . . From where he stood amid the bright illumination of stars, he pointed down at Carthage, and began speaking once more'. From Cicero's 'The Dream of Scipio', p. 10, in Michael Grant (trans. and ed.), 1971, *Cicero: On the Good Life*, London: Penguin, p. 342.

62 See Gless, *Interpretation and Theology*, p. 99.

63 Janet Adelman, 2005, 'Revaluing the Body in *The Faerie Queen* I', *Spenser Review* 36 (1), pp. 22–4, notes the anagramic play of Orgoglio with George, the name Red Crosse eventually is given. She misses, however, the linking of the names with a true and false deification.

64 Bond, '*Faerie Queene* and *Paradise Lost*', p. 209.

as Mutabilitie, 'Proud Change', wages a war on the heavens. Bemoaning the fall of humankind, she maligns the state of divinekind (VI.11). Rebellion is in her bloodline, since 'She was, to weet, a daughter by descent/ Of those old Titans, that did whylome striue/ With Saturnes sonne for heauens regiment' (2). Anticipating Milton's Satan, she 'wrong of right, and bad of good did make'; anticipating Shelley's Prometheus, 'she gan to cast in her ambitious thought,/ T'attempt th'empire of the heaunes hight,/ And Ioue himself to shoulder from his right' (7).

Jove finds himself, as with Io of old, allured by her beauty ('sich sway doth beauty euen in Heauen beare' [31]). Therefore, deterred from striking her down, he reminds her of Prometheus's fate, and makes what seems at first to be an offer of deifying grace:

> Then ceasse thy idel claime thou foolish gerle,
> And see by grace and goodnesse to obtain
> That place from which by folly Titan felle
> There-to thou maist perhaps, if so thou faine
> Haue Ioue thy gratious Lord and Soueraigne. (34)

Mutabilitie does not take this to be an offer of a peaceful road to Godlikeness, however, since the place that Jove offers is the one Prometheus abandoned: subordination to Jove's sovereign rule. Rejecting this offer, Jove agrees (still swayed apparently by her beauty) to take the matter to trial, in the court governed by the queenly Nature.

So Nature stands as judge between Proud Change and the Olympian Gods. Mutabilitie appeals to her, already stealthily making her case, that 'heaven and earth are both alike to thee' (15). Her claim that 'Jove usurps unjustly' his own rule by overthrowing the Saturnine regime of her ancestors (16) goes unrefuted even by Jove himself.[65] In fact, although the reader might have begun the first Canto with sympathy for Jove, Mutabilitie's case grows stronger throughout her argument to Nature. 'All that moveth doth mutation love' (55), she says, and as the Titanes scrolls through the ways in which all the Olympians are affected by movement, we recall that the very graciousness of Jove in allowing the matter to go to trial is evidence of change: at her beauty he 'chang'd his cheare' (31). Like Prometheus's own failed coup, the case of Change against Jove may in fact be sound, finally making right a disorder within Nature's realm that reaches back to the original injustice of the Olympian rebellion.

Nature's judgement, after hearing the case, is remarkably simple. She gives 'her doome in speeches few':

> I well consider all that ye haue sayd
> And find that all things stedfastnes doe hate
> And changed be: yet being rightly wayd

---

65 See Fowler, *Literary Character*, pp. 238–9.

They are not changed from their first estate;
But by their change their being doe dilate:
And turning to themselues at length againe,
Doe worke their own perfection so by fate:
Then ouer them Change doth not rule and raigne,
But they raigne ouer change, and doe their states maintain. (VII.58)

Mutabilitie is right: even the gods are subject to change. But she fails to
see that all change is ruled by the constancy of fate, so that perfection is a
dilation back to an original immutable stillness. This is just as true for Jove
as for the creatures of earth, the seasons, and the hours. With these words
'was the Titanesse put downe and whist' (VII.59).

What does the Christian poet mean to convey by this pagan narration?
The final fragment explains that although change 'beares the greatest sway'
and makes the poet 'loath this state of life' (1) still the 'pillours of Eternity'
are contrary to her rule:

For, all that moueth, doth in Change delight:
But thence-forth all shall rest eternally
With Him that is the God of Sabbaoth hight:
O Thou great Sabbaoth God, graunt me that Sabaoth sight.
Finis (VIII.2)

This brief authorial apostrophe contains the clearest suggestion of how to
read the entire poem. Red Crosse, Calidore, Arthur and the rest are mortal souls who seek a static perfection within a landscape ruled by change.
There is a perfection which exceeds human limit, but this is ultimately
because it exceeds human form all together. Our nature alone is tragically
imperfectible, even if it is poetically improvable. It is only because we are
changelings, cross-bred with a nature of an entirely different sort, that we
can acquire the theological virtues and press on toward a Sabbath perfection. *Theosis* is not, as in Maximus, a Sabbath rest in God's perichoretic
movements *ad intra*; rather it is a pre-Christian dilation and return. 'We'
go on beyond the earthly realm into union with the heavenly, but it is the
always-already heavenly part of us, like the unfallen Plotinian soul, that
goes on, while the part ruled by change remains behind, bound in the Caucasus. Thus change is our governor in all things but the protological and
eschatological. Elfin stillness becomes our destiny; this though will mark an
annihilating end to the humanity with which it is crossed.

In a sense, Spenser simply goes too far in attempting to solve the Thomistic paradox of a nature-perfecting supernatural gift. Our final end is in
God, Spenser says, and then assumes that this end must imply cessation of
creaturely motion. Had Thomas, Maximus or Cusanus written the poem,
Jove would have blessed Mutabilitie as an *imitatio dei* and invited her into
heaven despite her insurrective designs. Red Crosse and Arthur would
have quested straight on into the eternal Sabbath, with knightly adventures

caught up into the adventure of the eternal Son's Spirit-quest into the Far Country and his long journey home into the Father's embrace. This is divine perfection, and if it is truly the human end as well, then somehow our nature must find here its true home, rather than its ultimate exile.

By abandoning mutable nature, *The Faerie Queene* likewise carries on the rapid inflation of the virtue of humility. Despite its appearance as the porter to the theological virtues, humility reappears in the Cantos in the only way it can: as the final acceptance of our fated lot. Mutabilitie approaches Nature in 'obaysance and humilitie' (VII.13), because natural judgement will always rule the day; the elfin, meanwhile, has no need of humility, since it is fated to return to its native home in God. All the rest must bow before Nature's rule. We may not like the usurpation behind Jove's throne, nor the tragic state of humankind, dwelling in a flux where 'blisse may not abide' (I.viii.44). Justice may, in fact, be on our side. Still, Nature has passed her judgement, and our mutability must return to Camelot with Lancelot, making the best of a less than perfect end.

The Whiteness of Excrement

Of Man's First Disobedience, and the Fruit
Of that Forbidden Tree, whose mortal taste
Brought *Death into the World, and all our woe*,
With loss of Eden, till *one greater Man*
Restore us, and regain the blissful Seat,
Sing Heav'nly *Muse* . . . (Paradise Lost I.1–6)[66]

As we turn finally to Milton's epic poem, our story of perfection's emergence and distortion returns to the beginning. It was, after all, in the demonic 'hero of *Paradise Lost*' that Shelley found his proto-Prometheus, 'the type of highest perfection of moral and intellectual nature impelled by the purest and truest to the best and noblest ends'. True, Milton's Satan is a bit too tainted by 'ambition, envy, revenge and a desire for personal aggrandizement' to be counted as the type itself; but like Blake before him, Shelley can overlook these taints as accruals of 'religious feeling' that fight against the more important insights of the poet: they are Satanic vices that 'interfere with the interest' of his own poem (Shelley, 'Preface').[67]

Thus *Paradise Lost* takes on the role in the nineteenth century – and more subtly in the twentieth as well, as we have seen – of a kind of itinerary for the mythopoetic imposition. Taking Milton to suggest that human perfection is at heart a Promethean insurrection against divine order, these later readers see his poem as enabling two possible trajectories: one either sides with Milton and refuses perfection, as the Christ of *Paradise Regain'd* refuses Satan's offer

---

66 All references are from Milton, *Paradise Lost*, Merritt Y. Hughes (ed.), 1935, New York: The Odyssey Press.

67 See Exposition, above.

to 'aim at the highest' (IV.106),[68] or else, with Blake, Shelley, Freud and De-leuze, one grasps for perfection (or at least for a perfect anti-perfection), in hopes that the very act of grasping will serve to empty heaven's throne and finally usher in humankind's ultimate transcendence. Though Milton chooses the former, they say, he does so in spite of the true thrust of his own epic creation. He is, as Blake puts it, 'of the Devil's party without knowing it'.[69]

To what extent, though, does Milton reject the earlier perfection inheritance? While it is difficult to argue against the point that his Satan is the real hero of Paradise Lost,[70] still, the fallen angel moves in a landscape that is more Catholic than Blake or Shelley are ready to acknowledge. Has Milton really lost the classically Christian account of perfection as the receiving of a gift, so that he can only imagine it in order to reject it, as illicit theft? Have the Danaan belts severed entirely in his poem?

There is, in fact, a good bit of evidence to the contrary. When Satan, escaping his place of exile, first infiltrates the created earth, he is moved at the sight of

> Two of far nobler shape erect and tall,
> Godlike erect, with native Honour clad
> In naked Majestie seemd Lords of all,
> And worthie seemd, for in thir looks Divine
> The image of thir glorious Maker shon,
> Truth, wisdome, Sanctitude severe and pure,
> Severe but in true filial freedom plac't; (IV.288–94)

The traits of Adam and Eve so much remind Satan of the God whose favour he has lost that he wavers in his rebellion for a moment (neither the first nor last time in the poem he will do so), finds himself lost in wonder at their grace, and even suggests that he could love them for their 'Divine resemblance' (IV.362–65).[71] Adam strides about paradise with these perfections following him like a parade of virtues (V.352–53), and the fallen one admires the spectacle in spite of himself.

If Milton sees the original creation as fashioned 'all/ such to perfection' (V. 471–720), he does so in a way that calls to mind the Augustinian 'perfect universe'. This is a world in which perfection is not a frozen sublimity

---

68 *Paradise Regained*, at http://www.gutenberg.org/cache/epub/58/pg58.html, accessed 21 October 2010.

69 William Blake, *The Marriage of Heaven and Hell*, in J. Hayward and G. Keynes (eds), 1941, *The Complete Poetry and Selected Prose of John Donne and the Complete Poetry of William Blake*, New York: The Modern Library, p. 652. See Peter J. Kitson, 'Milton: The Romantics and After', in Thomas N. Corns (ed.), 2001, *A Companion to Milton*, Oxford, UK, and Malden, MA: Blackwell Publishers, pp. 469ff.

70 See Sayers, *Whimsical*, pp. 267–68.

71 See also VIII.230 and especially 430–2, where Adam links his uprightness ('erect and tall', as in the quote above at IV.288) with his readiness for deification. Thanks to Tarah Van De Wiele for pointing this out.

but a dynamism of ascending and descending signifiers. The angel Raphael explains over dinner in Eden that as his own body can condescend to partake of the fruits of the garden, human bodies will ascend into a higher state, so as to eat the *panis angelicus*:

> Time may come when men
> With angels may participate, and find
> No inconvenient Diet, nor too light Fare:
> And from these corporal nutriments perhaps
> Your bodies may at last turn all to Spirit,
> Improv'd by tract of time, and wing'd ascend
> Ethereal, as wee, or may at choice
> Here or in Heav'nly Paradises dwell; (V. 493–500)

Humans have their own *dunamis* and their own perfection, and this may be equally called the earthly or heavenly paradise, since 'then the Earth/ Shall all be Paradise, far happier place/ Then this of Eden, and far happier daies' (XII. 463–65). The *telos* of God's finest work on earth will not abolish the natural shape and agency of the creation, and the Father explains to the Son in heaven that 'I formd them free, and free they must remain,/ Till they enthrall themselves: I else must change/ Thir nature. . . '(III.124–6).

In all of this, Milton follows the classical account of a nature-perfecting grace, the grace that works by inviting humans to fulfil themselves in a *telos* that is beyond their own capabilities. It is for him not the desire to soar up to the heavens that is condemnable, but the attempt to do so in a non-human way. What Milton rejects is a pathway into the divine being that would destroy human nature. When Christ, in *Paradise Regain'd*, responds to Satan's invitation to begin his eternal reign sooner rather than later, his reply is entirely Irenaean: 'All things are best fulfil'd in their due time' (*PR* III.182). By recapitulating Adam and Eve's haste toward union with a patient performance of union mediated through the actions and receptions of temporality, Christ has 'aveng'd/ Supplanted Adam, and by vanquishing/ Temptation, hast regain'd lost Paradise' (*PR* IV.606–8).[72]

Further, Milton demonstrates the natural bent towards deifying union in taking up the New Testament theme of human work as a perfection of God's work. At day's end, Adam and Eve make their hymn to the Creator:

> Maker Omnipotent, and thou the Day,
> Which we in our appointed work imployd

---

72 See Regina Schwartz, 2002, 'Redemption and Paradise Regained', *Milton Studies* 42, pp. 26–49. Schwarz, however, overly influenced by the post-metaphysical prejudice of Continental philosophy, applauds only the passivity of Christ, who simply 'says no' to his own redemption. 'In PR, it is Satan who offers what we can know and what we can think about redemption. When that is denied, when he is refuted, we have entered a realm beyond knowing and beyond speech' (p. 42). Thus for Milton, she says, redemption depends on the refusal of redemption (p. 44).

Have finisht happie in our mutual help
And mutual love, the Crown of all our bliss
Ordain'd by thee, and this delicious place
For us too large, where thy abundance wants
Partakers, and uncropt falls to the ground. (IV.725–31)

God is the 'Maker Omnipotent', and the human gardeners are appointed to 'sub-create':[73] to employ their labours in corresponding creativity. In doing so, they perform the reflecting capacity that is the key, as in Athanasius, to both their likeness and their distinction from God. 'Uncropt', divine abundance 'falls to the ground', just as Adam and Even themselves will. Their daily work is to grace the vines and flowers of Eden with spatial and temporal limit, and in doing so to enact their own created path to Godlike abundance. This is, perhaps, the real danger of the forbidden tree, and why it is not only off limits for consumption, but apparently for pruning as well (IX.651). It grows as a sublime and unmediated event of divine abundance in a garden meant for mediation and participation. Unmediated divinity is poison for bodily and temporal creatures.

Seen thus, the paradise poems are more classically Christian than Shelley and Blake can recognize. If the voice of the poet already makes Satan into a Prometheus (I.196–8), and the voice of Satan anticipates almost exactly the defiance of Shelley's hero,[74] the Romantic Satan occludes completely the ironies embedded in the Restoration Era prototype. It is, after all, the 'Father of lies' who speaks the Titanic dialect throughout the poem. His pride and swagger on the rock in pandaemonium are empty deceptions, as he himself admits in his soliloquy later (IV. 82–6).[75] In the early books, Satan still sees God's truth clearly enough to waver in his rebellion, even to consider asking for pardon (IV. 74–81), and, as an effect of this vision, retains a hint of his heavenly form. As the narrative progresses, so does his defiance, and his appearance devolves reciprocally. So he bids 'farewell Hope, and with Hope farewell Fear,/ Farewell Remorse', and

while he spake, each passion dimm'd his face,
Thrice chang'd with pale, ire, envy and despair,
Which marr'd his borrow'd visage, and betray'd
Him counterfeit, if any eye beheld. (IV.114–17)

Before the poem's end, we will find him in various manifestations of the grotesque: 'squat like a toad' (IV.800) and whispering into Eve's ear,

---

73 The phrase comes from J. R. R. Tolkien's *On Fairy Stories*, in J. R. R. Tolkien, 1966, *The Tolkien Reader*, New York: Ballantine Books, p. 47. I owe my awareness of this essay and this very useful term to Nathan Jennings.

74 '. . . Peace then is despair'd,/ For who can think Submission?' (I.651–61). Cf. Shelley: 'Submission, thou dost know I cannot try' (*Prom Bd.* 396).

75 See C. S. Lewis, 1942, *A Preface to* Paradise Lost, London, Oxford, and New York: Oxford University Press, pp. 94–103.

hideous and unrecognizable to his erstwhile companion Gabriel, and finally foiled by his own falsely humble ruse of stuffing himself into a snake's mouth, with the effect that he and all hell's mighty demons are permanently rendered serpentine. If so many commentators have found the Satan of *Paradise Lost* to be more heroic and magnanimous than is theologically warranted,[76] this is only because they, like the fallen angels, have been deceived by the false Satanic triumphalism. Indeed, Milton wants us to see that the very desire to 'reign in hell' rather 'than serve in Heav'n' (I.263) already reveals in Satan a tragic blindness to the divine light, as Abdiel attempts to warn him (V.809ff). Satan misses the important theological point that submission to God is not a self-denial, since to serve in heaven is his glorification. Submission of the self-destructive sort is the end-game (as Satan still from time to time recognizes[77]) of the self-glorifying rebellion, of 'hurling defiance toward the Vault of Heav'n' (I.669). As in the scholastic mind, so in Milton: we rebel against divine order not by desiring too much, but too little, by refusing the glorifying fire that comes as a gift.

Does Milton then stand out as a seventeenth-century exception to the late medieval and modern distortion of perfection? We must make him answer a series of questions about the theological vision of his poem before we can make any judgement on this question.

First, is there any sense in which, as Shelley suspects, Satan's claim to injustice is a legitimate one? If we can dismiss his self-victimizing claims in the early books by simply noting that the devil *would* say that, the question becomes rather more complex later, when the story of heaven's war is narrated to Adam by the angel Raphael. Satan's envy first burns, as Raphael tells it, on the day that God gathers the angels to a coronation ceremony and makes the decree: 'This day I have begot whom I declare/ My only Son, and on this holy Hill/ Him have anointed. . .' (V.603–05). All angels are Sons of God, and the Nephilic reference here appears intentional.[78] The fallen angels are both the Titans who wage war on Olympus and the Sons whose false desires sire the giants. But the great war, we now discover, was not initiated by a sudden desire to dethrone the Almighty Father; rather, it began with the exaltation from the ranks of angelic

---

76 Along with Shelley and Blake, see Baker, 'A Man of Wealth and Taste: The Strange Career of Hannibal Lecter', pp. 125–6, 130–1, in Christopher Partridge and Eric Christianson (eds), 2009, *The Lure of the Dark Side: Satan and Western Demonology in Popular Culture*, London and Oakville: Equinox Publishing, pp. 125–7; also Mark Edmundson, 1997, *Nightmare on Main Street: Angels, Sadomasochism and the Culture of Gothic*, London, and Cambridge, Massachusetts, pp. 80–1.

77 So Satan says to Christ, in *Paradise Regained* IV.9–1: 'Worst is my Port,/ My harbour and my ultimate repose,/ The end I would attain, my final good'.

78 See Basil Willey, 1953, *The Seventeenth Century Background: Studies in the Thought of the Age in Relation to Poetry and Religion* (Garden City, NY: Doubleday), p. 236. See also John P. Rumrich, 2004, *Milton Unbound: Controversy and Interpretation*, Cambridge: Cambridge University Press, 127ff., who traces Milton's figure of 'allegorical anarchy' from Nimrod the hunter.

beings of one who had no obvious claim to this novel enthronement. So Satan (or Satan 'so call him now, his former name/ is heard no more in Heav'n' [V.658–9]) was,

> If not the first Arch-Angel, great in Power,
> In favour and præeminence, yet fraught
> With envie against the Son of God, that day
> Honour'd by his great Father, and proclaimd
> Messiah King anointed . . . (V. 658–64)

It is beyond dispute that the Milton of *De doctrina* embraces an explicitly Arian position on the Son's generation, or at least what passes for Arianism in the seventeenth century.[79] In *Paradise Lost*, though, we discover a subtlety to his Christology that ought to give us at least some hesitation in affirming this label. The angel Abdiel, whose words Raphael relates to Adam, challenges Satan's jealousy of the Son, first on the basis of God's unwavering sovereignty ('Shalt thou give Law to God?' [V.822]) and then by a more careful logic. The anointed Son is the one

> . . . by whom
> As by his Word the mighty Father made
> All things, ev'n thee, and all the Spirits of Heav'n
> By him created in thir bright degrees,
> Crownd them with Glory, and to thir Glory nam'd
> Thrones, Dominations, Princedoms, Vertues, Powers,
> Essential Powers, nor by his Reign obscur'd,
> But more illustrious made, since he the Head
> One of our number thus reduc't becomes,
> His Laws our Laws, all honour to him done
> Returns our own. (V. 835–45)

This response suggests, on the one hand, that Satan is correct, the number of angels was reduced by one when the Son was exalted, and the laws he establishes are novel rather than aboriginal. On the other hand though, all the created heavens, and even Satan himself, were made through this Son. If Christ is 'by merit more than birthright Son of God' (III.309), his agency is still implicit in the originary creative work of God. The Christology of the poem is in this sense a blend of Arianism, Nicenism and Adoptionism.[80] Satan, of course, scoffs at this response, and his claim to be self-created is a kind of facetious counter-argument, I have got just as much right to a logically absurd pre-existence as he does, Satan seems to say (V.832ff).

---

79 See Lewis, *Preface*, pp. 89ff.

80 Lewis, *Preface*, pp. 85ff, disagrees. But this is perhaps because his own dependence on an uncompromising substitionary atonement, by which the Son is at the mercy of the Father's will, amounts to a 'soft' Arianism.

This is parallel to a self-typologizing from earlier in the poem. When Satan asks, 'is there no place/Left for Repentance' (IV.79–80), he echoes Hebrews 12.17's synopsis of the Esau story, thus casting himself in the role of the rightful heir whose birthright was stolen away.[81] Satan is the heavenly Esau: but even if true, does this justify his claim? We must still interpret with caution: we are inclined to side with Esau in Genesis, if for no other reason than that his own mother did not (Gen. 25.28). But in the New Testament epistle, Esau is a 'profane person', whose bitterness ruins him for true repentance (Heb. 12.15–16). Satan is right again, Milton seems to say, in the substance of his complaint that God chose a Son who had no primordial right to that position; he is wrong to allow his own divinely willed subordination to turn him monstrous and reptilian.[82]

The nineteenth century's question about whether Milton was on the side of the devils or the angels thus comes down to an interpretive hinge. If the subordination of all things to the 'merited' Son is an unwarranted cosmic event, as Satan insists, then the satanic impulse to transcend this order is a legitimate claim. Shelley is correct, and Miltonic perfection is, in this case, the pursuit of deification beyond the false limitations of the natural order. If, on the other hand, as Abdiel argues, Christ was 'virtually' in God all along, and if besides this God's sovereignty automatically legitimizes any divine decree, then Christic transgression is ruled out, and perfection is equivalent to submission as such.

This ambiguous scenario may sound familiar: Milton's account of the relation of Father to Son to creation is less like the Christian accounts of a Trinitarian origin, and more like the Saturn–Jupiter–cosmos progression, in which the question of the legitimacy of the Olympian rule all depends on how you look at it. Jupiter is 'in' his father, even before Saturn swallows him, as not-yet-issued persona. Once born, he asserts his rule over his Father's creation. But if Aeschylus and Plato leave the question of Olympian legitimacy hovering, as the great mystery of universal justice, the partially Christianized reading allows the Father and the Son a harmony of will, so there is no more question of which one wins in the Son's coronation: the secondary rule of the Son of God is cosmically and morally warranted. The God who 'formd the Pow'rs of Heav'n/ Such as he pleasd' (V.824–5) also appoints one of the angels as his heir.

In Milton then we find a bifurcation of Themis and Dike, such as would have rendered Argos's depth dive a fruitless labour.[83] Here Themis, heavenly justice, pits the Father's will for the Son's deification against Satan's will for his own. She rejects the subordinate creature's claim, since it is sublimely refuted by the Father's desire. Dike, on the other hand, still stands

---

81 Hebrews 12.17, in the Authorized Version: 'For ye know how that afterward, when he would have inherited the blessing, he was rejected: for he found no place of repentance, though he sought it carefully with tears'.

82 I owe this reading of Satan as a self-proclaimed Esau, and the link to Hebrews entirely to Tarah Van De Wiele.

83 See First Movement, above.

on the side of Satan/Esau, or at least stands shrugging with confusion between the two. Earthly justice cannot fully accept the spurning of Esau or the refusal of Satan's transcendence, since it is founded at least partially in a just claim. Heaven thunders against Prometheus, while earth wonders if perhaps his ill-fated coup was at least a just war. Milton himself sides unequivocally with Themis, as he makes clear in an earlier writing on the primordial 'symphony of the stars': 'the fact that we are unable to hear this harmony seems certainly to be due to the presumption of that thief Prometheus, which brought so many evils upon men' (*Prolusions* II).[84] The Danaan girdle binding human justice to the divine is severed entirely here, and it is not difficult to make out the accelerated paganism of the Middle Ages in the background. *Prometheus Bound*'s division of earth and heaven, divorced of the participatory plea of the *Suppliants*: this is the framework for perfection's modern distortion.

A severed girdle is reparable only by an extraordinary act of imputation, and so Milton's Christ solves the problem of human sin in a way reminiscent of Scotus's 'primacy of Christ' argument. Adam and Eve are 'created . . . to a nobler end' than their nature allows (XI.604–5), but this means that their reception of supernatural grace will recall Christ's own sovereignly decreed coronation. They will receive deification as an eschatological gift that they are protologically unfit to receive. When the Father tells the Son to 'ascend my chariot', and shines on him 'with Rayes direct' (VI. 711,19), the allusion to Phaethon and Phoebus is more than a poetic flourish. Adam and Eve do not share in the Father's glory so fully as to allow them to steer; they are Phaethon, and by nature will always wreck the chariot. Only the supremely anointed Son can make the journey, and thus overcome the lack that is hard-wired into the earthly creation.

What does this mean for a perfection of human nature? *Paradise Lost* certainly retains a strong sense of the tragic, and this in itself is enough to disallow any straightforward reading of the fall from grace as a *felix culpa*.[85] But is this the ultimate note of the poem? Human nature, prior to that morning at the Tree, is already prone to narcissism, and only Reason's (that is Adam's) constant governance over Desire (that is Eve) can steer it away from self-absorption. This, indeed, is the thread that unravels Eden, since the serpent is both crafty enough to exploit her Narcissus complex (why should only one man see your beauty, when you move among us as 'a Goddess among Gods?' (IX. 545–48))[86] and lucky enough to find her wandering far from Adam's watchful eye. In this sense, creation is already

---

84 Don M. Wolfe (ed.) 1953, *Complete Prose Works of John Milton*, Vol. I, New Haven and London: Yale University Press, pp. 238–9.

85 Gale H. Carrithers, 1994, *Milton and the Hermeneutic Journey*, Baton Rouge: Lousiana State University Press, pp. 23–4, 100ff.

86 See William Poole, 2009, *Milton and the Idea of the Fall*, Cambridge and New York: Cambridge University Press, pp. 168ff. On the complex characterization of Eve, see John P. Rumrich, pp. 113ff.

a kind of fall. The second fall at the tree is *infelix*, in that it loses them Paradise, but also *felix*, in that it allows them to recover from the natural imperfections of the first. So, when Michael explains to Adam that the end will be more blessed than the beginning, Adam replies: 'full of doubt I stand,/ Whether I should repent me now of sin/ By mee done and occasiond, or rejoice/ Much more, that much more good thereof shall spring . . .' (XII. 473–76). Significantly, Michael does not reprimand him for this doubting of his repentance, but moves on in the conversation, apparently accepting it as the appropriate response.

A second implication of Milton's severed girdle aligns *Paradise Lost* with the post-1277 bifurcation of metaphysics and theology. Though the prohibition of knowledge 'higher than my lot' is first spoken by Satan (IX. 690),[87] and as such is not a trustworthy bit of information, in the end a version of the prohibition is voiced by Michael and accepted by Adam, as if, once again, Satan is at least partially accurate in his complaint. So Adam says:

> Greatly instructed I shall hence depart,
> Greatly in peace of thought, and have my fill
> Of knowledge, what this Vessel can contain;
> Beyond which was my folly to aspire. (XII.557–60)

And Michael: 'Thus having learnt, thou hast attain'd the sum/ Of wisdom; hope no higher . . . '(XII.575–6).

How does the poet want us to remember this injunction to 'hope no higher?' Milton is, as Basil Willey puts it, a Promethean as much as he is an anti-Promethean.[88] The scriptural narrative compels him to treat the eating of the fruit as the source of all human failings; and yet the proto-sin is also in some sense inevitable and even beneficiary, in both Eve's case and Adam's: Eve because of her natural bent toward Narcissus, Adam because of his natural bent toward Eve. Natural imperfection is linked, in fact, to Milton's Arianism, since only absolute unity is perfect, while number manifests imperfection.

---

87 Poole, *Milton and the Idea*, pp. 175–6.

88 'Milton is thus caught in the tangle of his biblical imagery. He is bound to represent the unfallen Adam as perfect, made in the image of God; and he is bound to represent the act of disobedience as a calamity engineered by the devil. And yet that act represented the liberation of man from the beneficent determinism of Jehovah, and the birth, accompanied, indeed, by the throws of sin and suffering, of his capacity for true "liberty". Milton was a Promethean, a Renaissance humanist, in the toils of a myth of quite contrary import, a myth which yearned, as no Milton could, for the blank innocence and effortlessness of a golden age'. Willey, *Seventeenth*, p. 251. Willey seems to think, though, that the original Genesis account is Promethean, and so in Milton's internal oscillation between rebellious Romantic and submissive servant we are in fact seeing the war of the poetic imagination against a strict literalist hermeneutic. I have tried to show above that this is a misreading of Genesis.

Man by number is to manifest
His single imperfection, and beget
Like of his like, his Image multipli'd,
In unitie defective, which requires
Collateral love, and deerest amitie. (VIII.420–25) [89]

Because God is perfect, he is eternally alone (and thus there was a time when the Son was not); because Adam is not perfect, he needs Eve. In this sense, ironically, Adam's belaboured decision to eat the fruit and die with Eve rather than to go on without her and 'live again in the wild Wood forlorn' (IX.910), is the humble decision, the rejection of the Promethean impulse.[90] Only God could live alone in bliss. Adam's lot is tied to Eve, and by choosing her over heaven, he makes a choice that we must take, if vaguely and perversely, to be the right one. Despite Milton's complaint about the tediousness of heroic poems which bring tribute only to 'fabl'd Knights/ In Battels feign'd' (IX.30–31), he repeats here the signature theological construction of the courtly love poem. Adam is the originary Lancelot, choosing the Lady over deification. If this decision is tragic and devastating, it is also the only one we can imagine generating good poetry, and so seems to be the poet's final hesitating argument for a Saturn-respecting humility. We were made for the forests of earth, and to hope for higher would constitute an egregious insubordination.

The difference between the two Lancelots, however, is that Malory's tragedy is historical while Milton's is ontological. Something has gone awry in our age, Malory laments, and the grail has passed beyond human grasp perhaps forever. For Milton, the errancy is our natural bent, created multiples that we are. So there was never a grail, never a Galahad, no lost age of Arthur to which we might hope to return. The meadow of humility has only ever pastured speckled cows. 'Hope no higher' is not simply a way forward when humans have lost the cultural ability to name their Creator; it is the injunction that takes effect on the first dawn in Eden.

This injunction is, finally, a key to Milton's fondness for Spenser, whom he calls 'a better teacher than Scotus or Aquinas'. In the errancy of Red Crosse and Guyon, Milton finds a poetic account of a humanity made for struggle, for the psychomachia of holiness in a fallen world. We may and even must imagine Eden, and humans in that Paradise, as an omega point of the struggle, and perhaps even a kind of fictive alpha point of our existence. But these fictions are not what we call 'human'. This is the trouble, for Milton, with the theology of the Schools, it always treats a

---

89 Milton studies have long pointed out the influence of Origen on Milton's understanding of divine unity. See Harry F. Robbins, 1963, *If This Be Heresy: A Study of Milton and Origen*, Urbana, IL: University of Illinois Press, especially pp. 65ff. See also Douglas Trevor, 2009, 'Milton and Oneness', *Milton Studies* 49, pp. 87–9. What is missing, though, in Milton, is the hypostatic relationality by which Origen orders the divine unity.

90 See Lewis, *Preface*, pp. 125–8.

pure *humanum*, before turning to that human as *viatorum*. We do not originate, for Milton, in abstract purity, but rather in the militant arena of sin and salvation:

> We bring not innocence into the world, we bring impurity much rather. That which purifies us is trial, and trial is by what is contrary. That virtue therefore which is but a youngling in the contemplation of evil, and knows not the utmost that vice promises to her followers, and rejects it, is but a blank virtue, not a pure; her whiteness is but an excremental whiteness; which was the reason why our sage and serious poet Spenser (whom I dare be known to think a better teacher than Scotus or Aquinas), describing him in with his palmer through the cave of Mammon, and the bower of earthly bliss, that he might see and know, and yet abstain. (*Areopagitica* II.67–8)[91]

But this is precisely where the brilliant Milton ceases to function as a trustworthy theological guide. It is certainly the case that human virtue emerges in struggle. But the moment we allow the struggle to name the human form itself, we have lost the ability to imagine the perfection of this strangely suspended nature. What would a paradise regained look like for creatures who only become themselves 'hand in hand with wandering steps and slow' (XII. 648–9) beyond Eden's gates? If those creatures were to receive the extraordinary grace of deification, it would be the sort of gift that annihilates the very form that receives it. Satan is again speaking truthfully when he tells Christ that human nature is not fit for perfection (*PR* 229–30). In the final analysis, Milton's humans are not for Milton simply imperfect, but imperfection itself.

Making Merry in Middle Earth

The poets of the late medieval and early modern world craft a new imaginative realm of interiority. In so doing they generate new literary pathways for human perfection, since the themes of questing and journeying seem appropriate allegories for the human 'passage' through the world and into God. As this new landscape develops, however, the poet's internal gaze begins to lose sight of the external grounding of Christian perfection. If Alysoun of Bath can bring all her imperfections with her on the way to Canterbury, this is because human imperfection is simply a name for the various incompletions that make up the human passage toward the highest good, a good breathed into the original creation and restored, through sacrament and pilgrimage, by Christ. Once the poets begin to give priority to the interior experience of imperfection, however, they sell the farm before the harvest. Humans are naturally temporal and incompletable, and so will

---

91 Quoted in Willey, *Seventeenth*, p. 241.

always experience the Canterbury road as imperfect. The point though is that perfection is prior to this human experience of imperfection, and so the two are not polarities at all, any more than the human and divine natures in Christ are a polarized conflict. One way of attending to the modern turn, as C. S. Lewis puts it, is to notice the way in which the priority of perfection gives way to a priority of imperfection.[92] This change, as I have demonstrated, mutually supports another change, the ascension of humility beyond charity as the human virtue par excellence. If imperfection is more basic to the human creature than perfection, then humility is the most basic virtue. If, however, divine perfection is the cause that always inheres in the effect of human imperfection, then humility is only ever relative to charity: it is the creaturely mode of participating in divine glory.

But if Lewis diagnoses the reversal of perfection with his characteristic insight, he misses the corresponding point about humility entirely. The Renaissance, which brings back a variant form of classical perfection, gives Spenser and Milton the tools to say, insofar as they were able to say it, that deification is a thing crafted from human incompleteness. For Lewis, on the other hand, it is precisely this return of a perfecting *poesis* that renders the early moderns culpable and post-Christian. So, missing the double excess in Spenser that I explored above, Lewis remarks on 'the astonishing absence of humility' in the knights of The *Faerie Queene*, and suggests that rather than the virtue-questers of Spenser, it is the earthbound knights in Malory who recover the authentic Christian path.[93] Between the animal indulgences of civilization and the angelic hopes of the sanctified, Lewis celebrates the middling path of human 'civility', a kind of perfection that stabilizes at a halfway point:

> The round table is pressed between the upper millstone (Galahad) and the nether (Mordred) . . . . As long as we live in merry middle earth it is necessary to have middle things. If the round table is abolished, for every one who rises to the level of Galahad, a hundred will drop plumb down to that of Mordred . . . . It has all been tried before.[94]

Lewis is right to suggest that Spenser and Milton alter something significant in their construction of perfection. This novelty is not, however, a pre-Christian magnanimity which replaces Christian humility; in fact, they manage to reintroduce an element of pre-modern excessive grace into their texts, thus situating the virtue of humility, already eroding from the later Middle Ages, nearer to its classical locus. Lewis's inability to see this only shows the extent to which he himself was captivated by a distorted image of Christian perfection. Still, Spenser and Milton are haunted by a post-

---

92 C. S. Lewis, 1964, *The Discarded Image: An Introduction to Medieval and Renaissance Literature*, Cambridge: Cambridge University Press, pp. 85, 220.

93 Lewis, *English Literature*, p. 53.

94 Lewis, *Preface*, p. 137.

Christian account of perfection, in the suggestion that deification is no end for human nature. Union with God does not signify a transformation that humans naturally anticipate, but rather a return to the *monos* from which multiplicity first issued. Lady Change and her realm must be overruled if humanity is united to God: Spenser in this sense favours a kind of deification over perfection, since what we call human ceases to exist as soon as we abolish motion and change. Edenic Adam should satisfy himself with earthly knowledge and 'hope no higher': in so saying, Milton ultimately casts aside both perfection and deification, and identifies human nature as the endless struggle of Reason against Narcissus. In these poetic visions perfection's distortion is complete, and the stage is set for a Romantic protest, the modern Prometheanism set forth above, which announces to the world that 'middle things' are not nearly perfect enough.

9

Second Interlude:
Perfection, Modernity and John Wesley

Experience makes you sad.

Rosalind, in Shakespeare's *As You Like It*

Languishing Perfection

At the twilight of the Middle Ages, a new metastasis imposes itself in the theological and philosophical imagination: heaven is now too high for any kinship with creatures. Humans collectively awake to find themselves locked into the character of the weaned soul of Psalm 131, never the panting hart of Psalm 42.

As a staging for the salvation narrative, this metastasis ensures that any communion between heaven and earth will take the form of a violation of orders, this violation itself giving birth to a new orthodoxy that is fully in place by the seventeenth century. If humans attempt to climb Sinai toward the heavens above, the new orthodoxy charges them with marching in the footsteps of Pelagius, the ancient Prometheus transposed for this modern static ontology.[1] Only God can violate the natural orders by crossing the boundary, like a Titan in reverse; when the new orthodoxy spots evidence of this, it celebrates the atoning substitution, the Scotist 'primacy of Christ' similarly transposed. In this way the new theology loses perfection entirely, since the atoning event is effective precisely by introducing a saving end foreign to human nature. The recipient of grace may express bewildered gratitude, but she can never find this new environment to be the Sabbath's rest for which her nature was made.

---

1 This is especially true for Protestant accounts of sin and grace, and John Pass-more, 2000, *The Perfectibility of Man*, Indianapolis: Liberty Fund, pp. 130ff, falls into this trap: see Exposition, above. For an insightful critique of the exaggerated anti-Pelagianism of Reformed theology, see Brian Gerrish, 2003, 'Sovereign Grace: Is Reformed Theology Obsolete?', *Interpretation* 57 (1), pp. 45–57. Catholic thought is of course also affected by modern static conceptions of nature, as de Lubac in particular has demonstrated: Henri de Lubac, 1969, *Augustinianism and Modern Theology*, trans. Lancelot Sheppard, London: G. Chapman.

Many of the great works of spirituality from the early modern era, though insightful and theologically adept in other respects, still express this sentiment in one form or another. In de Caussade's *L'Abandon à la Providence Divine*, holiness is 'produced in us by the will of God', and our 'ready acceptance of all that comes to us at each moment' (1.4).[2] God's activity, and primarily his activity on the cross, makes us holy, but all this activity is veiled in shadow, manifest to us only as 'murky rays from a clouded sun' (2.4). Job is holy insofar as he regards his ruin itself 'as one of God's names', and so learns to take his own unhappiness as divinely ordained will (2.10). The abandoned soul is 'perfectly satisfied with what it knows is suitable for it, . . . never attempting to tread beyond the boundaries laid out for it. It is not inquisitive about the way God acts. It is quite happy to submit to his will and makes no attempt to find out his intentions'. The sanctified soul is 'like metal poured into a mold, or a canvas waiting for the brush, or marble under the sculptor's hands' (2.12). As the human and liturgical alphabet for naming and speaking of God's activity falls into disrepair, so does our ability to communicate with one another, and so to form communities around the interpretation of God's will. Abandonment is an isolated and isolating practice. The sanctified soul who 'wants to know only what every moment says to it listens to what God utters in the depths of its heart and does not ask what has been said to others' (2.12).

In a rather different vein, the achingly beautiful poetry of John of the Cross centres on the image of a union of creatures to their divine Lover, a marriage which mystically spans a fathomless division. The world is made for the sole purpose of union with its bridegroom: 'My Son, I wish to give you / a bride who will love you' ('Romances' 3).[3] The world is not, however, made fit for this union. Unlike the angels, who 'possessed the Bridegroom in gladness', human creatures posses their Lover only in hope that he will one day span the gap that now keeps him distant, a hope

. . . founded
on the faith that he infused in them,
telling them that one day
he would exalt them,
and that he would lift them up from their lowness
so that no one could mock it any more;
for he would make himself wholly like them . . . ('Rom.' 4)

---

2 Jean-Pierre de Causaade, 1975 [1861], *Abandonment to Divine Providence*, trans. John Beevers, New York: Image Books. References are to chapter and section.

3 All references to John of the Cross are taken from Kieran Kavanaugh and Otilio Rodriguez (trans.), 1991, *The Collected Works of Saint John of the Cross*, revised ed., Washington, DC: ICS Publications.

Second Interlude: Perfection, Modernity and John Wesley

There is no fall in John of the Cross, only the emergence of creation into an existence already tragically distant from its true home.[4] The incarnation is not so much an act of God to undo sin, as a revising of this natural lacuna for the ends of a more 'perfect love' ('Rom' 7).[5] The beloved creature's ascent, cast as the ascent of Elijah up Mount Carmel, is therefore a journey up a 'secret ladder' in 'darkness and concealment' ('Noche Oscura' 2) accomplished in the 'obscurity of faith' (*La Subida al Monte Carmelo*, 2.1). The pilgrim is at the mercy of the fathomless God, and left 'without understanding/ transcending all knowledge' ('Coplas del mismo hechas sobre un éxtasis de harta contemplación' 4). Language itself fails, and utterly now, beyond the hierarchical mediations of Denys. The union is one that can occur, in spite of the creature's unsuitedness, in view of the 'sheer grace' (*Subida* 15.1) of the God who overcomes nature. *Theosis* for John is, alternatively, a natural creature gone into a slumbering state (*Subida* 15.2), a fish who has left its home in the water ('Coplas del alma que pena por ver a Dios' 4), or a mortal wound:

When the breeze blew from the turret
As I parted his hair,
It wounded my neck
With its gentle hand
Suspending all my senses. ('Noche Oscura' 7)[6]

New life in God is an entirely novel order of existence that abolishes the old. Fray Juan is here in a surprising harmony with the *theosis* promised by Milton's Satan: 'So ye shall die perhaps, but putting off/ Human, to put on Gods, death to be wisht' (*PL* IX.712–14). Union with God is understood by both to entail the destruction of the human form.

In the holiness literature of England we find a similar theology, if less lyrically expressed. The immensely popular anonymous devotional, *The Whole Duty of Man*, describes a constant humility that ought to characterize human beings, not simply in light of our sinfulness, but our very

---

4 This lack is glossed over in otherwise careful and insightful readings by Rowan Williams, 1990, *The Wound of Knowledge: Christian Spirituality from the New Testament to John of the Cross*, revised ed., Cambridge, MA: Cowley Publications, pp. 171–91, and David Bentley Hart, 2003, 'The Bright Morning of the Soul: John of the Cross on *Theosis*', *Pro Ecclesia* 12 (3), pp. 324–45.

5 'Now you see, Son, that your bride/ was made in your image, and so far as she is like you/ she will suit you well; yet she is different, in her flesh,/ which your simple being does not have./ In perfect love/ this law holds: that the lover become/ like the one he loves . . .'

6 The masculine pronoun refers to 'the wind', but appears to hesitate, as if to hint that perhaps the beloved is the one who does the wounding: 'El aire de la almena, cuando yo sos cabellos esparcía,/ con su mano serena/ en mi cuello hería/ y todos mis sentidos suspendía.', p. 51. Thanks to Horacio Peña for helping me understand the proper translation.

createdness. 'If we be not thoroughly perswaded that God is infinitely above us, that we are vileness and nothing in comparison of him, we shall never pay our due obedience.' Echoing the Franciscan claim that God's infinity is itself the real problem that the incarnation is to overcome, the author advises us to 'consider him as he is a God of infinite Majesty and glory, and we poor worms of the earth; He infinite in power . . . and we able to do nothing . . .' Collapsing the problem of sin into this ontological divide, he continues: 'He of infinite purity and holiness and we polluted and defiled, wallowing in all kind of sins and uncleanness; he unchangeable and constant, and we subject to change and alteration every minute of our lives.'[7] Mutability and sin are thus interchangeable; our nature is unfit for *theosis*. In light of this divide, we find that our *telos* is not to become like God so far as we are able, but to follow a law divinely ordained for humanity in God's inscrutable will.[8]

No less popular through the late seventeenth and eighteenth centuries is Jeremy Taylor's *Holy Living* and *Holy Dying*, the latter of which is a surprisingly familiar and occasionally witty tract that describes human limitations in the quest for divine favour.[9] 'Death meets us everywhere' (*Holy Dying* 1.1),[10] and for this reason it is 'a great art to die well' (*Holy Dying*, 'Dedication'). This art includes the limiting of hopes and designs, since 'every morning creeps out of a dark cloud, leaving behind it an ignorance and silence deep as midnight' (2.2). We are 'the heritage of worms and serpents', as the friends of a young German gentleman learn when they procrastinate a bit too long in having his portrait done for the great room, commissioning it finally a few days after his entombment. They find 'his face half eaten, and his midriff and backbone full of serpents; and so he stands pictured among his armed ancestors' (2.2). We make our limited existence into an advantage by making of each activity, whether eating or plowing, praying or dying, an 'action of religion' (*Holy Living* 1), 'hallowed by a holy intention' (1.1). This holy intention and consequently holy activity becomes our security, the hope that we will be saved from our natural end by Christ's resurrection; as Taylor says in another place, 'He who endeavors most is most secure' (*Discourse IX*. 28). The saving act of God thus turns 'our nature into grace' (*Holy Living* 1), and our part of the covenantal agreement is to live a holy life in response:

---

7 Richard Allestree, 1659, *The Whole Duty of Man*, London: T. Garthwait, pp. 35–6. I am indebted to Alan Gregory for first bringing this text to my attention. See Umphrey Lee, 1936, *John Wesley and Modern Religion*, Nashville: Cokesbury Press, p. 26.

8 Preface, paragraphs 12–22.

9 See Edmund Gosse, 1968 [1904], *Jeremy Taylor*, New York: Greenwood Press Publishers, pp. 90–3.

10 All Taylor references are from Thomas Carroll (ed.), 1990, *Jeremy Taylor, Selected Works*, New York and Mahwah: Paulist Press.

But then we, having received so great a favour, enter into covenant to correspond with a proportionable endeavour; the benefit of absolute pardon, that is, salvation of our souls, being not to be received till 'the times of refreshing shall come from the presence of the Lord': all the interval we have promised to live a holy life, in obedience to the whole discipline of Jesus. That is the condition on our part. (*Discourse IX.* 8)

God's grace cancels our sins and takes our earthly duties as deserving of heaven; we, left with a severely limited nature, must answer by living beyond our means, so to speak, destined to run up debts we will not be able to pay off.[11]

In all of these great works of spirituality we find a common appraisal of the human *telos*. Our proper end is no longer perfection: by an odd transposition of the term out of the philosophical register and into one of piety, now only God retains the privilege of having a perfection (Allestree, p. 36). The end of the imperfectible human would be a languishing in finitude were it not for the super-legal and super-verbal work of God who, out of sheer love, takes the creature as deserving of union with the Creator. In the earlier vision, an economy of kinship and desire between God and God's creatures reflects an economy of kinship and desire within God himself; in the later, God alone is perfect, and he graciously and voluntaristically declares that humans will have an end foreign to their beginning, a *telos* transposed onto an unfamiliar origin. The human as such will evaporate as she is united to the divine. What will remain in her place? A beloved cipher that God takes as a stand-in for a creation now annihilated by its own tragic limitedness?

Happiness and Holiness

There is of course one striking instance of a modern theology built entirely on the rehabilitation of this term. Even if 'there is scarce any expression in Holy Writ which has given more offence than this,' if 'the word "perfect" is what many cannot bear' (*Sermons*, p. 70),[12] if even this father of modern perfection admits late in life that he himself has 'no particular fondness for

---

11 Taylor's fear of sins after baptism connects with his rejection of original sin. See *Discourse IX.* 10–16. However, it also surely connects with the destruction of crown and cathedral in the Civil War and Interregnum period. Taylor writes with a kind of tragic despair reminiscent of Malory, two centuries prior. There is a good account of the relationship between Taylor's theology and the political turmoil of his times in Henry Trevor Hughes, 1960, *The Piety of Jeremy Taylor*, London: Macmillan; New York: St. Martin's Press, pp. 3 1ff, as well as in Reginald Askew, 1997, *Muskets and Altars: Jeremy Taylor and the Last of the Anglicans*, London and Herndon, Virginia: Mowbray Press.

12 Albert C. Outler and Richard P. Heitzenrater (eds), 1991, *John Wesley's Sermons: An Anthology*, Nashville: Abingdon Press.

the term' (*Works* XI, p. 450),[13] still John Wesley's legacy consists largely in a reconfiguration and proclamation of 'a plain account of Christian perfection'. In an age well practiced in 'the art of forgetting God' (*Works* VII, p. 263), Wesley's hymns and sermons gesture toward a divine vocation for the human creature. To what degree do his teachings manage to correct the distortions of modernity and the late Middle Ages?[14]

Among the most significant revisions that Wesley makes to eighteenth-century theology is in returning humility to its proper place as a pathway toward the higher ends of faith, hope and love. Though citing Taylor's

---

13 *The Works of John Wesley*, Grand Rapids, MI: Zondervan Publishing House (reproduction of 1872 edition).

14 I set aside here the questions surrounding Wesley's actual reading of and reliance on the Fathers. Though much has been made recently of his Patristic sources, I find the conclusion of Heitzenrater and Campbell to be largely persuasive: like nearly all theology of the eighteenth century, Wesley's actual acquaintance with the Fathers was rather thin. See Ted Campbell, 1991, *John Wesley and Christian Antiquity: Religious Vision and Cultural Change*, Nashville: Kingswood Books; and Richard Heitzenrater, 2002, 'John Wesley's Reading of and References to the Early Church Fathers', in S. T. Kimbrough, *Orthodoxy and Wesleyan Spirituality*, Crestwood, NY: St. Vladimir's Seminary Press. Heitzenrater (p. 32, n. 16) notes Campbell's conclusion that Wesley intentionally removed references to deification in his collections of the Fathers' works. See also Randy Maddox, 1990, 'John Wesley and Eastern Orthodoxy', *Asbury Theology Journal* 45 (2), pp. 29–53. Though he consistently recommends readings from the Fathers to clergy, his reason for doing so seems to be more that these writings are chronologically nearer the writing of Scripture than any sense that they bear particular theological insight for his century. 'Can any who spend several years in those seats of learning, be excused, if they do not add to that of the languages and sciences, the knowledge of the Fathers[, t]he most authentic commentators on Scripture, as being both nearest the fountain, and eminently endued with that Spirit by whom all Scripture was given[?] It will be easily perceived, I speak chiefly of those who wrote before the Council of Nice. But who would not likewise desire to have some acquaintance with those that followed them? [W]ith St. Chrysostom, Basil, Jerome, Austin; and, above all, the man of a broken heart, Ephraim Syrus?' 'An Address to the Clergy,' Wesley Center for Applied Theology at Northwest Nazarene University: http://wesley.nnu.edu/john_wesley/in dex.htm, accessed 28 July 2010. This characterization of Ephraim is particularly significant, as it gives support to an argument that Wesley's understanding of the Fathers was heavily channelled through historians such as William Cave, whom he read in 1732. Cave passes over Ephraim's doctrinal and ecclesiological mediations entirely, and makes of him a kind of mystic of pious devotion of the type for which certain strands of Anglicanism were given to pine. William Cave, 1683, 'An Appendix Containing a Brief Account of Some Other Eminent Fathers that Flourish'd in this Fourth Century', pp. 26ff, in *Ecclesiastici: Or, The History of The Lives, Acts, Death, and Writings of the Most Eminent Fathers of the Church that Flourisht in the Fourth Century*, London. Indeed a 'man of a broken heart'. My research on this issue has proceeded in tandem with that of my friend Doug Harrison, in particular for a paper we presented together at the Wesleyan Theological Society's Annual Meeting in 2005, entitled: 'What Has London to do with Syria? Or Maybe Wesleyans Really *Don't* Need the Church'.

treatises as influential on his own understanding, he comes to challenge Taylor's idea that 'we ought, in some sense or other, to think ourselves the worst in every company where we come' as neither reasonable nor carrying with it the possibility of sincerity.[15] Annoyed by 'the mock humility of Protestants', who evade moral responsibility behind a veil of justification by faith, he saw rightly that faith is itself a kind of work: 'For if it be really true that you can do nothing, then you have no faith.' Even his own father was startled by the rigour of John's pursuits while a student at Oxford and questioned what sort of Icaran folly the 'Holy Club' was ascending toward: 'What would you be? Would you be angels? I question whether a mortal can arrive to a greater degree of perfection, than steadily to do good, and for that very reason patiently and meekly to suffer evil. For my part, on the present view of your actions and designs, my daily prayers are, that God would keep you humble . . .' (*Works* I, pp. 8–9). But John insists that Christian humility is not self-degradation, but the intellectual and practical habit of refusing autonomy:

Q. May not, then, the very best of men adopt the dying martyr's confession: 'I am in myself nothing but sin, darkness, hell; but Thou art my light, my holiness, my heaven'?

A. Not exactly. But the best of men may say, 'Thou art my light, my holiness, my heaven. Through my union with Thee, I am full of light, of holiness, and happiness. But if I were left to myself, I should be nothing but sin, darkness, hell.' (*Plain Account*, p. 73)[16]

Humility of this sort is in no way contradicted by a pursuit of boundless perfection, and here Wesley echoes the *epectasic* vision of Gregory of Nyssa:

As to the end of my being, I lay it down for a rule that I cannot be too happy, or therefore too holy; and thence infer that the more steadily I keep my eye upon the prize of our high calling the better, and the more of my thoughts, and words, and actions are directly pointed at the attainment of it. (To his Brother Samuel, 17 November 1731).[17]

---

15 See the quotation and commentary in Southey's 1820 *Life*: Robert Southey, 1925 [1820], *Life of Wesley and the Rise and Progress of Methodism*, London, Oxford University Press, 1925, p. 74.

16 Wesley, 1968 [1766], *A Plain Account of Christian Perfection*, 1968 [London, Epworth Press].

17 http://wesley.nnu.edu/john_wesley/index.htm. See Stephen D. Long, 2005, *John Wesley's Moral Theology: The Quest for God and Goodness*, Nashville: Kingswood Books. Long's treatment of the question of humility and *theosis* (pp. 138, 143ff, 220) is, to my mind, unsurpassed.

This connection of happiness and holiness, which he holds throughout his long public career, is another important revision Wesley makes to contemporary holiness theologies. He could never have said, with Caussade, that Job found his own misery to be the lot to which God asked him to submit, or with John of the Cross that the ultimate moment of union is a mortal wound of our own humanity. To be sure, his own poetry does not ignore the experience of distance between the soul and its divine lover, as evidenced by his revision of the first stanza of a 1712 hymn by Joseph Addison. The original read:

When all Thy mercies, O my God,
My rising soul surveys,
Transported with the view, I'm lost
In wonder, love and praise.

Wesley includes it in his 1737 hymnal, now reading

When all Thy mercies, O my God,
My rising soul surveys,
Why my cold heart, are thou not lost
In wonder, love, and praise?

Though Wesley himself never returned to re-edit the stanza,[18] during the nineteenth century the Methodist hymnal would revert to the original Addison lyrics.[19]

Wesley understands, however, that despair cannot have the final word without doing damage to a Christian account of creation. God 'made all things . . . not "as if he needed anything . . ." He made all things to be happy. He made man to be happy in himself' (*Sermons*, p. 533). Just as in Thomas, where our creation for divine blessing carries with it the logical imperative that the path to this blessing be open to us, 'lest such a noble creature might seem to be created to no purpose' (see *Summa contra Gentiles* IV.1),[20] Wesley insists that all created natures reach their end when they are perfected, and not destroyed or even suspended, by grace. Lions, lambs, scorpions and daffodils are made for this happiness too, for the end in which 'violence shall be heard no more, neither wasting or destruction seen on the face of the earth' (*Works* VI, p. 295). The role of humankind on God's eschatological mountain is consciously and wilfully to rest in the life of its Creator.[21]

Here Wesley provides us with another key insight that does indeed return to the vision of cosmic perfection from the Fathers. The coming of Christ

---

18 Lee, *Modern Religion*, pp. 96–7.

19 1889 Hymnal, http://wesley.nnu.edu/charles_wesley/hymns/index.htm.

20 See Long, *Moral Theology*, pp. 64, 106, 171ff.

21 See Theodore Runyon, 1998, *The New Creation: John Wesley's Theology Today*, Nashville: Abingdon Press, pp. 8–12.

into the world is not a negligible instance of grace that might just as well have been demonstrated naturally throughout history, as John Tolland and others of the era would have it. Nor, though, is it a radically novel event to which all the laws of nature are opposed, as the more aggressive interpreters of Calvin and Luther said.[22] Christ came 'not to destroy, but to fulfil' the Law of Moses. Wesley's 13 discourses on the Sermon on the Mount, in many ways the heart of his literary output, unfold this excessive New Testament perfection.[23] The typological excess for Wesley, however, is double, since the words written in stone for Moses and Israel already refer to the writing 'on the hearts of all the children of men, when they came out of the hands of their creator' (*Works* V, p. 311). Wesley thus finds it easy enough to pass from the moral law given in Moses to the natural laws governing all creation, 'unknown indeed to men, but doubtless enrolled in the annals of eternity, when "the morning stars" first "sang together," being newly called into existence' (*Sermons*, p. 257). This Law is the 'everlasting fitness of all things that are or ever were created' (*Sermons*, p. 260) to the mind and being of God; 'the copy of his inimitable perfections' (*Sermons*, p. 265), '"the streaming forth" or outbeaming "of his glory, the express image of his person"' (*Sermons*, p. 260). In noting that Scripture speaks of Law the same way that Saint Paul describes the Son of God (*Sermons*, p. 261), Wesley arrives at the classically Christian understanding of the Nativity: Creation itself is an imperfect incarnation of God, and the Son's journey to dwell among us is neither identical to nor different than the grace of creation. Christ comes to fulfil the law, which is to say he incarnates the divine perfections perfectly.

Furthermore, it is in this light that we should read his account of a spiritual sensorium, a doctrine of which Wesley first perhaps heard in his 'Holy Club' readings of Malebranche in the 1730s.[24] 'Before a child is born into the world he has eyes, but sees not; he has ears, but does not hear.' Similarly, before a creature experiences new birth in Christ and is thus 'in a mere natural state', 'he has, in a spiritual sense, eyes and sees not; a thick impenetrable veil lies upon them. He has ears, but hears not; he is utterly deaf to what he is most of all concerned to hear. His other spiritual senses are all locked up' (*Sermons*, p. 339). Like the unelicited desire for the supernatural in Thomas, the spiritual senses are fashioned in order to perceive a reality that they are no longer able to name. Though made to manifest God to humankind in all sorts of ways, the world now is largely silent, and its maker invisible (*Works* VII, p. 257). But the eyes to see and ears to hear are still ours by nature: even if having such sensory organs that one cannot use places him in exactly 'the same condition as if he had them not', the difference they make is essential. The grace through which 'the "eyes of his understanding are opened" (such is the language of the Apostle)' (*Sermons*, p. 339) perfects the man who was created to receive

---

22 See Lee, *Modern Religion*, p. 164.
23 See Long, *Moral Theology*, pp. 141ff.
24 See Long, *Moral Theology*, p. 108.

this grace; it does not replace this man with another, one who enjoys an utterly novel communion for which he never before longed.[25]

Through these emphases - spiritual senses which perfect the natural, a gospel which perfects all forms of law, holiness which completes rather than negates happiness, and humility which has its *telos* in divine union rather than nihilistic self-effacing - John Wesley sails against the winds of modern theological anthropology.

Why John Wesley Was Not a Christian

While a more rigorously philosophical mind might have been capable of leaving the question of perfection to hover in this theoretical–eschatological space, Wesley engages in abstract questions of this sort only as a means to inform himself and others in matters of 'practical divinity'. If it is worth talking about, perfection must be a practice-able experience. As his journal shows, he is constantly tortured by his own inability to experience the co-incidence of happiness and holiness. He writes here of multiple conversions to a life of godly righteousness, beginning when he 'gladly received' the Christian teachings of salvation as a child (*Works* I, p. 98). At age 22, he took orders and at the same time began reading Taylor's *Holy Living* and *Holy Dying*. His describes this experience as a kind of conversion: 'In reading several parts of this book, I was exceedingly affected; that part in particular which relates to purity of intention. Instantly I resolved to dedicate all my life to God, all my thoughts and words, and actions' (*Plain Account*, p. 9). The following year, while reading Thomas à Kempis and simultaneously meeting a friend for religious conversation, he experienced another life-altering moment: 'I began to alter the whole form of my conversation, and to set in earnest upon a new life' filled with public and private prayer, regular Eucharistic worship, and attention to holiness (*Works* I, p. 99). More dramatic still was his encounter with William Law's *Christian Perfection* and *A Serious Call to a Devout and Holy Life*:

> The light flowed in so mightily upon my soul, that every thing appeared in a new view. I cried to God for help, and resolved not to prolong the time of obeying him as I had never done before . . . I am persuaded that I should be accepted of Him, and that I was even then in a state of salvation (*Works* I, p. 99)

In light of these several conversion experiences, and the famous attention to habits of holiness already developed at a young age, why does he write in 1738, on the occasion of his less than triumphant return from a two-year mission to Georgia, 'that I who went to America to convert others, was never myself converted to God' (*Works* I, pp. 75–6)? A few weeks

---

25 See Long, *Moral Theology*, pp. 132–3.

later he angered his brother Charles by telling him that he (John) had never had saving faith in Christ (*Works* I, p. 91). Throughout the next several weeks, it is a troubled man who journals: 'I had continual sorrow and heaviness in my heart . . . God is holy; I am unholy. God is a consuming fire; I am altogether a sinner, meet to be consumed' (*Works* I, p. 97).

The logic of these statements is, in fact, rather straightforward: 'O let no one deceive us by vain words, as if we had already attained this faith. By its fruits we shall know. Do we already feel "peace with God," and "joy in the Holy Ghost?" Does "the Spirit bear witness with our spirit, that we are the children of God?" Alas, with mine He does not.' Ergo, I am not a Christian (*Works* I, p. 102).

All of this sets up the famous Aldersgate Street experience of Wednesday, 24 May 1738. In the early morning, looking for assurance from Scripture, he found 2 Peter 1.4: 'There are given unto us exceeding great and precious promises, even that ye should be partakers of the divine nature' (*Works* I, p. 103). At the meeting that evening, at 'about a quarter before nine . . . I felt my heart strangely warmed. I felt I did trust Christ, Christ alone for salvation: And an assurance was given me, that he had taken away my sins, even mine, and saved me from the law of sin and death.' This experience marks at least a fourth conversion, or perhaps a fifth, if we count from his reception of the gospel as a child. This time the assurance lasts for exactly one week: 'Yet on Wednesday did I grieve the Spirit of God, not only by not watching unto prayer, but likewise by speaking with sharpness instead of tender love, of one that was not sound in faith. Immediately God hid his face, and I was troubled' (*Works* I, p. 105).

Still, for some time he maintains, as to his brother Samuel, that 'I was not a Christian till May the 24th' (30 October 1738).[26] A few months later though, the notion that a tree is known by its fruits returns to haunt him: 'I have not the fruits of the Spirit of Christ,' 'I do not love either the Father or the Son,' and am still 'hankering after a happiness'. Conclusion: 'Though I have constantly used all means of grace for twenty years, I am not a Christian.' In fact, 'That I am not a Christian at this day I as assuredly know as that Jesus is the Christ.'[27] Twenty-seven years later, the logical argument still torments him: 'I do not love God. I never did. Therefore I never believed, in the Christian sense of the word . . . . I never had any other evidence of the eternal or invisible world than I have now; and that is not at all . . .'[28]

---

26 http://wesley.nnu.edu/john-wesley/the-letters-of-john-wesley/wesleys-letters-1738/ See Lee, *Modern Religion*, p. 90.

27 4 January 1739, as quoted in Lee, *Modern Religion*, pp. 90–1. Oddly, this letter is omitted from the Wesley Center website. Stanley Hauerwas, 1998, *Sanctify Them in the Truth: Holiness Exemplified*, Nashville: Abingdon Press, pp. 123ff., gives an admirably critical appraisal of this 'pragmatic' demand in Wesley's thought.

28 As quoted in Lee, *Modern Religion*, p. 92, and Richard Heitzenrater, 1995, *Wesley and the People Called Methodists*, Nashville: Abingdon Press, p. 224. This letter is also omitted from the Wesley Center site.

Commentators often deal with the ambiguities of these tormented journals by attempting to answer the question of whether he believed that the experiences of justification and perfection come instantaneously or progressively.[29] This indeed is a difficult question to answer, not the least, apparently, for Wesley himself. There is some evidence that he came to believe his own conversion was gradual, and that all the above narratives were 'true' instances of his progressive turning to God. So, for instance, his later insertions into the Georgia journal attempt to show that he 'had even then the faith of a servant, though not that of a son', a distinction he relies upon heavily in his late writings (*Works* I, p. 76; see VII, p. 256).[30] He told his brother Charles, at around this same time, to 'press the instantaneous blessing, I will enforce the gradual'.[31] However, in his late writings he says 'it is given instantaneously, in one moment' (*Plain Account*, p. 50). That no clarity on this question is forthcoming[32] ought to be obvious after reading his 'Brief Thoughts on Christian Perfection':

As to the manner. I believe this perfection is always wrought in the soul by a simple act of faith; consequently, in an instant.

But I believe in a gradual work, both preceding and following that instant.

As to the time. I believe this instant generally is the instant of death, the moment before the soul leaves the body. But I believe it may be ten, twenty, or forty years before.

I believe it is usually many years after justification; but that it may be within five years or five months after it, I know no conclusive argument to the contrary.

If it must be many years after justification, I would be glad to know how many. (*Works* XI, p. 446)

This rather muddy explanation satisfied him as clear and straightforward enough to include later in *A Plain Account of Christian Perfection*.

Still, though, the question in Wesley's own mind seems larger than whether a 'second blessing' comes instantaneously or gradually. As he gathers together the many terms for various Christian experiences (new birth, justification, initial sanctification, full sanctification, perfection, assurance, servant-like faith, child-like faith) under the single experience of 'salvation', he really appears to be asking whether he himself has any claim to a share in the latter. In order to gain clarity into what Wesley means by salvation, and why his own inability to experience it led him constantly to

---

29 See Randy Maddox, 1994, *Responsible Grace: John Wesley's Practical Theology*, Nashville: Kingswood Books, pp. 159–60. See also R. Newton Flew, 1934, *The Idea of Perfection in Christian Theology: An Historical Study of the Christian Ideal for the Present Life*, London: Oxford University Press, pp. 315ff.

30 See Lee, *Modern Religion*, pp. 97ff.

31 Quoted in Lee, *Modern Religion*, p. 93.

32 See Flew, *Idea*, p. 325.

the conclusion that he was neither perfect nor even a Christian, we must pause to consider what he understood 'experience' itself to signify.

John Locke's *Essay Concerning Human Understanding*, which Wesley read and commented upon (*Works* XIII, pp. 455–64), outlines an epistemology originating with a mind like 'white paper, void of all characteristics, without any ideas'. Against the argument that logical or moral precepts lie innate in the mind, waiting to be discovered, Locke insists that 'to imprint anything on the mind without the mind's perceiving it, seems to me hardly intelligible,' as this amounts to saying that a thing is and is not in the understanding. The mind is an 'empty cabinet'; how does it come to be filled with ideas? 'How comes it to be furnished? When comes it by that vast store which the busy and boundless fancy of man has painted on it with an almost endless variety? Whence has it all the materials of reason and knowledge? To this I answer, in a word, from EXPERIENCE' (*Essay* I, pp. 121–2).[33] All that we know and understand, we know and understand from experience, from sensory information gathered and sorted out according to our reasoning faculty.

Wesley, as is widely acknowledged, follows Locke implicitly and even explicitly in this epistemology.[34] He sees, perhaps, that Locke's *Essay* links up better with classical Christianity's account of illumination than does Descartes' theory of innate ideas.[35] In addition, Locke gives him a framework for describing the *sine qua non* of Protestantism: we are justified by faith in God's work, not by anything innate within us.[36] On this theory, however, internal experience becomes the only means to verify an extrinsically originating idea. Locke cites the internal awareness of happiness as evidence for a true and verifiable encounter with a happiness-causing external reality: 'For to be happy or miserable without being conscious of it, seems to be utterly inconsistent and impossible . . .' Compare this with what Wesley recalls of his Moravian friend's understanding of justification:

1. When a man has living faith in Christ, then he is justified:
2. This is always given in a moment;
3. And in that moment he has peace with God;
4. Which he cannot have without knowing that he has it:
5. And being born of God, he sinneth not:
6. Which deliverance from sin he cannot have without knowing that he has it. (*Works* I, p. 111)

---

33 A. Fraser (ed.), 1959, *An Essay Concerning Human Understanding*, New York: Dover Publications.

34 Long, *Moral Theology*, pp. 62–66; Lee, *Modern Religion*, p. 122; Albert Outler, in his Introduction to his own edited volume, 1964, *John Wesley*, New York: Oxford University Press, p. 29.

35 Long, *Moral Theology*, pp. 64, 78–80.

36 This is perhaps lurking in the background of Locke's theory already.

From this logic, Wesley was persuaded, and remained persuaded through-out his life, that true deliverance from sin, and the perfection that comes of having the love of God shed abroad in one's heart, cannot occur without a full consciousness that it has in fact occurred.

Or, perhaps better stated, the one in whom such a work has occurred can expect full consciousness of it. Locke suggests, in the second volume of his *Essay*, that intuition, while still a kind of knowledge gathered from experience, is the highest sort of experiential knowing possible. It is also immediate, in that our intuitions rely on no intervening ideas.

This part of our knowledge is irresistible, and, like bright sunshine, forces itself immediately to be perceived, as soon as ever the mind turns its view that way; and leaves no room for hesitation, doubt, or examination, but the mind is presently filled with the clear light of it. It is on this situation that depends all the certainty and evidence of all our knowledge. (*Essay* II, p. 177)

This intuition, which Wesley assumes, dubbing it 'plerophory', 'a clear conviction that *I am now* in the favour of God as excludes all doubt and fear concerning it' (To Hester Ann Roe, 10 April 1781),[37] is precisely the assurance he associates with perfection and without which he cannot claim to have received full salvation. The argument for immediacy, as in the fol-lowing excerpt, has to do less with his rather tortured mixture of verb tenses than it does with the implicit assumption that perfected salvation ought to align with Locke's highest form of knowledge, and thus come entirely unmediated by temporality and community:

My comfort stands . . . not on the remembrance of anything wrought in me yesterday; but on what is today; on my present knowledge of God in Christ, reconciling me to himself on my now beholding the light of the glory of God in the face of Jesus Christ . . . that I personally for myself, and not for another, have an hope full of immortality; that I feel the love of God shed abroad in my heart, being crucified to the world, and the world crucified to me. My rejoicing is this; the testimony of my conscience, that in simplicity and godly sincerity, not with fleshly wisdom, but by the grace of God, I have my conversation in the world. (*Works* X, p. 295)

Thus holiness for Wesley will always involve happiness, and happiness in turn will involve assurance, or the immediate intuitive awareness of 'the love of God shed abroad in my heart'. Without this awareness, which Wesley is never able to sustain for any length of time, there is no experience of hap-piness; and without the experience of happiness there is no holiness.[38]

---

37 http://wesley.nnu.edu/john-wesley/the-letters-of-john-wesley/wesleys-letters-1781a/. See Lee, *Modern Religion*, p. 157.

38 See Flew's treatment of this dynamic, *Idea*, pp. 328–9.

Second Interlude: Perfection, Modernity and John Wesley

What Wesley is unable to see in Locke's *Essay* is the way in which its very *raison d'être* lies in the sort of humility that Wesley is so concerned to reject. 'Men have reason to be well satisfied', says Locke in his Introduction, 'with what God hath thought fit for them, since he hath given them (as St Peter says) πάντα πρὸς ζωὴν καὶ εὐσέβειαν, whatsoever is necessary for the conveniences of life and information of virtue; and has put within the reach of their discovery, the comfortable provision for this life and the way that leads to a better' (*Essay* I, p. 29). The citation is from 2 Peter 1.3, just prior to the '*theosis* passage' that Wesley himself read on the morning of Aldersgate. For Locke, though, the 'all things' that God has given us are merely human and earthly, the very opposite of 'participation in the divine nature'. The many intellectual disputes come when humans, like Icarus again, ignore 'the horizon . . . which sets the bounds between the enlightened and dark parts of things; between what is and what is not comprehensible by us' (*Essay* I, p. 32). The *Essay* is intended to turn us away from 'things to which our understandings are not suited', and toward those ideas of which we can form 'clear and distinct perceptions' (*Essay* I, p. 29). There is little room here for the invisible world for which Wesley tells us our spiritual senses are suited; in Locke, all experience begins in a metastatic reduction to the empirical.

Wesley's mistake, then, is to accept a Lockean understanding of experience, one to which his own more classically rooted description of sanctification is ill-suited. So in his late sermon 'Spiritual Worship', he says, 'He who is not happy is not a Christian; seeing if he was a real Christian he could not but be happy. But I allow an exception here in favour of those who are under violent temptation; yea, and of those who are under deep nervous disorders . . .' (*Sermons*, p. 439). Clearly he understands happiness here in the unrefined 'common' sense of immediate emotive response.[39] Is this really the New Testament of classically Christian understanding of happiness? It would be odd to hear Saint Paul say that he was 'feeling rather comfortable' about his imprisonment in Rome; *caras* through suffering has to do, as we have seen, with the mediations of hope that come from his communications with other believers, including his own memories

---

39 Though in other places his conception is less tied to empirical evidence, notably in his sermon 'The Unity of the Divine Being', where he characterizes happiness as communion with the Creator that allows the communers to become 'patterns to all of true genuine morality, of justice, mercy and truth. This is religion, and this is happiness, the happiness for which we were made' (*Sermons*, pp. 532–9). See Long, *Moral Theology*, p. 112. Long, though, overlooks the ways in which Wesley's understanding of happiness diverges from the classical philosophical and theological accounts, and in doing so he distances Wesley too much from Locke, as on p. 106. It is interesting to note that in the sermon mentioned, essentially a discourse on the one human happiness as a corollary of the one divine being, Wesley challenges Rousseau, Voltaire and Hume, for a religion 'independent of any revelation whatever' (p. 537), but does not challenge Locke's conception of happiness. I suspect, as I am suggesting above, that this is because he simply transfers a Lockean notion of experiential happiness into a classically Christian account of the soul's journey into God.

of and expectations for them, far more than it depends upon his emotional state at any given moment. Likewise, the *makarios* of the Sermon on the Mount subverts the very idea that Christian happiness can be discerned in the normal way. 'Blessed are you who weep . . .' (Luke 6.21). Are the mourners conscious, at the moment of their mourning, of full assurance? And what about Jesus himself? Does he experience plerophory in the Garden, or from the cross? Wesley has undercut here the Aristotelian principle, so important to the Christian understanding of perfection: a single moment of happiness does not make one blessed, any more than one swallow makes a summer.

In short, Wesley accepts a Lockean definition of happiness, which serves to undercut his theological vision of human perfection. Lacking the experience, he finds he can either say *there is no happiness*, or *there is a happiness, and I lack it*. Again following Locke, who says that 'we may as rationally hope to see with other men's eyes, as to know by other men's understandings' (*Essay* I, p. 115), he finds he can draw no final conclusions from the testimonials of Charles, of Mr Fletcher or even of Paul and Cornelius regarding a verifiable experience of perfection. An eroded sense of Christian community convinces him that the witness of the Spirit is primarily and finally a matter of personal conviction, hence his siding with the Donatists as 'the real Christians' of the fourth and fifth centuries (*Works* XI, p. 453).

So Wesley can say only that instantaneous perfection is likely a trustworthy doctrine, and then go off like Bunyan's Pilgrim, turning over stones in search of the lost scroll on which is written his assurance of salvation. Happiness is, to repeat, essential to an understanding of perfection that completes rather than destroys nature. But this happiness too must be perfected, so that like natural bodies transformed by the resurrection, what Christian happiness/full salvation/perfection is 'has not yet been revealed' (1 John 3.2).

What Wesley Nearly Said

Had Wesley avoided Locke's reduction of reality to what can be epistemologically regulated, how far might he have recovered the classical doctrine? If the notes in his Georgia journal are any indication, he might have given 'a plain account of Christian perfection' that came closer to Alysoun of Bath's account on the Canterbury Road. He came to see, at least partially, his own *via salutis* as a complex narrative, and his 'conversion' to Christ as a lifelong event. If Paul and Augustine experienced a radical turn to Christ in the midst of a world in which Christianity was one of many competing orders of devotion, the same could hardly be expected of a 'cradle Anglican' of the eighteenth century. Even for Paul, conversion was a complex experience that he could only narrate in a series of fictionalizations, as his own understanding of the event unfolded throughout his life (Acts 22 and 26; Gal. 1; 1 Cor. 15). Similarly, the Wife tells a fictional narrative of perfect redemption while making her way toward the place of perfect worship, all the while dismissing perfection out of hand as something that holds no interest whatsoever for her. For both, 'conversion' is a kind of perfection, an event that takes place once, and yet one that will continue to take place throughout a lifetime of imaginative retellings.[40]

Immediacy, after all – immediacy of the Lockean sort that avoids all the interruptions of language and ideas – is not a human experience. Salvation, from prevenient grace through to the beatific vision, is a storyline mediated endlessly by language, by experience, by the interpretations and interruptions of others. The free and unmerited grace of God, that is, must be 'worked out' through time and space as a tapestry of salvation.

Does Wesleyan perfection go this far? Very nearly, but no. George Herbert's poetry, anticipating Wesley in many ways, is in this respect more theologically astute. While Herbert can, like Wesley, lament his own lack of fulfilled experience of grace, and moreover refuse any easy consolation, 'Ah my God, though I am clean forgot/let me not love thee if I love thee not!' (*Affliction* I.65–6),[41] he can at the same time recognize that any experience of assurance would fail to deliver on its promise. How can supernatural perfection fit into a traceable human experience of assurance? This poetry in fact, as Rowan Williams argues, pushes the Reformation era's eroded language of justification to its very limits, using the term to name an event of grace that resists any nameable experience, as in the final 'approval' of 'A True Hymne' at lines 19 and 20: 'As when th'heart sayes (sighing to be approved)/ O *could I love!* And stops: God writeth, *Loved.*'[42] The perfect approval from God does not cancel the human longing, and sighing is the heart's own life-rhythm: therefore God's response is not even a humanly discernible sentence, just a simple monosyllabic sound. But 'Loved' is still God's judgement on the whole, the *tetelestai* of a human life that would be tragically unfinished were it not joined to Christ.

Wesley's quest for immediacy, even where it saves space for working out the dynamics of faith over a lifetime, thus dismantles his own account of perfection. In one of his sermons he quotes Augustine, favourably, as saying *Qui fecit nos sine nobis, non salvabit nos sine nobis*: 'He that made us without ourselves, will not save us without ourselves' (*Sermons*, p. 491). Armed with this excerpt, Wesley is able to say that sanctification is a saving grace within which humans have a co-operating agency. But the Lockean cult of immediacy holds even here, since he insists, as he ever did, that humans are justified immediately, while sanctification, as a secondary

---

40 'Even though Wesley's account of sanctification is inherently teleological, he was unable to find the appropriate means to suggest how our being on a journey also . . . results in the particular kind of singleness characteristic of Christians.' Hauerwas, *Sanctify Them*, p. 126.

41 C. A. Patrides (ed.), 1974, *The English Poems of George Herbert*, London: Dent and Totowa, NJ: Rowman and Littlefield.

42 I am following the analysis in Rowan Williams, 2003, *Anglican Identities*, Cambridge, MA: Cowley Publications, pp. 57–72.

work, involves human habitual action. Herbert would perhaps want to ask Wesley, especially in light of the ambiguities of his journal entries, to describe the instant in which he was justified: was this an experience which he could be sure to have had? In fact, Wesley here misquotes Augustine, who neither had an idea of a grace that precludes active human mediation, nor maintained any sharp distinction between justification and sanctification. The original text is a commentary on Romans 4.24–5: 'It will be reckoned to us who believe in him who raised Jesus our Lord from the dead, who was handed over to death for our trespasses and was raised for our justification.' Augustine is explaining here that human fellowship and labour mediate the grace of Christ's resurrection at every point, from conversion through glorification, and thus he writes, *qui ergo fecit te sine te, non te iustificat sine te*:[43] 'He who made us without ourselves will not *justify* us without ourselves.'[44] God will not justify us without our mediating involvement in that work, because to do so would be a destruction of the human form. Had Wesley grasped this key insight of the Fathers, his account of Christian perfection may have been, if not plainer, at least more theologically persuasive.

43 J. P. Migne (ed.), 1958–74, *Patiologia, Series Latina*, Paris: Éditions Garnier Fièies, Vol. 38, p. 923.

44 For this point, see Geoffrey Wainwright, 2001, 'The Lutheran–Roman Catholic Agreement on Justification: Its Ecumenical Significance and Scope from a Methodist Point of View', *Journal of Ecumenical Studies* 38 (1), pp. 20–42. Maddox, *Responsible Grace*, pp. 148–51, explores the co-operative dimensions of Wesley's account of justification, but fails to see how the modern dialectic of immediacy/mediation affects Wesley. He also misses the misquote: see p. 148.

Emergence (Reprise)

Diagonal Advance

The Truth must dazzle gradually
Or every man be blind—

Emily Dickinson

Pilgrims and Poets

If it is generally the poets from the Middle Ages forwards who provide the most suggestive accounts of perfection, this is because a trajectory emerges among them with which philosophy has only recently begun to catch up. The work of Alain Badiou, which bridges disciplinary divisions between science and the humanities, as well as between English and Continental philosophy, aligns with many of the concerns of the Third Movement, above, suggesting that a human subject emerges in simultaneity with the pathway towards her own perfection. The work of Jean-Louis Chrétien, which bridges disciplinary divisions between Continental Philosophy and Catholic theology, construes perfection as life of prayerful responding, in which the divine call is constructed within the human response. Both Badiou and Chrétien come up short, as we shall see, in their attempt to escape the distortions of modern teleology; still, their writings can be read as inheriting the poetic project, and thus gesturing beyond the Promethean dialectic with which this book began.

What Dante, Chaucer and Spenser suggest regarding human emergence is not, as I have demonstrated above, entirely new. In implying that perfection is always a matter of *poesis*, they are in an important sense simply unfolding and nuancing the implications of ancient Prometheanism, which sees the gap between heaven and earth as more tragic than ontological, and thus as one that can be traversed, but only at great risk. In the ancient texts, we are invited to weep for Io, Arachne and Icarus, all of whom were at the same time Godlike and tragically flawed. Though the New Testament subtracts the teleological tragedy from the classical verses, the poetic nature of human striving remains. So Christ speaks in parables, not in order to offer his gospel as a code for a new humanity so much as to indicate that a new humanity materializes only in a series of encodings: in the wandering of a son, or the complaints of vineyard workers. Becoming perfect for Saint John and Saint

Paul is about completing God's creative work through the ad hoc tinkerings of a human life. Likewise, in Gregory of Nyssa, the only proper answer to the question 'what is Christian perfection?' is a treatise on turning the name of Christ into allegories, which in turn provide sites for the reinterpretation of all human activity. If all the activity of creatures is ultimately, as Maximus has it, a way of coming to rest in the perichoretic motions of the Trinity, then the only appropriate language for perfection is an existential poetry, linking inexhaustible temporal possibility to the fathomless embrace of divine actuality. In Thomas's vision, the metaphors of Scripture are appropriate means of conveying this grace to us, because we ourselves are metaphors, perfected by our encounter with the divinizing earthiness of the sacred text.

Dante and the poets, then, extend this deeply Christian idea that perfection is the unscripted recipe of a dump-cook, that the good life is always an uncharted pilgrimage, that 'real knights don't need maps'. These poetic constructions take shape, however, in a world that is increasingly arrested by its own attempts to define and classify the human subject. The late medieval return to pagan allegory becomes part of this attempt, insofar as writers like our Franciscan poet reinterpret the lyrical strivings of the archetypal characters as a set of morality tales: so the *Ovide moralisé* scolds Arachne, and, through her, the reader as well, for hoping to compromise the distance between us and God (*Ovide moralisé en prose* 6.iv).[1] Arachne must limit herself to her own natural sphere: the subject is itself only when it refuses to bleed over into another, and especially into the divine other. As the drive to define and sterilize a transcendental subject increases, we find ourselves miles removed from those characters who awaken 'mid-way through life' to find themselves in a wood, in a pigsty or in a travel inn on route to Canterbury. As I indicated above, a vein of Catholic and late Protestant philosophy remains true to this older ideal, beginning with Renaissance Catholicism and appearing again to a certain degree in post-Enlightenment Romanticism.[2] In the mainstream of intellectual development, though, it is the still-life that dominates, and reduces the question of perfection to ruins. For how can we inquire after the suitable end of a character which is fundamentally static, transcendental to all development, mutability and temporality?

It is in this sense that philosophy has recently begun to catch up to the idea of an emergent subjectivity,[3] a subject whose history can be traced more like the arc of a character in a novel, and less like the adventures of an element of the Periodic Table. So Alain Badiou, for instance, can say that a subject is not a substance, a point of origin, or even a result of a becoming, but rather a process that shuttles between an event, like the October Revolution or Christ's resurrection, and a 'procedure of fidelity'

---

1 A fifteenth-century prose synthesis of the longer poem: C. de Boer (ed.), 1954, *Ovide moralisé en prose*, Amsterdam: North-Holland Publishing Company.

2 See, for example, John R. Betz, 2009, *After Enlightenment: The Post-Secular Vision of J. G. Hamann*, Oxford: Wiley-Blackwell.

3 I take the term from Catherine Pickstock, 2004, 'Eros and Emergence', *Telos* 127, pp. 97–118.

to that event.[4] Saint Paul becomes a unified subject by taking up the multiple fragments of the gospel *kerygma* and 'cobbling together'[5] a trajectory towards a universal truth. The point is not that Paul achieves perfection by realizing this universal truth, since 'truth alone is infinite,' and 'the subject is not co-extensive with it'. Rather he is himself a 'fragment of the process of a truth'.[6] Thus the subject emerges through an event which she comes to love:[7] only passion gives rise to subjectivity, as Kierkegaard put it.[8] It is not simply that 'being there' (when resurrection was first proclaimed, when the Red Army stormed the Winter Palace) allows one to come to be as a subject.[9] Fidelity to the event gives rise to any number of subjects, individual and collective, as later generations interpret the event, and constantly rediscover themselves as a kind of 'diagonal of the situation', traced between it and the yet-to-come universal truth that extends outward from it.[10] In describing this path of becoming, Badiou uses language reminiscent of the daughters of Danaus, who refuse to found themselves anywhere but in suspension from an elusive presence: a subject is one 'taken up in fidelity to the event, and suspended from truth; from which it is forever separated by chance',[11] chance: that is, the many contingencies that lie between any given instance of finite fidelity, and the universal articulation of the faithfulness for which the subject strives.

Does this account of emergent subjectivity align with the perfection which Alysoun of Bath 'refuses'? She articulates a gospel perfection which she cannot imagine, and yet her pilgrimage itself is a kind of suspension from an unimaginable end. Perfection calls her, and her drama of refusal fashions a certain fidelity to it, an attempt to become faithful to the gospel's injunction: 'If ye would be perfect . . .' Canterbury is a diagonal line drawn between the event of a call and the ultimate realization of a subjectivity that is all at once individual, social and universal (Alysoun, the Pilgrims, Becket's catholic shrine).

Yet Badiou guards himself against this kind of reading, not least by challenging the poetic quest itself. Poetry 'exhausts itself' by searching for the presence of a nothing, a voice of being or a voice from beyond being, which calls to the poet and asks to be made to come forth into language. Plato is right to banish the poets from the city, since they insist on propagating

---

4 Alain Badiou, 2005, *Being and Event*, trans. Oliver Feltham, London and New York: Continuum Press, pp. 239, 392.

5 Badiou, *Being and Event*, p. 403, 2003, *Saint Paul: The Foundation of Universalism*, trans. Ray Brassier, Stanford: Stanford University Press, pp. 45–47, 98ff.

6 Badiou, *Being and Event*, p. 15.

7 Badiou, *Being and Event*, p. 16.

8 Søren Kierkegaard, *Philosophical Fragments*, trans. Howard Hong and Edna Hong, Princeton: Princeton University Press, pp. 47–8.

9 Badiou, *Being and Event*, p. 237.

10 Badiou, *Being and Event*, p., 392; see also p. 210, and Badiou, 2000, *Deleuze: The Clamor of Being*, Minneapolis: University of Minnesota Press, pp. 52–3.

11 Badiou, *Being and Event*, p. 406.

the ideal 'of an intuition of the nothing in which being would reside when there is not even the site for such an intuition.'[12] By making something of this nothing, they construct a false sovereign, and then call for fidelity to this falsehood as though it were transcendence itself. The trouble, Badiou insists, is with the very idea that truth, and therefore subjective emergence, is somehow written into being or transcribed in some unwritten language as that which gives rise to being. Being is rather an array of uncollected multiples whose proper name is the void, and whose sign is the empty set.[13] The event (resurrection, revolution), which alone gives rise to a set by gathering multiples from the void and counting them as one, is never permitted, always refused by being.

So the poets make us believe they are calling for a perfection of human character that will bring us into alignment with being itself. In fact, the nature for which they pine is not being, but rather a normal, stabilized state of affairs within the discipline of fidelity to a super-ontological event. Nothing calls to the poets except this contingent naturalism, fully immanent to the counted set, itself a product and process of historical choices. Nature (and what is perfection but the blossoming of a nature?) is generated by set-counting, not by being, and this brings it under the purview of the mathematician rather than of the poet. Poetry is 'the *temptation* of a return' which we wrongly take 'to be a nostalgia and a loss, whereas it is merely the permanent play induced in thought by the unrelenting novelty of the *matheme*. Mathematical ontology - labour of the text and of inventive reason – retroactively constituted poetic utterance *as* an auroral temptation, *as* nostalgia for presence and rest.'[14] This retroaction fools the poets into thinking that their quest for emergence is the response to a call that precedes their own labours; in fact the call itself is crafted by the event, as well as by our subsequent interpretation of the diagonals of fidelity to which it gives rise. For this reason, Badiou's subjects emerge without the poetic categories of 'the auroral and the opening-forth'.[15] Nature does not stand sovereign over the trajectory of the subject any more than does God; there is no call from the depths of being into which the subject can quest.

Fidelity is the 'discipline of time',[16] and patterns of fidelity are routes to perfection;[17] but if the situation is not that of a composite entity responding to a transcendent call, what disciplines the career of the subject? For Badiou, it is the event itself: Saint Paul emerges as a subject in his fidelity

---

12 Badiou, *Being and Event*, p. 54; see Peter Hallward, 2003, *Badiou: A Subject to Truth*, Minneapolis: University of Minnesota Press, pp. 199–200.

13 Badiou, *Being and Event*, pp. 66–9, 184–90.

14 Badiou, *Being and Event*, p. 126; see Hallward, *Badiou*, pp. 13, 209ff.

15 Badiou, *Being and Event*, p. 128.

16 Badiou, *Being and Event*, p. 211.

17 I hyphenate here in order to emphasize the etymological sense of the term as a complete-making, since I find this to be compatible with Badiou's language of fidelity and completed trajectories of truth. See *Being and Event*, pp. 394–5. Badiou himself does not make significant philosophical use of the term.

to Christ's Resurrection.[18] And the event? Does it answer a prior call? Surprisingly, Badiou answers this question affirmatively. There is a call for an event, though it is still the *matheme* rather than the poem that it activates. The call issues from an 'excrescence', a site within a unified multiple (a political state, a standard theory of music, a religion) that is presented by the multiple, but whose individual members are unpresented.[19] So for example, within a political state there is a place for the recognition of the peasants; but suppose these represented peasants are, due to the political machinery that supplies them with this place, entirely un-present within the legal decisions of the state? Within a tonally centred orthodox musicology there is a site for an avant garde; but suppose the avant garde suggests an atonality that is ipso facto unrecognizable within the musical academy? Within first-century Roman–Jewish Palestine there is a place for Messianic cults; but suppose one such cult proclaims a Messiah who subverts the social and civic arrangements that permit its existence? Within these historical situations, the sites – 'peasants', 'avant-garde musical theorists' and 'Messiah-cults' – all teeter on the edge of an explosive encounter. Through them, the uncounted void (being) threatens to erupt within the counted multiple of state, theory and religion.[20] And while the unstable site does not render this eruption necessary, still it is only here that such an eruption can happen, as it alone is 'open to the possibility of the event'.[21]

It is precisely here, though, that we find Badiou's revolution to be rather disappointing, since the historicizing of the call only serves to limit the horizons of the event itself. The chance emergence of a pattern of fidelity relies upon this contingent beginning point, the evental site, whatever it may be, and generates itself as an infinitely composable answer to the question this site asks. The evental site of the gospel of resurrection is the sociopolitical situation of first-century Palestine, while the October Revolution's is the collapse of Tsarist Russian under the pressures of war and isolation; the events themselves cannot be predicted by these sites, but they still answer to them alone. So for instance, in order to determine Alysoun of Bath's trajectory of fidelity, we first must determine what event or events situate her world, which means at the same time determining what world situates these events. She herself is a non-teleological subject whose track of becoming is validated retroactively by fidelity to the course that history actually and contingently takes. Her nature is perfected as she emerges as a fidelity to an event, which is in turn a kind of perverse fidelity to an evental site. Likewise the pilgrims together constitute a practice of this fidelity that perfects their mathematically generated nature. The revolution, not answerable to being, responds to its site, and this site continues to direct

---

18 Badiou, *Saint Paul*, pp. 55–74.

19 Badiou, *Being and Event*, p. 207–11.

20 Badiou, *Being and Event*, p. 174–5; Alain Badiou, 2001, *Ethics: An Essay on the Understanding of Evil*, trans. Peter Hallward, London and New York: Verso, pp. 6off. See Hallward, *Badiou*, pp. 116–22.

21 Badiou, *Being and Event*, p. 203.

the course of fidelity, of nature and thus of perfection. The event itself is thus relativized: if he is practising a fidelity to the gospel of resurrection, Saint Paul still remains fully within the horizon of first-century Palestine. In spite of the event that is the object of his passion, Paul is the perfection of pre-resurrection Palestine, the site which situates his pilgrimage like a super-ego governing the journey of a subject.

Badiou thus attempts to articulate a theory of becoming in which no transcendent (unnameable, super-linguistic, posited-though-never-experienced) character whatsoever rides sovereign over the subject's trajectory, including even the 'character' of a Deleuzian virtual. This sort of becoming is, as I have argued throughout this book, of the highest importance for a theory of perfection, since a raw encounter with a pure transcendent can never invite a perfection, only an abolition. Yet Badiou fails to deliver, precisely by immanentizing the event within a historical site. In fact, he never considers the possibility of a One that is neither an anti-multiple sovereignty, negating all language and multiplicity, nor a product of a count within the multiple. Badiou never asks, that is, if there might be a truth that is neither a positivistic transcendence nor a self-perpetuating immanence. No Cusanian *non-aliud* ever complexifies his sets. In the end, his attempt to free Prometheus from the tyranny of eternity fails, because his insurrection is limited to an ever-developing response to an event which is itself called forth by poor parliamentary representation or a narrow-range of acceptable musicologies. This is, admittedly, a kind of perfected nature, given that Badiou redefines nature as the stabilization point within the history of an event, in which no new unpresented multiples threaten eruption. In fact, it is the perfection of a Just-So story: the fidelity provides a subject who emerges as the very thing that the situation itself was calling for, though no one was able to see it at the time. The refrain of the Exposition, above, continues to hold true: Prometheus freed is Prometheus bound, since an immanentized sovereign is just as limiting as a wrathful Jupiter ruling from Olympus.

Divine Modulations

Something calls the temporal creature towards a *summum bonum*; but if it is not the historical setting within which we emerge, what is it? The Catholic phenomenology of Jean-Louis Chrétien bears more promise as a philosophical grammar for perfection since, in the first place, Chrétien allows for a response that answers a far more universal call. Creation itself, the primordial experience of coming-into-being, is the call to which all beings are a response: 'springing into being, we answer'.[22] Granted, one could easily construe this relationship between calling and responding in a positivistic fashion, as if the priority of the call were a temporal or pre-temporal

---

22 Jean-Louis Chrétien, 2004, *Call and the Response*, trans. Anne. A. Davenport, New York: Fordham Press, p. 17.

priority, and the subsequentiality of the response made the creature into an endless quest for the right answer to an unheard question. Chrétien will not let us structure the relationship like this, arguing instead that call and response mutually embrace one another.[23] The bodily forms of creatures are but 'modulations of the initial call',[24] thus rendering beings as fundamentally percussive: the various vibrations we formulate within our organs and cavities can only ever be responses to the variety of touches - a light tap, a violent pound, a gentle rub, the stroke of a brush - that call us into being.[25] The accidental touch of a stranger's hand on my arm is a reminder, a distance echoing, of the original calling-into-being of creation, and if I respond by acknowledging the existence of the stranger, I have in this small respect come to be. Thus 'any radical thought of the call implies that the call is heard only in the response'.[26] The *poesis* through which a creature emerges as a history of response constructs, without constituting, the very voice that invites her to be: our poetic labours are 'the perpetual memorial of what exceeds us'.[27]

Like the stranger at my arm, the muse speaks in a voice that the poet can hear only in his own crafted poems, otherwise the excess would destroy the medium. But 'grace does not come to abolish nature but to perfect it'.[28] The musician stands in the place of muse for her own music-making: so if the skin of a drum can respond to the palm's invitation, this is only because it has a prior kinship with the surface of the hand. The drum comes to be as a materialized desire to sing back to the taut skin of the drummer. Following Philo, Chrétien suggests that the unique place of the human within creation is as that being who lives as a self-offered response and thus as the voice through which 'the world offers itself to God'.[29] So 'when the world was finished, God asked an angel if there was any creature missing. "He, it is said, made answer that all were perfect and complete in all their parts, and that he was looking for one thing only, namely the world to sound their praises . . ."'[30] In response to this lack, God made human beings.

In this way, Chrétien acknowledges, with Badiou, that the world is a multiplicity – even ungathered multiples – which must be counted-as-one in order to actually become a unity, and so also to trace a unified trajectory toward a *telos*. For both, there can be no simple givenness of a *telos*, and so the subject emerges precariously through this very count-as-one, diagonalized between the immemorial and the unhoped for: 'Every utterance trembles

---

23 Chrétien, *Call and the Response*, p. 5.

24 Chrétien, *Call and the Response*, p. 16.

25 Chrétien, *Call and the Response*, p. 56.

26 Chrétien, *Call and the Response*, p. 30.

27 Jean-Louis Chrétien, 2002, *The Unforgettable and the Unhoped For*, trans. Jefrey Bloechl, New York: Fordham University Press, p. 39.

28 Jean-Louis Chrétien, 2004, *The Ark of Speech*, trans. Andrew Brown, London and New York: Routledge, p. 120.

29 Chrétien, *The Ark of Speech*, pp.123–4.

30 Chrétien, *The Ark of Speech*, p. 122, quoting Philo's *De Platatione*.

and resonates between two abysses, the abyssal origin of the call that makes utterance possible and the abyssal final term of the perfected answer . . .'[31] This response is always choral, establishing *ecclesia* as a community of fidelity, a communion that exists through intentionally guessing at God through the various poetic constructions of a life.[32] The difference between this count and Badiou's count is that a transcendent call, constituted nowhere but in the count, can also for Chrétien be 'proper', ontological, and thus the resting place of a nature which the call always exceeds. The count, in other words, is a hymn of praise: 'Even a detailed enumeration of things does not make a world. It is by being sung that the world is properly a world, grasped in its unity.'[33] So humans construct their own perfection in crafting the call within their response; but this is also the perfecting of the world, which awaits the singing of its own song in the human hymn.

Theorizing that *poesis*, as hymnody, is secondary, Chrétien can acknowledge that it simply does not register on the grid of Promethean *mythos*. A responsive *telos* is not 'something to be wrenched away from the gods, conquered or stolen from them in a hostile manner.' Rather, it is always humanly crafted, but humanly-crafted-as-divinely-given.[34]

The question then must be – and the plot of this entire book hangs on this question – how does the poetic hymn that humans compose construct a divine call that perfects and does not destroy the natural creation? Can Prometheus offer himself, and through himself can he offer the world, as a response to an originary call, without thereby voiding the contingencies, limitations and becomings of creaturely life? Can he praise Jupiter? Or by doing so does he tragically acknowledge that the only human *telos* is the anti-*telos* of a non-celestial career, an obedience to a sovereign that asks only for the self-annihilation of human language, human culture, human desire?

'To sing the song of the world in the chorus is to become oneself, irreplaceably.'[35] Chrétien's project is, in one sense, the quest for a non-Promethean perfection (as opposed to an anti-Promethean, which is to say he seeks a perfectionism dependent on gift rather than on avoidance of theft), a vision of a sacramental community whose history and emergent essence is the reception of the gift of sanctifying fire. Even as he gestures toward such a perfection, however, his phrases and arguments shroud this vision with ambiguity. Prayer, he says, is 'the religious phenomenon par excellence',[36] and the human act in which the creative call and creative response are most fully sounded. Here listening is perfected, since speaking takes place only by the forming of words that precede it, to which we must

---

31 Chrétien, *Call and Response*, p. 20; See *Unforgettable*, p. 37: 'Recollection . . . makes us catch hold of ourselves from out of the immemorial truth.'

32 Chrétien, *Call and Response*, p. 20.

33 Chrétien, *The Ark of Speech*, p. 32.

34 Chrétien, *The Ark of Speech*, p. 144.

35 Chrétien, *The Ark of Speech*, p. 147.

36 Chrétien, *The Ark of Speech*, p. 17.

give ear. Machines cannot pray because they cannot listen.[37] But how does this listening happen when we pray? For Chrétien, it is centrally a matter of self-effacement, of annihilating all language and rhetoric that might shade the message of the call. 'To listen with my particularities, in other words with my habits and prejudices, with my predilections and my resentments, with my memories and my dreams', always implies 'forcing the words of the other into the Procrustean bed of everything that is most contingent and most accidental about me'. Over against this failed praying/listening, it is only 'when a man burns in the fire of attention the dead wood of his particularities, when he allows the words of the other to unfold in a silence that is rustling with meaning', that he truly listens: 'by effacing himself, he becomes properly himself'.[38]

Prayer, then, is a matter of standing down before the voice, coming to a kind of ontic silence that ends all rhetoric, since rhetoric is fundamentally a reliance on phrases and linguistic rhythms too familiar to allow us to hear alterity through them.[39] However, in this case, what has become of the responding that perfects human *energia*? Though critical of any conception of the call and response that 'makes use of our voice by dispossessing us entirely in order to keep the origin unaltered',[40] Chrétien himself seems at a loss as to how precisely to conceive the relation any other way. Human creativity itself becomes theologically problematic for him, and its old enemy *humilitas* returns to put it in its place. When he recounts the history of the relation of divine creativity and human making, he points to a movement through the ages that subtly and gradually erases the theologically fundamental dissemblance between them. Early on, in Augustine, the notion of human *poesis* as a kind of creation 'does not issue from a profane tradition wherein rebellious man takes the place of the God he rejects', and is thus not incompatible with Christian humility.[41] By the time we come to Ficino and Cusanus, though, this analogy issues in theological disaster. The 'victory of "creating" over the "making of a work" '[42] takes shape in these texts as an impious quest for Godlikeness. The work of human hands comes to resemble too much the work of divine hands: 'the distance between the two arts is reduced'.[43] In tandem with this reduction, Chrétien faults a contemplative fellowship within the life of the Trinity which, while 'intellectually thrilling', is nonetheless a stage in the undoing of proper *humilitas*. For this mystical notion allows us to think of the Father as artist, bringing forth the Son in a way that resembles too much the painter 'begetting' an image onto a canvas.[44] The only properly

---

37 Chrétien, *The Ark of Speech*, p. 15.
38 Chrétien, *The Ark of Speech*, p. 10.
39 Chrétien, *The Ark of Speech*, p. 13.
40 Chrétien, *Call and Response*, p. 27.
41 Jean-Louis Chrétien, 2003, *Hand to Hand: Listening to the Work of Art*, trans. Stephen E. Lewis, New York: Fordham Press, p. 113.
42 Chrétien, *Hand to Hand*, p. 124.
43 Chrétien, *Hand to Hand*, p. 115.
44 Chrétien, *Hand to Hand*, pp. 111–12.

Christian construction of human and divine activity for Chrétien is finally a dialectical one, where the human maker, naturally and eschatologically *ad extra* to the Triune God, knows her activity to be perfect precisely insofar as it is human rather than divine. Likewise divine perfection is discernible only in its refusal of analogy. But here we are back to Prometheus after all, though siding with the Olympians over the Titan. Our perfection lies in accepting our lack of participation in the divine; the road to human destruction is in the over-reaching aspirations of deification.

Chrétien's view of poetry in this is the opposite of Badiou's, Plato was wrong, for him, to exile the composers of verse. Significantly, both Badiou and Chrétien have Heidegger in mind when they consider poetry and the poets. The 'presence' that Badiou refuses, as the natural unveiling of being, is the Heidegerrian *Ereignis*. Heidegger's 'poetic-natural orientation, which lets-be-presentation as non-veiling' eclipses emergence and the diagonal struggle to the point even of its insistence on the passive voice.[45] Likewise, though reciprocally, Chrétien argues that it is Heidegger, rather than Eriugena, Ficino and Cusanus, who points the way toward a theologically proper relation of human handiwork to divine creativity.[46] In 'that saying which speaks in the elements of a poem', Heidegger indicates the possibility of an aboriginal speech 'devoid of creativity'.[47] While Heidegger errs in suggesting the possibility of a correspondence between our poetic silence and being's primordial call, since the call is always excessive of the response, he is fundamentally correct in positing an access to the origin through a kind of anti-poetic poetry.[48]

This Heideggerian fulcrum reveals an important element to the narrative of mythopoetic intrusion: namely, that the dialectic of the Promethean/anti-Promethean does not correspond, as we might assume, to the modern division of philosophy/theology. In fact, there is a rather easily discernible division in the last century within Continental philosophy, between Bergsonian Prometheans, Delueze (Badiou, Žižek, Brassier) and Heideggerian anti-Prometheans (Derrida, Levinas, Marion, Chrétien). If the former proceed with the assumption that subjects emerge only by throwing off all forms of sovereignty, the latter follow the Heideggerian imperative to 'let something else arrive and come to presence'.[49] Subjects only come to be by withdrawing before the other, by refusing all assertion in a quest for a *telos* that completes only by annihilating, by losing oneself while 'saving the unconcealedness of what is'.[50] In Chrétien's final rejec-

---

45 Badiou, *Being and Event*, p. 125.

46 Chrétien, *Hand to Hand*, p. 125.

47 Chrétien, *Call and Response*, p. 6.

48 Chrétien, *Call and Response*, pp. 27–31.

49 Martin Heidegger, 'What Calls for Thinking?', in David Farrell Krell (ed. and trans.), 1993, *Basic Writings*, San Francisco: Harper Publishers, p. 388.

50 Martin Heidegger, 'Origin of the Work of Art', in *Basic Writings*, p. 74; See also 'What are Poets For?', in Heidegger, 1971, *Poetry, Language, Thought*, trans. Albert Hofstadter, New York: Harper Collins, p. 135.

tion of human creativity as too analogous to the inner-workings of the Trinity, the dialectic is still intact: perfection is either the titanic rebellion against sovereignty, which always amounts to a new sort of binding, or the surrender of a nature-perfecting *telos* in favour of a nihilistic humility. Significantly, both options refuse deification: the Bergsonian, because naming God as *telos* limits human freedom;[51] the Heideggerian, because a supernatural *telos* dethrones the humility that has become the principal human virtue. Our perfection lies either in refusing God in order to be divine ourselves, or in refusing godliness in order to allow God to be perfect. Contemporary philosophy, even the discipline-bending philosophy considered here, is unable to imagine a trajectory beyond the forked path of modern Prometheanism.

Making the Unmakeable

A Christian account of perfection requires a construal of human activity as mediative of a supernatural end. The philosophical work of Badiou and Chrétien point in the direction of this construal, even if ultimately without success. How might theology proceed, taking cues from their constructions, and correcting them where they come up short?

The failures of theological accounts of perfection most often involve the conception of human activity as deifying-to-a-degree, before that activity comes up against the limit at which humanity would encroach too much on the insular divine perfections. At this point, wherever that limit lies, humanity stands down and allows divinity to complete the task. Human enquiry ceases in the pre-revelatory end of metaphysics (Scotus); human agency returns to earth after a mid-level flight (*Ovide moralisé*); human holiness rests in the meadow of humility where we can finish our days as in an earthly cud-chewing repose (Malory).

This failure is in the first place a Christological one, implying as it does that Christ's humanity itself had to stand down at some point in order to refuse infringement upon his divinity: *humilitas malum* is thus an anthropological Nestorianism.[52] The life of Christ suggests, instead, that human perfection is always a human craft, though this craft does not reduce the excessive and uncrafted divinity. So Jesus is fully divine on earth, and yet makes enquiries and intercessions to his Father in heaven, often experiencing and expressing the painful tension between the God-above and his own

---

51 See for instance Žižek, in Creston Davis (ed.), 2009, *The Monstrosity of Christ*, Cambridge, MA and London: MIT Press, pp. 82–9, 242–3, where he associates the receptiveness of supernatural deification, negatively, with a feminizing character of mainstream religious thought.

52 Aaron Riches, 2008, 'After Chalcedon: The Oneness of Christ and the Dyothelitic Mediation of His Theandric Unity', *Modern Theology* 24 (2), pp. 199–224, and also the forthcoming *Christ the End of Humanism*, Grand Rapids: Eerdmans.

God-craft below.[53] Jesus emerges in the Gospels as a different character from God; this is not because he is human rather than divine, but because his human relation to God is already founded in the eternal relation of Logos to *Theos*, of *Huiou* to *Pater*. The incarnate Son can turn to the Father, long for the Father, pray to the Father, only because the Second Person of the Trinity is eternally distinct from and consubstantial with the Father (Augustine). The hypostatic distinctions erect religious gaps within God, the religious gap that separates Jesus of Nazareth from his Father in heaven is but an earthly refraction of this division-for-union (Origen). By not-being-the-Father, the heavenly Son can be an *energeia* of the Father's love; by this same not-being-the-Father, the earthly Son can be this divine *energeia* in an earthly way. Thus what appears in Galilee is divine poetry: a human journey that constructs life as the way-into-God. That this poem says 'God is other' does not install an uncrossable division between heaven and earth; rather, it makes the gap present only by constructing a causeway across it. While Christ's divinity is always excessive of his humanity, this does not supply it with a separate faculty within his being. The outcome of several centuries of Christological debate led to the conclusion that the divinity of the incarnate Son does not appear at all: divine perfection only manifests itself in his life as a hidden excess of human perfecting. The babe in the manger governs at the creation; the man who progresses in virtue is the unchanging God. The humanity of Christ thus makes use of all the spatial and temporal limitations of the creature to diagonalize his humanity into his kenotically-absent-but-ontologically-basic divinity.

This Christic diagonal provides the structure for all Christian speculation on human perfection. To conceive of the gap between heaven and earth as a barrier that protects the integrity of God from human incursion, or the integrity of humanity from divine incursion, is to conceive of it in a post-Christian way. Likewise, to conceive of the gap in as a tragic situation that will make the human *telos* into a self-defeating one is to conceive of it in a pre-Christian way. The revolutionary anthropology that the Christ-event initiates orients itself on the diagonal, so that human cultural activity can become a mediation of divine grace. Said otherwise: in light of Christ's own *poesis*, we can now see divine grace as perfecting, rather than destroying, the lives that humans make. 'Christian perfection', first in Christ, then through Christ for all humanity, is 'the temporal form of eternal life'.[54]

We are now in a place to see the importance of the too-perfect God of Israel's priestly redactors for a proper understanding of Christian perfection. The God of the Elohist, like the Athenian gods, could be affected, appeased and seduced, and so was also a God unable to save humanity from the evils hovering around materiality. The priestly conception of God in the Old Testament allows us to imagine, for the first time, a God

---

53 See Ira Brent Driggers, 2007, *Following God through Mark: Theological Tension in the Second Gospel*, Louisville, Westminster John Knox, especially pp. 99ff.

54 Alan Gregory, 2008, *Quenching Hell: The Mystical Theology of William Law*, New York: Seabury Books, p. 18.

utterly beyond *genesis*. The priests themselves must eat the shewbread, because Yahweh cannot be moved by the smell of rising dough or grilled meat. A God who is in this way beyond earthly intrigue is also beyond competitive entanglements with his own creatures. The path is thus open for an earthly progress up Sinai's slopes that will never in any conceivable fashion violate the otherness of God. When the scribes of the Holiness School reassert the Elohistic dynamic, they do so in light of these priestly concerns, and thus are able to imagine Israel's holiness as a movement toward the God who is immovably holy. Only after the Elohistic emphasis on imitative holiness collides with the priestly insistence that God's holiness separates him forever from human imitation, can the Holiness School transcribe a God who extends the invitation to 'be holy because I am holy.' All three schools are finally mutually supportive, since only one whose holiness is perfect beyond compare is able to grant to his people a comparative holiness.

Taken up into Christian reflection, this becomes the insight that human perfection is a sharing in a super-teleological perfection. The commerce between divinity and humanity that is the life of Christ makes participation in divinity a human-perfecting end. God has no *telos*, no 'perfection' at all, in so far as this implies completion-through-making (Thomas). God is perfect only metaphorically, similar to the way in which God is said to be moved with anger, pity or compassion: he is this 'motion' in an immovable way, and upon which we can only speculate. And it is precisely this insight into divinity that allows creaturely perfection. Motion itself is a trajectory towards God's immovability. To suggest that creatures are imperfectible because they are always changing is already to confuse the teleological orientation and the super-teleological *telos*. The paradox of perfection then is this: to have a perfection is to be in motion toward a particular end; humans have no such perfection, insofar as the end toward which we move is perfect only by being beyond perfection. Our end is to rest in the super-*telos* of God, and for this we rely on the grace for which our nature is most suited. Only a God who knows no becoming can share himself in such a way as to make becoming itself a path toward being divine; only a God beyond perfection can invite us to become perfect as he is perfect.

The holiness-sharing God never encounters creation in raw and sublime divinity, since this would annihilate the gifts that make creatures who they are. Satanic deification asks the human to die to humanity in order to become God (Milton, John of the Cross); Christ's way is to invite the human to become God by becoming more human. But this means that human invocations of the divine will always have the character of the hypothetical about them. Chrétien is entirely right to say that the divine call never encounters us anywhere but in the human response. He falters though, through a concern that the human response will always taint the call which it constructs. Is this not the deep secret of divine grace? God shares himself, even his intra-Trinitarian relatedness, in relating to creation, so that the impurities of human creation – motion, language, mutability, desire – do not simply taint our construction of the divine, but can also mediate the divine to us. The stock phrases[55] and imaginative images that populate our prayers do not simply get in the way of grace, since God's gifts always take the shape, as Paul says, of a Spirit who interprets our humanity through the text of the Son's (Rom. 8). It is not by neglecting or denying our humanity that we are made gods, but by invoking the divine Spirit to modulate our humanity in harmony with Christ's, since Christ's humanity is already a modulation of divinity. Thus humans achieve perfection through the remarkably translative act according to which our prayers, which consist of human language, human speculation and enmeshment in human culture, come to God's ears in a supremely divine, deifying act of speech: 'Our Father, who art in heaven . . .'

This translation would indeed be an annihilation, if God's perfection were something creatures could 'become'. But prayer never changes God, as Thomas argues (*ST* II–II.83.2), precisely because God is beyond the threat of any genetic encroachment. Becoming God is not something God can do at all; it is the ultimate creaturely act. If all human work is potentially a sharing in divine *poesis*, primarily in the Father's eternal generating of the Son, then prayer is the thin place of human–divine poetry, the site where heavenly and earthly activity come to be most entangled with one another. That we can encounter God through human praying is not evidence that we are able to forget ourselves. Rather it shows that God has imbued our language at its fullest with the ability to make us perfect, through making the unmakeable name of the beyond-perfect God. So to lose oneself in prayer to the Creator is to find oneself as a creature (Mark 8.35), because the name 'made' by our prayers is our own. This is what it means to share in the life of the Triune God, and to become perfect by resting in the divine perfection.

---

55 Lewis, *Preface to Paradise Lost*, pp. 21–2.

Postlude

Theosis and Insurrection:
A Non-Lyrical Drama
Or
Prometheus Perfected

> Man is . . . a revolution.
>
> G. K. Chesterton

Preface

If the preceding chapters are correct, modern Christianity has got the wrong *mythos*, and so is no longer capable of understanding what the New Testament and the Church Fathers mean by 'perfection'. Philosophers have unwittingly accepted this intrusive mythology, and indeed fed it back to theologians, so that its aporetic human *telos* seems now to be an unquestionable axiom of our being.

If the Prometheus of the tragedians, translated into the static ontology of the moderns, is the wrong myth for Christian perfection, what is the right one? How might we retranscribe the ancient myth in a way that aligns with the anthropology of the Sermon on the Mount, and with the pre-modern conception of a grace that perfects rather than destroys? Spenser, Milton and even Shelley were all on the track of something of this sort, though all demonstrate in various ways a failure of theological imagination that limits their craft. If I attempt something of this sort here, as a way of correcting a theological error, I harbour no presumptions – I should hope it goes without saying – of improving upon their artistry. They were master poets; I am a hack. I hope only to suggest that a deeper theological vision could have greatly improved their art, without myself attempting to approach their heights.

Thus I humbly offer the following Promethean drama as the final word of this argument. Like Shelley's, my Prometheus is not a Titan once thrown down from heaven, but the archetypal human, attempting to come to terms with his own *telos*. The reader will observe many phrases and ideas in the dialogue taken from the preceding chapters, and I hope the allusions will be obvious.

Diagonal Advance

Dramatis Personae: Prometheus, a Stranger, Vesta
Setting: A cliff midway up a peak in the Caucasus Mountains. Morning. Prometheus is chained to a rock. Alongside him is the Stranger, also chained.

Theosis and Insurrection

Prometheus: The sun's rays break upon us, my friend, and so begins another day in our eternity of torment. Shall we begin with our rite of morning ministrations?

Stranger: Yes, I'm never ready to face the day before I've splashed water in my face and bent down to touch my toes at least six times.

P: I'll do those things in a slightly adapted version. With arms far from toes as from face, I'll greet the morning in the way that I can, seeing to the waking of face and limbs by the curses that tumble off my lips.

S: As you see fit.

P: Well then:
Sunlight, have you come again to taunt me with your scalding rays and your freedom of motion? I, Prometheus, curse you today as I did yesterday, and will be so true as to follow-up tomorrow as well.

Illuminated world, do you now glow in the sun's rays in order to taunt me with your change? While I stay fastened interminably here, your flowers open then close, then wilt, then are reborn. Midway up a peak I shall neither surmount nor descend, I sit and watch the display that you wish me to praise as beauty and I curse it as futility. There is no change – you are as locked into your existence as I mine. Neither of us were free to begin to be, neither of us free to be as we will. Our only freedom is suicide, and I will not grant the creator such pleasure as to take this course. But you, world, I would welcome you to give it some thought. Perhaps it would be the best course for us all. I curse you, world.

Creator, have you hung me here, halfway between heaven's perfection and earth's tediousness, in order to give me just enough of a glimpse into your abode as to know what I lack? You have hung me with a rope round my throat, not dropping me from your palace walls so as to break my neck – no, you would not be so merciful – but easing me into place so as to watch me asphyxiate for all eternity. Have you made a show of granting me a share in your attributes of science and power, all the while holding back the real gifts for yourself? I curse you, Creator. Better to have made a stone shaped like a Human, or never to have made one at all, than to set a living, breathing, desiring creation here, chained to this misery. You ask that I accept my plight? You know I cannot submit. And the reason you know it is because you created me with this desire to be, to know, to encompass the world, and then you commanded me to rebuke these very desires. So is my lot to wear either the chains of a prisoner, or the chains of a humble slave? I'll take the former, you wretch of a tyrant. You'll get no humility from me, having cheated me out of the very gifts you mock me by displaying. I curse you, Creator, with every breath and every sinew, I curse you!

S: That bit about death by hanging was new, wasn't it?

P: Yes, it was in fact. Did you like it?

S: A particularly nice touch. It accents the entire thing beautifully. You should remember that one for tomorrow.

P: Thanks, Stranger. I think I will.

S: I've been meaning to ask, by the way, what you mean when you say the Creator has granted you a share of his attributes, but held the good parts back?

P: All these years, hanging side by side, and you've never asked me that question. What have we been talking about all this time, anyway?

S: Yes, strange to think, isn't it? We should really talk more, you know, to pass the time more pleasantly. Anyway, about the attributes?

P: The Creator, who is infinite in knowledge, power and governance, made the cosmos as a symphonic display of all his virtues. Each particular creation was given its place, becoming a finite reflection of the God's infinity. And as part of this reflecting, each thing was given an end to achieve. When flowers bloom, when antelope leap, when waves hit the shore, all these things come to their ends, and rest in a happiness of their own kind, thereby praising the Creator who contains all ends in his simplicity.

S: That's lovely. This is the same Creator you just finished cursing?

P: But you see, the one creature for whom this didn't work out so well was the Human. He made me higher than the rest of the natural world, giving me a mind capable of reflecting upon the cosmos, and reflecting on my own place within it.

S: I am corrected: that wretch of a tyrant.

P: But you don't see yet. A wave can reach its own perfection, will, in fact, when it touches the shore. An antelope when it has leapt about, or whatever those ridiculous and perennially adolescent things do. But the creature that is given the ability to see what it all means can never be happy. I know just enough to know that I will only die ignorant, I see just enough to see my own nearsightedness. I am the only one created without any perfection.

S: And so you are chained?

P: All things are chained, Stranger. It's just that I embrace mine, and other beings carry on as if they are not bound to their own misery. There they are, down in the lowlands, submitting to the laws governing their existence. These chains I can live with; those would destroy my spirit.

S: Yes, I see that now. Now I see. You know, not being native to this valley, I never have got quite familiar with its way of explaining things.

P: Now that you mention it, I thought I was picking up an accent of some sort. Elea is it?

S: Not far from there.

P: Nice in the summers there, isn't it? Maybe a bit breezy in the evenings?

S: Yes, a mixture. I was about to say, though, that we too have a story we tell of how we came to be the creatures that we are. If you've got some time free, I'll tell it to you.

P: Well, alright, as long as it won't take a minute longer than forever.

S: I'll watch the time then. But I'm afraid I'll have to present you with a little prologue first, as my people never can say what a Human is without first explaining why a Human is.

P: I'd pray to be hanged if I thought it would change anything.

S: Our story goes like this. When Jupiter was first born from Saturn's belly, he lived in Saturn's palaces, at Saturn's table, and laughed upon Saturn's lap. The father loved this son immensely, and rarely spoke of anything else. In the evenings, they would sit together around the hearth, and, while its fires warmed them, Saturn would tell his beloved son stories of the ancient ones, and the son would sing the songs or recite the poems he had learned in court.

P: Who was Jupiter's mother?

S: Not the point.

P: Apologies. Continue.

S: One day, as he was just coming of age, Jupiter came into his father's throne room and asked permission to go abroad, and discover the far ends of heaven. Now, Saturn was greatly troubled by this request, and for two reasons. First, because he knew of the dangers lurking in the shadows in these remote parts, but also simply because he had become so accustomed to his son's presence that he could no longer imagine passing a day without him. Later that evening, after Jupiter had left the room, Saturn discussed the matter with Vesta, keeper of the heavenly hearth, who had come in as she always did to tend the fire. After hearing her advice, Saturn decided to allow his son to go, and blessed him, though his worries were far from dispelled.

P: Are the Gods of Elea chronic worriers, would you say?

S: A few days later young Jupiter left, and made his way beyond the castle walls, and out into the open plains of heaven and beyond. Saturn wept to see his son go, and then again each night that he was away. Night after night, till weeks, then months went by, and Saturn heard nothing from his child. Finally he could endure the crushing sadness no more. 'Vesta,' he said, as she came to stoke the fire one evening, 'I fear for my beloved son. Will you go to him?' 'My king,' she said, 'you know I will give my very life for him. But how am I to find him?' 'Go and search the ends of heaven for him. Into every cave, onto every beach, upon every hilltop and down in every gulley. Take my hearth fire with you, so that when you find him you may keep him warm.'

So Vesta too made her departure, journeyed out beyond the castle walls, and headed out into the open plains of heaven and beyond. She took coals from her hearth with her, carrying them in an urn on top of her head. She searched for many weeks, into every cave, on every shore, upon every hilltop, and down in every gulley. At last, nearly giving up hope, she came upon a deep cavern that opened in the earth, and there at the bottom, many fathoms down, she found the boy. He was thin as a rake, and shivering from fear as much as from cold. Vesta called to him, and then began climbing down the steep cavern wall to where he had fallen. Finally reaching the base of the hole, she hugged the boy close to her, and built up her hearth fire until he was warm and comforted.

So great was Saturn's joy when he saw Vesta coming down the road with the boy in her arms that he ran out to greet them when they were still a long way off. 'My son!' he cried. 'My son is alive! There will be feasting in heaven tonight!' And a feast there was, the way my people tell it. The next year, on that night, and each year after, the Gods held an annual feast to mark the great event of Jupiter's return.

Many years later, on the night of the great festival, Saturn, whom I suspect had taken in a bit too much wine . . .

P: I'm beginning to think I like the sound of your gods better than ours.

S: . . . stood at the traditional point of the toast, and said, 'My friends, this year, in honour of my beloved son's return from the far reaches of heaven, I will do something more than feast in his honour. With my son and my faithful Vesta, I will create a world modelled on his very journey. I will call this world 'earth', and as the shadowlands of heaven are far from my throne, so the earth itself will come to be across an immeasurable distance from all of heaven. I will form creatures there on this earth, and give them life, as my own son found new life across the heavens. And as Vesta, true and loyal keeper of my hearth, found my beloved there in the cavern and brought him back to me, so she herself will journey into this earth, and give my own hearth fire to all the creatures that awaken to life upon it.'

There was great applause at this idea, though I'd imagine Saturn got a rather punctuated glare from Vesta, as she tended the fire in the midst of the party. But Saturn wasn't finished yet. 'And finally, upon the earth I will place one, whom I will call the Human, who will be upon it as my own son is here in heaven to me. All these other creatures will receive my hearthfire in view of their very existence; the Human will receive it with the consciousness that its very warmth is my love. As my son received in the heavens my love from the hand of Vesta that day, so will my Human form receive it, and so will this creature alone receive the gift of offering back to me its love.'

The very next morning, they set about this work, a task such as no heavenly beings before had ever undertaken. Standing on the palace walls, Jupiter recounted his journey into the hinterlands, sentence by sentence, describing each day, each encounter, each new discovery with careful detail. Each time he paused for a breath, his father, seated as his side, spoke the words, 'Let it be so.' Each sentence thus gave birth to a new created form, until by evening a land stretched out in the emptiness beyond the heavens, filled with great oaks and sycamores, mountains, seas, land animals and insects and monsters of the deep waters.

All was formed, full of colour and definition, but all was still and quiet, like a painting of a basket of fruit. Then, in that very first evening of the world, Saturn turned to Vesta and asked, 'Will you go then?' So Vesta went, carrying her coals in an urn upon her head. As she passed through the land, all the creatures around her surged forth with life and longing, the sycamores stretching up out of the river banks toward the heavens, the oaks swelling thick and strong, the oceans moving to a constant rhythm, all the while teeming with the chaos of life within. Other heavenly beings followed after Vesta with joy, and they became the nymphs and sprites that choreograph earth's motions. They danced along the riverbanks, rising and falling, changing steps and singing together the music of creation.

At this display, all the heavens erupted in applause. But Saturn silenced them all with a wave of his hand, a stern look of concentration on his brow. 'All is not yet perfect,' said he. 'Tell me, my son, of that day when she found you in the cavern.' So Jupiter told of that day, of the fear, the despair, the cold and the loneliness, but also of the hope in his father, of his trust in him and of his joy in seeing Vesta and the warmth and comfort he received from her. As he told of all this, Saturn reached into his creation, and gathered up from the four directions the four elements that gave it substance and placed them in a great iron kettle in the middle of the newly formed land. As Jupiter's words rolled over the heavenly walls and down into the creation, they passed over the top of the kettle. When the elements within began to mix and mingle, Saturn said, 'Let it be so.' And as the mingled elements came to rest, all saw there draped over the rim the still form of a Human. Naked and beautiful, neither man nor woman; soft and vulnerable, without any protective shell, fur or scales. And there was silence in heaven for a period of the evening.

Then Saturn turned to Vesta once again. 'This is my beloved. Will you go to it?' 'I would give my very life for it,' she whispered back. And so the Human awoke, and the fire of Vesta was in its soul and in its eyes. But her coals were also in the creature's home: the Human built a dwelling place to take shelter from the winds and rains, and Vesta's fire burned gently in the Human hearth. She herself came into the dwelling every evening, as she does in Saturn's own abode, to stoke and tend the fire. And she would stay late into the night hours, talking and laughing with the Human, hearing its stories and poems, its plans and its memories. Then she would depart, and though the Human would fall into a sleep, like the stillness of death, it would awaken the next morning, like Jupiter reborn that day in heaven's far country, to the glow of Vesta's embers. As it awoke, the Human confessed each morning its love for Saturn.

P: Well, at least Vesta kept him company for a few hours. Still though, it sounds like a lonely existence. Was this first Human, in the way that you Eleatics tell it, happy with the straw that it drew?

S: Happy in a perfectly Human sort of way, which is to say that it was not in a constant state of bliss, for nothing in Saturn's creation is constant: its very beauty is in its mutability. So the Human too, as we tell it, would often feel the chill of loneliness in the twilight hours, as it went about its work, just as Jupiter had in the far reaches. But the hearth fires would then greet it, and Vesta would bring comfort and companionship to it.

P: And what was the work to which this first Human set about? In the way that you of Elea tell it, I mean?

S: The hosts of heaven used to sing of the magnificent labours of Saturn's crowning creation. All other creatures had as their calling the performance of a particular rite, celebrating a stage of Jupiter's heavenly journey. But to the Human alone Saturn gave the task of crafting the journey itself.

P: I don't see what you mean.

S: All things are, in the depths of their being, the story that Jupiter told at the dawn of the world. But the Human became Jupiter himself to the world, the storyteller, whose task it was to craft a journey to the ends of the earth, as Jupiter had before it journeyed to the ends of heaven. The Human made the earth itself into a journey from and to Saturn's dwelling, by giving a name to each and every creature, each turn of the path, each new day, as a way of marking its place in Jupiter's story. Heavenly abundance fills the earth, but it fills it like the harvest fills an orchard: an abundance that falls to the ground when it is untended and unnamed. This is what Saturn meant by saying that the world was not yet perfect before his final creation. The Gods made the world, but the Human made the world into a hymn to the Gods.

P: But if the rhythms of creation are in its nature, then all was in a state of passing away. Even the Human could do nothing but identify the particular path towards death that each thing, including itself, must take. All comes from nothing and returns to nothing, like the blooms of spring and the breath of a child. You might argue that all the earth is a rhythm of becoming, I'll say this same thing by arguing that all is in a state of decaying. And if the Human is the one conscious of this, then it is its fate to lose everything, even eventually itself. I've heard this song before, my friend. It names the world that I've come to hate.

S: But we do not simply say that all was made to become, we say that all was made to become God. Saturn gave to the Human not simply a genesis, but a *telos*, so that the work it did, pruning vines, tending animals, baking bread, weaving cloth, making tents and ships for its longer journeys . . . all this was patterned on Jupiter's narrative. They were perfect tents and ships and names, not in that they were flawless in an earthly sense, since again, earthly perfection has nothing to do with permanence or flawlessness. The cloth had snags, the ships needing patching. But they were perfect in that they were suited precisely for an earthly telling of Jupiter's story. In a sense then, yes, as you say, the Human was created for loss. The cloth it wove, the cities it built, the names it invented, the friendships it forged, it would lose or forget it all and watch much of it decay before it. The only thing, in fact, the Human could ever possess, is union with the one beyond losing. And this was to be its perfection. Its energies and labours, its rest by the fire, all of this amounted to a striving after Saturn, which, by Saturn's own gift, the Human was to achieve in due time. Time itself is this gift, in fact. Perhaps you imagine that we strive for union with the Gods in ways that are accommodated to worldly time? In my land we say that time is the name of this human labour. We stretch forward toward our reunion with Saturn, and we call 'time' the periods and eras of the striving. So each night, when Vesta departed from the Human's house and her fire waned to embers, creation was found to be nearer to heaven, and another moment in the earthly telling of Jupiter's journey home was perfected.

P: I think I see, Stranger, though your story and your gods may be more interesting and dynamic than mine, still the human role is the same. We hover above creation, but under the supreme authority of the Gods. We are like governors and task masters who fear the constant presence of an emperor. Thus we name and create, but never freely. All our work is decreed to us by the God, and human morality consists in nothing but submission to these inscrutable decrees. You see now why rebellion is the only perfection for me? I will not submit, I will use my very boundedness as the occasion for the only freedom that I have: the freedom to curse. An insurrection of words and will, if not of motion and action.

S: But my friend, you don't yet see what we mean to say about the place of the Human. You imagine the Gods to interact with their creation like, as you say, a king or emperor commands serfs and task masters. But we imagine the heavens to be utterly separate from the earth, and the Creator to be utterly distinct from creation.

P: And how does this make a difference in the way that they interact? A king at a distance is still sovereign.

S: True, but this is no king at a distance. Jupiter in the hinterlands was outside the palace and fields of his father, and so the boy had to imagine anew what a son of Saturn would do and say, and where a son of Saturn would go, as he travelled those untrodden paths. The Human likewise is placed in a land of utter novelty. What decree could command the deeds of a day, when each day is a new invention, in which the powers of the Gods, the rhythms of nature, and the mind and hand of the Human all cooperate? No moment has occurred before it is already past, and so the world must be named and made anew a thousand times and more a day. And this is the labour of the Human. To make Jupiter, you might say, out of the chance encounters, the wild growths, the torn blanket, the fragmentary moments of each day. Since Jupiter's journey occurred in the heavens, beyond the time and space of earth, the worldly repetition of this journey can only be unscripted, utterly new, beyond strange. Created existence is itself revolutionary, and the Human is the pulse of this revolution. Humanity is the true insurrection.

P: But how can a revolutionary existence pattern itself on anything at all, even a journey across the span of heaven? No one gives law to a revolutionary; a revolutionary is his own lawgiver.

S: Are you certain of that principle? Under the unbending will of sovereign, I agree, no one is truly free. But are we any more free if all become a law unto themselves? Does that not bind us ever more securely, like Narcissus, whose freely chosen path led him into an intorted existence, and eventually to eternal captivity? The Human is much freer than either the occupied inhabitants of a city or the self-proclaimed lawgiver. We receive a human law that is born from the law of heaven, as Dike is born from Themis. But this is not sovereignty of an earthly sort, precisely because this birth spans the gap from heaven to earth. The pattern, as you call it, is a transcendent one. The gap that divides the human journey from the Jovian is not a gap of sovereignty, which is still an intra-worldly divide, but a gap of religion. The Human was led and informed by Vesta's hearth fires. But this informing was not a matter of receiving a new command, or an itinerary for the next day's labour. It was, you might say, an illumination. Each evening, as she spoke to the Human, bringing it comfort and conversation, the flames in her hearth rekindled the flames in the human heart and hand and eye. The Human received this flame in its inner depths, so that the world that the Human imagined, the bread that it baked, the poems that it composed, were fully human and also fully divine. The Human's revolutionary imagination told the heavenly story perfectly, because the Human was radically illuminated by Vesta's fire.

P: What is that orange light I see on the horizon? I would say it is the sunrise, if the sun weren't high in the sky already.

S: So we say that in creating Humans on the pattern of the heavens, Saturn handed over his own name to them, by handing over the name of his son.

P: Just there! Did you see it that time? It was there a moment ago. A sort of flickering, and then it was gone.

S: So human perfection is an imitation, but not the sort of imitation you get when I pretend to be a rooster, or a child makes a rumbling of thunder in her throat. It's a spoken imitation of silence, a poetic imitation of heavenly hush. 'Be holy,' Saturn says, 'as I am. Though my perfection is utterly removed from genesis and progression, I invite your genesis and progression to imitate me. Be perfect like me.' This is Saturn's gift.

P: But then we're like one who must forever push a rock up a slope, though in this case perhaps it's worse. We never even reach the peak in order to watch our stone roll back to the base of the mountain. How is this perfection?

S: You still imagine a perfection that occurs outside of time, the sort of end that would destroy creatures for whom time charts the journey toward God. We are mixed beings, always in motion, always seeking rest. To be perfect for us, as for the things we make, is not to be flawless, not to achieve permanence, not even, in fact, to be complete. Even as we come to rest by Saturn's hearth, we will have our perfection outside ourselves. This is the mystery of the Human creature and the reason the Human is always a mystery to itself. Our perfection is not simply in the energizing of our internal powers; rather we are perfect as our own energy links into the motion of the heavens. When we discover ourselves to be loved as Saturn loves Jupiter, ignited with and warmed by the fire that belongs in their own drawing room, then we are perfect.

P: No doubt I am far from perfect then, as I have made no such discovery. Should I expect an epiphany along these lines in the next few days?

S: I'm not sure. Do you expect to have finished becoming Human by then?

P: How strangely you Eleatics talk.

S: One moment of contentment does not make one happy, any more than the appearance of a single swallow comprises an entire summer. The discovery of oneself as perfected in the divine energies is inseparable from the discovery of oneself as a good Human. By this I don't mean that perfection is nothing more than the practice of human goodness. But being Human is a practice, and takes a great deal of practice. We learn to bake and mend, to welcome one another into our homes, to plan cities and educate our young. All of this is involved in becoming Human. Becoming Human is becoming perfect, since this becoming, the human genesis, is not self-guiding. The end comes first. Our goal is, after all, the motion of the Gods, who are themselves pure motion, pure actuality.

P: I suppose, then, that you would no longer be welcome in your native country.

S: Why do you say this?

P: Humans are made, the Eleatics say, to move, to create and so to link themselves into the movements and creations of Jupiter, Saturn and Vesta. And yet here you and I are chained to a cliff, unable to move at all. Rather imperfect, wouldn't you say?

S: I would. By the way, I don't believe I've ever asked you how you came to be here.

P: We really must talk more. But there's nothing to tell. I was born here, I'll draw every breathe here, I'll die here. What about you? One morning as I awoke, there was another here with me. You never told me what brought you and these chains together.

S: I believe the charge was 'corrupting the youth' of my land.

P: Cheers. I suppose your perfect ending was a nice dream while it lasted, anyhow.

S: Oh, I wouldn't put it like that.

P: No?

S: I may have been exiled from my city, but only because they've forgotten the parts of our ancient stories that I remember.

P: And now I suppose you are going to tell me what comes next in the Eleatic Chronicles?

S: If you have no other pressing duties?

P: Still available, for a short while anyway. Narrate on, oh verbose one.

S: Life in the created earth went forward, recounting day after day the primordial journey of young Jupiter, and every evening the created order became perfect, as Saturn said, when Vesta and the Human conversed together by the fire. But then one evening, though she stoked the fires and sat waiting, the Human never came. All that night she waited, and then throughout the following day, and again, for several days and nights on end. During this time, the motions of creation began to grow strange. Creatures began to turn violently on one another, not simply in search of food, but out of fear and aggression. Wood nymphs departed from their forests, and fruit-bearing trees produced diseased fruit. The spirits of winds and rains turned vicious, and escaping the rhythm of seasons and cycles, they attacked the earth as though bent on destruction. After several days, Saturn summoned Vesta to find out what event gave rise to all these signs. 'My own sons and daughters, the nymphs and sprites who care for earth and sea, have rebelled against us. What news, faithful Vesta, do you bring from the world you inhabit?'

'Ancient Saturn,' Vesta said, 'I come with troubled soul. The Human, crown jewel of our creation, with whom I have conversed every evening since the dawn of time, has not returned home. My hearth fire was ready for it, and I kept the flames strong for several days and nights while I waited for the beloved one to return. But now the fire has gone to ash, and the house has grown cold. You know that I would give my very life for the Human. But I do not know where to go to find it.'

P: Again, the light on the horizon! How can you not see it? It flickered for several moments that time.

S: Saturn was deeply grieved by this news, and the servants of heaven say that he entered a state of gloom like only once before he ever had, and that during the long absence of young Jupiter. Finally, he called Jupiter and Vesta into his drawing room to speak with them. 'Dearest ones, there is evil at work in our created world. The Human, whose very existence is a crafting of the story of my heavenly son, has not returned to its hearth. Whether the Human wandered off first, or the spirits began their rebellion before it wandered, I cannot say. Perhaps both actions have somehow mutually caused the other. At any rate, the Human has ceased its timely path to perfection, for how can it perform the story of Jupiter's journey, if it does not meet with Vesta, and so, in due time, return to me? And how can creation itself sing its ballad of the reunion of Saturn, Jupiter and Vesta, if creation's bard cannot to be found?'

'I will go,' Vesta said, 'and seek him, as I did once before. I will enter every cave, walk every beach, climb every hilltop and descend to every gulley, as I did once before. I will search the ends of creation until I find our beloved child of earth.'

But Saturn shook his head sadly at her offering. 'Not this time, faithful Vesta. Our creation was formed the morning after the great heavenly Feast of the Return, and that story comprises the very fabric of its being. My son wandered far, but never forgot his father's house. If the world now ceases to tell that story, it begins a long and agonizing process of self-unravelling.'

'But surely if I went and found the Human, I could convince it to come home, and resume its place again,' she protested.

'Perhaps you could,' Saturn answered, 'but by going to where it was, you would go to were Jupiter never went. Your coming would inspire it with a life that was not my son's, and that would replace the creation we know with something entirely new. My grace perfects, it never replaces. You would give a new fire to the errant creature, and it would live on and on as something unrecognizable to any of us. The Human is telling its own story now, and is forever bound to itself rather than to us. Vesta's fire will still flash in its heart and eyes, but it will forget what this means, and what this warming force is that drives it, even as it forgets its own name. We fashioned the Human to move freely through the world as a revolutionary image of ourselves; now it will bind itself into a long deceleration, until it fails to move at all.'

P: The fire there; it's constant now. Can't you see? It's so bright.

S: Then Jupiter spoke to them both. 'We could revise the story,' he said. 'What do you mean?' Saturn asked. Jupiter turned to Vesta, and then to Saturn. 'Vesta always comes to where I am. That is the secret at the heart of creation's story, isn't it?' 'Yes, Son, that is the secret.' 'And Vesta cannot go now to the Human, because the Human has begun telling a story that is not mine?' 'Yes.' Jupiter then knelt before his father. 'My father, I ask your blessing.' 'Son?' 'I wish to go out beyond your castle walls, beyond your fields, in search of the ends of earth.' 'Haven't you heard anything I have said?' Saturn retorted angrily. 'We cannot go to the Human and overtake the story it is now telling. What do you propose, to go and blind the Human with your majesty and drag it back to hearth and home? Before it wandered, perhaps you could have visited its home and spoken with it as Vesta did, accommodating your brightness to the eyes of a creature. But now, when it is unmaking its very creatureliness? Even if you went under a veil to hide your face, the wandering one could not bear it. What you saved would be a lifeless thing. If you, a god, encounter the world that rejects your image, you will destroy it. My grace perfects, it never destroys.'

'No Father,' Jupiter answered. 'I don't mean to go as a God at all. I mean to go as one of them.' Saturn looked at Vesta in alarm. 'You can't! You are no creature of earth. You are the Creator, you were there when it was made. Your very words are the world.' 'Father, I ask your blessing.' Saturn looked again to Vesta, but she only stared at Jupiter in silence, with wide eyes. 'They won't know you', Saturn whispered. 'None of them will know you. It's all gone monstrous, and the Human wouldn't even know the primal story if you, the storyteller, walked into its rooms. None of them know the story now, the rocks, the trees, the land creatures, the Human. You'll go to the world that is your own, and it won't even know you.' 'Father, I ask your blessing,' Jupiter repeated. Saturn looked at Vesta once again, as he had that evening long since passed, in that same room, by that same fire. Her eyes met his, and she nodded. 'Then you have it,' Saturn said, eyes shut, his hand on his son's bowed head. 'Go. Find your way to the ends of the earth. Go with my blessing.' The son stood to his feet and nodded to his father. As he turned toward the door, Vesta grasped his shoulder. 'I will find you,' she said. 'I will search every cave and walk every shoreline, I will climb every hill and descend into every gulley on the earth, until I find you.'

P: You Eleatics are renowned for your storytelling, and now I see why. You have almost persuaded me to believe your myth. But tell me, is there a second sunrise that I've been missing all these years? It's blinding me now. How can you bear it?

[*Enter Vesta with her urn.*]

S: Jupiter journeyed far into the earth, and he found that his father was right. The world no longer knew him. Jupiter himself could hear the distant echo of his own words as he walked through the forests and seas, but he knew that the world itself no longer knew what story it was telling. His journey was difficult, as the errant spirits now fought against him, buffeting him with wind and rain, and sending ferocious beasts into his path. Where once the mountains were wooded and inviting, now they were rocky and hostile; where once there were soft grassy meadows, now there were barren desserts. And it was over these mountains and through these deserts that the son passed. And he journeyed through all with the flesh of a Human, knowing fatigue and illness and fear. And then one morning, just before the sun rose over the mountains in the east, he found the ends of the earth, and the object of his journey.

P: Are my eyes scarred by the brightness of this fire from the horizon? Are they creating false images in my soul? Or is it true that where there were tongues of fire, there is now the figure of a woman?

S: Tell me, my friend, what do you recall of our conversations that morning that I first came to be bound alongside you on this cliff?

P: What? Oh. Not much, really. I think you were simply there when the sun rose, and joined me in my ritual greeting of the day.

S: I recall every word. You began: 'Oh Gods of highest heaven, do you tantalize me with another morning in this suspended state? Do you assign me to a middle course, and then rain down coals on my head for desiring too much, when all the while you are the fashioner not only of my hands and feet, but of my desire as well? Is your edict then that I lessen my desire, and ascend not to the heavens, but dwell below, in the meadow of humility? I curse you Gods, even as I know this curse is my own condemnation. Yes, even as I know that my condemnation brings you pleasure in your own sovereignty, seeing that you now may wear my ruin as one of your many names. You bind me to this rock as punishment for my desire? I tell you that I was ever bound, as a creature in whom hope and limit made war on one another. Your punishment, at least, is fitting to your pathetically incoherent creation. You made me naked and weak, you bind me to ensure that I never grow armoured and strong.'

And I said, 'My friend, who told you that you are naked?'

You told me then, perhaps you have forgotten it now, that you once laboured upon the earth below, pruning vines, weaving wool and binding the wounds of the creatures around you.

P: Have the years of captivity finally cost me my sanity? Is there not a woman here, building a fire at your feet?

S: A spirit of that world – one of the muses, as I recall – met you one morning as you went about your labours. 'Blessed Human,' she said. 'How long will you make your labours, and what do you hope to accomplish by them?'

P: Perhaps you are right, yes, I seem to recall something of that nature. But this woman, with this urn and these flames, is she not like the figure from the Eleatic story?

S: You told the muse that you were labouring toward union with the gods of heaven, and that you dared not cease to work, else you might cease to live, and ceasing to live you would not in due time make your approach there.

P: Perhaps. Yes, perhaps I did say that once.

S: She responded, did she not, 'Human child, you misunderstand the purposes of the Creator?'

P: She did. 'You hope for the heavens', the Muse said, 'but the Gods have ordained this realm to exist on its own plane, forever separate from theirs. The tasks assigned to you are to keep your hands from telling your soul that all ascent is futile. The fire in your hearth is but a consolation prize, a false warmth that numbs your senses and slakes your own restless longing for a higher order of being. The Gods have made you higher than the beasts, but lower than the angels. They have ordained to you a middle course. Stay to it, and hope no higher.'

S: As you told me once before. I wanted to say then what I could not say, as you could not hear it. I wanted to say that this muse, a daughter of the Gods sent to keep time in the creation, had looked upon your blessing lustfully, jealous that a creature so vulnerable as you might be the most highly favoured to walk the paths of earth. She wanted your birthright; knowing that she could not have it, she did the next best thing: she deprived you of it. She saw that your weakness is your strength: the softness of your skin allows you to touch the lilies and sheep without the intervening layers of scale and fur; the vulnerability of your emotions allows you to sense their joy and pain. Your nakedness in the world is in fact the world's nakedness to you. In this lay your royalty. In this you were the great reader of creation, and the speaker of the divine word.

P: Your hands . . . how is it that you are no longer bound to the mountain?

S: I wanted to tell you these things then, but these words were not mine to give, lest by revealing the purposes of heaven to you, I annihilated the very agency that makes you a creature of earth. Come, woman, rest yourself here.

Vesta: Greetings beloved one. Did I not long ago promise that I would come to you, searching cave and crest, valley and shore?

S: You did.

P: Eleatic Stranger, will you not tell me who you are?

S: Who would you say that I am?

P: I would not have said you were anyone of consequence, just a man bound to earth, as all ever shall be bound. But if she has come to you and brought you this fire, then you are Jupiter, the son of highest Saturn. I have seen strange things today.

S: (*Ascending the mountain*) Stranger things yet will you see.

P: Wait, Stranger. Where are you going? I wish to go with you!

S: You cannot come to where I am going. My labours here are finished; your labours are ready to begin. Remember all I have said to you. And she will lead you into all truth. (*Exits.*)

V: Prometheus, do you recall my face?

P: Only from a stranger's story, my lady, not from my own.

V: Not the many nights we sat together by your hearth, laughing, conversing, knitting our garments and resting our feet?

P: No, my lady. I do not recognize you.

V: Still, there is a remembering that is beyond the forgetting and a recalling beyond recognition. My form is no longer in your soul, but I remain the form of your soul.

P: What is it that I have become?

V: You have for ages now practised the art of forgetting God, and so you have forgotten yourself. Your language has gone lifeless, and your morning liturgies are now spoken through a frozen alphabet. You have spoken this language so long that by it you have bound yourself here to these hills. And yet as it is your language that is a dead thing, you can no longer hear the truth that it is you, and no other, who fastened these chains round your body.

P: How can that be? How can I have done this?

V: When you refused the gift of my fire, my fire turned to poison in your soul.

P: What am I, sister?

V: Who does the Stranger say that you are?

P: Will you speak to me in only riddles?

V: Will you speak to me in only curses?

P: You are like him, answering me in prose. Why can't you speak plainly?

V: Because I do not wish to destroy the ears that no longer hear.

P: Give me what I have lost then. The eyes to see you as I once did, the ears to hear, the tongue to speak a language I have forgotten.

V: Make them for yourself.

P: You give them to me. Soak the language into a sponge and hold it to my mouth and I will drink it. Write the language in a book and I will eat it.

V: This is your work.

P: No, it is yours.

V: Yes, it is mine. And I will not engage in it without you.

P: Tell me Fire-bringer, why has he gone?

V: Because his work was perfected.

P: His work done, and me still in chains. How blessed I am to see a god descend from the skies for my love.

V: Do you think then that he came for you?

P: Did he not?

V: No. It is for you that he left. He came for me.

P: How do you mean that?

V: I once begged Saturn to allow me to come to you, but he refused, saying that this encounter would unmake creation. Jupiter came to you, to retell his own story through your own. I can only go to where Jupiter is; so Jupiter came here, that I might come to you as I wished.

P: And why do you come?

V: To bring you my fire, so that you may rediscover it as the gift that has illuminated your hands and hearth and eye from the day you first took breath. To remind you how to speak the language of the Gods.

P: Am I made for ascent into the heavens?

V: You are.

P: Am I originally divine then? Or a chimera, earthly in form, heavenly in descent? Does the blood of immortality flow in my veins?

V: No, though by the lust in your eye I can see that the thought moves you.

P: What am I then?

V: The creature called Human, no more no less.

P: So little?

V: So little.

P: You are not helping.

V: Have I come here to help?

P: If what you say is true, then I am ruined.

V: Ruined.

P: For I know what it is to be Human. It is a loathsome thing. I have experienced the fatal imperfections, the inconstancies. I know myself too well. I could never go to where he has gone.

V: Perhaps you know yourself not well enough.

P: Speak on Fire-bringer, as this is the first word that has not encouraged despair within me.

V: You experience yourself as imperfect; why should this take precedence over our naming of you as perfect? Is your experience at any moment ever so complete that you should grant yourself authority to name it? Are you a sealed container, so that what you find locked within your own soul is the truth of all reality?

P: My experience is all I have. I name myself as I experience myself, I name the trees and clouds and rules of the natural world as I experience them.

V: And by doing so you reduce the world, yourself and all discoverable truth of the world to a dead form. I cannot breathe life into this dead form, as it stands closed to my revealing truth. I could only then encounter it with a blinding revelation of an anti-nature. Your work is to remind the world that your experience of it, and its experience of itself, is not the higher truth that it tells. Perhaps the world experiences itself as slaked and violent; the Gods experience it as festival. This is the greater experience, and your philosophical inquiries kill the creation if they close it off from this truth.

P: If the Gods wanted me to tell of this higher experience, perhaps they should have made me a higher being.

V: Can't you see that your false rebellion is the offspring of your misguided piety?

P: No, I cannot see this.

V: You think the divine pastureland is closed off to you, and so you imagine that a godly life must refuse to climb the fences into this forbidden zone. But then your desire for beatific vision turns sour, finding that the very thing you want is off limits. So now this desire turns to a show of insurrection, you'd have the vision of God, whether God wants you to or not. All atheism reduces to this irony. You imagine God to have fenced you out, so you reject him in order to be united with him.

P: Fabulous. Even my curses have come to God's ears as praise. A slave, in spite of all.

V: Your curses have not come to God's ears at all.

P: I was being facetious.

V: I see. Sorry to spoil the taste of it in your mouth.

P: Not at all. I only mean that I do not think I can unlearn this language, and turn my words into praise. Perhaps I could somehow receive it from you?

V: But I've told you. You are receiving it from me, and this is the way I give it. The Human is a made maker, a maker of ideas and poems, of gardens and machines. This is the form of the Human. Do you wish to cease making in order to be perfect? You may as well say you wish to cease being a Human in order to finally be Human. It's nonsense, and I'll hear no more of it.

P: There's not that much I can make, though, bound in this way.

V: In what way?

P: But my hands . . . how long have the chains been off me?

V: Were you chained?

P: How strange. I can still feel their weight. My hands and feet can move now freely, and I can't even say when or how. Should I not follow him up the mountain?

V: You must follow him. But up the mountain? Alone? With soft hands, atrophied muscles?

Postlude: Theosis and Insurrection

P: How then?

V: Follow him by creating a world that follows his journey.

P: But the world no longer wants to be made into his journey. *I'm* not so sure I want to either. I do this moment, I may not the next. I'm a fool, too foolish to journey to God.

V: Travel the route to holiness anyhow, and bring your foolishness with you on the road. We have revised the story, you see.

P: Revised it?

V: So that fools can tell it. It's all perfect again, as it once was. Perfection was once the entire world, the asymmetry of a nutshell, the chaos of storms, the hormonal volatility of the adolescent, the failure of language to communicate with any finality or clarity, the Human's tendency to snort when laughing and its inability to concentrate when tired or intoxicated. This was its perfection from the beginning, since the revolutionary Human was made to take all this chaos, energy, raw emotion, all this life, and send it heavenward. When you bound yourself here, you ceased your work, and made yourself unfree to ever begin working again. It was not simply that the world through your failure stopped desiring to be the creation; the world through your failure became unfree to ever be the creation again. It all went monstrous.

P: Oh dear.

V: But Jupiter made a journey through that monstrous world, like he once made a journey through the heavenly one. Guessing at God on a hostile sea, he refashioned the wind and waves into creatures who hear the divine voice. Now even the monsters can be perfect, and through your work they will be. If the earthly Jupiter, bound to the Caucasus, can faithfully tell of the heavenly Jupiter's return to Saturn's house, then Prometheus, once bound upon this same mountain, can do the same. The violent world will aid you in telling the story that will save it. By overcoming the monsters both within your foolish soul and within this foolish world, you will rename them all. The labour before was simple, though not easy, like a journey up a ladder. Now the journey is a complicated one, a winding path through forested slopes hiding greedy beasts. But this world is no less perfect than that one, now that the Stranger has found you here, and I have found him.

P: Will you not tell me where to begin my journey?

V: I'll do more than that: I'll tell you where to end. Recall the Stranger's story, warm yourself at my fire and create. This is who you are.

Diagonal Advance

P: What shall I create?

V: Make a world, make cities and fill them with your progeny. Organize your children round squares and markets that allow the fragmented world to become one. Make families and neighbourhoods. Make instruments for singing and tools for building and pens for writing. Craft a world that perfects rather than destroys the one you've been given, and give names to all that you make.

P: What shall I call this making?

V: Call it Culture: this is the proper name of the saving work of the Human within the world.

P: How am I to know if Culture tells the proper story?

V: Take my fire with you, and use it to light your kitchen fires, the torches with which you explore caverns and castles, the candles by which you read and the chandeliers under which you dance. If you read blueprints of your crafting under the light of my crafting, then what we create will be humanly divine: an earthly shaping of the heavenly journey. I can go nowhere that he is not.

P: And if I, the fool, happen to weave a bit of cloth that testifies against Jupiter?

V: Then my fires will act also as a proving flame: when your making turns to tearing down, my fires will reduce it to ash. Trust my flames not only to give light, but to engulf every word, every chiselled stone. Burn them all. Do so, and you will find that though you do not ascend immediately towards Saturn's drawing room, yet you are advancing diagonally toward a place you think yourself unfit to go, and bringing the creation along with you.

P: Can I truly advance thus?

V: It's what you were made for.

P: I go then, though I descend instead of climb. With this urn I remake a world, and so doing I make my own justification. The creation can no longer hear the tune it sings; but I go to create from its own wreck the thing it secretly contemplates. I go to make my insurrection.

(*Exit Prometheus.*)

Epilogue

Vesta:

> The soul of man thus quickens to creation
> In holy works crafts he his own salvation
>
> Inventing the yeast that rises in leaven
> Which mortals consume as bless'd bread of heaven
>
> Sculpting an artform with no earthly pattern
> Save Fire and Word, beloved of Saturn
>
> Prometheus thus to his great insurrection
> Bound to and toward God, goes he on to perfection.

(*Exit Vesta*)

Index

Index

Index

Index

Narrative 8, 10–11, 15, 18, 25, 70–5, 77–9, 84–5, 89–91, 97, 99, 106, 108, 118, 136, 162, 178, 199, 225, 232–3, 235, 237, 240, 245, 257, 262, 267, 278, 282, 308
Nephilim 72, 76, 82, 84, 91, 106, 115
Niditch, Susan 73–4
Nohrnberg, J. C. 246
Noth, Martin 72

Oates, Whitney 39, 41, 73
Obedience 23, 31, 33, 58, 77, 81, 94, 97–8, 103, 168, 254, 262, 270–1, 294
O'Brien, Denis 151–2
O'Donnell, James 158
Olson, Glending 235–8
O'Malley, John W. 233
O'Neil, Charles J. 211
O'Neill, Eugene 39, 41, 73
Ontology 25, 92, 147, 267, 290, 301
Origen 147–54, 156, 158–9, 161, 163, 168, 176, 186, 194, 263, 298
Ousia 22, 108–9, 159, 194
Ouspensky, Leonid 24
Ovid 179, 197–8

Pabst, Adrian 46, 48, 50, 54
Palamas, Gregory 22, 24, 25, 229–30
Pannenberg, Wolfhart 83
Participation 22, 24, 30, 32, 41, 48–52, 58, 60–1, 66, 89, 94, 98, 100–2, 110–1, 128, 134–5, 140, 144, 151, 153, 155, 163–4, 167, 169, 172, 174, 176, 178–9, 184, 200–1, 225, 228–9, 234, 244–5, 257, 281, 296, 299
Passmore, John 21, 29, 31, 199
Pegis, Anton C. 210, 212
Peña, Horacio 269
Peterson, David 116, 119–20
Philo of Alexandria 100–11, 118–9, 121, 141, 144, 161, 171, 176, 293
Philosophy 19, 39, 48, 57, 59, 70, 74, 83, 149, 183, 199, 201, 210, 212–4, 219, 256, 287–8, 296–7
Pickstock, Catherine 45–6, 217, 224, 225, 288
Pieper, Josef 199–200, 202, 204–5, 220

Plato 2, 39, 44–51, 53–61, 63, 65–6, 68–70, 83, 101–2, 104, 109–11, 122, 130, 133–5, 137, 141, 144, 146–7, 149, 151–2, 168–70, 172, 180, 183, 185–6, 192, 200, 235, 260, 289, 296
Plotinus 149–52, 181, 183, 185
Poesis (Making) 9, 18, 48, 56, 68, 72, 75, 81, 84, 89–90, 94, 98, 103–4, 106–7, 110–1, 119–20, 126, 129, 141, 145–6, 177, 182, 189, 193, 208, 210, 216, 219, 225, 240–1, 249, 252, 265, 270, 287, 290, 293–5, 297–300, 313, 322
Poetry 8, 16, 19, 34, 48, 50, 56, 63, 65, 102, 197–8, 216, 232, 245–9, 253–5, 257–61, 263, 268, 274, 283, 288–91, 293, 296, 298, 300, 304, 307, 310, 320
Poole, William 261–2
Poorthuis, Marcel J.H.M. 81
Porphyry 152, 184
Positivism 11–2, 28, 33–4, 292
Prometheus 5–8, 10–13, 19–21, 25, 33–5, 39–41, 44–5, 50, 54, 59, 69, 73, 128, 136, 154, 179, 232, 252, 254, 257, 261, 267, 292, 294, 296, 301–2, 317, 321–23
Propp, William H.C. 78, 91

Rahlf, Alfred 128
Ramelli, Illaria L.E. 152
Rappe, Sara 150
Ratzinger, Josef 121–3
Reason 58, 144, 150, 158, 165, 181, 187, 192, 200–1, 204–8, 210, 212–5, 219–21, 226–7, 234, 241, 261, 266, 279, 290
Redemption 19, 160, 198, 217, 256, 283
Reed, Walter 71
Resurrection 124–9, 139–41, 244, 270, 282, 284, 288–92
Revelation 26, 30, 78–9, 81, 83, 88–9, 91, 98, 100–1, 103, 107, 133–4, 208, 210–2, 214–6, 221, 226–8, 230, 245, 281, 319
Riches, Aaron 297
Richmond, Velma Bourgeois 233
Ridderbos, Herman N. 118
Righteousness 19, 41, 43–4, 47, 75,